Innovations in Sustainable Consumption

ADVANCES IN ECOLOGICAL ECONOMICS

Series Editor: Jeroen C.J.M. van den Bergh, *ICREA Professor, Universitat Autònoma de Barcelona, Spain and Professor of Environmental and Resource Economics, Vrije Universiteit, Amsterdam, The Netherlands*

Founding Editor: Robert Costanza, *Gund Professor of Ecological Economics and Director, Gund Institute for Ecological Economics, University of Vermont, USA*

This important series makes a significant contribution to the development of the principles and practices of ecological economics, a field which has expanded dramatically in recent years. The series provides an invaluable forum for the publication of high quality work and shows how ecological economic analysis can make a contribution to understanding and resolving important problems.

The main emphasis of the series is on the development and application of new original ideas in ecological economics. International in its approach, it includes some of the best theoretical and empirical work in the field with contributions to fundamental principles, rigorous evaluations of existing concepts, historical surveys and future visions. It seeks to address some of the most important theoretical questions and gives policy solutions for the ecological problems confronting the global village as we move into the twenty-first century.

Titles in the series include:

Conflict, Cooperation and Institutions in International Water Management
An Economic Analysis
Ines Dombrowsky

Ecological Economics and Sustainable Development
Selected Essays of Herman Daly
Herman E. Daly

Sustainable Welfare in the Asia-Pacific
Studies Using the Genuine Progress Indicator
Edited by Philip Lawn and Matthew Clarke

Managing without Growth
Slower by Design, Not Disaster
Peter A. Victor

Carbon Sinks and Climate Change
Forests in the Fight Against Global Warming
Colin A.G. Hunt

Macroeconomics and the Environment
Essays on Green Accounting
Salah El Serafy

Innovations in Sustainable Consumption
New Economics, Socio-technical Transitions and Social Practices
Maurie J. Cohen, Halina Szejnwald Brown and Philip J. Vergragt

Innovations in Sustainable Consumption

New Economics, Socio-technical Transitions and Social Practices

Edited by

Maurie J. Cohen

New Jersey Institute of Technology, USA

Halina Szejnwald Brown

Clark University, USA

Philip J. Vergragt

Tellus Institute, Clark University, USA

ADVANCES IN ECOLOGICAL ECONOMICS

Edward Elgar

Cheltenham, UK • Northampton, MA, USA

Published by
Edward Elgar Publishing Limited
The Lypiatts
15 Lansdown Road
Cheltenham
Glos GL50 2JA
UK

Edward Elgar Publishing, Inc.
William Pratt House
9 Dewey Court
Northampton
Massachusetts 01060
USA

A catalogue record for this book
is available from the British Library

Library of Congress Control Number: 2012949251

This book is available electronically in the ElgarOnline.com
Social and Political Science Subject Collection, E-ISBN 978 1 78100 134 9

FSC
www.fsc.org
MIX
Paper from
responsible sources
FSC® C018575

ISBN 978 1 78100 125 7 (cased)

Typeset by Servis Filmsetting Ltd, Stockport, Cheshire
Printed and bound by MPG Books Group, UK

Contents

Figures

Tables

Contributors

Michael M. Bell is Professor of Community and Environmental Sociology at the University of Wisconsin-Madison. Three central foci can be found in all of his work: dialogics, the sociology of nature and social justice. These concerns for the world have led him to studies of agroecology, the body, community, consumption, culture, development, food, democracy, economic sociology, gender, inequality, participation, place, politics, rurality, the sociology of music and more.

Halina Szejnwald Brown is Professor of Environmental Science and Policy at Clark University in Worcester, Massachusetts. After earning a doctoral degree in chemistry from New York University, she served during the 1980s as the chief toxicologist and public health advisor to the commissioner of the Massachusetts Department of Environmental Protection. For the past two decades, Brown's research has covered health risk assessment and policy, corporate management of environmental and occupational health, and international comparative environmental policy. She currently works on socio-technical transitions, sustainability policy, sustainable consumption and small-scale experimentation and learning and has a special interest in energy and buildings. Brown is a co-founder of the Sustainable Consumption Research and Action Initiative (SCORAI), a Fellow of the American Association for the Advancement of Science and a Fellow of the International Society for Risk Analysis. She has authored over 60 journal articles and two books entitled *Corporate Environmentalism in a Global Economy* and *Effective Environmental Regulation*.

Maurie J. Cohen is Associate Professor at the New Jersey Institute of Technology where he is Director of the Program in Environmental and Sustainability Policy and the Program in Science, Technology and Society. He is also Associate Fellow at the Tellus Institute and has held prior academic positions at the University of Leeds, Binghamton University (State University of New York), Mansfield College (Oxford University) and Indiana University. Cohen is a co-founder of the Sustainable Consumption Research and Action Initiative (SCORAI) and Editor of *Sustainability: Science, Practice, and Policy*, an open-access e-journal dedicated to the wide dissemination of scholarly research and professional insights on sustainability. His prior books include *Exploring Sustainable Consumption: Environmental Policy and the Social Sciences* (with Joseph Murphy), *Risk in the Modern Age: Social Theory, Science, and Environmental Decision Making* and *The* Exxon Valdez *Disaster: Readings on a Social Problem* (with J. Steven Picou and Duane Gill). He received his PhD in regional science from the University of Pennsylvania in 1993.

Bente Halkier is Professor of Communication in the Department of Communication, Business, and Information Technologies at Roskilde University. Her empirical research focuses on change communication and food consumption in everyday life. Halkier is the author of *Consumption Challenged: Food in Medialised Everyday Lives* and co-editor of a special issue of the *Journal of Consumer Culture* devoted to social practice theories. She has also published on the methodological implications of using a practice theoretical perspective and her work has appeared in *Qualitative Inquiry, Critical Public Health*, and *Food, Culture, and Society* as well as other journals.

Jonathan M. Harris is Director of the Theory and Education Program at the Global Development and Environment Institute at Tufts University. He is author of *Environmental and Natural Resource Economics: A Contemporary Approach* and co-author of *Environmental and Social Issues in Economics* (with Cutler Cleveland) and *Macroeconomics in Context* (with Neva Goodwin and Julia Nelson). He is editor of *Rethinking Sustainability: Power, Knowledge, and Institutions* and co-editor of *Twenty-first Century Macroeconomics: Responding to the Climate Challenge* (with Neva Goodwin), *New Thinking in Macroeconomics: Social, Institutional, and Environmental Perspectives* (with Neva Goodwin) and several of the volumes comprising the series *Frontier Issues in Economic Thought*. His current research focuses on the implications of large-scale environmental problems, especially global climate change, for macroeconomic theory and policy.

David J. Hess is Professor in the Department of Sociology at Vanderbilt University where he is Associate Director of the Institute for Energy and Environment and Director of the Program on Environmental and Sustainability Studies. He has recently finished a three-volume series with MIT Press on strategies for opening political opportunities for sustainability policies in the United States. The first volume, *Alternative Pathways in Science and Industry*, studies industry-oriented social movements, both in favor of alternatives and against aspects of existing regimes, and the historical tendency for them to achieve only partial success; the second, *Localist Movements in a Global Economy*, analyses the strengths and weaknesses of small businesses and community enterprises in developing more sustainable and fair regional economies; and the third, *Good Green Jobs in a Global Economy*, develops a political sociological approach to green-energy transition policy by examining the role of actors such as the fossil fuel industry, Tea Party movement and labor-environmental coalitions.

Sabine Hielscher is Research Fellow in the Science and Technology Policy Research Unit (SPRU) at the University of Sussex. She is currently working on the Community Innovation for Sustainable Energy project that examines the diffusion of community-energy projects in the UK. Hielscher's research interests center on everyday practices, technologies and consumption. Her PhD investigated the potential of applying an approach inspired by practice theory to ordinary routines at home to engage with the dynamics of socio-technical systems that impact on resource consumption.

René Kemp is Professorial Fellow at the United Nations University's Maastricht Economic and Social Research Institute on Innovation and Technology (UNU-MERIT) and Professor of Innovation and Sustainable Development at the International Centre for Integrated Assessment and Sustainable Development (ICIS) at Maastricht University. He was formerly research director of STEP – Centre for Innovation Research (now the Nordic Institute for Studies in Innovation, Research, and Education) and has been a visiting researcher at the Institute for Prospective Technological Studies (IPTS), the Belfer Center for Science and International Affairs at Harvard University, the Science and Technology Policy Research Unit (SPRU) at Sussex University and the Center for Innovation Research in Utility Sectors (CIRUS). Kemp is well known for his work on eco-innovation, environmental policy, strategic niche management and transition management and he has authored numerous articles and books on these themes. His research interests are focused on environmental policy and technical change, technological transitions, innovation policy, evolutionary theories of technical change, the politics of knowledge production and reflexive governance for sustainable development. He is a multidisciplinary researcher whose expertise covers several domains including energy, mobility, waste and water. Kemp is a member of the advisory board of the European Eco-innovation Observatory, Advisory Editor of *Research Policy* and Editor of both *Sustainability Science* and *Environmental Innovation and Societal Transitions*.

Emily Kennedy is Assistant Professor in the Department of Resource Economics and Environmental Sociology at the University of Alberta. Her research interests include sustainable consumption, social networks, urban sustainability and the intersection of these three lines of inquiry.

Kennedy uses both qualitative and quantitative methods in her research and is interested in mixed methodology. Her work has appeared in *Human Ecology Review*, *Rural Sociology*, *Canadian Journal of Sociology*, *Agriculture and Human Values* and other journals.

Harvey Krahn is Professor and Chair of the Department of Sociology at the University of Alberta. His research interests include social inequality, sociology of work, sociology of education, environmental sociology and political sociology. He typically uses quantitative research methods and has directed a number of longitudinal studies of school-work transitions, but has also participated in studies employing qualitative and historical methods. His work has appeared in *Rural Sociology*, *Youth and Society*, *Developmental Psychology*, *Work, Employment and Society*, *International Migration Review*, *Criminology* and other journals.

Naomi T. Krogman is Professor of Environmental Sociology in the Department of Resource Economics and Environmental Sociology at the University of Alberta. She is also serving as the university's Academic Director of the Office of Sustainability from 2012–15. Her research interests are in sustainable consumption, environmental policy implementation, social impacts of resource development, and gender and international development. She regularly teaches courses in environmental sociology, social theory of the environment and the sociology of environment and development. Emerging interests in sustainable consumption include the role of local food production in triggering supportive sustainable consumption behaviors, the embedding of sustainable consumption behaviors in other healthy lifestyle choices, and the environmental and social justice implications of consumptive lifestyles in the global North. She enjoys working with Emily Kennedy and Harvey Krahn, long-term collaborators on the sociology of consumption.

Stephen M. McCauley is Research Associate at the George Perkins Marsh Institute at Clark University. Trained in human-environment geography and economic geography, his research is on human-environment systems as systems in transition. His recent work has focused on urban and regional-scale energy systems and emergent interactions involving capital, the state, civil society and technological configurations as localities recognize the necessity of shifting toward more sustainable energy systems. He embraces an action research approach that seeks to both understand and advance sustainability transitions, and he works closely with policy makers and other practitioners on economic development and sustainability initiatives.

Inge Røpke is Associate Professor in the Department of Management Engineering at the Technical University of Denmark. She trained as an economist and holds a PhD in social sciences. During her early career she worked on the economics of innovation and technological change in the shipbuilding industry, but since the late 1980s her research has focused primarily on environmental issues. Røpke has written about the development of modern ecological economics and various related topics such as trade and economic growth. In particular, she has specialized in the ecological economics of consumption and the environmental aspects of technological change in everyday life. She has also studied the use of information and communications technologies from a practice theoretical perspective, focusing both on the energy impacts as a new round of household electrification and the potential for transition to a low-carbon society. She is the co-editor of *The Ecological Economics of Consumption* (with Lucia Reisch) and has published in *Ecological Economics*, *Journal of Consumer Policy*, *Research Policy* and other journals.

Gill Seyfang is Senior Lecturer in Sustainable Consumption in the School of Environmental Sciences at the University of East Anglia. Her research links sustainability policy agendas with new economics theories and cutting-edge community-based practice. She is particularly interested in grassroots innovations for sustainable consumption and their potential to grow and spread from green niches and to influence wider society. Recent research has investigated local food systems, community energy, low-impact eco-housing, complementary currencies and Transition Towns. Seyfang leads the Sustainable Consumption strand of the Science, Society, and Sustainability (3S) Research Group, co-leads the Grassroots Innovations Research Group and is Editor of the *International Journal of Community Currency Research*. She is the author of *The New Economics of Sustainable Consumption: Seeds of Change*.

Adrian Smith is Senior Researcher in the Science and Technology Policy Research Unit (SPRU) at the University of Sussex. His research considers the politics and governance of innovation for sustainability and has generally addressed one or more of three themes: grassroots innovations for sustainable development, transformation of socio-technical systems and transitions to sustainability, and critical policy analysis for sustainability. Smith's work draws upon theories and methodologies from political science, innovation studies and science and technology studies and involves studies in both 'developed' and 'developing' countries.

Gert Spaargaren is Senior Researcher and Professor of Environmental Policy for Sustainable Lifestyles and Consumption in the Environmental Policy Group at Wageningen University. His main research interests are in environmental sociology, sustainable consumption and behavior, and globalization of environmental reform. His work has appeared in *Global Environmental Change*, *Environmental Politics*, *Society and Natural Resources*, *Organization and Environment* and other journals. Spaargaren's most recent books are *The Ecological Modernisation Reader* (with Arthur Mol and David Sonnenfeld) and *Food in a Sustainable World: Transitions in the Consumption, Retail, and Production of Food* (with Peter Oosterveer and Anne Loeber).

Jennie C. Stephens is Associate Professor of Environmental Science and Policy in the Department of International Development, Community, and Environment at Clark University and a Research Affiliate of the Energy Technology Innovation Policy Group at the John F. Kennedy School Government at Harvard University. Her teaching, research and community engagement focuses on the socio-political aspects of energy technology innovation, renewable energy, carbon capture and storage technology, public perception of energy technologies and climate change education/awareness. Her work also explores stakeholder engagement in sustainable innovation and communication among different actors including 'experts' and the public. Stephens received a PhD in 2002 and a Master's degree in 1998 from the California Institute of Technology in Environmental Science and Engineering and a Bachelor's degree in 1997 from Harvard University in Environmental Science and Public Policy. Before joining the faculty of Clark University, she did postdoctoral research at the Kennedy School and taught courses at Tufts University, Boston University and the Massachusetts Institute of Technology.

John Stutz is Senior Fellow and co-founder of the Tellus Institute and over the past three decades has addressed regulatory, economic and environmental issues on behalf of numerous clients in the public sector, including the United States Environmental Protection Agency and the Organisation for Economic Co-operation and Development. He is the author of hundreds of technical reports, monographs, papers and items of expert testimony. Since 2004, Stutz has been an active participant in the Great Transition Initiative spearheaded by the Tellus Institute and is co-founder of the Sustainable Consumption Research and Action Initiative (SCORAI). Stutz received a PhD in mathematics from Princeton University in 1969. From 1969 to 1976, he taught and did research at the Massachusetts Institute of Technology, the State University of New York at Albany (where he received tenure and helped establish a new college offering an interdisciplinary degree program) and Fordham University (where he was Associate Professor of Mathematics and Co-director of the program in mathematics and economics).

Emanuel Ubert is a PhD student in the Department of Sociology at the University of Wisconsin-Madison. His research focuses on how ecological disruptions affect political-economic stability and on how societies subsequently reconstitute themselves.

Harro van Lente is Socrates Professor of Philosophy of Sustainable Development at the International Centre for Integrated Assessment and Sustainable Development (ICIS) at Maastricht University and Associate Professor of Innovation Studies at Utrecht University. He is also currently Program Director of Technology Assessment at NanoNextNL, a leading Dutch nanotechnology research consortium. Van Lente has studied physics and philosophy and published widely on the dynamics of expectations in science and technology. He teaches courses on innovation theories, knowledge production and technology dynamics and his research interests concern how emerging technologies – such as nanotechnology, hydrogen fuel cells and medical devices and equipment – produce novelty and needs. This work involves technology assessment, foresight, intermediary organizations, politics of knowledge production and philosophy of technology. He was previously Research Manager at the Inspire Foundation, a think tank of the KPMG consulting firm, and Visiting Professor at the University of Oviedo.

Philip J. Vergragt is Professor Emeritus of Technology Assessment at Delft University of Technology, Research Professor at Clark University and Fellow at the Tellus Institute. During the 1990s, he served as Deputy Director for the Dutch government's Sustainable Technology Development Program. His research interests include technological innovation for sustainability, sustainable consumption, housing and community development, backcasting and technology assessment of emerging technologies. He has published widely in academic journals, written book chapters and co-authored three books. He is a co-founder of the Sustainable Consumption Research and Action Initiative (SCORAI) and the Worcester Housing, Energy, and Community (WoHEC) group and a founding member of the Greening of Industry Network (GIN). Vergragt is also a co-founder of the Global Research Forum on Sustainable Consumption and Production. He obtained a PhD in Chemistry from Leiden University in 1976.

Abbreviations

ANT	Actor-network Theory
AOO	*Afval Overleg Orgaan* (Waste Management Council) (the Netherlands)
BLA	Better Life Approach
CO_2	Carbon Dioxide
CRAG	Carbon Reduction Action Group
DCCCP	Danish Commission on Climate Change Policy
DECC	Department of Energy and Climate Change (UK)
DRE	Distributed Renewable Energy
EE	Emotional Energy
EE	Energy Efficiency
EEA	European Environment Agency
EROI	Energy Return on Investment
ESI	Economic Security Index
EU	European Union
FHFA	Federal Housing Finance Agency (United States)
FiT	Feed in Tariff
GAP	Global Action Plan
GCA	Green Communities Act (Massachusetts)
GCP	Green Communities Program (Massachusetts)
GDP	Gross Domestic Product
ICLEI	International Council for Local Environmental Initiatives (which later became Local Governments for Sustainability)
IES	Institute for Energy and Sustainability (Worcester, Massachusetts)
IPCC	Intergovernmental Panel on Climate Change
IR	Interaction Ritual
LEED	Leadership in Energy and Environmental Design (United States)
LOHAS	Lifestyles of Health and Sustainability
MBRI	Massachusetts Biotechnology Research Institute (United States)
MLP	Multi-level Perspective
MTC	Massachusetts Technology Collaborative

NESTA	National Endowment for Science, Technology, and the Arts (UK)
NGO	Nongovernmental Organization
OECD	Organisation for Economic Co-operation and Development
PACE	Property-Assessed Clean Energy
RE	Renewable Energy
REC	Regional Environmental Council (Worcester, Massachusetts)
RGGI	Regional Greenhouse Gas Initiative (United States)
SCORAI	Sustainable Consumption Research and Action Initiative
SCP	Sustainable Consumption and Production
SDC	Sustainable Development Commission (UK)
STS	Science and Technology Studies
UNEP	United Nations Environment Programme
WCAC	Worcester Community Action Council
WEB	Worcester Energy Barnraisers
WGJC	Worcester Green Jobs Coalition
WoHEC	Worcester Housing, Energy, and Community
WPI	Worcester Polytechnic Institute (Massachusetts)

Preface

A joint statement issued in 1992 by the Royal Society of London and the National Academy of Sciences of the United States asserted that '[u]nrestrained resource consumption for energy production and other uses, especially if the developing world strives to achieve living standards based on the same levels of consumption as the developed world, could lead to catastrophic outcomes for the global environment.' Agenda 21, the action plan adopted at the Rio Earth Summit, conveyed this concern to a wider audience later that same year. The report specifically noted that 'the major cause of the continued deterioration of the global environment is the unsustainable pattern of consumption and production, particularly in industrialized countries, which is a matter of grave concern, aggravating poverty and imbalances.'

Sustainable consumption was again a key focus of attention in 2002 at the World Summit on Sustainable Development held in South Africa. The key outcome of this event, the Johannesburg Plan of Implementation, stated that '[f]undamental changes in the way societies produce and consume are indispensable for achieving global sustainable development. All countries should promote sustainable consumption and production patterns, with the developed countries taking the lead and with all countries benefiting from the process.' As we complete this book, thousands of representatives from both governments and civil society organizations have recently convened in Rio on the twentieth anniversary of the first Earth Summit to again tackle the challenges of sustainable development and have adopted a Ten-Year Framework of Programs on Sustainable Consumption and Production.

It has not just been international mega-events that have sought to engage with the deeply problematic ways in which our material and financial economies fuse together to constitute current systems of consumption. The issue of sustainable consumption has over the past 20 years occupied the attention of prominent institutions such as the United Nations Environment Programme, the Organisation for Economic Co-operation and Development, the World Economic Forum, the World Business Council for Sustainable Development and numerous others. National scientific councils have amply funded extensive research programs and several countries have even formulated their own sustainable consumption plans. We have moreover seen the deployment of countless eco-labeling schemes, energy-efficiency programs and educational campaigns encouraging ordinary consumers to 'green' their shopping practices.

Common to all of these familiar strategies is a hopeful emphasis on technology. There is though growing recognition that such approaches will not bring about the required drastic reductions in consumption by the wealthy countries of the global North and, increasingly, the rapidly growing economies of the South. In addition to technological changes, fundamental shifts will have to take place in how people satisfy their needs and wants through the heedless appropriation of scarce materials, sources of energy and assimilative biophysical capacity.

Over the course of the past two decades, European policy makers have tended to demonstrate greater interest in engaging with the concept of sustainable consumption than their counterparts in the United States, but political progress has been minimal everywhere. In many domains of consumer activity (and in some notable countries) resource volumes flowing through global supply chains have continued to increase without pause, in certain cases markedly so.

Part of the problem is the emotionally loaded nature of the idea of sustainable consumption, which for many people conjures images of retreat and loss in terms of wealth, freedom of choice, aspirations for intergenerational progress and overall well-being. In addition, consumption in everyday life is a complex phenomenon, tied to cultural norms, prevalent technologies and infrastructure, established habits, formal and informal institutions and market forces. Furthermore, the prevailing economic system seems to be profoundly dependent on ever-larger amounts of material and energy throughput that neither policy makers nor proponents of political change have a vision of how to decouple without triggering an economic disaster. Devising interventions that can address such systemic complexity is an unprecedented, and possibly unachievable, goal. Indeed, the experience so far with government efforts to encourage citizen-consumers to 'downshift' their consumption has been unsuccessful; it has become evident that traditional policy approaches predicated on regulations, financial incentives, subsidies and information disclosures are ill-suited to the problem at hand.

It is equally clear that a deeper understanding of the multidimensional nature of consumption is required. This observation has two implications from the standpoint of the social sciences. First, more research is needed, drawing on a wide range of disciplines, from science and technology studies to economics, sociology, anthropology and many others. Second, new platforms must emerge for bringing together in novel and insightful ways the knowledge that is developing from these diverse areas of scholarship. The Sustainable Consumption Research and Action Initiative (SCORAI) is an effort to create such an institutional form. Its history is both short and telling.

In 2008, a small group of researchers began to meet in Boston on a monthly basis under the auspices of the Tellus Institute, initially with a vague idea of forging in the United States (and soon afterward in Canada as well) a community of scholarship and policy practice focused on sustainable consumption. Over the course of half a year or so, the meetings expanded to encompass a widening circle of interested participants. Several of us involved in this effort were personally familiar with a prior project called SCORE! that played an important role in building a robust network of European academics and policy makers engaged in work on sustainable consumption. Our aim was to draw inspiration from this project while at the same time taking advantage of the distinct circumstances in North America. A tangible outcome of these deliberations was establishment of SCORAI and the first step of the founders group was to convene a workshop in October 2009 at Clark University in Worcester, Massachusetts.

This event ultimately brought together three-dozen participants from the United States and Canada around the theme of 'Individual Consumption and Systemic Societal Transformation.' Attendees included sociologists, anthropologists, political scientists, geographers, ecological economists, environmental social scientists, industrial ecologists, urban planners, marketing and management specialists and scholars in science and technology studies. The outcome of the workshop was broad recognition that consumption in a technological society is not an individual act performed by rational 'sovereign' consumers, but rather a set of practices embedded in dominant socio-technical systems and, as such, heavily entrenched in culture and habituated routines. Accordingly, it is futile to think that households might be able to significantly advance sustainable consumption on their own. They are themselves deeply entrained in the dominant socio-technical systems that provision goods and services, the structure of daily life and the economics of work-and-leisure time. It was also generally observed that the evolution of new, more sustainable lifestyles will require harmonized changes in several domains including civil society, political and economic institutions, culture and government policies.

To further explore these issues, SCORAI organized a second workshop in Princeton, New Jersey in April 2011 and it was at this meeting that most of the chapters in this volume were first presented. This event was conceived around three promising theoretical perspectives: new economics, socio-technical transitions and social practice theories. Each of these approaches seeks to address different issues and to date there has been limited cross-fertilization across the relevant scholarship communities. Work in 'new economics' (a composite of ecological macroeconomics and environmental political economy with consumption positioned as a key organizational focus) interrogates the privileged position of economic growth in contemporary policy making. The 'socio-technical transitions' approach asks how it might be possible to transform seemingly stable and obdurate large-scale systems such as agrofood, energy, housing and transportation. 'Social practice theories' examine the routine patterns that develop around consumer goods and services. By highlighting advances to bridge these three perspectives, this book seeks to identify viable new pathways toward a more sustainable future.

At the time this book is going to press the SCORAI network encompasses nearly 500 researchers and other professionals working at the locus of material consumption, human fulfillment, lifestyle satisfaction, and macroeconomic and technological change. In addition to the North American group, a sister network – SCORAI-Europe – was launched following the first SCORAI-sponsored trans-Atlantic workshop in Austria in May 2012. One month later, with the support of SCORAI, approximately 85 people convened in Rio to establish the Global Research Forum on Sustainable Production and Consumption (GRF-SPC).

The success of SCORAI to date is largely attributable to the enthusiastic scholars and policy practitioners who have attended its workshops or evinced support in various other ways. We are particularly grateful for the collegiality of Jeffrey Barber and John Stutz with whom we have worked in close partnership on the SCORAI Executive Committee. In addition to the authors whose work is represented in the following pages, we express our appreciation to all of the participants in the Princeton workshop: Nicholas Ashford, Erik Assadourian, Bruce Biewald, Karla Cook, Jaime Ewalt, Joshua Farley, Jim Freund, Ethan Goffman, James Goldstein, Jonathan Harris, Alex Haxeltine, Anders Hayden, Debbie Kasper, Gabriela Kütting, Benjamin Linder, Janet Lorenzen, Christa McDermott, Diana Mincyte, Robert Rattle, Lucia Reisch, Viccy Salazar, Juliet Schor, Rachael Shwom, Eleni Sotos, Sarah Van Gelder, Ashwani Vasishth, Josefin Wangel, Michael Weinstein and Edward Woodhouse. Special thanks also to Tom Hargreaves, Marlyne Sahakian, Adrian Smith and Peter Victor for input at critical stages of this project and to Alan Sturmer at Edward Elgar for his patience during the book's overly long gestation. We also take this opportunity to acknowledge the financial support of the Tellus Institute, the New Jersey Institute of Technology (Provost's Office), the Netherland-America Foundation, ProQuest, LLC and an anonymous donor.

1. Societal innovation in a constrained world: theoretical and empirical perspectives

Halina Szejnwald Brown, Philip J. Vergragt and Maurie J. Cohen

INTRODUCTION

Several recent scientific assessments have offered persuasive evidence that the physical demands of contemporary patterns of energy and material consumption have begun to exceed critical biogeochemical thresholds and to jeopardize planetary systems (IPCC, 2007; Rockström et al., 2009; Aaronson, 2010). Current debates on appropriate policy responses evince skepticism about whether improvement in technological efficiency, including enhanced reliance on renewable energy sources, will alone be adequate to meet the demands of a global population projected to exceed nine billion by 2050.[1] Although not impossible, in the words of Paul Raskin and his colleagues (2010, p. 2648) 'the sustainability challenge presents, as well, the prospect of transcending technological solutions with a transformation in human values and restructuring of economic and governance institutions.' Under these circumstances, a new conception of the future is gaining traction in the scientific community, one in which far-reaching innovations in both industrial production and societal consumption patterns are likely to be required.

Systemic changes in the prevailing social-technical-cultural-economic-political system are necessary to move in the direction of such a vision. This book will show that there are different dynamic forces that could help shape a comprehensive transition, which will imply a transformation of present arrangements for production and consumption. Some commentators argue that government policies should be the overriding force to help shape this transition, given the urgency of the problems and the need for swift, coordinated and effective actions. Others do not deny the important role of governments, but also contend that due to the complexity of the issues government policies alone will not suffice, and other actors and dynamics need to play an important role. It is this latter perspective that this book takes.

An important set of approaches for moving forward on this front has been developed over the past two decades by social scientists, environmental scientists and engineers, and policy makers working within the interdisciplinary field of sustainable consumption. This work integrates across industrial ecology, ecological design, ecological economics, sociology, psychology, science and technology studies (STS) and consumer studies. Understanding what is meant by sustainable consumption, or how to study and advocate for it, varies widely within this community of scholars, practitioners and policy entrepreneurs. At one end of the spectrum, the emphasis is on the nature of the 'stuff' that we consume, with calls for more durable and less resource demanding consumer products and services. At the other end, priority is given to human behavior, with calls to reduce the volume of material goods and energy-intensive activities that people engage in while searching for a fulfilling life. A distinct and important line of thinking explicitly recognizes the social construction of technology (and the stuff we consume), as well as the mutual interaction and coevolution of technologies, human behaviors, societal institutions and economic arrangements. But even here, there are pronounced differences in perspectives, research approaches and related action alternatives.

This book comprises contributions by scholars from three domains of scholarship at the intersection of societal innovation and sustainable consumption: new economics, socio-technical transitions and social practices.

First, the new economics is a broad, emergent area of research that forges new understandings of the macroeconomics and political economy of consumption (Speth, 2008; Victor, 2008; Jackson, 2009; Seyfang, 2009; Cohen, 2010; Schor, 2011). Propelled by the financial crisis that began in 2008, new economists are formulating novel approaches with which to model production and consumption and how changes in social and economic policy might affect, for example, employment and economic growth. Absent to date from this work, however, has been much consideration of the role of technology as a driver of human behavior and societal change.

Second, work on socio-technical transitions is grounded in evolutionary economics, studies of the social construction of technologies and research on technological innovation and diffusion (Kemp et al., 1998; Schot, 1998; Rotmans et al., 2001; Geels, 2002; Vergragt, 2005, 2010; Loorbach, 2007). These investigations unambiguously recognize the importance of nonlinearity and the role of social context in large shifts of dominant technologies and focus on the coevolution of technologies, societal institutions and culture. However, to date this scholarship has been relatively silent on the political and economic context of the underlying changes and the nature of technology-human behavior interactions.

Finally, social practice theories focus on the mutual interactions between technology and ordinary daily human behavior and examine how more resource-intensive practices emerge and become stabilized in response to technological innovations (Shove, 2004; Hand et al., 2005; Røpke, 2009). This research though has not been concerned with the evolution of new technologies from a complex system perspective or issues pertaining to prevailing political and economic frameworks. Moreover, it has not actively considered how technological innovation could lead to more sustainable social practices.

This book seeks to forge intellectual bridges across these three perspectives with the aim of enriching each one through novel framings, new analytical lenses and development of a shared language of discourse. A second objective is to deepen the body of knowledge on how consumption patterns evolve in a technological society and the role of policy interventions, grassroots initiatives, small-scale experiments and market actors in affecting changes that are consistent with the requirements of the twenty-first century. We do not claim that these are the only, or necessarily the best, three perspectives for achieving a better understanding of sustainable consumption. Indeed, several of the contributors to this volume remind us that social movement theories may provide another fruitful and complementary perspective, and thus may help policy makers, civil society actors, progressive businesses and other innovators to sharpen their interventions.

THREE THEORETICAL PERSPECTIVES

The linkages across the new economics, socio-technical transitions and social practices have to date not received adequate attention.[2] Each perspective has its respective strengths and weaknesses, but jointly there is potential that they might provide useful ways to formulate new intellectual framings, to deepen the pertinent body of knowledge and to inform policy processes. We explore more explicitly the capabilities of this interdisciplinary approach later in this chapter and use the case of passive houses to illustrate its utility in elucidating the complex technological, institutional, economic and behavioral dimensions of a shift in the socio-technical system for housing construction. We first though elaborate on the three theoretical perspectives that inform this chapter and the book as a whole.

New Economics

The new economics, by drawing together insurgent ideas from ecological macroeconomics and environmental political economy, effectively demonstrates that intensifying environmental stress, growing economic volatility and widening social inequality are interlinked trends. Furthermore, the dominant economic model, predicated on growth in gross domestic product (GDP) and improvements in resource efficiency, is being increasingly challenged because of its inability to maintain full employment, to ensure financial and political stability and to facilitate ecological sustainability (Speth 2008; Victor, 2008; Boyle and Simms, 2009; Jackson, 2009, 2012). Moreover, social surveys have shown that over the past few decades, despite multifold increases in material consumption, most affluent countries have experienced little improvement in subjective well-being (Layard, 2006; Engelbrecht, 2009; Hanlon et al., 2010). This work suggests that beyond a relatively modest level of average annual per capita income – generally understood to be approximately US$15 000 – consumer economies become relatively inefficient in converting resource throughput into gains in personal lifestyle fulfillment. Other studies of objective indicators of well-being have shown similar leveling off in such variables as infant mortality, life expectancy and educational achievement (see, for example, Wilkinson and Pickett, 2009).

Drawing on these insights, an alternative paradigm has begun to emerge, one that seeks to improve individual and societal prosperity under conditions of ecological constraint. This so-called 'new economics' draws attention to the drivers (overproduction, relentless marketing and illusory fixation on growth through consumer spending) and the side-effects (premature product obsolescence, chronic indebtedness and unsustainable exploitation of planetary life-support systems) of current modes of consumption. A key point of awareness is how consumerism creates and perpetuates a culture of 'working and spending,' a development that has become especially prominent in the United States over the past several decades (Schor, 1998; Whybrow, 2005). Such observations have led new economists to consider models based on decreased throughput of energy and materials, as well as low or no growth of GDP (or even degrowth).

New economics is still emerging as a societal vision, an economic theory and a research area. Nonetheless, over the past few years, a growing number of authors and working groups have made progress defining its contours (see especially Boyle and Simms, 2009). This innovative way of considering social progress includes an emphasis on equitable distribution of paid employment, a reduction of economic inequalities, a shift from individual consumption to public investment, a distinction between benign forms of growth (for example, renewable energy, cultural activities, education, healthcare) and environmentally damaging modes such as nonrenewable resource extraction, and a restructuring of major societal institutions that influence government policies (especially the financial markets that over the last few decades have come to overwhelm the real economy).

Some prominent sustainability proponents – and indeed some socially responsible companies – are calling now for a complete restructuring of the economic system toward one that is both more conscientious and green, while simultaneously predicated on new understandings of ownership, growth and the role of a corporation (Korten, 2009; Alperovitz, 2011; see also WEF, 2012). Other commentators stress the need to expand our understanding of technology as more than simply a means with which to enhance labor productivity and to move toward multidimensional analyses of how the actual functioning of dominant technological systems – agrofood, transportation, housing, energy and others – affect the overall economy.

From a quality-of-life perspective, the economy envisioned by some new economists will translate future increases in labor productivity into large-scale investments in education and other public goods, shorter working hours with living wages and improved balance between work and leisure. From that perspective, un- and under-employment created by improvements in labor productivity are offset not by consumption-driven GDP growth, but through greater reliance on an informal economy and self-provisioning that strengthens communal linkages and by more equal distribution of working hours and income. In addition, consumers are likely to begin under such circumstances to develop more expansive societal roles as 'prosumers' (producer-consumers) on a community scale.

Examples of these novel forms of communal interdependency include sharing networks, time banks, complementary currencies, urban farming, vocational reskilling and community-based energy generation (see, for example, Seyfang, 2009; see also Crawford, 2009). Popular interest in these activities has been catalyzed by new social networking tools that make it relatively straightforward and inexpensive to acquire instructional materials, to develop skills and to seek out collaborators. While the emergence of these practices may be viewed by some readers as the perpetuation of deeply rooted (but socially marginal) traditions of utopian communalism or as simply the result of constrained economic circumstances, the prominent (and in some cases pervasive) role of technology in many of these societal innovations is a notable development.

These lifestyle experiments are also of interest because of their potential to engender new (or new kinds of) social movements. However, the durability of these innovative provisioning routines, as well as the extent to which they are likely to diffuse spatially and in scale – and in what form – remain open questions. It is presently unclear how these nascent practices fit into existing socio-technical regimes, economic structures and social practices and how they might contribute to change. Finally, it is indeterminate what role, if any, public policy might play in encouraging the uptake of these new consumer routines.

Socio-technical Transitions

Scholars conceptualize socio-technical systems (or regimes) as configurations comprising technologies, infrastructures, policies, cultures, institutions, actors and networks (Geels, 2002; Geels and Schot, 2007). For example, the agrofood system, the transportation system and the electric power system all constitute socio-technical systems. These systems are complex, operate on a relatively efficient and optimized basis and, despite prominent flaws, are highly stable. However, insurgent alternatives can emerge to challenge them as a result of internal tensions and external pressures. When successful, such changes are called socio-technical transitions and are driven by processes that can dramatically alter the structure, culture and practices of relevant societal systems of provision.

The socio-technical transitions perspective is deeply rooted in evolutionary economics (Nelson and Winter, 1977; Dosi, 1982; Rip, 1995). Evolutionary economists tend to view technological innovation as a process guided by variation (through, for example, laboratory experiments and research and development) and societal selection (primarily through market competition and government regulation). On the macro level, these dynamics give rise to technological trajectories that are relatively durable and further develop in path-dependent directions, leading to a high degree of entrenchment and lock-in (Unruh, 2000).

Historians of technology have explored the temporal and geographical evolution of numerous socio-technical transitions (see, for example, Schot, 1998; Geels and Schot, 2007). The most notable case studies include transitions from the horse-drawn carriage to the automobile, from sailing ships to steam ships, from cesspools to sanitary sewers, from traditional factories to mass production and from chemically cultivated food to organically grown produce. Key insights from these studies are the significance of niche-level processes (such as experimentation and higher-order learning); the coevolution of technologies, institutions, cultures and infrastructures; and the importance of interactions and timing of these different processes.

Socio-technical transitions are commonly understood to evolve slowly and, in accordance with what is referred to as the multi-level perspective

(MLP), to occur across three levels: niche, regime and landscape (Geels, 2002). First, landscape developments occur at the scale of macroeconomics, cultural patterns and political relationships. Prevalent understandings of the linkages among global climate change and greenhouse gas emissions, future resource availability and human-environment interactions more generally constitute landscape-level considerations. Second, these evolutionary changes at the landscape level put pressure on incumbent regimes, but such stress is generally not sufficient to destabilize regime-scale actors who tend to have considerable capacity for resilience. Finally, socio-technical experiments and more expansive innovations gestate in niches as alternatives to the incumbent system of provision. These nascent technologies and practices could – if the incubated innovations were to be adopted on a sufficiently wide scale – mature to a point where they might eventually transform an existing socio-technical regime.

A transition to a new socio-technical regime becomes feasible if pressure from and opportunities within the landscape, along with internal fissures in the incumbent regime and new developments in niches, align so that the insurgent technologies and practices come to be regarded as more attractive than the prevailing alternatives (Geels and Schot, 2007). This process though is rarely rapid and numerous factors can intervene to refortify extant relationships and circumstances. Historical case analyses suggest that transitions evolve over a long period of time – one or two generations – and include the concomitant transformation of societal institutions, technologies and practices. It is however not clear if this protracted time-frame is generalizable over different sectors and for ongoing and future transitions.

Transition management is an applied variant of this more conceptual work on socio-technical transitions that actively aims to orient or steer ongoing processes of transformation toward socially desirable goals (including sustainability) (Rotmans et al., 2001; Loorbach, 2007). Proponents of this approach argue in favor of policy interventions to promote niche activities, where experimentation and learning can take place (Brown et al., 2003; Brown and Vergragt, 2008), by way of 'strategic niche management' (Kemp et al., 1998; Schot, 1998; Hoogma et al., 2002; Raven, 2005). Methods for improving the efficacy of niches have been described as 'transition arenas.' Related approaches are captured by the notion of 'reflexive governance' that entails conscious attempts to align landscape pressures on socio-technical regimes and niches to accelerate regime-level change (Voβ et al., 2006; Murphy, 2007; Kemp and van Lente, 2011).

Much of the socio-technical transitions research – both historical and contemporary – has been conducted from the perspective of technological innovation and diffusion, emphasizing the coevolution of technologies, cultures, institutions and infrastructures in the emergence of new regimes. Although socio-technical transitions also implicate the demand side – predicated on consumer behaviors and consumption patterns – scholars and policy practitioners have not to date explored these dimensions in detail. In particular, research on socio-technical transitions, especially within the context of the MLP, has been mostly silent on the specific roles of consumers and their regularized daily practices. The economic and political dimensions of socio-technical transitions, both on the landscape and regime levels, have also received limited attention. Outstanding research questions include: What roles could consumers play in transition processes (for instance, by participating in transition arenas and socio-technical experiments)? How does demand for new products and services develop in niches and then upscale to the mainstream? What roles do civil society, economic considerations and deeply embedded cultural attitudes and practices have in fostering and facilitating transitions? Social practice theories, the third perspective taken up in this book, usefully engages with these issues.

Social Practice Theories

Social practice theories complement research on new economics and socio-technical transitions because this perspective focuses on the coevolution of technology and human behavior. The unit of analysis is on individual practices, as constituted in a social context (Shove, 2004; Hand et al., 2005; Kennedy and Krogman, 2008; Røpke, 2009). Social practice scholarship views consumers of goods and services (and the attendant use of resources) as practitioners immersed in the affairs of everyday life. Practices are the ways that people constitute the ordinary tasks of working, cooking, washing, socializing and relaxing. Moreover, most individuals typically regard themselves as practitioners engaged in the business of living, rather than as consumers of scarce commodities.

Technology can be an important driver in the rise and change of social practices. Research by Shove (2004) on evolving practices over the past few decades with respect to personal cleanliness and home cooking effectively illustrates this point. For instance, as technology made it easier to shower at home, people abandoned the less convenient custom of weekly bathing and also began to cleanse themselves more often. This change transformed collective ideas about personal hygiene and expected norms of cleanliness. The social practice of daily showering, in turn, had the effect of creating 'bottlenecks' in access to bathrooms among family members for which a commercially mediated answer has been the construction of larger homes with a greater number of bathrooms (see also Quitzau and Røpke, 2008).

Developments in the kitchen offer other examples relevant to considering the growing demand for energy, water and materials by ordinary 'consumers.' During the past few decades, the prototypical kitchen has been transformed from a production center, with free-standing labor-saving appliances, to a large and comfortably appointed 'living' space where appliances are built in accordance with the latest fashions in interior design. An analogous story can be told about the evolving idea of indoor comfort. With technological developments in central heating and cooling, and based on scientific studies of what constitutes a comfortable ambient temperature, came the idea that indoor temperature should be fixed within a particular narrow range (69–72 °F, 20–22 °C) regardless of climate and season. Social practices for dressing and choosing various activities developed around this notion of comfort, and so have various institutional rules such as those mandated in many cities regarding minimum wintertime temperature in rental apartments, as well as expectations of building performance.

These illustrations highlight the strengths of looking at consumption from the perspective of social practice theories. First, they reveal that there is strong path-dependence in the emergence of ordinary social practices and that technology and social practices coevolve such that current practices appear normal and inevitable. Second, this work stresses the importance of attributing cultural meanings to everyday technologies in the evolution and stability of social practices. Shove (2012) notes, for example, that showering is now associated with freshness and cleanliness while bathing is part of a set of practices connected to relaxation. Third, social practice theories make it clear that education, outreach and incentives will have limited effect on people's behaviors if they are determined by routine patterns of everyday life. Finally, this perspective shows that the coevolution of technology and social practices includes not only individual behaviors in a cultural context, but also the larger elements of socio-technical systems such as infrastructure and institutional rules. These insights were clearly presaged by the landmark study by Hughes (1983) showing how utility companies created demand for electricity by appealing to cultural attitudes, needs and expectations, and how growing demand, in turn, facilitated emergence of the infrastructure and the institutional rules governing it.

This latter observation is a promising point of departure for conceptually bridging the other perspectives highlighted in this book with social practice theories. This integration is still in its infancy. In particular, markets, economics and technological innovation and diffusion are not well incorporated into social practices approaches. Furthermore, social practice theories have to date been less helpful in explaining how technology can influence the emergence of social practices that lead to reduced usage of constrained resources. Importantly, they have not to date provided ways out of current circumstances of 'lock-in' or shed light on the roles of markets or economic contexts in changing practices. If consumers are fixed in their habitual behavior, which is determined by the incumbent socio-technical regime, how does change occur? Studying the relationships spanning everyday practices, socio-technical systems, and the macroeconomics and political economy of consumption may offer a way out of this conundrum.

PASSIVE HOUSES AS AN INTEGRATIVE CASE STUDY

To illustrate the complementary analytical powers of our three theoretical perspectives – new economics, socio-technical transitions and social practices – we consider the case of an incipient shift from the current building-construction regime to one based on passive house technology. A passive house is a building that requires minimal external energy input, largely owing to holistic design that includes an extremely well-insulated building envelope, an innovative system of air circulation based on heat-exchange technologies, an appreciation of the importance of careful positioning with regard to the external environment and an emphasis on high-quality materials and construction techniques (see Klingenberg et al., 2009).

The reason for focusing on passive houses is that a putative transition in the types of structures presently being built in the United States and elsewhere touches in many interconnected ways on the main foci of the three perspectives: a change in the prevailing economic system, a transition of a dominant socio-technical system and a shift in routine social practices. Furthermore, buildings account for approximately one-third of the greenhouse gas emissions produced in most affluent countries and have other huge direct and indirect environmental impacts in terms of timber, plastics and minerals, and through their implications for transportation and mobility. The construction sector has moreover been during the post-World War II era one of the most reliable engines for generating employment and growing GDP in these countries (though the situation is obviously quite different in the aftermath of the Great Recession). And a home is a central anchor in people's lives: an expression of their values, aspirations and social position; a determinant of access to education and public services; a lifetime financial investment of considerable consequence; and, at least until recently, a crucial source of financial security in old age.

The concept of the passive house was first introduced in Germany during the early 1990s and defined by the Passivhaus Institut as a residential structure that uses less than 15 kilowatt hours of energy per square meter (kWh/sq m) for heating (compared with approximately 220 kWh/sq m in customary construction). To achieve this stringent performance standard, passive houses entail different architectural, material and engineering strategies than conventional buildings, and may place new demands on occupants in terms of how they relate to the house as a technological artifact. Proponents of passive houses also encourage – for technical reasons as well as a matter of principle – a size not exceeding 500 square feet per person (sq ft pp) (compared with an average of 800 sq ft pp for the current middle-class 'dream house' in the United States (Wilson and Boehland, 2005), as well as site locations that promote higher density land development than is common in most contemporary suburban communities and alternatives to personal mobility based on the automobile.

It is reasonable to ask at this point how relevant this case is at a time when the housing sector in the United States and parts of Europe is in shambles, few new houses are being built, and more and more people are expected to forgo the prospect of home ownership. Doherty and Leinberger (2011) address this question with respect to the American context by noting that the baby-boom generation and its children (the so-called millenials or members of 'Generation Y' born between approximately 1977 and 1994) together comprise half of the American population. These two age cohorts are redefining their housing needs and will, over the next two decades, become a powerful driver for the 'next real estate boom' in the country. For different reasons – boomers are downsizing while Generation Y-ers are confronting rising energy and material costs, traffic congestion and personal costs of long commutes – these two demographic groups are looking for smaller homes located in walkable, transit-friendly, economically dynamic and job-rich areas (Glaeser, 2011; Cohen, 2012). According to recent surveys, 77 percent of millenials plan to live in city centers (Doherty and Leinberger, 2011), but housing in such places is at present unaffordable for most people. Over time, though, this demand will lead to new construction in cities and their proximate suburbs and to restructuring of more distant exurbs into more spatially compact and economically viable and culturally vibrant places (Dunham-Jones and Williamson, 2008).

Examples of the changing priorities for housing in the United States abound, and are not related to political ideology. In Denver, the values of homes in the car-dependent suburb of Highland Ranch dropped by half while those in the Lower Downtown Historic District (dubbed LoDo) have increased. In Maryland, suburban McMansions with vaulted ceilings and granite countertops are being converted into small apartments for the needy; locally financed public transit is emerging in improbable cities such as St Louis and Salt Lake City (Doherty and Leinberger, 2011). Foremost perhaps, a recently inspired cooperative movement in Cleveland is resulting in a remarkable – if long awaited – process of urban renewal (Alperovitz et al., 2009; Bond, 2012).

These changes will, of course, necessitate significant investments in new or retrofitted infrastructure – especially transportation – and require a radical shift in current policies that privilege the automobile as the primary means of personal mobility, but such changes are already in evidence. To be sure, numerous other policy adjustments will be needed over an extended period of time to bring this change to full fruition. But more to the point, the anticipated 'next real estate boom' will lead to new construction and create opportunities to replace current building technologies with drastically different ones. The shift from the presently dominant model for a single- or multi-family dwelling to this fundamentally different one is neither going to be easy nor assured because housing construction is a socio-technical system that fiercely resists change.

The remaining discussion on the passive house case is explored from the standpoint of each of the three perspectives pursued in this book (though in the interests of coherence in a slightly different order from the sequence above): socio-technical systems, social practices and new economics.

Socio-technical Transitions Perspective

There has been considerable progress over the past two decades in the design and implementation of passive houses. In 2011, 32 000 passive houses were reported worldwide, mostly in Germany and Austria, and the numbers have been increasing exponentially (Rosenthal, 2008; Zeller, 2010; Gregor, 2011). Advocates of passive houses – a minority among architects, building and materials scientists, engineers and homebuilders – regard such structures as a technical innovation that deserves wide adoption. Ornetzeder and Rohracher (2009) analyzed the adoption of passive houses in Austria as a socio-technical transition, and found that starting in the 1990s the number of passive houses in the country had been increasing at a rate of more than 40 percent per year. By 2010, about 25 percent of new houses in the leading Vorarlberg province met the passive house performance standard, making Austria the world leader in the per-capita number of structures of this type.

The two-decade process in Austria has gone through four distinct phases. During the first phase, the technical concept was defined and developed, championed (mostly in a bottom-up fashion) by innovators from the architectural and engineering professions.

The second phase was marked by the emergence of a community of practice in the country's westernmost province of Vorarlberg. This process was driven and nurtured by Energieinstitut Vorarlberg, a local education and outreach organization with a mission to foster technological innovation and to disseminate knowledge. From a socio-technical transitions perspective, these developments can be seen as institutionalization of a bottom-up process and the emergence of a thriving niche. The community of practice grew over time to encompass not only technical innovators but also mainstream actors such as builders, developers, planners, building materials manufacturers and others. Moreover, because the emphasis was on building practical, high-quality houses for ordinary occupants, feedback from users was incorporated into evolving practices, sowing the seeds for eventual emergence of a market for passive houses.

The third phase entailed the diffusion of passive houses in Austria from niche toward mainstream through the nationally funded scaling up (in terms of magnitude, geographic reach and diversity of actors) of provincially based efforts. This process of transmission and dissemination of formal knowledge and accumulated experience contributed to improvements of the technology, the circulation of knowledge and the expansion of the community of practice.

Finally, in the fourth stage, the new socio-technical system started to stabilize as a result of government policies aimed at nurturing the niche-to-mainstream transition, including direct regulations, financial incentives, subsidies and other regulatory instruments (Krapmeier, 2012). For example, in Vorarlberg, all so-called social housing (similar to low-income housing in the United States) must meet the passive house standard while in Vienna, where developers compete fiercely for expensive permits to build on mostly municipally owned land, priority is given to low-energy buildings. All of these activities were fostered by landscape pressures: the threat of climate change, the quest for energy security and the advent of concern about peak oil. The emergence of an influential national interest group to disseminate the passive house concept through lobbying and outreach campaigns was a sign of maturation of the new socio-technical regime. And the increasing number of these structures, diffusion of knowledge and growing availability of materials have lowered the cost differential between a passive and conventional large occupancy building from about 15 percent only a few years ago to 5–8 percent at the time of this writing (Krapmeier, 2012).

The Austrian passive house case, analyzed through the lens of the MLP, highlights the complexity of the system, the spatial clustering of pre-niche and niche activities and actors, the harmonization of bottom-up and top-down initiatives at different stages, the importance of government support for small-scale experiments and learning, and the institutionalization of the innovation by strategic government policies and emerging interest groups. It also demonstrates the centrality of champions and the role that they can play in framing the issue at various stages and for different actors – for example, as cutting-edge innovation for early professional movers, as an expression of progress and environmental action for initial adopters and as a statement of progress for later adopters – and the relevance of user feedback in optimizing the technology and creating a market.

The Austrian example also contributes to our understanding of why the passive house niche in the United States is developing much more slowly (as of 2010 there were just 13 passive houses completed in the country, with approximately 130 more either under review or underway (Klingenberg et al., 2009). Some of the factors holding back construction of these homes are: the lack of market demand; the greater technical complexity (owing to the presence of eight different climatic zones); the sheer size of the country (which slows down the emergence of geographically clustered communities of practice); the absence of government support for research and development and small-scale experimentation (that inhibits the aggregation of proximate experts); the absence of supportive public policies; and the inability thus far to resolve conflicts with existing building codes.

The socio-technical transitions perspective concomitantly draws attention to important indicators of niche-level developments such as the institutionalization of various practices with respect to construction and performance and dissemination of knowledge.[3] Accordingly, it merits observing that public subsidy programs are beginning to emerge in the United States on local and regional levels with Baltimore County (Maryland) providing but one illustrative example (Hindle, 2010; Weber, 2011).

More conceptually, using the socio-technical transitions perspective to understand the status of a putative new housing construction system in the United States elucidates the progress (and its absence) on the three levels: the niche in the country, as explained above, is still quite weak; the tensions in the incumbent system – such as questioning of the prevalent model of a 'good life' in the form of a large single-family suburban home requiring heavy energy inputs – has emerged only in the past few years; and the landscape pressures (such as demographic shifts or high energy prices) are only now beginning to garner attention in the housing market.

The analysis of the Austrian experience from a socio-technical transitions perspective also has limitations. For example, it does not enable us to understand why market demand developed earlier in Austria than elsewhere. Or, why the market for passive houses is so undeveloped in the United States, despite a very active community of practice. One might be prone to ask whether there are opportunities to frame the passive house more appropriately and how it might be made more consistent with prevalent (and changing) conceptions of a 'dream home': one that is smaller, differently designed, less energy intensive, connected to an economically vibrant locale and within reach of vital services and amenities. These limitations stem from an emphasis in the socio-technical transitions perspective on the supply side of new regimes and from limited consideration of demand-side factors such as lifestyles, social practices and coevolutionary formulations of normal consumption, as well as a tendency to underplay the role of civil society and cultural trends.

Social Practice Theories Perspective

In the United States, nearly all passive houses built to date are free-standing, single-family suburban constructions. This mode of development is in marked contrast to Europe where most passive houses thus far built have been multi-family houses and institutional buildings. This distinction has implications for the lifestyles of the occupants. Inhabitants of apartments in a large passive house building are barely aware in their daily lives of the uniqueness of the building's design. The situation is quite different in the case of a free-standing, single-family passive house. For one thing, in the absence of artificial heating and cooling, the interior temperature is not constant but rather varies with the external temperature and occupant behavior. Because interior thermal conditions are very sensitive to the level of physical activity undertaken by occupants, residents need to be more deliberate about their daily practices of cooking and entertaining. In addition, a passive house requires replacement of a gas-burning stove with an electric one to avoid air pollution in the tightly insulated structure. And simple acts such as making a pot of tea, using a hair dryer or taking a shower or a bath influence the indoor temperature, as does the presence of many people. Indoor cooking on hot summer days (which in a conventional house can be easily remedied by turning on an air conditioner) needs to be minimized. In short, when living in a passive house the social practices related to cooking, socializing and personal hygiene require recalibration. And the notion of a house inhabitant as a passive consumer of its technologies and amenities needs to be recast in favor of a more active producer-consumer (similar to the vision of a prosumer in the new economy).

The relationship with the outdoors also differs in a passive house from a conventional structure. Since the building is designed to maximize the use of natural light, occupants tend to be more aware of weather and lighting conditions. They open and close windows and shades more often to adapt to external conditions. The large southern exposure windows that are typical in a passive house also encourage more connection with the outdoors. Some residents of passive houses note that they spend more time gazing out the windows into their backyards, watching nature and changing lights, and enjoying the experience of merging interior and exterior space. Under such circumstances, common notions of relaxation are likely to change.

There is also a push among passive house advocates to make the structure smaller than a customary home, both for technical reasons and as a matter of principle. This idea challenges the long-standing trend in the United States (but also prevalent elsewhere), one that has persisted for more than a half-century, toward larger suburban houses (from approximately 900 sq ft in 1950 to 2400 sq ft in 2010 (USCB, 2011; see also Diamond and Moezzi, 2004). On the one hand, a passive house may be viewed as unacceptable by many householders because of the tight relationship that customarily pertains among perceived levels of comfort, social status and home size. On the other hand, the ongoing post-2008 housing crisis has led to an apparent trend reversal. Between just 2009 and 2010 the average square footage of a new house actually declined by 100 sq ft and, in some communities, outsized homes with high cathedral ceilings are losing their appeal (Hurst, 2010).

Other emerging social practices may presently be influencing our notion of privacy and house design toward smaller spaces. New electronic personal devices give members of a household the capacity to share the same room while being in their own 'private space' and lessen the need for large, personally customized rooms outfitted with entertainment and communication equipment. Passive house design can respond to these new practices in ways that are perceived as gains rather than losses, which may increase the relative attractiveness of these homes. Further developments along these lines would have an effect on the home-furnishings industry, reversing the decades-long trend toward larger household accoutrements. In doing so, new furnishing designs and novel conceptions of comfort and elegance in suburban and urban interiors would converge.

In short, the development of a market for passive houses would likely be accompanied by changes in the ideals that have since World War II dominated conceptions of what constitutes a 'dream house,' and that process of evolution may be consistent with an already changing set of practices and sensibilities, including the demographically driven interest in urban lifestyle.

New Economics Perspective

Conventional wisdom places the cost of building a single-family suburban passive home at about 15 percent above traditional construction. However, these approximations do not include the extra time required by highly trained professionals who must work as a team with the homeowner to develop the design, to secure the necessary materials (many presently imported from Europe and Canada) and to build the structure. Inclusion of these expenses would create a greater differential between the construction of a conventional and a passive house. So far, at least in the United States, each passive house is a unique construct. Over time, with growing expertise and increasing demand, some aspects of design and construction could be streamlined in the future, but since passive houses must be adapted to their external surroundings, it may always be the case that some level of customization will be required. And that adds to the costs. To be affordable, a single-family suburban passive house may therefore need to be smaller in size and sited on a more modestly proportioned lot.

In the case of multi-family buildings, the differential in construction costs is much smaller: about 5–8 percent, and dropping. The customization and attendant additional expenses are less of an issue in a multi-family building as is the need to adjust to a more compact living space: both are accepted as part of an urban lifestyle. The value of an apartment in an urban passive structure would derive from its low operating costs, high-quality construction, aesthetic features such as large windows and interior design focused on multifunctionality in a compact space, all especially attractive for people with more leisure time but less discretionary income. For this reason, it is possible that in the future the concept of a passive house will diffuse into the mainstream in the form of an urban apartment located within reach of public transit and basic amenities. Stated differently, the socio-technical transition to passive houses may also be a socio-economic transition from suburban to urban living. This point brings us full circle to the forecasted 'next real estate boom' and its drivers (Doherty and Leinberger, 2011).

Would this socio-technical transition be consistent with, and facilitative of, the defining lifestyle characteristics of the 'new economy' as characterized by more leisure time, less discretionary consumption, reduced emphasis on material throughput as the key to well-being, greater grounding in local communities, more self-provisioning and emergent understandings of 'prosperity'? Would it be consistent with its macroeconomic features, such as a shift from consumption-based growth to public investment, making distinctions between different types of growth and different types of socio-technical systems? The answer will partly depend on how we frame this new technology. On the one hand, passive houses can be viewed as nothing more than an energy-efficient version of the current dominant building technology. In this framing, this development will be another case of ecological modernization, with minor cultural impact and the potential for perverse rebound effects.[4] On the other hand, the community of practice emerging around the putative shift toward the passive house has an opportunity to rethink the design of these kinds of (very likely) urban dwellings, with an eye toward creating public spaces for civic engagement and informal economies, urban agriculture and other types of self and communal provisioning, and various modes of what has come to be known as 'collaborative consumption.' For the most part, these questions are still open. What is clear is that one cannot contemplate a regime shift toward passive houses without considering the broader social and economic context.

The passive house case provides a starting point for how in combination the three theoretical perspectives featured in this book – new economics, socio-technical transitions and social practices – can enrich our understanding of what is required to affect a regime shift from conventional home construction to an arguably more sustainable mode of development. It illustrates the roles of diverse actors – from innovators to local governments to citizen-consumers going about their daily lives, to urban planners and economic development specialists – in such a transition and the complex relationships among them. No single perspective alone can offer this level of explanatory power. We now turn our attention to a summary of the other contributions that comprise this volume.

ORGANIZATION OF THE BOOK

The chapters of the book are organized into three parts that correspond to the conceptual perspectives outlined above. The first part is devoted to the emergent field of new economics and brings together work on the macroeconomics and political economy of sustainable consumption. The second part comprises four contributions that draw on research on socio-technical transitions to explore opportunities for change in prevalent mobility and energy systems. The final part considers both conceptual and applied scholarship on social practice theories.

Part I of the book on new economics begins with a chapter by Jonathan M. Harris who makes an explicit case for a new macroeconomic theory, a need made only more urgent by the Great Recession and its aftermath. Since 2008, a political debate has raged calling for, on the one hand, reassertion of Keynesian prescriptions or, on the other hand, belt-tightening austerity. Focusing specifically on the former set of strategies, Harris reminds us that Keynesianism is not about growth per se, but a broad set of societal objectives including the pursuit of full employment, the satisfying of basic needs, the allocation of sufficient resources for public investment and the need to ensure income equality. Harris notes that all of these objectives are compatible with sustainability and then proposes the formulation of a new economics that makes a sharp distinction between environmentally benign growth (for example, renewable energy, cultural activities) and environmentally problematic growth. He asserts that it will be necessary to redefine basic concepts such as consumption (to be more multidimensional), labor (to provide opportunities for reduced working hours) and capital (to distinguish between environmentally sustainable and unsustainable investments). A transition to a sustainable economy would proceed in two steps: an initial transition to sustainable technology during the first half of the twenty-first century driven by growth while a steady-state economy could become manifest during the second half of the century.

Inge Røpke then explores the connections between an emergent new economics and ecological macroeconomics and discusses the role of citizen-consumers in this framework. She identifies various interdependent problems, most notably ecological degradation, inequality and poverty, security and crises at various scales. Her narrative is illustrated with a critical discussion of a recent Danish report championing 'green growth.' Røpke observes that customary macroeconomics is mostly concerned with national and international developments and does not adequately consider global inequalities and the social and environmental costs of growth. For instance, GDP is widely recognized as an inadequate measure of progress and most macroeconomists fail to distinguish between the 'financial' economy, the 'real' economy in which ordinary people work and live, and the 'real real' economy of material and energy flows. Critical challenges include how to shift from consumption to investment, how to change consumers into prosumers and how to combine top-down policies with bottom-up experiments.

John Stutz's chapter contributes to the new economics perspective by offering a prospective scenario for individual and societal well-being. He explores the conditions under which an envisioned future – referred to as the Better Life Approach (BLA) – could unfold. The BLA is predicated on higher productivity, more effective education, stable (or reduced) working hours (with wages that keep up with productivity growth), diminished economic volatility and less income inequality. Although these dimensions are not ordinarily formulated in ecological terms, if comprehensively implemented, attention to such matters would yield manifold environmental benefits. While education is at the core of the BLA, curtailment of working hours, without concomitant income decline, and reductions of both economic volatility and income inequality could be attained through a combination of general insurance, tax policies and other forward-looking interventions.

Our treatment of new economics concludes with a chapter by Emanuel Ubert and Michael M. Bell who approach sustainable consumption from the standpoint of political economy. They identify four commonly used stances for studying consumption – neoclassical, competitive, sentimental and productivist. Each of these perspectives captures only a limited view of the consumption process and they contend that a more satisfactory approach is to look at the interdependencies between production and consumption: producers are dependent on the expenditures of worker-consumers but at the same time are under economic pressure to minimize the wages that they pay to the same worker-consumers. This paradox creates codependence and conflict between producers and consumers that Ubert and Bell refer to as the 'wage-price gap.' This gap is overcome by two types of 'stretching.' 'Financial stretching' occurs by accessing consumer credit and 'ecological stretching' takes place by depleting natural capital. Both forms of stretching are reliant on 'consumption lines' that discipline consumers in much the same way that producers are subject to the control of production lines.

Part II of the book comprises four chapters devoted to charting socio-technical transitions in the areas of mobility and energy. René Kemp and Harro van Lente argue that transformations toward sustainability actually entail two challenges: the need to impart long-term change to various technologies and infrastructures and the need to ensure that cultural values and consumer criteria evolve in a consistent direction. They relate the experience of two sustainability transitions in the Netherlands: the hygienic transition from 1870 through the 1930s and the waste management transition from 1970 through 2000. In both of these cases changing societal norms, cultural values and social practices were instrumental to the overall transition because they led to a shift in how the problem – and its solution – were framed and how the criteria for judging the success of a technological shift were defined. In contrast, the ongoing effort to transition toward a more sustainable mobility system has generated neither a shared vision nor much progress on how to gauge the societal suitability or desirability of such a system.

Sabine Hielscher, Gill Seyfang and Adrian Smith then discuss the linkages between strategic niche management and community initiatives premised on grassroots innovations. This perspective lays the groundwork for analyzing the potential of local projects to catalyze changes in current energy systems. This is a particularly timely and topical endeavor as interest in such community-led initiatives has been growing in recent years among academics, nongovernmental organizations (NGOs) and policy makers. There has been considerable speculation about the potential of these grassroots innovations to prevail where traditional interventions have failed: changing social practices and attitudes toward consumption as well as creating market pull for low-carbon technologies.

The third contribution in this part is by David J. Hess who provocatively asserts that the sustainability transition has already failed, at least in terms of mitigating global climate change, and an adaptation transition is now underway. He claims that this breakdown is likely to have profound effects on the landscape level of the MLP because adaptation responses will seek to enhance systemic resilience and lead in turn to different design parameters. For instance, diversification of energy sources may imply a portfolio containing fossil fuels to augment resilience. But the relationship is not (or at least does not have to be) zero-sum. Hess describes 'zones' of compatibility and conflict between resilience and sustainability. He observes that efforts to reduce consumptive throughput are consistent with both objectives while efficient technologies dependent on just one resource input are likely inconsistent. At the household level, enhanced resilience would call for the accumulation of savings to weather difficult periods, as well as access to multiple sources of paid employment. Hess draws on examples from the building industry to demonstrate how distributed renewable energy and energy efficiency could simultaneously support both sustainability and resilience.

The fourth and final chapter of Part II is by Jennie C. Stephens and Stephen M. McCauley who combine insights from work on sociotechnical transitions with theories of industrial cluster development. The planned concentration of firms in particularly dynamic industrial sectors has to date been a useful strategy for technological innovation in a number of places. The chapter provides a case study of Worcester, Massachusetts, a former manufacturing center with older building stock that has considerable potential for both sustainable energy production and energy conservation. Stephens and McCauley maintain that a focus on sustainable energy is likely to engage more heterogeneous constellations of stakeholders than is typically the case in cluster initiatives: educational institutions, social movement organizations, business leaders, local politicians and administrative staff of government agencies. The resultant aggregation is likely to bring together agents of grassroots social innovation with proponents of more traditional technology-policy priorities. While such diverse configurations hold some interesting opportunities, there is a strong likelihood that these participants will harbor irreconcilable visions that could also undermine a transition.

Social practice theories are the third innovative perspective for sustainable consumption considered in this book. Bente Halkier begins Part III with a critical appraisal of dominant policy approaches for conceiving of sustainable lifestyles. Campaigns based on deficient public understanding of relevant issues, or that seek to customize communication to specific target groups, fail to engage with the complexities of everyday life. She traces the intellectual development of social practice theories and defines a practice as a set of interconnected elements comprising bodily and mental activities, things and their uses, background knowledge and know-how, states of emotion and motivational knowledge. More sustainable consumption is dependent on the organization and conditions associated with the relevant practices that constitute people's ordinary experiences. Moreover, different practices invariably intersect and working toward less resource-intensive lifestyles entails developing different types of achievable practices and identifying their institutional, technological and social preconditions.

Gert Spaargaren then further examines the conceptual basis of social practices from the standpoint of reconciling the dichotomy between structure and agency and he addresses the question of how to develop governance capacity to facilitate sustainable lifestyles. This chapter also contends that most policy interventions have approached the consumer from an individualist perspective and have neglected the systemic aspects of consumption. In contrast, a systemic approach focused primarily on the supply side and technology obviates the potential of human agency. There is a need for a balanced way forward and practice theories offer a possible useful way forward because they understand social life as 'a series of recursive practices carried out by knowledgeable and capable agents.' The primary societal challenge is how to transition to low-impact practices and Spaargaren offers two suggestions: through technologies and objects or through culture, images, norms and ideas. The former artifactual alternative relies heavily on insights from STS while the ideational perspective remains substantially underdeveloped. He proceeds to highlight the relevance of 'interaction rituals' and 'emotional energy' as ways to comprehend how objects and human actions constitute one other. This contribution conceptualizes innovation as new, more sustainable ways of doing, saying, knowing and thinking and provides novel pathways for analyzing technologies, infrastructures, objects and products that coshape prevalent consumption routines.

The book's final chapter by Emily Kennedy, Harvey Krahn and Naomi T. Krogman operationalizes the concept of social practices by designing and implementing a mixed-methods empirical study to explore how life choices – in this case of whether to live in an outlying suburb or a city center – influence transportation behavior. This work represents a pioneering attempt to use quantitative tools to examine social practices and how the location of one's home shapes mobility. Kennedy and colleagues demonstrate the reciprocal influences surrounding social practices pertaining to residential choices. The chapter also reveals how these factors lead to the proximate aggregation of similarly minded individuals and how such propinquity can foster grassroots innovations that contribute to the emergence of new lifestyles.

ACKNOWLEDGMENT

We thank Alicia Cavanaugh, a graduate student in the Environmental Science and Policy Program at Clark University, for her work collecting data for the passive house case discussed in this chapter.

NOTES

1. For reviews of the drawbacks of singularly focusing on technological efficiency, see Huesemann (2006), Speth (2008), Jackson (2009) and Tukker et al. (2010).
2. A notable exception is McMeekin and Southerton (2012).
3. In the United States, the Passive House Institute US (PHIUS) has played a visible role in disseminating knowledge on the general concept and convening events and training programs. Also notable to varying degrees have been the activities of a number of other organizations including New York Passive House, the Northeast Sustainable Energy Association, the National Association of Homebuilders and the US Department of Energy.
4. Refer to David Owen (2011) for a comprehensive overview of rebound effects induced by efficiency improvements.

REFERENCES

Aaronson, J., J. Blignaut, R. De Groot et al. (2010). 'The road to sustainability must bridge three great divides', *Annals of the New York Academy of Sciences*, **1185**, 225–36.

Alperovitz, G. (2011). 'The new economy movement: activists and socially responsible firms are rethinking business as usual', *The Nation*, **292**(24), 20–4.

Alperovitz, G., T. Howard and S. Dubb (2009). 'Cleveland's worker-owned boom: rust-belt to recovery', *Yes!*, 5 June, available at http://www.yesmagazine.org/issues/the-new-economy/clevelands-worker-owned-boom (accessed 16 October 2012).

Bond, C. (2012). 'ReImagining Cleveland seeks to reclaim vacant lots in the city', available at http://reimaginingcleveland.org/about/ (accessed 16 October 2012).
Boyle, D. and A. Simms (2009). *The New Economics: A Bigger Picture*, London: Earthscan.
Brown, H. and P. Vergragt (2008). 'Bounded socio-technical experiments as agents of systemic change: the case of a zero-energy residential building', *Technological Forecasting and Social Change*, **75**(1), 107–30.
Brown, H., P. Vergragt, K. Green and L. Berchicci (2003). 'Learning for sustainability transition through bounded socio-technical experiments in personal mobility', *Technology Analysis and Strategic Management*, **15**(3), 291–316.
Cohen, M. (2010). 'The international political economy of (un)sustainable consumption and the global financial collapse', *Environmental Politics*, **19**(1), 107–26.
Cohen, M. (2012). 'The future of automobile society: a socio-technical transitions perspective', *Technology Analysis and Strategic Management*, **24**(4), 377–90.
Crawford, M. (2009). *Shop Class as Soulcraft: An Inquiry into the Value of Work*, New York: Penguin.
Diamond, R. and M. Moezzi (2004). *Changing Trends: A Brief History of the US Household Consumption of Energy, Water, Food, Beverages, and Tobacco*, Berkeley, CA: Lawrence Berkeley National Laboratory.
Doherty, P. and C. Leinberger (2011). 'The next real estate boom', *Washington Monthly*, November/December, available at http://www.washingtonmonthly.com/features/2010/1011.doherty-leinberger.html (accessed 16 October 2012).
Dosi, G. (1982). 'Technological paradigms and technological trajectories: a suggested interpretation of the determinants and directions of technical change', *Research Policy*, **11**(3), 147–62.
Dunham-Jones, E. and J. Williamson (2008). *Retrofitting the Suburbs: Urban Design Solutions for Redesigning Suburbs*, New York: Wiley.
Engelbrecht, H. (2009). 'Natural capital, subjective well-being, and the new welfare economics of sustainability: some evidence from cross-country regressions', *Ecological Economics*, **69**(2), 380–8.
Geels, F. (2002). 'Technological transitions as evolutionary reconfiguration processes: a multilevel perspective and a case study', *Research Policy*, **31**(8–9), 1257–74.
Geels, F. and J. Schot (2007). 'Typology of sociotechnical transition pathways', *Research Policy*, **36**(3), 399–417.
Glaeser, E. (2011). *Triumph of the City: How Our Greatest Invention Makes Us Richer, Smarter, Greener, Healthier, and Happier*, New York: Penguin.
Gregor, A. (2011). '"Zero-energy" construction crosses the ocean', *New York Times*, 1 December.
Hand, M., E. Shove and D. Southerton (2005). 'Explaining showering: a discussion of the materials, conventional, and temporal dimensions of practice', *Sociological Research Online*, **10**(2).
Hanlon, P., S. Carlisle, D. Reilly, A. Lyon and M. Hannah (2010). 'Enabling wellbeing in a time of radical change: integrative public health for the 21st century', *Public Health*, **124**(6), 305–12.
Hindle, M. (2010). 'The making of the Baltimore County High Performance Homes Bill', Presentation at the Fifth Annual North American Passive House Conference, Portland, Oregon, 5–6 November.
Hoogma, R., R. Kemp, J. Schot and B. Truffer (2002). *Experimenting for*

Sustainable Transport: The Approach of Strategic Niche Management, New York: Spon.
Huesemann, M. (2006). 'Can advances in science and technology prevent global warming? A critical review of limitations and challenges', *Mitigation and Adaptation Strategies for Global Change*, **11**(3), 539–77.
Hughes, T. (1983). *Networks of Power: Electrification in Western Society, 1880–1930*, Baltimore, MD: Johns Hopkins University Press.
Hurst, T. (2010). 'Despite recession, U.S. green building sector soars', *Earth and Industry*, 15 November, available at http://earthandindustry.com/2010/11/despite-recession-u-s-green-building-sector-soars.
IPCC (Intergovernmental Panel on Climate Change) (2007). *Fourth Assessment Report of the Intergovernmental Panel on Climate Change*, Geneva: IPCC.
Jackson, T. (2009). *Prosperity Without Growth: Economics for a Finite Planet*, London: Earthscan.
Jackson, T. (2012). 'Let's be less productive', *New York Times*, 26 May.
Kemp, R. and H. van Lente (2011). 'The dual challenge of sustainability transitions', *Environmental Innovation and Societal Transitions*, **1**(1), 121–4.
Kemp, R., J. Schot and R. Hoogma (1998). 'Regime shifts to sustainability through processes of strategic niche formation: the approach of strategic niche management', *Technology Analysis and Strategic Management*, **10**(2), 175–95.
Kennedy, E. and N. Krogman (2008). 'Toward a sociology of consumption', *Journal of International Sustainable Society*, **1**(2), 172–89.
Klingenberg, K., M. Kernagis and M. James (2009). *Homes for a Changing Climate: Passive Houses in the U.S.*, New York: Aspen Publishers.
Korten, D. (2009). *Agenda for a New Economy: From Phantom Wealth to Real Wealth*, San Francisco, CA: Berrett-Koehler.
Krapmeier, H. (2012). Personal communication with H. Brown, Bregenz, Austria, 2 May.
Layard, R. (2006). *Happiness: Lessons from a New Science*, New York: Penguin.
Loorbach, D. (2007). *Transition Management: New Mode of Governance for Sustainable Development*, Utrecht: International Books.
McMeekin, A. and D. Southerton (2012). 'Sustainability transitions and final consumption: practices and socio-technical systems', *Technology Analysis and Strategic Management*, **24**(4), 345–61.
Murphy, J. (ed.) (2007). *Governing Technology for Sustainability*, London: Earthscan.
Nelson, R. and S. Winter (1977). 'In search of a useful theory of innovation', *Research Policy*, **6**(1), 36–76.
Ornetzeder, M. and H. Rohracher (2009). 'Passive houses in Austria: the role of intermediary organizations for the successful transformation of a socio-technical system', in C. Broussous and C. Jover (eds), *Act! Innovate! Deliver! Reducing Energy Demand Sustainably*, Conference Proceedings, Stockholm: European Council for an Energy Efficient Economy, 2009 Summer Study, pp. 1531–41.
Owen, D. (2011). *The Conundrum: How Scientific Innovation, Increased Efficiency, and Good Intentions Can Make Our Energy and Climate Problems Worse*, New York: Riverhead Books.
Quitzau, M.-B. and I. Røpke (2008). 'The construction of normal expectations: consumption drivers for the Danish bathroom boom', *Journal of Industrial Ecology*, **12**(2), 186–206.

Raskin, P., C. Electris and R. Rosen (2010). 'The century ahead: searching for sustainability', *Sustainability*, **2**(8), 2626–51.
Raven, R. (2005). *Strategic Niche Management for Biomass: A Comparative Study on the Experimental Introduction of Bioenergy Technologies in the Netherlands and Denmark*, Eindhoven: Eindhoven University Press.
Rip, A. (1995). 'Introduction of new technology: making use of recent insights from sociology and economics of technology', *Technology Analysis and Strategic Management*, **7**(4), 417–31.
Rockström, J., W. Steffen, K. Noone et al. (2009). 'A safe operating space for humanity', *Nature*, **461**(24), 472–5.
Røpke, I. (2009). 'Theories of practice: new inspiration for ecological economic studies on consumption', *Ecological Economics*, **68**(10), 2490–7.
Rosenthal, E. (2008). 'No furnaces but heat aplenty in "passive houses"', *New York Times*, 26 December.
Rotmans, J., R. Kemp and M. van Asselt (2001). 'More evolution than revolution: transition management in public policy', *Foresight*, **3**(1), 15–31.
Schor J. (1998). *The Overspent American: Why We Want What We Don't Need*, New York: Harper Perennial.
Schor, J. (2011). *Plenitude: The New Economics of True Wealth*, New York: Penguin.
Schot, J. (1998). 'The usefulness of evolutionary models for explaining innovation: the case of the Netherlands in the nineteenth century', *History of Technology*, **14**(3), 185–200.
Seyfang, G. (2009). *The New Economics of Sustainable Consumption: Seeds of Change*, New York: Palgrave Macmillan.
Shove, E. (2004). *Comfort, Cleanliness and Convenience: The Social Organization of Normality*, New York: Berg.
Shove, E. (2012). 'Energy transitions in practice: the case of global indoor climate change, in G. Verbong and D. Loorbach (eds), *Governing the Energy Transition: Reality, Illusion, or Necessity?* New York: Routledge, pp. 51–74.
Speth, G. (2008). *The Bridge at the Edge of the World: Capitalism, the Environment, and Crossing from Crisis to Sustainability*, New Haven, CT: Yale University Press.
Tukker, A., M. Cohen, K. Hubacek and O. Mont (2010). 'The impacts of household consumption and options for change', *Journal of Industrial Ecology*, **14**(1), 13–30.
Unruh, G. (2000). 'Understanding carbon lock-in', *Energy Policy*, **28**(12), 817–30.
USCB (United States Census Bureau) (2011). *Median and Average Square Feet of Floor Area in New Single-Family Houses Completed by Location*, Washington, DC: USCB, available at http://www.census.gov/const/C25Ann/sftotalmedavgsqft.pdf (accessed 16 October 2012).
Vergragt, P. (2005). 'Backcasting for environmental sustainability: from STD and SusHouse towards implementation', in M. Weber and J. Hemmelskamp (eds), *Towards Environmental Innovation Systems*, Berlin: Springer, pp. 301–18.
Vergragt, P. (2010). 'Sustainability future visions: impacts and new strategies', Paper presented at the Learning Network on Sustainability Conference: Challenges and Opportunities for Design Research, Education, and Practice in the Twenty-first Century, Bangalore, 29 September–1 October.
Victor, P. (2008). *Managing Without Growth: Slower by Design, Not Disaster*, Cheltenham, UK and Northampton, MA, USA: Edward Elgar.

Voβ, J.-P., D. Bauknecht and R. Kemp (eds) (2006). *Reflexive Governance for Sustainable Development*, Cheltenham, UK and Northampton, MA, USA: Edward Elgar.
Weber, V. (2011). 'Passive house in local, state, and national codes: successes and others', Presentation at the Sixth Annual North American Passive House Conference, Silver Spring, Maryland, 28–29 October.
WEF (World Economic Forum) (2012). *More with Less: Scaling Sustainable Consumption and Resource Efficiency*, Geneva: WEF.
Whybrow, P. (2005). *American Mania: When More is Not Enough*, New York: Norton.
Wilkinson, R. and K. Pickett (2009). *The Spirit Level: Why More Equal Societies Almost Always Do Better*, New York: Penguin.
Wilson, A. and J. Boehland (2005). 'Small is beautiful: U.S. house size, resource use, and the environment', *Journal of Industrial Ecology*, **9**(1–2), 277–87.
Zeller, P. (2010). 'Can we build in a brighter shade of green?', *New York Times*, 25 September.

PART I

New economics

2. The macroeconomics of development without throughput growth

Jonathan M. Harris

INTRODUCTION

Serious discussion has begun of policies to promote the goal of increasing well-being without material growth. The idea of a steady-state macroeconomics was introduced into the modern economics conversation by Herman Daly (see, for example, Daly, 1973, 1991a, 1991b). Daly built on the fundamental analyses of Georgescu-Roegen (1971), although, of course, the origins of the concept go back much further, at least to John Stewart Mill,[1] with significant echoes in the work of John Kenneth Galbraith.[2] In the growth model presented by Robert Solow (1970), economic growth theoretically converges to a steady-state rate of growth based on the rate of growth of the labor force and technological progress – but would reach an absolute steady state (with no economic growth) only if the rates of population growth and technological progress were both zero. Interestingly, Solow, the originator of modern growth theory, has recently stated:

> There is no reason at all why capitalism could not survive with slow or even no growth. I think it's perfectly possible that economic growth cannot go on at its current rate forever . . . it is possible that the US and Europe will find that . . . either continued growth will be too destructive to the environment and they are too dependent on scarce natural resources, or that they would rather use increasing productivity in the form of leisure . . . There is nothing intrinsic in the system that says it cannot exist happily in a stationary state. (Solow, quoted in Stoll, 2008)

Peter Victor (2008) has recently introduced a model that shows scenarios for 'managing without growth' in the Canadian economy. This interactive macroeconomic model indicates that with a level of high social investment, a reduced work week and a substantial carbon tax, a transition to low and then no growth could be accomplished simultaneously with declining poverty, unemployment, lower carbon emissions and a reduced debt to gross domestic product (GDP) ratio. Tim Jackson (2009) similarly suggests that 'prosperity without growth' can be achieved by a shift from consumption to investment, with a specific investment focus on resource conservation, energy efficiency, clean technology and ecosystem restoration.

In a comparable vein, Neva Goodwin and I have proposed a reorientation of consumption toward basic needs, health services and education, and of productive technology toward resource-conserving investment (Harris and Goodwin, 2003). More specifically, I have advocated an ecologically oriented revival of Keynesian theory, 'deconstructing' the macroeconomic C + I + G + (X − M) equation into, on the one hand, categories representing energy- and resource-intensive sectors and, on the other hand, energy- and resource-conserving and human capital-intensive sectors (Harris, 2007, 2009). A focus on environmentally friendly technology and social investment then allows a revised Keynesian growth model, indicating the possibility of full employment without increased material consumption, or 'throughput,' a term introduced by Herman Daly (1973, 1996) to denote the combined economic processes of input of resources and output of wastes.

Moving toward the goal of prosperity without material growth requires a profound restructuring of macroeconomic theory. Importantly, the call by ecological economists to move away from traditional growth-oriented models comes at a moment when standard macroeconomics is in considerable turmoil. The financial crisis of 2007–09, with its legacy of continued high unemployment, seriously undermined the basis for mainstream macroeconomics and brought renewed attention to various forms of Keynesian analysis and policy previously regarded as outdated.

THE CURRENT CRISIS IN MACROECONOMICS

Paul Krugman (2009), in an overview of the crisis of macroeconomics, pointed out that as recently as 2008 there was something approaching a consensus among macroeconomists. Within the profession, most economists believed there was a 'broad convergence of vision,' according to Olivier Blanchard (2008), and that 'the central problem of depression-prevention has been solved,' according to Robert Lucas (2003). This confidence was based both on theoretical models that envisioned a self-equilibrating economy and a long period of relative stability and fairly steady economic growth from roughly 1985 to 2007. As Krugman observed, events like the Asian macroeconomic crisis of 1997–98 made little impression on this United States-centered consensus. It is true that there were differences between New Keynesian economists, who recognized some imperfections in the process of economic adjustment, and so-called New Classicals, whose theory of efficient markets essentially recognized none. But no crucial differences on policy arose while economic growth progressed smoothly.

The macroeconomic consensus was rudely interrupted by the Great Recession of 2007–09 and its aftermath. Not only was the severity and depth of the recession unprecedented since the 1930s, the very aggressive fiscal and monetary policies used to counter it came straight out of the 'old Keynesian' playbook, in contravention to everything that the new consensus – certainly the New Classical part of it – believed. New Keynesians adapted rapidly to the urgency of the policy needs, and some of them were at the forefront of formulating the emergency policies put into place by the Obama administration. But nothing in their theories had predicted or explained these dramatic developments. As Krugman describes it, this process of scrambling to catch up with reality has left macroeconomic theory in a state of confusion.

According to Krugman (2009), the first step back to reality is for economists to admit that 'Keynesian economics remains the best framework we have for making sense of recessions and depressions.' This would mean, at the least, extensive changes in the way formal macroeconomic theory is presented. In our text, *Macroeconomics in Context* (Goodwin et al., 2009), researchers at the Tufts University Global Development and Environment Institute have tried to formulate the approach of taking Keynesian economics seriously as a fundamental framework for understanding the macroeconomy. We also included in the book sections on 'Renewable resources, non-renewable resources, and sustainability,' 'Accounting for the environment' and 'Macroeconomics and ecological sustainability' to emphasize that environmental issues are an essential part of macroeconomics. But these initial steps are only the beginning of efforts in the task that now confronts us – a complete reorientation of macroeconomic theory and policy.

There is potential for close complementarity between a revived Keynesian and an ecological perspective. While older Keynesian analysis was oriented toward promoting growth, a Keynesian analysis of the relationship between investment and consumption does not depend on a growth orientation. What this analysis has in common with an ecological perspective is the rejection of market optimality assumed in classical models. Moving away from the neoclassical goal of inter-temporal utility maximization allows for different, pluralistic economic goals: full employment, provision of basic needs, social and infrastructure investment, and income equity. These goals are compatible with environmental preservation and resource sustainability, whereas indefinite growth is not. But they require a revitalization of the sphere of social investment, seriously neglected (indeed often omitted completely) in standard models.

There is good precedent for this approach in Keynes's own writings. In 'Economic possibilities for our grandchildren' he envisioned an end to economic growth. He suggested that a different structure of economic incentives and values would be appropriate for a world in which material economic growth had ceased. In his essay on 'The end of laissez-faire' he also recognized the importance of the social direction of investment in achieving what he anticipated to be a better economic system.

> I believe that some coordinated act of intelligent judgement is required as to the scale on which it is desirable that the community as a whole should save . . . and whether the present organization of the investment market distributes savings along the most nationally productive channels. I do not think that these matters should be left entirely to the chances of private judgement and private profits, as they are at present. (Keynes, 1930 [1963], 'The end of laissez-faire' and 'Economic possibilities for our grandchildren')

Keynes also famously proclaimed that '[t]he outstanding faults of the economic society in which we live are its failure to provide for full employment and its arbitrary and inequitable distribution of wealth and incomes' – a statement that seems to have particular contemporary resonance (see Keynes, 1936 [1964], Chapter 24, 'Concluding notes on the social philosophy towards which the General Theory might lead'). This observation suggests that we could do worse than look to the (neglected) heritage of Keynes as we struggle for solutions to today's social, economic and environmental problems.

NEW APPROACHES TO MACROECONOMIC POLICY

In previous work, I have suggested that a new breakdown of the major sectors of aggregate demand is useful in thinking about alternatives to current economic growth patterns (Harris, 2007, 2009). Specifically, the three major sectors of consumption, investment and government spending can be divided into subsectors representing material goods, services, resource-intensive and resource-conserving investment, and investment in human and natural capital. The idea is that we can then distinguish between those macroeconomic aggregates that should be strictly limited – resource-intensive consumption and investment and energy-intensive infrastructure – and those that can expand over time without negative environmental consequences. The latter would include large areas of health, education, cultural activity, and resource- and energy-conserving investment. The conclusion is that there is plenty of scope for growth in economic activity, concentrated in these categories, without growth in resource throughput, and with a significant decline in the most damaging throughput, that of carbon-intensive fuels.

A major shift in the direction of 'greener' economic growth will not, of course, come about without activist government policy. This is where the updated Keynesian view of economic policy is central. To some extent, the kind of transition to a low-carbon, resource-conserving economy that I am suggesting could be accomplished through market incentives – 'green taxes' and ecological subsidies aimed at internalizing environmental costs and promoting environmentally beneficial sectors. The combination of these taxes and subsidies could be revenue neutral. But there is also a large and necessary role for social investment, both in human capital and infrastructure. Fiscal policy is essential here. The discrediting of fiscal policy among economists has played a major role in enabling many of our current problems, from growing inequality to environmental degradation. If the 'free market' is solely responsible for resource allocation, and government fiscal intervention is seen as ineffective or harmful, then these negative trends seem simply inevitable. Reversing this bias is essential, and the current disarray among mainstream economists provides an excellent opportunity to do so – at least in the realm of theory.

What about in the realm of practical policy? There are some recent examples of the effective uses of fiscal policy for environmental objectives. The Obama administration's $787 billion dollar stimulus package – the first clearly Keynesian expansionary fiscal policy in many years – included about $71 billion for specifically 'green' investments, together with $20 billion in 'green' tax incentives. Specific provisions directed spending on energy efficiency in federal buildings and defense facilities ($8.7 billion), smart-grid infrastructure investment ($11 billion), energy and conservation grants to state and local governments ($6.3 billion), weatherization assistance ($5 billion), energy efficiency and renewable energy research ($2.5 billion), grants for advanced battery manufacturing ($2 billion), loan guarantees for wind and solar projects ($6 billion), public transit and high-speed rail ($17.7 billion), environmental cleanup ($14.6 billion) and environmental research ($6.6 billion).[3] According to a recent analysis by Alan Blinder and Mark Zandi (2010), the aggressive federal policy action including these 'green' investments 'probably averted what could have been called Great Depression 2.0 . . . without the government's response, GDP in 2010 would be about 11.5% lower, payroll employment would be less by some 8.5 million jobs, and the nation would now be experiencing deflation.'

Unfortunately, fiscal stringency in Europe has had the opposite effect, resulting in, for example, cutbacks for solar and wind power subsidies. It remains to be seen whether the deflationary effects of this fiscal austerity will force some rethinking among European governments. A standard Keynesian analysis would certainly suggest that at a time of high unemployment and near-zero inflation, deficit reduction should not be the prime concern. Prior to the onset of a misplaced doctrine of austerity in Europe, Portugal had achieved an impressive government-led transition from fossil fuels toward renewable power, with the percentage of renewable supply in the country's grid up from 17 percent in 2005 to 45 percent in 2010 (Rosenthal, 2010). This achievement involved a $22 billion investment in modernizing the country's electrical grid and developing wind and hydropower facilities. Portugal will recoup some of its investment through European Union carbon credits and will save about $2.3 billion a year on avoided natural gas imports. This example seems to indicate that major progress toward a sustainable energy system can be made in a relatively short period of time, without crippling costs or inflationary effects. Electricity prices are up about 15 percent, partly as a result of the investment in renewables, but of course this is justifiable and even desirable from the point of view of internalizing environmental costs and creating incentives for conservation.

These examples just scratch the surface of what is possible with a more aggressive approach to promoting an environmental transition. With continuing high unemployment, programs that create jobs directly seem especially appropriate, either in the government sector (along the lines of President Roosevelt's Civilian Conservation Corps, an early environmental Keynesian undertaking) or through government programs carried out by private sector contractors. Continued timidity on the part of deficit-conscious governments can only retard this transition, and prolong the period of high unemployment that we are now suffering.

GREEN GROWTH OR NO GROWTH?

One interpretation of the revised Keynesian perspective outlined here is that there is no need to worry about limits to economic growth. Rather, the issue is one of redefining economic growth in terms of energy-efficient, low-resource throughput, service-oriented activities. After all, it is the unrestrained growth of physical production that Daly and others have warned is incompatible with the Earth's ecosystems. Can we not grow the nonmaterial aspects of consumption while limiting or reducing physical throughput of resources?

Peter Victor's (2010) recent work gives an interesting perspective on this question. He distinguishes 'green growth,' 'brown growth,' 'black growth' and 'green degrowth' in terms of two dimensions: traditionally measured GDP and greenhouse gas emissions per unit GDP. 'Green growth' is growth in GDP with lower total greenhouse gas emissions. 'Brown growth' is growth with declining greenhouse gas intensity but rising overall greenhouse gas emissions. 'Black growth' is growth with rising greenhouse gas intensity. 'Green degrowth' is a decline in both GDP and greenhouse gas emissions.[4] This formulation leaves open the possibility of a large wedge of 'green growth,' with the growth rate of GDP more than offset by the rate of decline in emissions intensity. A few countries, such as Sweden and the United Kingdom, have actually followed such a 'green growth' path, while the United States is in the 'brown growth' zone.[5] Some developing countries, most notably Indonesia and Brazil, have experienced 'black growth' with increasing emissions intensity associated with GDP growth (see USEIA, 2006).

Lest we get too excited about the possibilities for 'green growth,' Victor analyzes the carbon intensity reduction requirements for various growth paths needed to achieve targets such as the goal of atmospheric stabilization through an 80 percent reduction in greenhouse gas emissions by mid-century put forward by the Intergovernmental Panel on Climate Change (IPCC). At a zero growth rate for GDP, an 80 percent reduction target would of course require 80 percent reduction in intensity. But at a 3 percent GDP growth rate, the same target would require a 95 percent reduction in intensity, since GDP roughly quadruples over a 50-year period. Victor's point is that while there is significant potential for 'green growth,' if we are to achieve ambitious carbon reduction targets, economies would have to become virtually carbon-neutral to permit any growth at all. Whatever environmental target you choose, it is more difficult to achieve at faster growth rates – no matter how 'green' the growth. In effect, whatever progress is achieved through greater energy and resource efficiency is undermined or completely negated by the effects of exponential growth.

One conclusion from this discussion is that while economic growth is essential in the currently developing world, it can no longer be afforded in the industrialized nations. Programs to reduce carbon and resource intensity in those countries are essential, but even given an aggressive approach to a transition away from carbon, any economic growth, even 'green' growth, in already rich countries reduces the carbon budget available for the developing world.[6]

This logic is mathematically unassailable, provided we assume that increases in GDP and reductions in intensity are independent of each other. But this assumption conceals the economic realities involved in an economic transition to energy efficiency and renewables. Suppose, for example, that a particular economy implements a large-scale program to replace coal-fired power plants with wind power. By all standard measures, this will involve a lot of economic activity, raising the investment component of GDP and increasing employment. But it need not involve any added consumption. The power that was formerly supplied by coal plants will now be supplied by wind (as in the case of Portugal cited above). So the country will have experienced economic growth with both a decrease in carbon intensity and an absolute decrease in carbon emissions. Once the investment program is completed, however, any growth in consumption will increase carbon emissions, though by a smaller amount than it would have previously (assuming that there is still some carbon-based power production in the system). Only if carbon-based fuels have been completely eliminated will it be possible to have increased consumption with zero net emissions increase.

This suggests that certain kinds of GDP growth (for example, the growth in investment in wind power) are environmentally neutral or beneficial. A general increase in consumption is not. But it is also possible to conceive of kinds of consumption growth that are environmentally beneficial. Suppose, for example, that a family builds a fully solar, carbon-neutral house, and that the cost of this house is 20 percent greater than that of an ordinary house.[7] By a standard GDP measure, the family's consumption is 20 percent greater than it would have been had they built an ordinary house. Yet this choice to consume 'more' has led to lower carbon emissions. A similar logic might apply to, say, consuming organic food at a price premium. If the higher price of organic food is due primarily to more labor-intensive methods in production, then this additional GDP also represents increased employment – a Keynesian benefit in an economy operating at anything less than full employment.

So it appears that not all forms of economic growth are environmentally negative, and some may be beneficial. It is true, as Herman Daly has argued, that the 'angelization' of GDP has its limits – once we have maximized energy efficiency, use of renewables, organic food production and so forth, any increase in consumption must necessarily increase throughput (see Daly, 1973, 1991b; see also Jackson, 2009). It is also true that, broadly speaking, economic growth works against reduced throughput intensity, so that if we increase overall consumption while also improving resource efficiency, the net effect on the environment is less beneficial than if we had increased efficiency while holding consumption constant. Eventually the exponential effect of growth will overwhelm the gains.

Nonetheless, there are rather large opportunities for types of economic activity that involve a transition to more environmentally beneficial means of production.

REDEFINING CONSUMPTION, LABOR AND CAPITAL

If we are to think in terms of a revised macroeconomics for an environmentally constrained twenty-first century, we need to do some redefinition of basic concepts. The first of these is consumption. Juliet Schor (2010) has addressed this issue in her discussion of the 'economics of plenitude.' In standard economic analysis, well-being is identified with 'utility,' a one-dimensional measure of happiness or satisfaction. Utility in turn is primarily associated with consumption of goods. Thus to increase utility, goods consumption must rise, and the focus of economic theory is on which combinations of goods most increase utility.

A different approach, advocated by Schor, would recognize that well-being is multi-dimensional, involving such factors as a sense of community, a feeling of purpose in life and an opportunity to engage in fulfilling work. Increased consumption of goods can contribute to well-being, but it may also be ineffectual or have an actual negative effect, for example, in cases where consumption is just 'keeping up with the Joneses' or is an attempt to salve inner feelings of emptiness, a kind of addiction. While there is an extensive literature addressing this issue (including several of the chapters in this volume), it has made little impact on economic theory.

As economies struggle to recover from the 2007–09 recession, there is much concern about whether and when consumers will resume spending at levels similar to those prior to the crash. From Schor's point of view, as well as those of many ecological economists concerned with excessive resource use and carbon emissions, such a resumption of consumption would not appear as a positive development. Yet for standard macroeconomics it seems essential. Without increased consumption – about 70 percent of aggregate demand in the economy – recovery is seen as unlikely.

There is an interesting paradox here. On the one hand, economists proclaim that increased consumption spending is required for economic revival. But the same economists also argue that increased spending on 'entitlements' such as healthcare or discretionary government purchases poses a severe threat to the economy. Why is one kind of spending desirable and the other destructive? Should it not be possible to reorient consumption toward more socially beneficial services and infrastructure investment, generating increased aggregate demand, while reducing negative social and environmental impacts? Part of the resistance to this approach comes from an ideological opposition to any increased government role, evident in current Republican and 'Tea Party' politics. But another major factor is that macroeconomic theory fails to distinguish between different kinds of consumption, and therefore tends to rely on 'traditional' increased goods consumption as an essential engine of economic growth.

This issue also has a special resonance with Keynes's assertion in 'Economic possibilities for our grandchildren' that an addiction to increased consumption can be pathological. Commenting on Keynes's argument on excess consumption using more modern terminology, Joseph Stiglitz (2010, pp. 43–4) points out that:

> [O]nce we open up the possibility that preferences are endogenous, there is no presumption that private market solutions have any optimality properties. By the same token, while the kinds of policy prescriptions, calling for government interventions, that arise naturally from our analysis may not be as theoretically tight as those that arise in the context of market failures with well-defined preferences, at least in some instances the case for collective action is compelling.

A second redefinition would apply to the economic concept of labor. In utility terms, labor is seen as a 'disutility' for which workers require compensation in the form of wages. This would imply that a reduction in hours worked (an increase in leisure) should represent a net gain in utility. But at the same time, a reduction in working hours is seen in macroeconomics in the form of unemployment – definitely a major negative factor in economic well-being, and currently one of our major problems. As with consumption, there appears to be an internal contradiction here.

A possible resolution of this internal contradiction would be policies promoting shorter hours of work. Rather than having the burden of reduced work availability fall entirely on the portion of the population formally identified as being unemployed, reduced work hours for all could be a minimal hardship and potentially a net gain when we take into account the benefits ('utility' in economics-speak) of shorter work weeks and longer vacations. Implementation of 'work-sharing' policies in Germany has significantly mitigated the impact of the recent recession on unemployment levels. Victor (2008), Jackson (2009) and Schor (2010) all emphasize the essential role of reduced work hours in promoting full employment while reducing traditional consumption growth.

This proposition is actually completely consistent with standard neoclassical economics, since increased leisure time should be as conducive to greater well-being as increased consumption, but it is a route rarely explored in mainstream macroeconomics. It also echoes Keynes's own speculations on a reduced work week as a likely element of future economic systems. This prediction has thus far come about to some extent in Europe, and barely so in the United States, as Robert Solow (2010) points out in his commentary on Keynes entitled 'Whose grandchildren?' The European path may actually be a better indicator of a socially and environmentally sounder economic system.

The third fundamental economic concept that needs re-examining is capital. Capital investment is a key component of GDP, but there is no essential macroeconomic distinction between energy-using and energy-saving capital. From an environmental standpoint, this distinction is crucial. This is especially so because of the long life of many forms of capital. Investment today in, for example, coal plants increases a fossil fuel dependency that will continue for 50 years or more, depending on the timeframe of the plant. In contrast, investment in energy-efficient capital or renewable energy plants would reduce fossil fuel use over a similar period. For the purpose of promoting recovery from the current economic slowdown, either kind of investment would be effective, but clearly there are environmental, and possibly employment, benefits to the renewable path. Macroeconomics needs to recognize the distinction between environmentally sustainable and unsustainable forms of investment.

TOWARD A THEORY OF ECONOMIC TRANSITION

To reconcile ecological and economic growth perspectives, it is crucial to exploit environmentally beneficial forms of economic growth. Some ecological economists may regard this assertion as an oxymoron. But I think the examples cited above show that it is not. This is also extremely important from a political point of view. Most people associate 'economic growth' with jobs, income and opportunity. Is it possible, economically and politically, to revise the concept so as to preserve the positive concepts associated with growth while eliminating its negative effects on the environment?

The key to solving this conundrum is to think in terms of a global economic transition. We cannot continue indefinitely with exponential growth. But the transition to a steady-state economy must take place over a long period of time.[8] Suppose we think of two time periods, roughly the first and second halves of the twenty-first century. During the first of these periods, there are enormous opportunities for the kinds of beneficial investment and reorientation of the economy described in the simplified examples already given.

A recent study of ecological limits to growth identifies nine 'planetary boundaries,' of which the authors estimate that three have already been transgressed: climate change, rate of biodiversity loss and alteration of the global nitrogen cycle. Others that are close to the boundary include ocean acidification, global freshwater use, the phosphorous cycle and land-system change (Rockström et al., 2009).[9] Responding to all of these issues requires a combination of institutional/technological change and limits on resource demands and waste outputs. This could imply limits on economic growth, but it could also imply development of new economic activities to replace more ecologically damaging ones. For example, the excessive use of nitrogen and phosphate fertilizers could be remedied with a wide-scale shift to more organic agricultural methods. These would tend to be more labor-intensive, thus generating higher employment.

Biodiversity loss and land-system change are complex issues related to population growth, economic expansion and financial incentives. It will ultimately be essential to limit both population and economic growth to reverse the excessive appropriation by humans of the Earth's ecological productivity.[10] But much of the existing damage results from current market incentives and failure to internalize either negative externalities associated with ecosystem damage or positive externalities from ecosystem services. Creating an appropriate system of economic penalties for ecosystem damage and rewards for ecosystem services would vastly shift economic activity, but not necessarily lessen it. Such economic incentives have been implemented in small-scale projects with success, and could be vastly expanded, in combination with carbon-reduction schemes.[11]

Responding to climate change and ocean acidification requires massive changes in energy systems with significant implications for patterns of economic growth (Harris, 2009; Victor, 2010). There are certainly limits on technological solutions, but there is also a vast untapped potential in alternative energy and efficiency technology (McKinsey and Company, 2009). This point suggests that limitations on economic growth are not the first option for responding to climate change, though some growth limits may ultimately be necessary, as noted above.

In reviewing growth issues, we can start with population. During the twentieth century, rising economic output was accompanied by a steadily rising population, with the rate of population growth increasing during the second half of the century. This is an important element in standard models of economic growth. But now the rate of global population growth is slowing, and the absolute yearly increase has also begun to decline. Some nations have reached population stabilization, while virtually every nation has declining fertility rates. We can therefore foresee a stabilization of population by about mid-century.

The absolute increase in global population yet to come is, of course, a huge environmental issue, and sound ecological economics suggests that every noncoercive policy that reduces fertility and overall population growth is beneficial. But in any case, the transition to a stable global population is inevitable, and has begun. This in itself introduces a fundamental change in the nature of economic growth. It reduces the overall rate of growth, and it changes the nature of GDP in important ways.

A stabilizing population is a graying population. A larger cohort of older people requires more social security (or equivalent) payments and more expensive medical care, with fewer workers of prime working age to support them. There has been much hand-wringing about the budgetary implications of this trend. But from a Keynesian point of view it can be viewed as a positive development as it provides for plenty of employment in healthcare and other caring professions such as assisted living. These occupational opportunities are also, for the most part, in service industries with relatively low environmental impacts. A larger proportion of GDP in these sectors is environmentally beneficial, other things being equal.

As noted above, there are great opportunities for investment and employment in the transition to renewable energy. These are available both in developed and developing nations. The strong commitment of China to renewable energy development indicates that this is no luxury for rich environmentalists. The Chinese rightly see it as the economic wave of the future, and they are determined to be in the forefront. This is good for them economically and good for the world environmentally. The Portuguese example suggests that nations at any level of development can profitably jump on this bandwagon, if their governments have the foresight to resist the short-term lure of low fossil fuel prices. To the extent that carbon-trading regimes are established, there will be broad opportunities for poorer nations to participate in carbon-storage schemes that are environmentally beneficial in terms of carbon reduction, forest preservation, soil reclamation and employment generation.

There are also huge employment-generating opportunities in the area of social investment and infrastructure. If the infrastructure is energy efficient, and if social investment is directed toward education, health services and the development of human capital, there will be no conflict between economic activity generated and environmental protection. Both carbon-neutral infrastructure and a shift toward human services are environmental positives. Note, however, that this will not happen through market mechanisms alone. It requires government leadership in accordance with the New Deal model, but on a global scale.

Another theme of Keynesian economics is job creation and income redistribution to benefit lower-income workers. This commitment implies conscious policies to combat growing international and intranational inequity. But it is not a zero-sum game. Higher employment and higher wages and living standards for workers create greater global prosperity and a more stable basis for economic activity than a high dependence on consumption by the affluent. Rising wages (which we are beginning to see now in China, for example) also reduce the race-to-the bottom aspect of international competition. Of course, there are significant environmental dangers associated with rising mass consumption. As far as possible, this activity should be channeled into the consumption of more efficiently produced, less energy-hungry consumer goods. This again requires conscious government intervention. But the trend to development of a global middle class is hardly one which can, or morally should, be opposed.

During our 'first period,' roughly to 2050, economic growth is inevitable. The trick is to have environmental Keynesian policies that stabilize it and steer it toward a renewable energy transition and a human-capital, service-oriented economy. In the currently industrialized economies, growth should slow over this period, a trend that is already evident and will likely be reinforced by the aftereffects of the recession of 2007–09. The economies of the global South require vigorous growth, but this growth can be directed increasingly toward carbon-saving investment and energy efficiency.

How about the 'second period,' 2050 to 2100? Here the concept of a steady-state economy comes into its own. The population is likely to have stabilized, which is an essential element of steady-state economics. If the transitional period has been successful, middle-class standards of living will have been achieved by many, we can hope most, of the world's population, and the energy infrastructure shifted to a largely noncarbon-based system, with the industrial infrastructure oriented toward high efficiency. Thriving sectors will exist in healthcare, education and cultural activity, and – as Peter Victor (2008) has suggested – the work week can be reduced, at least in the richer nations, to spread labor and prevent unemployment. At this point it makes excellent sense to ask whether further progress requires increased consumption. If institutions have already been adjusted toward social investment and greater equity, the pressure for 'economic growth' is likely to be much less.

This pattern is reflected in the 'Great Transition' model developed by Paul Raskin and his colleagues (2010) in which income rises rapidly to about 2050, and levels off thereafter, while environmental indicators stabilize, work time declines and general quality of life rises. This model presents in a more technical form the kind of projection for the twenty-first century that has been discussed here in general and theoretical terms. The implications of such a revised approach to economic growth are that economic theory can look forward to Mill's, or Daly's, steady state, while helping to guide the essential transition that will make it possible.

CONCLUSION: THE WAY FORWARD

A combination of Keynesian theory and ecological priorities offers a path that promises higher employment, greater equity and a transition to a more sustainable economy. Eventually this will also lead to a steady-state economy, and clearly the most affluent nations must pioneer this transition. But given the high current levels of unemployment, the immediate task is to reinvigorate all economies using Keynesian methods oriented toward social and environmental goals. Reducing budget deficits would become an appropriate policy goal after full employment was achieved, but this would not preclude the types of transitional infrastructure investment discussed above. Rather, these investments would need to be financed with carbon and resource taxes, balanced by per-capita credits to preserve or increase income equity.[12] Carbon taxes, or cap-and-trade with auction, could be used to raise revenue as needed, being adjusted to become revenue-neutral or net revenue-generating as fiscal conditions required.

The continuing problems following in the wake of the global financial crisis cannot be resolved by a return to traditional growth patterns, but appealing to an immediate no-growth scenario will not meet the case either. Large-scale practical policies based on an ecological version of Keynesianism provide a way forward, and can initiate a transition to a stabilized, low-carbon, low-throughput world economy.

NOTES

1. On the stationary state, refer to Book IV, Chapter 6 of Mill (1848 [1994]).
2. See, in particular, Galbraith (1958).
3. See http://environment.about.com/od/environmentallawpolicy/a/econ_stimulus.htm (accessed 18 October 2012).
4. In theory, 'black degrowth' is also possible, with declining GDP but with greenhouse gas intensity increasing so fast that total emissions rise.
5. On the case of Sweden, see http://www.encharter.org/index.php?id=121&L=0 (accessed 18 October 2012).
6. For a perspective on the stringency of this global carbon budget and the tension between global North and South, see Baer et al. (2009).
7. My colleague, William Moomaw, has built such a house for his retirement in western Massachusetts. See http://enews.tufts.edu/focus/52/2008/04/04/LivingDeliberately (accessed 18 October 2012).
8. An ambitious modeling effort describing such a 'Great Transition' is presented in Raskin et al. (2010).
9. Other planetary boundaries not yet quantified include chemical pollution and atmospheric aerosol loading, while stratospheric ozone depletion is currently within acceptable limits as a result of international treaties restricting ozone-depleting substances.
10. A study by Vitousek et al. (1986) estimated that humans appropriated about 40 percent of terrestrial photosynthetic capacity and approximately 25 percent of total planetary

capacity as of that date. Since 1986, there has been a 40 percent increase in the global population while global GDP has roughly doubled.

11. See, for example, Kumar (2005) on payments for ecosystem services and Harris and Birjandi Feriz (2011) on carbon reduction, forest preservation and agriculture.
12. Refer to Boyce and Riddle (2009) for an exposition of 'cap-and-dividend' policies to reduce carbon and promote income equity.

REFERENCES

Baer, P., T. Athanasiou and S. Kartha (2009). 'The right to development in a climate-constrained world', in J. Harris and N. Goodwin (eds), *Twenty-first Century Macroeconomics: Responding to the Climate Challenge*, Cheltenham, UK and Northampton, MA, USA: Edward Elgar, pp. 75–112.

Blanchard, O. (2008). 'The state of macro', NBER Working Paper No. W14259, National Bureau of Economic Research, Boston.

Blinder, A. and M. Zandi (2010). 'How the Great Recession was brought to an end,' available at http://www.economy.com/mark-zandi/documents/End-of-Great-Recession.pdf (accessed 18 October 2012).

Boyce, J. and M. Riddle (2009). 'Cap and dividend: how to curb global warming while promoting income equity', in J. Harris and N. Goodwin (eds), *Twenty-first Century Macroeconomics: Responding to the Climate Challenge*, Cheltenham, UK and Northampton, MA, USA: Edward Elgar, pp. 189–225.

Daly, H. (ed.) (1973). *Toward a Steady-state Economy*, San Francisco, CA: W.H. Freeman.

Daly, H. (1991a). 'Elements of environmental macroeconomics', in R. Costanza (ed.), *Ecological Economics: The Science and Management of Sustainability*, New York: Columbia University Press, pp. 32–46.

Daly, H. (1991b). *Steady-state Economics*, Washington, DC: Island Press.

Daly, H. (1996). *Beyond Growth: The Economics of Sustainable Development*, Boston, MA: Beacon Press.

Galbraith, J. (1958). *The Affluent Society*, Boston, MA: Houghton Mifflin.

Georgescu-Roegen, N. (1971). *The Entropy Law and the Economic Process*, Cambridge, MA: Harvard University Press.

Goodwin, N., J. Nelson and J. Harris (2009). *Macroeconomics in Context*, Armonk, NY: M.E. Sharpe.

Harris, J. (2007). 'Reorienting macroeconomic theory towards environmental sustainability', in J. Gowdy and J. Erickson (eds), *Frontiers in Ecological Economic Theory and Application*, Cheltenham, UK and Northampton, MA, USA: Edward Elgar, pp. 36–52.

Harris, J. (2009). 'Ecological macroeconomics: consumption, investment, and climate change', in J. Harris and N. Goodwin (eds), *Twenty-first Century Macroeconomics: Responding to the Climate Challenge*, Cheltenham, UK and Northampton, MA, USA: Edward Elgar, pp. 169–86.

Harris, J. and M. Birjandi Feriz (2011). *Forests, Agriculture, and Climate: Economics and Policy Issues*, Medford, MA: Tufts University, Global Development and Environment Institute, available at http://ase.tufts.edu/gdae/education_materials/modules.html#REDD (accessed 18 October 2012).

Harris, J. and N. Goodwin (2003). 'Reconciling growth and environment', in

J. Harris and N. Goodwin (eds), *New Thinking in Macroeconomics*, Cheltenham, UK and Northampton, MA, USA: Edward Elgar, pp. 229–49.
Jackson, T. (2009). *Prosperity Without Growth: Economics for a Finite Planet*, London: Earthscan.
Keynes, J. (1930). *Essays in Persuasion*, London: Macmillan, reprinted 1963, New York: W.W. Norton.
Keynes, J. (1936). *The General Theory of Employment, Interest, and Money*, London: Macmillan, reprinted 1964, New York: Harcourt, Brace.
Krugman, P. (2009). 'How did economists get it so wrong?', *New York Times*, 2 September.
Kumar, P. (2005). 'Market for ecosystem services', International Institute for Sustainable Development, Winnipeg, available at http://www.iisd.org/pdf/2005/economics_market_for_ecosystem_services.pdf (accessed 18 October 2012).
Lucas, R. (2003). 'Macroeconomic priorities', *American Economic Review*, **93**(1), 1–14.
McKinsey and Company (2009). *Pathways to a Low Carbon Economy*, available at https://solutions.mckinsey.com/ClimateDesk/default.aspx (accessed 18 October 2012).
Mill, J. (1848). *Principles of Political Economy and Chapters on Socialism*, London: Longman, Green & Co., reprinted 1994, New York: Oxford University Press.
Raskin, P., C. Electris and R. Rosen (2010). 'The century ahead: searching for sustainability', *Sustainability*, **2**(8), 2626–51.
Rockström, J., W. Steffen, K. Noone et al. (2009). 'Planetary boundaries: exploring the safe operating space for humanity', *Ecology and Society*, **14**(2), 32.
Rosenthal, E. (2010). 'Portugal gives itself a clean-energy makeover', *New York Times*, 10 August.
Schor, J. (2010). *Plenitude: The New Economics of True Wealth*, New York: Penguin Press.
Solow, R. (1970). *Growth Theory: An Exposition*, New York: Oxford University Press.
Solow, R. (2010). 'Whose grandchildren?', in L. Pecchi and G. Piga (eds), *Revisiting Keynes: Economic Possibilities for Our Grandchildren*, Cambridge, MA: MIT Press, pp. 87–93.
Stiglitz, J. (2010). 'Toward a general theory of consumerism: reflections on Keynes', in L. Pecchi and G. Piga (eds), *Revisiting Keynes: Economic Possibilities for Our Grandchildren*, Cambridge, MA: MIT Press, pp. 41–86.
Stoll, S. (2008). 'Fear of fallowing: the specter of a no-growth world', *Harper's Magazine*, March.
USEIA (United States Energy Information Administration) (2006). *Energy Information Annual* 2006,Washington, DC: US Department of Energy.
Victor, P. (2008). *Managing Without Growth: Slower by Design, Not Disaster*, Cheltenham, UK and Northampton, MA, USA: Edward Elgar.
Victor, P. (2010). 'Ecological economics and economic growth', *Annals of the New York Academy of Sciences*, **1185**, 237–45.
Vitousek, P., P. Ehrlich and P. Matson (1986). 'Human appropriation of the products of photosynthesis', *BioScience*, **36**(6), 368–73.

3. Ecological macroeconomics: implications for the roles of consumer-citizens

Inge Røpke

INTRODUCTION

The economic decline that began in 2008 opened a window of opportunity for consideration about how to combine macroeconomic and environmental concerns. This discussion is far from new, as evidenced, for instance, by the European Commission's White Paper from 1993, which explained how a greening of the economy could go hand in hand with increased employment (European Commission, 1993). These ideas were not reflected much in actual policies, and – despite some green elements – the subsequent economic upturn was driven first of all by consumption, and in several affluent countries, fueled by credit expansion. The current revival of this discussion includes contributions from actors involved with efforts to advance a 'Green New Deal' (The Green New Deal Group, 2008; Schepelmann et al., 2009) that repeats the idea that the promotion of green innovation and government funding of greener infrastructure would improve competitiveness and increase employment.

This time 'Green Keynesianism' is accompanied by a more theoretical debate and increased interaction between the heterodox schools of ecological economics and post-Keynesian economics (Victor, 2008; Harris, 2009; Harris and Goodwin, 2009; Holt et al., 2009; Jackson, 2009; Pollitt et al., 2010). In addition, both the degrowth community and the research community organized around sustainable transitions of socio-technical systems have contributed to discussions on how to reconcile environmental and social concerns (Grin et al., 2010; Martinez-Alier et al., 2010; Schneider et al., 2010). Based on this broad variety of pieces in a jigsaw puzzle, a new ecological macroeconomics is emerging, but the contours are still vague. This chapter seeks to outline some of this topography and to add a few pieces of its own by highlighting the need to shift resources from consumption to investment and describing the role of consumer-citizens in such a change.

The chapter starts by identifying the problems and challenges for an ecological macroeconomics. The next section outlines some of the shortcomings of traditional macroeconomics and the requirements related to development of a new theoretical framework. Despite the complexities of such an initiative, many contributors agree on one important issue and this is dealt with in the third section: the need to shift from consumption to investment to transform the socio-technical systems related to energy, transport, housing, food and so forth. The fourth section outlines briefly the roles of consumer-citizens in relation to such sustainability transformations and the final section considers the possibilities for initiating the envisioned changes.

WHAT GOALS SHOULD AN ECOLOGICAL MACROECONOMICS PURSUE?

Traditionally, 'macro' in macroeconomics has referred to the national level: the theories – whether Keynesian or monetarist or some other 'breed' – are first of all applied as a basis for managing national economies. This makes good sense when 'the common good' is mainly conceived from a national perspective and when the possibilities for taking action are anchored in nation states. The customary concern for macroeconomic theory is, thus, the 'health' of the national economy: maintaining 'reasonable' economic growth, securing employment, avoiding long-term public deficits, inflation and balance of payments deficits that increase foreign debt and threaten the currency.[1] Other political issues, such as social concerns and care for the environment, are handled within the framework of these general matters.

The possibilities for national economies to stay healthy depend on the international institutional framework, but this does not alter the national focus. Although global institutions act at a supranational level, they are exactly international and formed as the path-dependent results of power relations among nation states (consider, for example, the establishment of the Bretton Woods institutions after World War II). Still, international institutions embody only to a very limited extent a global perspective of 'the common good' and challenge the predominantly national focus.

Since environmental problems increasingly call for a global perspective when conceiving 'the common good,' an ecological macroeconomics needs to have a global perspective on 'macro.' But at least for the foreseeable future, this must happen within a framework where most political power is still anchored at the national level. The global perspective accordingly calls for a redefinition of what is meant by a healthy national economy.

The core problems at the global and national levels can be translated into the goals with which an ecological macroeconomics should deal. At the global level, at least five main groups of challenges can be identified.

- Environmental challenges: climate change, destruction of ecosystems, overuse of core resources, such as land, water and phosphorus, and the use of problematic chemicals.
- Poverty, large inequalities and large-scale migration.
- Security: shifting global power relations imply instability. While this can be seen as a positive development, it may increase social and military conflicts, not least when combined with resource scarcity.
- Global economic crises, instability of the financial system, sudden breakdown, pervasive unemployment.
- The complexity of the global interrelationships presents a problem in itself. The prevailing institutions and mechanisms generate the problems mentioned above – destroying the environment, transferring resources from poor to rich – and they do so in ways so complex and subtle that both understanding and transformation is harder than 'just' challenging vested interests.

Translating some of these challenges into goals in a national context, and using Denmark as an example, implies a high priority for the issue of scale and distribution: the appropriation of resources for consumption in Denmark should be gradually reduced to make space for more consumption in poor countries and contribute to global redistribution. Data on the climate change issue, as well as data on material flows and land use, illustrate that this challenge is enormous and that its size depends particularly on the extent to which Denmark ultimately wants to deal with global redistribution (Jackson, 2009). When global redistribution is considered to be a necessary ethical concern, increased technological efficiency will not be sufficient to make room for others' consumption. Resource-consuming economic activity will have to be reduced and the challenge is to reconcile this objective with the achievement of other important societal goals.

A core aspiration should be to ensure the fulfillment of basic needs for all members of society, which should include a social position that enables acknowledgment as a citizen who contributes to society. In modern societies, this goal is often formulated as full employment in the formal economy, but this may have to be redefined. Simultaneously, relative economic stability is needed to avoid crises where people are driven from house and home. In a small economy with few natural resources, economic stability and reasonable living standards depend on imports and thus on the ability to export goods and services. Maintaining this ability is an important goal, but it should be combined with the aim of lessening dependence on imports to reduce complexity, national vulnerability and environmental pressures. In addition to global redistribution, an important target should be the gradual reduction of inequalities within individual countries because this will reduce social tensions and increase welfare.[2]

In mainstream economics, many of these nationally based societal goals are condensed into the goal of economic growth: constantly growing gross domestic product (GDP) is expected to ensure full employment, better living standards for most people, economic stability and the reduction of social tensions. The challenge of addressing climate change (which is usually seen as the main environmental problem) is thus formulated as the need to decouple GDP growth from carbon dioxide (CO_2) emissions. Since technological innovation may be able to contribute to both emissions reductions and economic growth, win-win solutions are expected to take us a long way. The challenge is of manageable size as long as rebound effects are downplayed, and, even more important, the need for global redistribution is not taken into account.

Ecological economists question this way of formulating the problem, because they, like many others, are skeptical about the relationship between GDP and well-being (Stiglitz et al., 2009), and even argue that GDP is best relinquished as a relevant measure of anything (van den Bergh, 2009). But giving up GDP does not change the need for reconciling the national goals related to well-being with the goal of preventing climate change, and since ecological economists cannot set aside the rebound and the distribution issues, the challenge is much larger than usually conceived by mainstream economists. To face this challenge, considerable transformations of both socio-technical systems and institutional structures are necessary (see the chapters in Part II of this volume). Fossil fuels must be replaced by renewable energy; ecosystems must be restored; systems of provision related to energy, food, housing, transport, healthcare and so forth have to be transformed; and economic mechanisms that allocate resources and distribute goods must be changed. To discuss these issues in an overall perspective, and not only as separate problems, a new ecological macroeconomics is needed.

THE CHALLENGE OF FORMULATING AN ECOLOGICAL MACROECONOMICS

Since an ecological macroeconomics redefines what is meant by a healthy national economy, it calls for new ways of theorizing or modeling the economy to analyze trade-offs and policy impacts. Macroeconomics has traditionally not dealt with environmental issues, and environmental economics is basically a microeconomic field. The introduction of satellite accounts (in relation to national accounting) on energy use and various emissions, as well as physical input-output tables, has made it possible to include environmental aspects in macroeconomic modeling, but this is mainly used for specialized studies that are added on to traditional analysis. As Victor (2008) has shown, interesting results can be achieved by applying conventional macroeconomics to address questions arising from ecological considerations, but there are substantial limitations to the kind of questions that can be addressed within this framework. Consideration of scale and distributional issues is not a common part of macroeconomic analysis and there are significant obstacles to the use of macroeconomic reasoning in relation to transformation processes. In the following discussion, some of the problems related to the use of traditional macroeconomic models for the purpose of ecological macroeconomics are outlined, and consequently, some requirements for a new ecological macroeconomics are formulated.

First, as already mentioned, macroeconomic models are typically based on a national perspective. It is not apparent in which ways and to what extent the national economy depends on foreign resources and the use of global absorptive capacity for emissions. Macroeconomic analysis should include two perspectives on resource use: a production perspective highlighting the use of resources in national production and a consumption perspective capturing the appropriation of resources for national consumption (private and public). Highlighting import dependency and environmental load displacement is important.

Second, macroeconomic models are built around the concept of GDP. As often pointed out, GDP is basically a measure of activities in the formal economy, and it is not really a relevant measure for any of the concerns of ecological macroeconomics. GDP mixes up costs and benefits, does not reflect the depletion of natural resources, does not correlate with well-being and so forth. In addition, GDP as a monetary measure is not very informative. Everything is added according to market value (or imputed value), independent of the character of the concrete activities being added. A distinction is made between consumption and investment, but it is not relevant for the functioning of the model whether investments are made in wind turbines or coal-fired power plants (see the chapter by Jonathan Harris in this volume). From an environment and transformation perspective, however, the concrete activities are decisive: it is not possible first to create GDP and afterward to find out how to spend the money, for instance, on welfare or environmental improvements. This is possible in a household's private economy, but at the macro level the process is simultaneous: we only get welfare services, for instance, if these are part of the activities included in GDP. The character of the output, the distribution of goods and services, and trade relationships are constituted in the process – embedded in the baking of the 'cake.' An ecological macroeconomics needs to focus on the character of the concrete activities – that is, how they contribute to transformation processes and important societal goals. Jackson (2009) emphasizes this point when he suggests distinguishing among various categories of investment.

Third, economic models are formulated in traditional economic terms – supply and demand, prices and quantities – and causal relationships are formulated as relationships between such variables. All sorts of transactions and relationships involve aspects of nature – flows of energy and materials – but these only exist as a hidden layer below the monetary relationships. When economists calculate something 'in real terms,' they just mean considering a trend adjusted for inflation. In relation to the financial crisis, they may also refer to the real economy as the actual production of goods and services, to distinguish it from the financial economy, which has completely outgrown the transactions in the real economy. However, as Kallis et al. (2009) point out, economists do not consider the real-real economy – the biophysical metabolism connected to economic processes.

An ecological macroeconomics must deal directly with natural flows and not only include them as add-on satellites. For instance, it should be clear that when resources are spent for increased consumption by the rich, they cannot, at the same time, be used for system transformation or for improving living conditions of the poor. Economic models tend to disguise this fact, since money can multiply without limits. Traditional reasoning would argue that economic benefit urges the high-income groups to work more and thus to create a larger GDP, which would also benefit the poor. But this makes sense only if resources are unlimited; when they are not, the economic carrot just gives high-income groups access to appropriating more resources and undermining the future living conditions for everyone.

Fourth, macroeconomic models are based on given institutions. Minor institutional changes may be analyzed in the models, such as changes to pension schemes, unemployment benefits or tax rates, but the transformations needed to cope with large challenges would involve more radical institutional changes – implying changes of the causal relationships.

An ecological macroeconomics thus needs to open up the discussion on institutional changes. Presently, many sensible political measures are 'shot down' because they would create problems within the given institutional framework. These recommendations may call for changing the set-up rather than giving up the measure. Free movement of capital across borders is an example of an institutional framework that limits the political space for action. When Denmark embarked on its liberalization process, deregulation was nicknamed 'insurance against socialism' because it would make socialist-inspired policies impossible; for instance, increased taxation of capital gains would encourage capital to leave the country and threaten the currency. To make progress toward sustainability, it is certainly necessary to abolish the financial markets as the highest judge with regard to the availability of policy options.

It would likewise be useful to understand and transform the institutions that are decisive for maintaining high-profit expectations – perhaps breaking up large firms would be useful to reduce power concentrations (Korten, 2009). Another example of political-economic mechanisms that make sensible change difficult relates to the vulnerability of pension systems and systems for housing loans; such systems call for institutional changes that diminish risks not to obstruct measures that may reduce economic growth (Seidl and Zahrnt, 2010).

In general, the concerns emerging from the basics of the real-real economy may conflict with the institutional set-up of the economy. Take the example of young people who decide to live on a low income level – for instance, by combining part-time work and educational activities for a long period of time. From an environmental perspective, it is desirable that they appropriate few resources and maybe delay having children, but considerable pressure is exerted to encourage young people to finish their education quickly so that they can earn more money and pay higher taxes to fund the welfare state. Of course, in the long run, citizens cannot, on average, command more services from the welfare state than it is possible to fund (which is presently the case in Denmark), but it is highly problematic when the funding depends on encouraging resource-intensive lifestyles. An ecological macroeconomics ought to be able to highlight such conflicts and consider how institutions can be changed.

Fifth, macroeconomics is weak with regard to technology and innovation. Technological change is black boxed and socio-technical systems are not thematized at all. This is problematic because it would be useful to conceive of resource use as emerging from the functioning of socio-technical systems rather than from the traditional statistical categories of production and consumption. Consumption and production are interwoven in socio-technical systems, and the dynamics of these systems are decisive for resource use (Elzen et al., 2004; see also the chapter by René Kemp and Harro van Lente in this volume). For instance, the food system includes the interplay between agricultural production, methods of cultivation, husbandry, provision of inputs for agriculture, industrial processing of food, distribution systems, trade relationships, diets and so forth. The system is extremely complex and is responsible for a large catalogue of disasters: homogenization and loss of biodiversity, diffusion of phosphorus, net use of energy (which is absurd in a process involving photosynthesis), eutrophication, maltreatment of animals, diffusion of pesticides, destruction of groundwater and water courses, resistant bacteria due to overuse of antibiotics, unhealthy working conditions, food-related health problems, obesity, hunger, underselling poor farmers in developing countries, enormous food waste, and the list goes on.

Obviously, there are large vested interests maintaining this system and current arrangements are legitimized by describing the system as high-productivity agriculture, which effectively provides high-quality food for the growing world population. Traditional macroeconomic reasoning only captures the contribution of agriculture to GDP and the balance of payments. In the Danish case, agriculture and related industries are usually considered to provide positive contributions to the overall health of the economy, in spite of the basic malfunctioning of the food system (the sector is currently coping with a number of economic challenges, but this has not led to problematization of the system as a whole). An ecological macroeconomics must take into account the functioning of socio-technical systems, including their interplay (for example, between the energy, food and transport systems), since they are decisive for the overall health of the economy. The theoretical framework should also open for consideration whether some general guidelines would be relevant for transformations of the socio-technical systems, such as localization and complexity reduction.

Although an ecological macroeconomics along the lines described above is not in place as a systematic framework, researchers who share these ideas do make suggestions regarding how to handle the multiple crises we are facing. The next section deals with a particular aspect of the insights advanced by many contributors, namely the need for a shift in resource use from consumption to investment (see the chapter by Jonathan Harris in this volume). An ecological macroeconomics could also emphasize other options, such as the reallocation of investments or an overall reduction of both consumption and investment – or various combinations of these approaches. In this chapter, however, the idea of shifting resources from consumption to investment is emphasized because it links up with the discussion about consumers in other parts of this book, and integrates the macroeconomic perspective with considerations of the roles of consumer-citizens in sustainability transformations.

THE SHIFT FROM CONSUMPTION TO INVESTMENT

The point of departure is in the need to reduce society's overall resource consumption (and related CO_2 emissions) and for restoring degraded ecosystems. In principle, this could be done by scaling down the level of activity and the standard of living within the framework of existing socio-technical and economic systems, but this option is not very attractive. To reconcile environmental improvements with other societal aims, system transformation is decisive – including transformed systems for energy, transport, food, housing and so forth. Such large-scale transformations require resources, and since the same resources cannot be spent twice in the real-real economy, consumption will have to make way for investments, just as the composition of investments has to change. In a traditional Keynesian model, natural resources do not constitute a limitation and investments can increase GDP and through the multiplier effect increase consumption as well, until full employment gives rise to wage push and problems with competitiveness. But from the perspective of ecological macroeconomics, limits to resource use have to be enforced, and unless large improvements in resource efficiencies are achieved through investments, consumption possibilities will be reduced. Transformative investments thus have to be combined with limitations on rebound effects and multiplier processes.

In programs for so-called green growth, consumption is often expected to continue increasing. Take, for instance, the plan from the Danish Commission on Climate Change Policy (DCCCP) that outlines how Denmark, by 2050, can become independent of fossil fuels and meet the target of reducing greenhouse gases by 80 to 95 percent compared with 1990 (Klimakommissionen, 2010; Richardson et al., 2011). The terms of reference for DCCCP state that this goal should be achieved simultaneously with continued economic growth and increased transportation. The main elements of the plan are energy savings, not least in relation to housing; a considerable increase in the use of wind energy for the provision of electricity, also to be applied for heating and transportation; and the use of biomass as the most important system backup (the DCCCP suggests that the use of biomass should be kept within the limits of national production capacity with unchanged food production, since it will become a scarce and probably expensive resource in the future; a scenario based on more biomass is also presented). This conversion of the energy system will require considerable investment in offshore wind turbines, electric cars, heat pumps, energy renovation of buildings and electricity infrastructure, but the DCCCP argues that this is compatible with increasing living standards – more cars, more housing space, more appliances. It assumes that GDP will more than double from 2008 to 2050 and calculates that the long-term additional costs of the conversion will be in the order of 0.5 percent of GDP in 2050. The low costs reflect that the reference scenario assumes increasing prices of fossil fuels and increasing costs of CO_2 quotas, which means that it will also be expensive not to convert the energy system. Although consumers will have to contribute to the investments in various ways – paying other actors as well as investing themselves – they are still expected to be much better off due to economic growth.

Before criticizing this result from an ecological economic perspective, it should be noted that the DCCCP may be passing lightly over the implications for consumption, even within a traditional modeling framework. If growth in GDP involves an increasing share of investments, consumption will not grow as fast as GDP; and in addition, part of the consumption may become tied to specific consumption categories that some consumers do not exactly find desirable, such as insulation, heat pumps and electric cars. Seen from the perspective of political legitimacy, investment-based GDP growth may serve the goal of increased employment, but it may not fulfill expectations regarding increasing consumption. The share of investment in GDP has historically been higher in earlier phases of economic development; and in quickly developing, more or less planned economies, the share has been very high, and still is – for instance, in China. But sooner or later, the population wants to benefit more from growth in the form of increased consumption and the investment rate tends to fall, as China now plans. While high investment rates seem to be acceptable in periods of rapid industrialization – when people have not yet become accustomed to high and growing consumption – and in periods of war, it is a new challenge to reverse the trend and convert from a consumption-driven to an investment-driven economy. It is sometimes argued that economic growth is decisive for the political legitimacy of sustainability transformations, but the question is whether higher employment is sufficient, if it is not combined with customary consumption increases over time.

Turning to the ecological economic critique of the DCCCP's idea that consumption can continue to increase, it should be noted that basically its result depends on two assumptions. First, the assumption of unlimited natural resources within the traditional modeling framework is maintained: fossil fuels are replaced by the resources needed for producing wind turbines, electric cars and all the other gear needed for the transformation (including, for example, rare earth minerals that are at the core of renewable energy technologies). Second, the plan only concerns Denmark's responsibility in relation to national production: there is no mention of the need to reduce the Danish share of globally appropriated resources. Therefore, it is not considered problematic that much of the equipment needed for the conversion, as well as the increasing volumes of consumer goods, will be imported and probably produced using fossil fuels and other resources elsewhere. When limited resources and global responsibility are taken into account, it is hard to see how increased investment can take place without reducing consumption – or at least hampering the growth of consumption.

The next question concerns how resources are actually directed toward investment instead of consumption. As Jackson (2009) emphasizes, some of the transformative investments are not profitable for private investors. Of course, investments and green innovation may be encouraged and made more profitable by taxing energy and other resources or emissions, but since the impacts of large price increases over a short period of time may be disruptive to the economy in other ways, it is difficult to make private investments profitable in the short term. Price signals are necessary, but it is better to phase them in gradually, complemented by many other instruments that include planning and public investment.

In addition to just signaling, green taxes may contribute to funding public investments, which is one of the ways in which consumers pay. The organization of consumers' payment is decisive for distribution of the burden. For instance, if pension funds were mobilized through legislation, part of the onus would fall on future pensioners, whose pensions would be lower due to the lower return on funds. When distributing the burden, it is important to protect the fulfillment of basic needs, including access to healthcare and education for everybody. This view implies that private consumption should bear the brunt of the transformation – less traveling, electronic gadgets, meat, housing space and so forth. It also suggests that high-income earners should pay a relatively larger share – thus turning the trend in the opposite direction of what has been dominant in most affluent nations for some time.

Consumption reduction is already coming for large groups of people in rich countries due to the economic crisis and tough global competition and labor migration that undermine the power of labor unions and lead to lower wages and deteriorating working conditions. The competitive pressure is increasingly diffusing to groups with higher education and the balance of power is shifting even more in employers' favor. From a global perspective, these forces work as equalizers for large groups of employees, but increase misery in the rich countries and go hand in hand with expanding inequality within nations, favoring profits and higher incomes for the privileged few. Furthermore, this redistribution does not provide resources for systemic sustainability transformations, but rather for extreme luxury consumption. The undesirability of this scenario emphasizes the need for an orderly and balanced shift from consumption to investment.

THE ROLE OF CONSUMER-CITIZENS

As emphasized above, system transformations are decisive in reconciling environmental improvements with other societal aims. This section considers the role of consumers in these transformations as well as in the more general institutional transformation of the economy. Obviously, the transformations call for much more than the traditional role of the green consumer as somebody who chooses green products and abstains from particularly resource-demanding practices. Consumers may have to develop their roles further to become investor-consumers, 'prosumers' (producer-consumers), cooperators and providers in the informal economy, contributors to the government budget, system actors and change agents. From a practice theory perspective, it could be argued that various practices need to be strengthened considerably (see the chapters in Part III of this volume).

In the DCCCP plan and related documents (Energinet.dk and Dansk Energi, 2010), the role of consumers is conceptualized in relatively customary ways (Nyborg and Røpke, 2011). A large increase in the use of wind energy is predicated on large-scale offshore wind farms, the extension of transmission cables to neighboring countries and the establishment of a complex smart grid system to introduce demand management. The conversion of the energy system is planned to occur completely within the formal economy and depends on public regulation of the process. As mentioned, the material standards for consumers are expected to increase, and the role of consumers is conceived as relatively passive: they are expected to react to price incentives that will make insulation, electric cars and heat pumps attractive investments (micro-generation at household level plays a marginal role). The plan does not rely on enthusiastic engagement on the part of citizens in developing novel solutions within the informal economy or in cooperating locally; they are rather expected to become sort of investor-consumers motivated by self-interest. Consumers are also expected to accept demand management, but planners hope to introduce it in ways that interfere as little as possible with consumers' customary everyday lives and standards.

Juliet Schor (2010) outlines a more radical perspective and focuses on more localized systems and more informal economies characterized by high-tech self-provisioning. The dynamic behind the sustainability transformation that she detects arises from the economic crisis and makes many people redundant in the formal economy. These individuals have to find a way to make a living, and thus may become entrepreneurs in a growing informal economy that focuses on self-provisioning and strengthens the socio-economic links within local communities. New advanced technologies – such as the so-called fabrication laboratories (or fab labs), where 3D printers can produce all sorts of products based on 'recipes' from software developers – can make the informal economy, as well as small businesses, highly productive. The sustainability of this vision is connected to increased localization, reduced complexity and transport, and the acceptance of lower (or at least not increasing) material standards in exchange for more time and closer social relationships in the local community. While Schor emphasizes the bottom-up perspective on social change, she also mentions the need for government regulation to raise the cost of energy and thus encourage the necessary green innovation.

The idea of localization as a core element in sustainability transformations is recurrent in the degrowth debate and elsewhere. It is worth noting, however, that Schor's idea of self-provisioning still relies on the use of microprocessors and several other technologies that can hardly be provided by the fab labs themselves. Moreover, raw materials for the high-tech equipment are seldom available locally. It can also be questioned whether local systems are necessarily more sustainable. For instance, the energy return on investment (EROI) may be much higher for bigger wind turbines than for small ones.

In Schor's vision, consumer-citizens are entrepreneurs for the new economy. They cooperate locally rather than just acting at the household level. In general, local solutions may be more effective in mobilizing citizens and in making increased effort, inconvenience or costs more acceptable (see the chapter by Sabine Hielscher, Gill Seyfang and Adrian Smith in this volume). Local solutions seem to call for more public engagement and to appeal to citizen responsibility rather than consumer interests, particularly in local communities where sustainability concerns go hand in hand with regard for the economic survival of the community (Späth and Rohracher, 2010). In Denmark, this is obvious on some of the islands and in other peripheral regions where ambitious local energy projects are carried out; but in many areas in modern societies, the notion of local community does not resonate because there is little inner coherence and contacts among residents and people are mostly oriented toward nonlocal activities. Localization as a more generally applicable strategy may thus face considerable challenges.

A related aspect of more sustainable consumer-citizens concerns labor time. In the degrowth debate, it is often stated as obvious that the number of working hours in the formal economy must decrease. Continued technological change will increase labor productivity, and since continued economic growth is impossible for environmental reasons, decreasing workloads and income from the formal economy should be shared. More work could be carried out in the informal economy, with less resource-demanding activities related to, for instance, care, culture and labor-intensive self-provisioning of food, and more time could remain for leisure. Increased leisure is often seen as an essential part of a more sustainable life, so that consumer-citizens could become more relaxed. While this sounds attractive, it may not be realistic in an economy investing in change rather than just bringing down consumption. The transformation of socio-technical systems in energy, transport, food, housing and so forth may require more work, and running the reformed systems may become more labor intensive. This possibility is all the more probable, since the rising prices of energy and raw materials will redirect the focus of innovation toward increasing energy and materials productivity rather than labor productivity. Furthermore, the demographic challenge facing many industrialized countries may militate against a shorter work week and eventually call for a higher pension age.

While more leisure is not as obvious a part of sustainability transformations as is often suggested (at least not in countries with relatively short work weeks and long holidays), work may shift partly to the informal economy – depending on the organization of socio-technical systems and socio-economic institutions. The macroeconomic implications of a shift toward increased reliance on the informal economy may be complex (see the chapter by John Stutz in this volume). A relative increase in the informal economy may give rise to difficulties funding the welfare state because more activities will not be taxed. For instance, visions of strengthened local economies sometimes include the introduction of local currencies that may imply avoidance of taxation of value added. Likewise, it may become more complicated to organize a certain equalization of incomes through government budgets if taxation becomes more difficult. New taxpayer roles may have to be developed.

While all these roles are or can become important, the role of making transformations politically legitimate is decisive. Unfortunately, as the following concluding remarks suggest, this will not be an easy task.

CONCLUSION: A WINDOW OF OPPORTUNITY?

As mentioned at the beginning of this chapter, the economic decline starting in 2008 opened a window of opportunity for discussions of how to combine macroeconomic and environmental concerns. There is presently widespread acceptance of the importance of both the climate change issue and the need for establishing economic stability, and the idea of dealing with the two issues together is often aired. The dominant perspective of the integration, however, is to return to economic growth and to use climate change as a stepping stone for national competitiveness by developing strong positions in various green technologies. Roughly speaking, this perspective includes two lines of action. The traditional Right wants to improve national competitiveness by clipping the wings of labor unions, reducing taxes, cutting back welfare services and encouraging environmental innovation through relatively minor government signals and leaving the rest to the market. Demand is expected to come from China and other rapidly growing economies and, when domestic growth picks up, from increased domestic employment. The traditional Left, supported by parts of industry, goes in for the 'Green New Deal,' where government intervention ensures a market for eco-technologies to improve simultaneously the environment, welfare, competitiveness and employment. This line of action tries to turn the trend of deepening domestic inequalities and to maintain domestic demand and social stability.

While the leftward leaning perspective is surely the most promising from an ecological economic perspective, it is still far from an honest appraisal of the challenge. It does not question the need for classic economic growth in the rich countries and investments are not expected to hamper consumption growth, except for the very wealthy. As a general rule, biophysical limits are not acknowledged and the need for global redistribution is not addressed. On an abstract level, it is not difficult to understand why. The process toward taking on more global responsibility involves risks and dilemmas in relation to national position in global competition: high living standards and good employment opportunities depend on producing the goods and services that allow generous remuneration – and thus ensure the transfer of resources from other countries. Lagging behind implies the risk of pronounced unemployment and a self-perpetuating decline – and the risk of ending up among the exploited. This is the classical 'Easter Island dilemma': giving up erecting statues would serve the common good but implies the risk of losing the battle altogether, and the privileged in the established society would be forced to surrender their advantageous position (Ponting, 1991). Or, as Andersson and Lindroth (2001, p. 121) formulate the dilemma for the core countries in international trade: 'A large footprint may be a condition for the preservation of their status vis-à-vis actual and potential rivals. Therefore, they may fear that to make ecological footprint reduction a priority can be used by less conscientious competitors. The laudable effort might end in a falling status and in eventually becoming a victim of ecologically unequal exchange.' The dilemma is exacerbated by the globally integrated financial system where the first steps toward, for instance, restricting profits may lead to outflow of capital and threats to currency stability. Likewise, limiting high incomes may encourage important specialists to migrate. As Victor (2008) observes, it may not be easy to manage without growth in one country.

Nonetheless, the shift from consumption to investment has to start in individual countries, and there is an extreme need for experiments. For some time, it will be necessary to rely on the complementarity between bottom-up initiatives and government intervention along the lines of a Green New Deal. In the meantime, work on ecological macroeconomics can contribute to the long-term change of discourse.

NOTES

1. The general concerns are different for a global superpower such as the United States where military expenses have priority and the role of the dollar as the primary international exchange currency has enabled cheap funding of balance-of-payments deficits.
2. In addition to such general goals, different countries face specific challenges. For instance, in a Danish context, it would be useful from an ecosystem perspective to reduce the high population density over time, and the present ageing population may be seen as an opportunity for a gradual demographic transformation toward a smaller population.

REFERENCES

Andersson, J. and M. Lindroth (2001). 'Ecologically unsustainable trade', *Ecological Economics*, **37**(1), 113–22.

Elzen, B., F. Geels and K. Green (eds) (2004). *System Innovation and the Transition to Sustainability: Theory, Evidence and Policy*, Cheltenham, UK and Northampton, MA, USA: Edward Elgar.

Energinet.dk and Dansk Energi (2010). *Smart Grid i Danmark (Smart Grid in Denmark)*, Fredericia: Energinet.dk (in Danish).

European Commission (1993). *Growth, Competitiveness, and Employment: The Challenges and Ways Forward into the 21st Century*, Brussels: European Commision.

Grin, J., J. Rotmans and J. Schot (2010). *Transitions to Sustainable Development: New Directions in the Study of Long Term Transformative Change*, New York: Routledge.

Harris, J. (2009). 'Ecological macroeconomics: consumption, investment, and climate change', in J. Harris and N. Goodwin (eds), *Twenty-first Century Macroeconomics: Responding to the Climate Challenge*, Cheltenham, UK and Northampton, MA, USA: Edward Elgar, pp. 169–86.

Harris, J. and N. Goodwin (eds) (2009). *Twenty-first Century Macroeconomics: Responding to the Climate Challenge*, Cheltenham, UK and Northampton, MA, USA: Edward Elgar.

Holt, R., S. Pressman and C. Spash (eds) (2009). *Post-Keynesian and Ecological Economics: Confronting Environmental Issues*, Cheltenham, UK and Northampton, MA, USA: Edward Elgar.

Jackson, T. (2009). *Prosperity Without Growth: Economics for a Finite Planet*, London: Earthscan.

Kallis, G., J. Martinez-Alier and R. Norgaard (2009). 'Paper assets, real debts: an ecological-economic exploration of the global economic crisis', *Critical Perspectives on International Business*, **5**(1), 14–25.

Klimakommissionen (2010). *Green Energy: The Road to a Danish Energy System Without Fossil Fuels: Summary of the Work, Results, and Recommendations of the Danish Commission on Climate Change Policy*, Copenhagen: Danish Commission on Climate Change Policy.

Korten, D. (2009). *Agenda for a New Economy: From Phantom Wealth to Real Wealth*, San Francisco, CA: Berrett-Koehler.

Martinez-Alier, J., U. Pascual, F. Vivien and E. Zaccai (2010). 'Sustainable degrowth: mapping the context, criticisms and future prospects of an emergent paradigm', *Ecological Economics*, **69**(9), 1741–7.

Nyborg, S. and I. Røpke (2011). 'Energy impacts of the smart home: conflicting visions', *ECEEE 2011 Summer Study,* June, 6–11.

Pollitt, H., A. Barker, J. Barton et al. (2010). *A Scoping Study on the Macroeconomic View of Sustainability: Final Report for the European Commission, DG Environment*, Cambridge: Cambridge Econometrics.

Ponting, C. (1991). *A Green History of the World*, New York: Penguin.

Richardson, K., D. Dahl-Hensen, J. Elmeskov et al. (2011). 'Denmark's road map for fossil fuel independence', *Solutions*, **2**(4), available at http://www.thesolutionsjournal.com/node/954 (accessed 1 December 2011).

Schepelmann, P., M. Stock, T. Koska, R. Schüle and O. Reutter (2009). *A Green New Deal for Europe: Towards Green Modernisation in the Face of Crisis*, Brussels: Green European Foundation.

Schneider, F., G. Kallis and J. Martinez-Alier (2010). 'Crisis or opportunity? Economic degrowth for social equity and ecological sustainability: introduction to this special issue', *Journal of Cleaner Production*, **18**(6), 511–18.

Schor, J. (2010). *Plenitude: The New Economics of True Wealth*, New York: Penguin.

Seidl, I. and A. Zahrnt (eds) (2010). *Postwachstumsgesellschaft: Konzepte für die Zukunft (Post-growth Society: Concepts for the Future)*, Marburg: Metropolis-Verlag (in German).

Späth, P. and H. Rohracher (2010). 'Energy regions: the transformative power of regional discourses on socio-technical futures', *Research Policy*, **39**(4), 449–58.

Stiglitz, J., A. Sen and J. Fitoussi (2009). *Report by the Commission on the Measurement of Economic Performance and Social Progress*, Paris: The Commission, available at http://www.stiglitz-sen-fitoussi.fr (accessed 1 December 2011).

The Green New Deal Group (2008). *A Green New Deal. Joined-up Policies to Solve the Triple Crunch of the Credit Crisis, Climate Change and High Oil Prices*, London: New Economics Foundation.

van den Bergh, J. (2009). 'The GDP paradox', *Journal of Economic Psychology*, **30**(2), 117–35.

Victor, P. (2008). *Managing Without Growth: Slower by Design, not Disaster*, Cheltenham, UK and Northampton, MA, USA: Edward Elgar.

4. Going for a better life

John Stutz

INTRODUCTION

During the late 1930s, economic growth emerged as a focus of national policy. At first this development was confined to the nations of Western Europe and North America. However, it rapidly spread throughout the globe. Writing in 1964, James Tobin described the situation in the following terms:

> In recent years economic growth has come to occupy an exalted position in the hierarchy of goals of government policy, both in the United States and abroad, both in advanced and in less developed countries, both in centrally controlled and decentralized economies. (Tobin, 1964, p. 1)

Today the performance of the American economy is generally viewed as a series of expansions and contractions (that is, recessions). Other features such as inflation and unemployment are addressed by situating them in relation to the economy's growth. This is true for the experience of the entire post-World War II period or the last few years (Samuelson, 2008; Lew, 2011).

In the United States, as in other nations, the effort required to maintain economic growth only becomes widely apparent when, as happened recently, the growth stops. However, the effort is ongoing and substantial. Much of it focuses on income; that is, real gross domestic product (GDP) per capita. The objective is not just that the economy should continually grow, but that the rate of increase should exceed population growth. Continual pursuit of growth in income has the support of the majority of those involved in the development of economic policy (Scherer, 1999). In contrast, this chapter joins with those who argue against this pursuit (Jackson, 2009; Simms et al., 2010). It calls for a transition to an economy in which there is no growth in income (Victor, 2008).

What rationale is offered for the continuing pursuit of growth in income? The claim is that such growth results in a higher standard of living. This assertion rests on the definition of real GDP. Standardized national accounts provide data that can be used to compute GDP in different ways. One is as the sum of all wages, rents and profits (BEA, 2007). It is this approach that justifies referring to real GDP per capita as 'income,' and, for some, using it as a measure of the standard of living. However, despite its apparently firm foundation, there are many problems with the use of income as a measure of living standards (Costanza et al., 2009). The most obvious is that income is an average. It is the share of wages, rents and profits that would be provided to each man and woman, adult and child, if real GDP were divided equally. However, in the United States the actual division of the economy's output is highly unequal (Salverda et al., 2009). Thus, to decide if there have been improvements in the standard of living one needs to look beyond averages, to the experience of typical workers and families. This chapter aims to do just that.

The chapter begins by reviewing a range of evidence to show that the increase in income in the United States over the last 40 years has not benefited typical workers and families. Environmental concerns and their relevance to American workers and families are an important aspect of the review. With that background, the Better Life Approach (BLA) is put forward. The point of reference for the development of the BLA is *Going for Growth* (OECD, 2011b), a well-known report prepared annually by the Organisation for Economic Co-operation and Development (OECD). This report recommends policies to foster growth in the two major components of income: productivity (the goods and services produced per hour worked) and labor utilization (the hours worked per capita). The policies recommended are specific to each OECD member nation including the United States. The BLA takes a similar, policy-oriented approach. However, rather than focusing on growth, it lays out goals that address the issues that the experience of the last four decades shows affect the lives of typical workers and families. Policies for meeting the goals – improvements in education and productivity that together create the possibility for better-paying jobs, shorter hours of work without loss of earnings leading to better quality of life, and changes in the tax and welfare systems to address income inequality and volatility and their adverse impacts – are discussed in some detail. While the BLA's goals focus on socio-economic concerns, its design and the policies it embodies address environmental concerns as well. The absence of growth in income that is built into the BLA is an important example of such 'design for the environment.'

The BLA is described in the language of GDP and income used in *Going for Growth.* There are substantial concerns that arise from the assumptions and techniques used to develop GDP. These were considered at length by a commission convened in 2008 for that purpose by former French President Nicolas Sarkozy. The commission's conclusion appears in the title of its report, *Mismeasuring Our Lives: Why GDP Doesn't Add Up* (Stiglitz, et al., 2010). While acknowledging these problems, *Going for Growth* continues to utilize the GDP/income framework. Unfortunately, this reflects the majority approach. This framework continues to provide the basis for most discussions of economic policy. So, this chapter uses it to frame a new policy approach for the United States and to argue for its adoption. Alternatives to the GDP/income framework are addressed elsewhere (see Stutz, 2011).

Successful implementation of the BLA will require substantial change. Fortunately, there are no insurmountable technical obstacles. Policies adopted in the past or currently in place in other high-income nations, together with those proposed by mainstream economists, are sufficient to achieve its goals. The challenge lies in developing political support sufficient to see such policies adopted and implemented in the United States. Such action will require the emergence of a coalition that brings together parts of the business community, typical workers and families and environmental interests in support of the BLA. In its design, the BLA seeks to balance and harmonize the interests of these groups, to make the emergence of such a coalition as likely as possible. Whether the BLA strikes the right balance is, admittedly, debatable. The need to achieve a compromise that makes the emergence of a broad-based coalition in support of the BLA likely is not.

The BLA is a proposal for the United States. However, with modest modification, it would be applicable to other high income nations. Adoption of an approach similar to the BLA by all the high-income nations is a part of a global approach – the Great Transition – that focuses on enhanced well-being, equity and a better environment (Raskin et al., 2002). The consequences of success and failure in achieving the Great Transition have been explored in depth (Raskin et al., 2010). The results make clear the importance of success. With a shift to the BLA in the United States the likelihood of similar movement in other high-income nations – and so of success for the Great Transition – is substantially increased. Without a shift in the United States the likelihood of these developments is greatly diminished (Stutz, 2010).

EXPERIENCE SINCE THE 1970s

Over the last 40 years, income has roughly doubled in the United States (Maddison, 2007; Mold, 2010). There has been high unemployment over the last few years, but based on the experience of the last four decades, this is quite atypical. Low unemployment has been the norm (Jacobs, 2007).

However, growth and low unemployment over the long term does not mean that all has been well in the world of work and beyond. For most it has not.

Roughly 80 percent of those in the American workforce are production workers in manufacturing or nonsupervisory workers in other sectors including government. For them the rent and profit included in income are largely irrelevant. What matters is the third component of income, namely 'wages.' Historical data show that real hourly compensation grew substantially from World War II through the early 1970s. Since that time, there has been little gain. Families have done better than individual workers, due in large part to the increase in the percentage of women in the labor force. Growth in median family income was substantial through the 1970s, but has been much slower since then (Mishel et al., 2008). Recently, families have fared particularly poorly. Looking over the period from 2000 to 2009, Paul Krugman (2009) commented, 'It was a decade with zero economic gains for the typical family.'

For some, economic gains have been possible. Since 1975, two-parent families have achieved an increase of 23 percent in median earnings. However, to do so the two parents typically increased their combined hours of work by 26 percent (Greenstone and Looney, 2011). In general, hours of work in the United States are long (OECD, 2009). Data on working hours include the hours of those in better positions. As a large-scale survey in 2000 showed, people in managerial, professional or technical occupations worked 9 percent longer than average (Jacobs and Gerson, 2004). Adding to the burden is the increasing intensity of the work effort required (Green, 2006). As one might expect, the result is a desire for shorter hours. In the survey, respondents were asked to compare their actual and ideal hours of work per week. On average, the ideal was ten hours less than actual. For about 20 percent of the respondents it was at least 20 hours less. Why is it not the case that those who are dissatisfied simply work shorter hours? In the United States, for most positions that option simply does not exist (EOP/CEA, 2010). And, even where shorter hours are available, such working arrangements often conflict with explicit or implicit requirements for success. Despite these obstacles, some people do choose to become 'downshifters,' making a choice to work less (Holbrook et al., 2006).

While growth has fallen off for typical families since the 1970s, those at the top of the income distribution have done extraordinarily well. This has resulted in a substantial rise in inequality (Garfinkel et al., 2010). It is of concern because inequality has been linked to a variety of adverse impacts (Wilkinson and Pickett, 2010). In addition, the year-to-year volatility in income has roughly doubled since the 1970s (Hacker, 2006). What sort of a social safety net do typical workers and families have to fall back on when hard times come? The most widely available source of public support is the Supplemental Food Assistance Program. For some, it is all that is available. The share of households receiving food stamps who had no other source of support was about 16 percent in 2008 (Pavetti and Rosenbaum, 2010). The newly developed Economic Security Index (ESI) draws together and systematizes the available information on income volatility and its impact. The results obtained using it show that during the period 1985 to 2009 the share of Americans who experienced substantial income declines and lacked adequate resources to fall back on grew by two-thirds (Hacker et al., 2010). The absence of resources significantly amplifies the adverse impacts that accompany a substantial drop in family income (Irons, 2009).

THE BETTER LIFE APPROACH

As Robert Samuelson (2008, p. xx) notes in his book addressing the last half century of economic developments in the United States, 'changes in ideas, institutions, values and beliefs can alter the way the economy works just as much as – and sometimes more than – new technologies, changes in prices or shifts in interest rates.' Most important among the ideas currently in need of change is the notion of a better life. As Galbraith (1958) famously pointed out, after World War II the United States became an affluent society. Through the early 1970s, the benefits of economic progress were broadly shared. The inflation-adjusted median family income increased by 104 percent from 1947 to 1973. However, for the period 1973 to 2009 the increase was only 15 percent (EPI, 2011a). And, as the discussion in the previous section showed, this modest increase was not accompanied by a better life. For typical workers and families over the last 40 years, growth simply stopped delivering benefits. Over the next four decades, rather than going for yet more growth, policy in the United States needs to focus directly on what Keynes (1963) called the permanent economic problem: living agreeably and well. This is the appropriate objective for an affluent society. The BLA does just that (see also the chapter by Jonathan Harris in this volume).

As its name suggests, the BLA will enhance the opportunity for typical workers and families to function in accord with their capabilities and so effectively pursue their interests and meet their obligations. To do so the BLA focuses on issues that have emerged during the last 40 years, and addresses them in three goals which together define the approach. The goals are as follows:

- Productivity and education. Foster productivity growth that creates the opportunity for good jobs and benefits the environment. Improve education to broaden the opportunity to benefit from productivity growth, and to improve the ability to lead a good life.
- Earnings and hours of work. Ensure that hourly compensation for typical workers grows at the same rate as productivity. Reduce typical hours of work in a complementary fashion to improve quality of life.
- Volatility and inequality. Change the welfare and tax systems to address income inequality and volatility and their adverse effects.

All three of the BLA goals address concerns related to employment. The first focuses on the creation of not just an adequate number of jobs, but good jobs in which the value added by workers justifies the payment of high and increasing hourly wages. The second addresses the ability of workers to receive the wage justified by their effort, and to reduce their hours to enhance their quality of life. The final goal addresses two key sources of adverse impacts, for typical workers and families in general and in particular those who, temporarily or permanently, need to rely on government support because their income from employment is inadequate.

The BLA has as its objective a better life for typical workers and families in the United States. Mainstream economic policy such as that formulated in *Going for Growth* fosters growth in income to achieve that same objective (Cotis et al., 2010). Given this overlap, it is not surprising that the BLA addresses many issues that are dealt with in *Going for Growth* as well. The 'common issues' are related primarily to the BLA's first and third goals. There, the OECD's treatment of issues such as education and the tax system is reshaped and the recommended policies modified to address the BLA's concerns. It is in its second goal that the BLA takes a 180-degree turn away from the approach articulated in *Going for Growth* – fostering growth in both productivity and the average hours worked per capita. Instead the BLA calls for growth in hourly compensation made possible by higher productivity but pairs it with reduced hours. Because this is a change from what is anticipated and what mainstream policy seeks to achieve, this chapter focuses particular attention on its feasibility.

While the BLA's goals are simple, the actions required to achieve them are complex. A separate section of this chapter addresses each goal, identifying policies that would foster success. Illustrative computations give a sense of the magnitude of the changes involved. In particular, they provide an indication of the upward pressure on income that might be created by productivity growth and the ability of the labor market policies to respond to it. However, before turning to the discussion of the individual goals, it is important to say a bit about the BLA's design and its treatment of the environment.

THE ENVIRONMENT

Since the 1970s, as the gains for typical workers and families from economic growth in the United States have diminished, the changes in the environment that accompany that growth and their effects on them have increased. Today the immediacy and magnitude of the threat from changes in the environment due to human activity is well known to those in the scientific community. The opening lines in a recent book by James Hansen (2009) convey the sense of urgency and concern quite clearly: 'Planet Earth, creation, the world in which civilization developed, the world with climate patterns that we know and stable shorelines, is in imminent peril.' Climate change – Hansen's area of particular expertise – is the source of the threat best known to the public. However, there are a number of other areas in which humanity's pressure on the environment is of serious concern (see, for example, Rockström et al., 2009).

There is a substantial literature linking pressure on the environment to adverse impacts on typical American workers and families. A recent report by the federal government concludes that health impacts due to heat stress, waterborne diseases, poor air quality, extreme weather events and diseases transmitted by insects and rodents will be associated with climate change (Karl et al., 2009). For other pressures on the environment there is a wealth of evidence that makes the adverse impacts crystal clear (see, for example, Burd-Sharps et al., 2008). In light of this, fostering improvement in the environment must be an integral part of any approach such as the BLA that seeks to improve the situation of typical workers and families. Of course, some environmental concerns are essentially global in nature. For them the BLA alone will provide a very limited response. However, because of the political centrality of the United States in the international system, a shift to the BLA will contribute substantially to the likelihood of a Great Transition which in turn will address issues at the global level.

The design of the BLA to produce no growth in income is motivated in part by concern about climate change. In his well-known book, Peter Victor (2008) provides an analysis of the restrictions on growth in income that are likely to be required to address climate concerns. For high-income nations such as the United States, the restriction is zero growth in income for the period 2002 to 2050. The goal incorporated into the BLA – zero growth for 2010 to 2050 – is similar. In addition to zero growth, the BLA will 'nudge' society toward more sustainable patterns of consumption

(Thaler and Sunstein, 2008). It will also address the wide range of adverse environmental impacts that can and should be reduced (Ackerman, 2008). Some will see a conflict here with the BLA's first goal, which includes enhanced productivity. In fact, there is none. As a recent survey of international experience by the Network of Heads of European Environment Protection Agencies concluded, good environmental management and regulation does not impede competitiveness and development (NHEEPA, 2005).

While the design of the BLA is strongly influenced by environmental concerns, that concern is not immediately apparent because the primary emphasis is on achieving better lives. However, the approach taken is that suggested by Keynes and developed in recent books by Juliet Schor (2010) and Tim Jackson (2009). The emphasis is on quality of life rather than quantity of stuff. This allows the BLA to incorporate environmental concerns in the policies chosen to address all of its goals. The fact that this is not highlighted reflects a judgment that, in the United States in particular, environmental gains are more likely to be achieved as a byproduct rather than through direct action. The hope is that those concerned primarily with environmental issues will understand that success for the BLA is in their interest and so will join businesses that can benefit from the productivity gains fostered by the BLA and typical workers and families in supporting it.

PRODUCTIVITY AND EDUCATION

The emphasis on productivity growth in the BLA reflects a concern common to economic policy proposals: the maintenance of an adequate level of employment opportunities ('jobs'). This concern arises from an understanding of the dynamics of the labor market. While net changes in the level of employment are generally small, they result from the near equality of much greater levels of job creation and destruction. For example, a recent study showed that between 1990 and 2003, net change in private (that is, non-governmental) employment in the United States averaged 0.3 percent per quarter. This amount was the difference between job creation of 8 percent and losses of 7.7 percent (Cahuc and Zylberberg, 2006). In recessions, job destruction is enhanced, the working-age population continues to grow and job creation declines, resulting in a 'job gap.' The recent recession created a 'job gap' that appears likely to last a decade or more (Greenstone and Looney, 2011). Looking ahead, the impact of globalization will make job creation an increasing challenge. While globalization has been underway for some time, its effect on American employment has thus far been modest (Lawrence, 2008). However, in the future, the impacts are likely to be much more substantial (Bhagwati and Blinder, 2009).

For the BLA, which incorporates a shift to zero growth in income, adequate job growth is a particularly important concern. In Peter Victor's (2008) memorable words, the transition to zero growth should be 'by design, not disaster.' For the BLA avoiding a dramatic drop in job creation is crucial. Much job creation arises from the founding of new firms (Haltiwanger et al., 2010). The ability to realize productivity gains is often what makes the establishment of new firms an attractive option. Policy choices have had and, with the BLA, will continue to have an important impact on the growth in productivity (Reinert, 2007). However, in an effort to foster productivity growth, careful attention to its impacts is essential. For the BLA, the focus will be on the creation of jobs that are desirable for those who hold them and for the environment

Today in the American job market, to earn a high and increasing hourly wage, a position that involves high and increasing productivity is generally required (Autor, 2010). Indeed, productivity growth is the source for most 'win-win' situations for business and workers. Without it their interests are generally in opposition. There are a number of opportunities for the BLA to foster the creation of such positions. Consider, for example, remanufacturing, that is, the refurbishing of used equipment so that it can be resold in place of new. Remanufacturing has the potential to create high productivity, high wage employment along with significant environmental benefits (Giuntini and Gaudette, 2003). To help achieve that potential, the BLA will ensure by regulation or incentive that, to the extent reasonable, equipment can be repaired and upgraded. There are also a variety of options to foster the development and use of clean energy technology that could provide environmental benefits and good positions (Urahn and Reichert, 2009). If we broaden the focus a bit, there are fundamental changes in technology taking place, such as the use of three-dimensional printing in industrial production, that offer improved efficiency in the use of materials, reductions in energy use and the creation of good jobs (The Economist, 2011). Moving beyond the manufacturing sector, consider education. Online courses could provide a significant boost to productivity in a sector famous for its low level. Facilitating the development and offering of online courses would likely be an important part of the BLA's effort to improve the quality of instruction at a reasonable cost. This effort is already underway (Markoff, 2011). Further progress will make additional good positions in education possible. A similar argument for productivity growth associated with the greater use of information and communications technology can be made for health care (Goldman and McGlynn, 2005).

In discussions of policy aimed at productivity growth there is often a concern expressed about efforts to 'pick the winners,' that is, to foster the commercialization of specific technologies or approaches (see, for example, Glaeser, 2011). However, well-designed efforts, such as 'golden carrot' programs leading to more efficient household appliances, have resulted in substantial positive change (NEEA, 2008). Care in the selection of the policies used to foster productivity will be required because such efforts can interact in unexpected ways (Metcalf, 2010). While productivity has long been a key focus of economic analysis, our understanding of it is still limited (Syverson, 2010). Thus, efforts to better understand productivity and its potential role in the creation of good jobs are likely to be an important part of the BLA, particularly in its early stages.

Opportunities for good jobs are only beneficial to those who can successfully qualify for and perform them. This turns the discussion to education. Historically, the United States has had a well-educated workforce. However, since the 1970s, key indicators have declined compared to other advanced nations (Goldin and Katz, 2008). This decline is relevant because in today's world productivity growth is often closely linked to the adoption and use of new technology, particularly computers (Choudhry, 2009). There is concern that a substantial part of the American labor force lacks the skills required to effectively utilize such technology (Partnership for 21st Century Skills, 2010). Experience supports this concern. Recently, despite high levels of unemployment, some businesses have not been able to fill high-wage positions because the applicants lacked the mathematics and other skills required (Rich, 2010). Mainstream policy proposals such as those in *Going for Growth* respond by suggesting changes in the primary and secondary schools often involving greater reliance on standardized testing. Such an effort is far too narrow. Poor performance in school often arises from problems in the family (Heckman and Lafontaine, 2008). The BLA will address these problems. A college degree is increasingly important in obtaining a good job. There are substantial difficulties in the United States with education at the college level. A large percentage of those who enter fail to complete their degree at all or in a timely fashion. The reasons for this are, in large part, financial. Many American college students work long hours, forcing them to attend on a part-time basis. Those who are enrolled part time often do not qualify for even minimal financial assistance, forcing them to work even more. Providing assistance to these 'part-timers' would increase degree completion rates, particularly among students from poor families (Johnson et al., 2009). The BLA will address this and other problems at the college level.

Discussion thus far of the BLA's education agenda has focused, as the OECD has done, on the development of a better educated workforce. That is important, but far from all that is required. For the BLA to be successful it is essential that education prepares students to be informed participants in the process of choosing and living a better life. To meet this objective, educators and concerned citizens will need to reconsider the aims, scope and content of education at all levels. Such issues are considered these days to be unproductive by much of the educational establishment, so not much of it takes place (Noddings, 2006). The BLA will revive such discussion and focus it on the notion of a better life.

EARNINGS AND HOURS OF WORK

The second goal of the BLA – shorter hours of work without loss of earnings – has been sought after in the United States for at least 20 years (Bowles et al., 1991). The goal embodies two separate objectives: first, ensuring that hourly compensation for typical workers rises at the same rate as labor productivity; and second, reducing the average hours of work per capita in a fashion complementary to the growth in productivity. Achieving these objectives will produce a future that differs dramatically from the experience of the last 40 years. Over that period, productivity more than doubled while hourly compensation remained roughly constant and hours of work increased modestly (EPI, 2011b). Assume for the moment that over the next four decades productivity increases at 1.5 percent per year, roughly the rate assumed in long-term, 'business-as-usual' projections for the United States (Maddison, 2007). This would add about 81 percent to the already substantial level of American productivity. If the first objective is met, typical hourly compensation would rise by the same percentage. If the second objective is also met, there would be a substantial reduction in the hours of work, about 45 percent.[1]

During the period from the late 1940s until the early 1970s, growth in hourly compensation in the United States was similar to that in productivity. So, linking the two is not something new. It is simply a return to what was common practice during what was a better era for typical workers and their families. Achieving that return will require a mechanism that ensures the sharing of the benefits that productivity growth creates. A negotiated national-level agreement is one natural choice. It would function in the same general fashion as a cost-of-living adjustment, such as that which governs Social Security payments. However, a variety of such mechanisms have been developed and utilized in Europe (Eichengreen, 2007). Examination of them shows that a wide range of formal and informal arrangements governing annual compensation changes are feasible.

How will the BLA achieve the second objective? Hours worked per capita are determined by the share of the population that is employed and the average hours put in by those who are employed. Policies would address these factors. The most important would change the annual hours for full-time work. In the United States today, over 75 percent of those employed work full time (United States Department of Commerce, 2008). Full-time workers put in roughly 40 hours per week for 46 weeks a year. Simply reducing the number of hours in the full-time work week to the current level in the Netherlands would contribute a 20 percent reduction. Phasing in requirements for annual vacation and other forms of leave similar to those in Norway would cut the typical weeks worked by 22 percent (Alesina et al., 2005). Taken together these two changes would reduce the annual hours for full-time employees in the United States by 38 percent.[2] There will also be beneficial demographic changes. Looking ahead to 2050, a reduction of over 10 percent in the share of working-age individuals in the United States population is anticipated (Bloom, 2011). Finally, changes that reduce the pressure to join the labor force or to increase one's hours of work will be part of the BLA. For example, to meet its third goal the BLA will require universal health care and more progressive taxation. Both have been identified as causes of the significantly lower share of the population that is employed and shorter hours worked in Europe compared to the United States (Mulligan, 2010). There is no way to show definitively that the policies discussed thus far would be sufficient to offset productivity growth. But achieving such an offset becomes a near certainty once one realizes that the most important policy option – reducing the annual hours for full-time work – is not restricted by practices elsewhere. Rather, the issue is whether the BLA will have the support required to make the needed changes.

Success in meeting the BLA's second goal will ensure that by 2050 typical workers will see their annual hours worked decline substantially. A reasonable expectation would be a 38 percent reduction, the same as for the hours of full-time employment. There are numerous benefits to such a pronounced reduction (Coote et al., 2010). And, the survey research on workers' ideal hours discussed earlier shows a desire for a sharp reduction (Jacobs and Gerson, 2004). This is quite understandable. When adults rank the activities on which they spend time by the contribution they make to their satisfaction with life, work and commuting to and from it come in dead last (Layard, 2005). Finally, recent research has shown that satisfaction with life has a causal effect on lifespan (Diener and Chan, 2010). This finding strengthens the case for action to enhance satisfaction with life beyond that found previously in the literature (Bok, 2010). Based on the productivity growth discussed above, the 38 percent decline in hours will be accompanied by a 12 percent increase in annual income.[3] When considering this modest increase there are three points to be kept in mind. First, policies the BLA will introduce to meet the third goal, and particularly to address income inequality, will enhance disposable income for typical workers and families. Second, the reduction in hours will lower the cost of living by shrinking the need for paid services and food from restaurants. Studies of retirees confirm that this allows the maintenance of a high standard of living despite significant reductions in household income (Aguiar and Hurst, 2009). Third, the value of one's income derives in part from its relation to that of others (Lyubomirsky, 2007). With the BLA, the focus of society will shift from material to time affluence. This will make gains in earnings less of a concern. Taken together, these points suggest that achieving the BLA's second goal should be attractive. Whether it will garner widespread support among typical workers and their familiar is, of course, an open question.

The BLA will create an environment favorable to the changes required to achieve the second goal. The quality of the workforce in the United States will be improved while the pressure to work will be reduced. This will tighten labor markets, shifting the balance of power away from businesses and toward workers. However, it cannot be labor alone that is pushing for change. The BLA will need the backing of a coalition that includes firms that can benefit from productivity growth while providing hourly compensation that increases in line with that growth and environmental advocates drawn by the opposition to income growth and the other 'pro-environmental' aspects of the BLA. The ability to forge a coalition broad and strong enough to force fundamental change also remains an open question. The discussion will return to this point and the previous open question in the final section of the chapter.

VOLATILITY AND INEQUALITY

This chapter began by examining the experience of typical workers and families since the 1970s. This led to the identification of a number of concerns. Here the focus shifts to the two concerns that have yet to be addressed – income volatility and inequality. To deal with them the BLA will make major changes in the welfare and tax systems in the United States. In general, the changes related to welfare will address volatility, while those pertaining to taxes will address inequality. However, the approach taken to welfare and taxes is more consistent than this 'division of labor' suggests.

Mention of the welfare system brings to mind the social safety net – government programs that aid those temporarily or permanently in need.

However, such programs are only a small part of the welfare system. Welfare is defined as 'publicly provided or subsidized goods that provide predominantly private benefits' (Garfinkel et al., 2010, p. 2). In the United States, what welfare provides is largely insurance. Roughly 40 percent of federal expenditures are for Medicare, Medicaid and Social Security (Klein, 2011). These programs focus on areas – health and retirement – in which individuals face risks and address them by spreading the cost. That is, insurance, pure and simple. As the examples just mentioned show, in the United States benefits from welfare are not limited to the needy. Indeed, there are very large welfare programs that provide benefits only to people who are reasonably well off. Here 'private' medical insurance provides an important example. Among high-income nations, the United States is unique in its absence of universal health care. Unless one falls into one of the narrow categories covered by Medicare and Medicaid, one obtains medical insurance privately, typically through one's employer. However, there is a substantial public contribution to the cost of this insurance because the value of the insurance is not considered taxable income. Society in effect contributes the value of the foregone tax revenue toward the cost of private health insurance.

To address income volatility and its adverse impacts, the BLA would shift welfare away from arrangements that provide benefits only to those with jobs. The ESI identifies loss or substantial reduction in household medical coverage as a key source of the adversity associated with income volatility (Hacker, et al., 2010). The BLA would replace private insurance with a system of universal coverage. Since the use of private health insurance causes the amount spent per capita on providing health care in the United States to be much higher than in nations with universal coverage, this shift would actually reduce costs. The savings would be used to help fund a better social safety net. For those whose incomes change dramatically year to year, and for the poor in general, a key issue is the floor for family income established by government transfer payments. With lower costs for health care, the BLA would be able to move such transfers toward higher European levels (Kenworthy, 2011). And, as noted earlier, universal health coverage would weaken the pressure to work or to move from part-time to full-time employment to 'get benefits,' thus making it easier to achieve the second BLA goal.

Reform of income tax provides a means to address income inequality. The most obvious approach would be to increase the rates applicable to successive increments of income. The BLA will certainly do this. However, it will not be the major focus. There are two reasons for this: increasing tax rates is difficult politically and it is not the most effective way to reduce inequality. Instead, the BLA will focus on the removal of features of the tax code that benefit the wealthy disproportionately. It is not possible to discuss all that the BLA would change. However, a key example – mortgage interest – provides a good indication of the general type of change that would be undertaken. In the United States, much of the interest paid on home mortgages is deductible from taxable income. Because 30-year mortgages are common, the total amount of such deductions can be massive. Through this mechanism society offsets a substantial part of the cost for an individual to purchase a home. The deduction has sharply increasing benefits as income rises (Glaeser, 2010). The BLA would replace the mortgage deduction with a fixed allowance that could be claimed by all those with a reasonable level of 'housing costs,' that is, expenses for rent or a mortgage. By carefully setting the size of the allowance, the current benefit could be preserved for typical workers and families while the incentive for the purchase of ever larger, more expensive and more energy-intensive homes is diminished. There are many other aspects of the tax code – provisions to tax income as capital gains, treatment of certain types of losses and so forth – all of which could be revised in ways that reduce inequality without making any changes in the politically sensitive tax rates. Going a bit further, Robert Frank (2011) has proposed sweeping changes in the tax system to benefit typical workers and families while reducing excessive consumption. Such recommendations would be adopted if political conditions permit.

Despite the fact that the policies to address the BLA's third goal will be carefully selected to benefit typical workers and families, they will likely be a 'difficult sell.' In the United States, there is a broadly held view that success and failure are primarily the result of individual effort and only marginally due to social and economic forces beyond individual control (Alesina and Glaeser, 2004). This leads to broad support for arrangements that reward the successful, giving grudgingly to those in need and avoiding 'universal benefits' such as health insurance because they might sap initiative. In light of these circumstances, the effort likely to be required to achieve the third goal is substantial. In thinking about this challenge, historic changes such as the New Deal and Great Society programs need to be kept in mind. Change is possible, but it requires far-sighted leaders capable of careful management of the political process (Newman and Jacobs, 2010). Indeed, with such leaders more radical change may be possible, giving all a bit of the security that currently only the wealthy enjoy. Building on an idea developed by Bruce Ackerman and his colleagues (2006), the BLA could arrange for each individual to have access to an 'emergency account.' Like a trust fund, the account would be established at birth. Usage would be limited to conditions of extraordinary need. This would give all in the United States 'something to fall back on.'

CONCLUSION: OPPORTUNITY AND CHALLENGE

Since the 1970s, the conditions facing typical workers and families in the United States have worsened. In the wake of the recent recession, things have become particularly bleak. *The Economist*, drawing on the results of a survey by the Pew Research Center (2010), commented at the end of July 2010 that '[f]ewer than half of all adults expect their children to have a higher standard of living than theirs, and more than a quarter say it will be lower.' This sad state of affairs creates the possibility that fundamental change may finally be possible. If the expectation of an ever higher standard of living has finally faded, support for the pursuit of a better life of the sort that the BLA would provide may have room to emerge.

The BLA and its goals provide an alternative to the growth-focused economic policy advice found, for example, in *Going for Growth*. However, many of the concerns addressed by the BLA are actually raised within mainstream discussion. A recent report by the World Bank's Commission on Growth and Development makes it quite clear that job creation and education, as well as arrangements to assist those between jobs, are all 'on the agenda' (Spence, 2008). Reducing income inequality is also addressed in some conventional economic analyses (Rajan, 2010). It is only in its thoroughgoing concern for the environment and its proposal to reduce the hours of work that the BLA makes a decisive break with the mainstream. And, even here, there is overlap with the discussion of quality of life and sustainability that are becoming part of the broader policy discussion at the OECD and elsewhere (OECD, 2011a; WBCSD, 2011).

Because it has not been part of standard economic policy there may be concern about the practicality of achieving the reduction in hours of work required for the stabilization of income. The approach anticipated is quite simple and workable. The BLA will, in a variety of ways, foster productivity growth. It is difficult to control the pace of such growth. The strategy will be not to try. Instead the BLA will apply a range of policies that reduce hours of work in a flexible fashion. In this it will be guided by a basic economic relationship: income is the product of productivity and hours of work. The BLA will proceed year by year in the way one drives a car, pressing the accelerator (that is, fostering productivity) and applying the brake (that is, reducing hours of work) as needed to maintain the desired speed (income). As the discussion in the section on 'Earnings and hours of work' makes clear, a substantial level of growth in productivity can be balanced by making changes consistent with practices in other high-income nations. These changes will be phased in as needed, targeting a constant level for income.

Achieving the goals that the BLA embodies is clearly feasible. The challenge is political: to motivate and then draw together the groups that stand to benefit from the BLA, to act in unison to make it reality. Motivation, cooperation and effective action all present significant challenges. For the groups in the 'BLA Coalition' one might expect that motivation would not to be an issue. After all, the BLA is designed to address their concerns and to improve their situation. Of course, each of the three groups may wish to go beyond the positions reflected in the BLA goals. For example, those concerned primarily about the environment may want zero growth in GDP rather than income, or even a reduction in GDP by 2050. However, this will make it very hard to maintain the support of business interests and the workers and families that desire the modest increase in earnings that the BLA would provide. Unfortunately, people find it quite hard to recognize what is in their interest (Folbre, 2011). And, even when they do recognize it, they may not support it, for a variety of reasons such as those indicated in the discussion of American attitudes toward welfare.

Even when groups wish to work together, it is often surprisingly difficult for them to do so. This is clear in past efforts by those in the labor and environmental movements. However, despite the difficulties, progress has been made. There is a long history of successful joint action by labor and the environmental movement when their interests are aligned and trust has been established (Obach, 2004). Finally, even if supporters of the BLA are able to elect representatives who support their cause, this will not assure action consistent with the BLA's goals and policy objectives. Such divergences can arise for a variety of reasons. Consider zero growth, for example. In his recent book, Barry Eichengreen (2011, p. 176), a well-known political economist, claims that '[a] nation whose economy does not grow loses political and strategic power.' It is all too easy to imagine a politician elected with the support of the BLA Coalition deciding not to support policies for zero growth based on such a view. This might occur despite the fact that, as others have pointed out, if there ever was a time when this view was relevant to the United States, it is long past (Cohen and DeLong, 2010).

Despite the obvious difficulties, the BLA should be the focus of substantial effort. Our affluent age cries out for a solution to Keynes's problem – living agreeably and well – not for another 'Great Prosperity' of the earn-and-spend type as suggested by Robert Reich (2011). Not only will another Great Prosperity fail to address quality-of-life issues just as the one from 1947 to 1973 did, it will push the United States and the world toward the environmental disasters that scientists warn us about with increasing frequency. Rather than working for reforms that simply set the stage for another boom-and-bust cycle, thoughtful individuals in the United States should work to put the BLA on the agenda. If not now, when?

NOTES

1. To see that a decline of 45 percent in hours worked is sufficient to offset an 81 percent increase in productivity, one simply checks that the combined effect is no change. Since income (GDP per capita) is productivity (GDP per hours worked) times hours worked per capita, the effect of changes in the two factors on income is multiplicative. The required calculation is as follows: (1 + 0.81) (1 – 0.45) = 0.9955.
2. The effects of a 20 percent reduction in hours per week and a 22 percent reduction in weeks per year are combined as follows: (1 – 0.2) x (1 – 0.22) = 1 – 0.38. One can combine them in this fashion because the policies that cause them – limits on the length of the work week and mandates for vacation and various types of leave – do not interact.
3. Here, as in the other illustrative calculations, effects are combined in a simple multiplicative fashion. Earnings per year are earnings per hour times hours worked per year. Their combined effect is computed as (1 + 0.81) (1 – 0.38) = 1 + 0.12, showing the net gain of 12 percent in earnings per year.

REFERENCES

Ackerman, B., A. Alstott and P. Van Parijs (2006). *Redesigning Distribution: Basic Income and Stakeholder Grants as Alternative Cornerstones for a More Egalitarian Capitalism*, Madison, WI: Real Utopias Project.
Ackerman, F. (2008). *Poisoned for Pennies: The Economics of Toxics and Precaution*, Washington, DC: Island Press.
Aguiar, M. and E. Hurst (2009). 'Home production, consumption, and labor supply', *NBER Reporter*, 4.
Alesina, A. and E. Glaeser (2004). *Fighting Poverty in the US and Europe: A World of Difference*, New York: Oxford University Press.
Alesina, A., E. Glaeser and B. Sacerdote (2005). *Work and Leisure in the U.S. and Europe: Why So Different?* Cambridge: National Bureau of Economic Research.
Autor, D. (2010). *The Polarization of Job Opportunities in the U.S. Labor Market: Implications for Employment and Earnings*, Washington, DC: Center for American Progress and the Hamilton Project.
BEA (Bureau of Economic Analysis) (2007). *Measuring the Economy: A Primer on GDP and the National Income and Product Accounts*, Washington, DC: U.S. Department of Commerce.
Bhagwati, J. and A. Blinder (2009). *Offshoring of American Jobs: What Response from U.S. Economic Policy?* Cambridge, MA: MIT Press.
Bloom, D. (2011). 'Population: 7 billion and counting', *Science*, **333**(6042), 562–9.
Bok, D. (2010). *The Politics of Happiness: What Government Can Learn From the New Research on Well-being*, Princeton, NJ: Princeton University Press.
Bowles, S., D. Gordon and T. Weisskopf (1991). *After the Waste Land: A Democratic Economics for the Year 2000*, Armonk, NY: M.E. Sharpe.
Burd-Sharps, S., K. Lewis and E. Borges Martins (2008). *The Measure of America:*

American Human Development Report 2008–2009, New York: Social Science Research Council and Columbia University Press.

Cahuc, P. and A. Zylberberg (2006). *The Natural Survival of Work: Job Creation and Job Destruction in a Growing Economy*, Cambridge, MA: MIT Press.

Choudhry, M. (2009). *Determinants of Labor Productivity: An Empirical Investigation of Productivity Divergence*, Groningen: University of Groningen.

Cohen, S. and J. DeLong (2010). *The End of Influence: What Happens When Other Countries Have the Money?* New York: Basic Books.

Coote, A., J. Franklin and A. Simms (2010). *21 Hours: Why a Shorter Working Week Can Help Us All to Flourish in the 21st Century*, London: New Economics Foundation.

Costanza, R., M. Hart, S. Posner and J. Talberth (2009). *Beyond GDP: The Need for New Measures of Progress*, The PARDEE Papers No. 4, Frederick S. Pardee Center for the Study of the Longer-range Future, Boston University.

Cotis, J.-P., A. de Serres and R. Duval (2010). 'Competitiveness, economic performance, and structural policies: an OECD perspective', in P. De Grauwe (ed.), *Dimensions of Competitiveness*, Cambridge, MA: MIT Press, pp. 19–94.

Diener, E. and M. Chan (2010). 'Happy people live longer: subjective well-being contributes to health and longevity', *Applied Psychology (Health and Well-Being)*, **3**(1), 1–43.

Eichengreen, B. (2007). *The European Economy Since 1945: Coordinated Capitalism and Beyond*, Princeton, NJ: Princeton University Press.

Eichengreen, B. (2011). *Exorbitant Privilege: The Rise and Fall of the Dollar and the Future of the International Monetary System*, New York: Oxford University Press.

EOP and CEA (Executive Office of the President and Council of Economic Advisors) (2010). *Work-life Balance and the Economics of Workplace Flexibility*, Washington, DC: EOP and CEA.

EPI (Economic Policy Institute) (2011a). '2000–07 business cycle was the first one on record where the typical family saw essentially no gain – median family income, 1947–2009 (2009 dollars)', *The State of Working America*, Washington, DC: EPI.

EPI (Economic Policy Institute) (2011b). 'Wages and compensation stagnating: hourly wage and compensation growth for production/non-supervisory workers and productivity, 1947–2009', *The State of Working America*, Washington, DC: EPI.

Folbre, N. (2011). 'Defining economic interest', *New York Times*, 8 August.

Frank, R. (2011). *The Darwin Economy: Liberty, Compensation, and the Common Good*, Princeton, NJ: Princeton University Press.

Galbraith, J. (1958). *The Affluent Society*, New York: Houghton Mifflin.

Garfinkel, I., L. Rainwater and T. Smeeding (2010). *Wealth and Welfare States: Is America a Laggard or Leader?* New York: Oxford University Press.

Giuntini, R. and K. Gaudette (2003). 'Remanufacturing: the next great opportunity for boosting US productivity', *Business Horizons*, November–December.

Glaeser, E. (2010). 'Housing policy in the wake of the crash', *Daedalus*, **139**(4), 95–106.

Glaeser, E. (2011). 'Why green energy can't power a job engine', *New York Times*, 18 January.

Goldin, C. and L. Katz (2008). *The Race Between Education and Technology*, Cambridge, MA: Harvard University Press.

Goldman, D. and E. McGlynn (2005). *U.S. Health Care: Facts About Cost, Access, and Quality*, Los Angeles, CA: The Communications Institute.
Green, F. (2006). *The Paradox of Job Quality in the Affluent Economy*, Princeton, NJ: Princeton University Press.
Greenstone, M. and A. Looney (2011). 'The great recession may be over, but American families are working harder than ever', *The Brookings Institution*, available at http://www.brookings.edu/opinions/2011/0708_jobs_greenstone_looney.aspx (accessed 18 October 2012).
Hacker, J. (2006). *The Great Risk Shift: The Assault on American Jobs, Families, Health Care, and Retirement and How You Can Fight Back*, New York: Oxford University Press.
Hacker, J., G. Huber, P. Rehm, M. Schlesigner and R. Valletta (2010). *Economic Security at Risk: Findings from the Economic Security Index*, New York: The Rockefeller Foundation.
Haltiwanger, J., R. Jarmin and J. Miranda (2010). 'Who creates jobs? Small vs. large vs. young', NBER Working Paper Series, National Bureau of Economic Research, Cambridge.
Hansen, J. (2009). *Storms of My Grandchildren: The Truth About the Coming Climate Catastrophe and Our Last Chance to Save Humanity*, New York: Bloomsbury.
Heckman, J. and P. Lafontaine (2008). 'The declining American high school graduation rate: evidence, sources, and consequences', *NBER Reporter*. 13 February.
Holbrook, K., A. Kim, B. Palmer and A. Portnoy (eds) (2006). *Global Values 101: A Short Course*, Boston, MA: Beacon Press.
Irons, J. (2009). *Economic Scarring: The Long-term Impacts of the Recession*, Washington, DC: Economic Policy Institute.
Jackson, T. (2009). *Prosperity Without Growth: Economics for a Finite Planet*, London: Earthscan.
Jacobs, E, (ed.) (2007). *Handbook of U.S. Labor Statistics: Employment, Earnings, Prices, Productivity, and Other Labor Data*, 10th edn, Lanham, MD: Bernan Press.
Jacobs, J. and K. Gerson (2004). *The Time Divide: Work, Family, and Gender Inequality*, Cambridge, MA: Harvard University Press.
Johnson, J. and J. Rochkind with A. Ott and S. DuPont (2009). *With Their Whole Lives Ahead of Them: Myths and Realities About Why So Many Students Fail to Finish College*, Seattle, WA: Bill and Melinda Gates Foundation.
Karl, T., J. Melillo and T. Peterson (eds) (2009). *Global Climate Change Impacts in the United States*, New York: Cambridge University Press.
Kenworthy, L. (2011). *Progress for the Poor*, New York: Oxford University Press.
Keynes, J. (1963). 'Economic possibilities for our grandchildren', in J. Keynes, *Essays in Persuasion*, New York: W.W. Norton, pp. 358–73.
Klein, E. (2011). 'The U.S. government: an insurance conglomerate protected by a large, standing army', *Washington Post*, 14 February.
Krugman, P. (2009). 'The big zero', *New York Times*, 28 December.
Lawrence, R. (2008). *Blue-collar Blues: Is Trade to Blame for Rising US income Inequality?* Washington, DC: Peterson Institute for International Economics.
Layard, R. (2005). *Happiness: Lessons from a New Science*, New York: Penguin.
Lew, J. (2011). 'The President's plan for economic growth and deficit reduction', *The White House Blog*. 19 September, available at http://www.whitehouse.

gov/blog/2011/09/19/president-s-plan-economic-growth-and-deficit-reduction-0 (accessed 18 October 2012).
Lyubomirsky, S. (2007). *The How of Happiness: A New Approach to Getting the Life You Want*, New York: Penguin.
Maddison, A. (2007). *Contours of the World Economy, 1–2030 AD: Essays in Macro-Economic History*, New York: Oxford University Press.
Markoff, J. (2011). 'Virtual and artificial, but 58,000 want course', *New York Times*, 15 August.
Metcalf, G. (2010). 'Tax policies for low-carbon energy', *VOX*, 20 July.
Mishel, L., J. Bernstein and H. Shierholz (2008). *The State of Working America 2008/2009*, Ithaca, NY: Cornell University Press.
Mold, A. (2010). 'Maddison's forecasts revisited: what will the world look like in 2030?', *VOX*, 24 October.
Mulligan, C. (2010). 'Look to Europe to understand why this U.S. recovery is jobless', *New York Times*, 29 September.
NEEA (Northwest Energy Efficiency Alliance) (2008). *Market Transformation and the Northwest Energy Efficiency Alliance: A Brief History*, Portland, OR: NEEA.
Newman, K. and E. Jacobs (2010). *Who Cares? Public Ambivalence and Government Activism from the New Deal to the Second Gilded Age*, Princeton, NJ: Princeton University Press.
NHEEPA (Network of Heads of European Environment Protection Agencies) (2005). *The Contribution of Good Environmental Regulation to Competitiveness*, Brussels: NHEEPA.
Noddings, N. (2006). *Happiness and Education*, New York: Cambridge University Press.
Obach, B. (2004). *Labor and the Environmental Movement: The Quest for Common Ground*, Cambridge, MA: MIT Press.
OECD (Organisation for Economic Co-operation and Development) (2009). *Society at a Glance: OECD Social Indicators*, Paris: OECD.
OECD (Organisation for Economic Co-operation and Development) (2011a). *How's Life? Measuring Well*-being, Paris: OECD.
OECD (Organisation for Economic Co-operation and Development) (2011b). *Going for Growth*, Paris: OECD.
Partnership for 21st Century Skills (2010). *Are They Really Ready to Work? Employers' Perspectives on the Basic Knowledge and Applied Skills of New Entrants to the 21st Century U.S. Workforce*, Washington, DC: Partnership for 21st Century Skills.
Pavetti, L. and D. Rosenbaum (2010). *Creating a Safety Net that Works When the Economy Doesn't: The Role of the Food Stamp and TANF Programs*, Washington, DC: Center on Budget and Policy Priorities.
Pew Research Center (2010). *A Balance Sheet at 30 Months: How the Great Recession has Changed Life in America*, Washington, DC: Pew Research Center.
Rajan, R. (2010). *Fault Lines: How Hidden Fractures Still Threaten the World Economy*, Princeton, NJ: Princeton University Press.
Raskin, P., T. Banuri, G. Gallopín et al. (2002). *Great Transition: The Promise and Lure of the Times Ahead*, Boston: Stockholm Environment Institute.
Raskin, P., C. Electris and R. Rosen (2010). 'The century ahead: searching for sustainability', *Sustainability*, **2**(8), 2626–51.

Reich, R. (2011). *Aftershock: The Next Economy and America's Future*, New York: Vintage Books.
Reinert, E. (2007). *How Rich Countries Got Rich . . . And Why Poor Countries Stay Poor*, New York: Public Affairs.
Rich, M. (2010). 'Factory jobs return, but employers find skills shortage', *New York Times*, 1 July.
Rockström, J., W. Steffen, K. Noone et al. (2009). 'Planetary boundaries: exploring the safe operating space for humanity', *Ecology and Society*, **14**(2), 32, available at http://www.ecologyandsociety.org/vol14/iss2/art32 (accessed 18 October 2012).
Salverda, W., B. Nolan and T. Smeeding (eds) (2009). *The Oxford Handbook of Economic Inequality*, New York: Oxford University Press.
Samuelson, R. (2008). *The Great Inflation and Its Aftermath: The Past and Future of American Affluence*, New York: Random House.
Scherer, F. (1999). *New Perspectives on Economic Growth and Technological Innovation*, Washington, DC: Brookings Institution Press.
Schor, J. (2010). *Plenitude: The New Economics of Wealth*, New York: Penguin.
Simms, A., V. Johnson and P. Chowla (2010). *Growth Isn't Possible: Why We Need a New Economic Direction*, London: New Economics Foundation.
Spence, M. (2008). *The Growth Report: Strategies for Sustained Growth and Inclusive Development*, Washington, DC: The International Bank for Reconstruction and Development and The World Bank.
Stiglitz, J., A. Sen and J.-P. Fitoussi (2010). *Mismeasuring Our Lives: Why GDP Doesn't Add Up*, New York: The New Press.
Stutz, J. (2010). 'The three-front war: pursuing sustainability in a world shaped by explosive growth', *Sustainability: Science, Practice, and Policy*, **6**(2), 49–59, available at http://sspp.proquest.com/static_content/vol6iss2/1001-001.stutz.pdf (accessed 18 October 2012).
Stutz, J. (2011). 'The quality of development index: a new headline indicator of progress', *Journal of Futures Studies*, **15**(3), 73–102.
Syverson, C. (2010). 'What determines productivity?', *VOX*, 25 June.
Thaler, R. and C. Sunstein (2008). *Nudge: Improving Decisions about Health, Wealth, and Happiness*, New Haven, CT: Yale University Press.
The Economist (2011). 'Briefing 3D printing: the printed world', *The Economist*, 12 February.
Tobin, J. (1964). 'Economic growth as an objective of government policy', *American Economic Review*, **54**(3), 1–20.
United States Department of Commerce (2008). *Statistical Abstract of the United States: 2009*, Washington, DC: Census Bureau.
Urahn, S. and J. Reichert (2009). *The Clean Energy Economy: Repowering Jobs, Businesses, and Investments Across America*, Washington, DC: The Pew Charitable Trusts.
Victor, P. (2008). *Managing Without Growth: Slower by Design, Not Disaster*, Cheltenham, UK and Northampton, MA, USA: Edward Elgar.
WBCSD (World Business Council for Sustainable Development) (2011). *A Vision for Sustainable Consumption: Innovation, Collaboration, and the Management of Choice*, Geneva: WBCSD.
Wilkinson, R. and K. Pickett (2010). *The Spirit Level: Why Greater Equality Makes Societies Stronger*, New York: Bloomsbury Press.

5. Welcome to the consumption line: sustainability, social organization and the wage-price gap

Emanuel Ubert and Michael M. Bell

INTRODUCTION

Consumption is the most everyday of acts. It is something we all do. It is a social phenomenon. And yet we typically understand it as a matter of individual action, using metaphors of choice, value and supply to describe its origin and aspiration. We are coming to understand that consumption has tremendous collective consequences for our economy, ecology and society. But we still have trouble understanding that the act of consumption is something that is socially organized, patterned by culture, economy, state and politics, and not merely an act of utilitarian satisfaction by a free-thinking and sovereign consumer.

Some authors have even gone so far as to state outright that a focus on consumption is at best a distraction from the real stuff that moves our lives. As none other than Karl Marx (1956) wrote in the second volume of *Das Kapital*, 'It is sheer tautology to say that crises are caused by lack of effective consumption, or effective consumers,' referring to the Marxist theory of economic crisis. Or, as another translation has it (Mehring, 1935), 'It is sheer redundancy to say that crises are produced by the lack of paying consumption or paying consumers.' For, as Marx goes on to argue (1956):

> [I]f one were to attempt to give this tautology the semblance of a profounder justification by saying that the working-class receives too small a portion of its own product and the evil would be remedied as soon as it receives a larger share of it and its wages increase in consequence, one could only remark that crises are always prepared by precisely a period in which wages rise generally and the working-class actually gets a larger share of that part of the annual product which is intended for consumption.

This view remains influential in some quarters. For example, Gould et al. (2004, p. 303) argue that 'producers, not consumers, are the major driving factor in the political economy.' Thus, the focus of analysis should be on where the decisions get made, they suggest. The important decisions are what gets produced, not what gets bought, Gould and colleagues contend.

In what follows, we by no means try to reverse the argument. Rather, we contend that production and consumption are social organizational phenomena of equal, and mighty, importance to our economy, ecology and society. But we place our emphasis here on the social organization of consumption, to balance our understanding and analysis. In a way, our analysis centers on observing that the current world economic crisis was by no means preceded by 'a period in which wages [rose] generally,' and in which the working class was getting a 'larger share,' as Marx had it. In this case, at least, it was quite the opposite; real wages fell and workers were getting a smaller share, as inequality increased, making it difficult for all that was produced to be bought and consumed, eventually resulting in the Great Recession and its, as we write, continuing aftermath (see the chapter by John Stutz in this volume). But we do not intend to replace Marx's overproduction argument with an underconsumption argument. Rather, as first outlined in Bell (2009), we argue instead that capitalists must contend with an ever-present wage-price gap that emerges from the double conflict between capital and workers and capital and consumers – or, rather, what we shall be calling worker-consumers. Because of this gap, capital is constantly under unrelenting pressure to speed consumption, as well as production, through the establishment of what we shall call consumption lines in parallel to, and interlocking with, the more familiar concept of production lines. The fate of much of great significance depends upon how we work through these interlocked pressures.

In what follows, we begin by adopting the concept of final consumption to measure the ecological impact of economic activity. We then review the debate on how best to conceptualize the economic organization of this impact. From there, we go on to introduce our theory of the consumption line and its intersections with the pressures of production via the double conflict of the wage-price gap.

ECOLOGICAL CONSEQUENCES OF CONTEMPORARY CONSUMPTION PATTERNS

The ecological boundaries necessary to maintain an environment in which humanity can safely exist are under increasing pressure. For the first time since the last ice age ended about 10 000 years ago, and as a direct result of human industrial activity and modern mass consumption over the last 150 years, geological scale changes are about to directly enter into and affect human history itself. Three critical environmental boundaries have already been breached (Rockström et al., 2009). First, failure to push the current (as of 2011) 396 parts per million (ppm) level of atmospheric carbon dioxide below the scientifically acknowledged safe upper limit of 350 ppm risks irreversible impacts such as the melting of the Greenland ice sheets and the widespread release of methane gases from permafrost, leading to runaway global warming. Second, biodiversity's current rate of about 100 species lost per million per year far exceeds the proposed safe boundary of ten, significantly damaging and reducing ecosystem services such as resistance against invasive species or pollination of plants. Third, the global nitrogen cycle has been greatly altered by human industrial activity, with about 121 million tons of nitrogen per year removed from the atmosphere (versus a safe boundary of about 35 million tons per year), threatening land fertility and plant life. Additional planetary boundaries close to being breached are ocean acidification, global freshwater use and land usage, all with dramatically negative consequences for today's highly interdependent, globalized social and economic life.

To assess the impact of modern consumption patterns on the breaching of those planetary boundaries, it is necessary to acknowledge that the ecological effects of consumption stretch back along the entire production cycle of a consumed good. As a result, in the context of their effects on the environment, the production and consumption sides of the economy should be viewed as closely interlinked and not just confined to the 'end-consumption' of goods. In what follows we adopt and extend the concept of final consumption as defined by the United Nations Environment Programme (UNEP) (2010) to account for the entirety of environmental effects of material lifecycles. Contrary to the concept of end-consumption, final consumption takes account of all the resources used, greenhouse gases emitted, and waste and pollution created during the lifecycle of a product that ends up being consumed by an end-consumer. Such a consumption lifecycle starts with the original resource extraction, includes the full production chain and ends with the actual consumption and discarding of a good. The ecological impact of the consumption of a soda, is, for example, not limited to waste created by the can, but also extends to the resources depleted by producing the can, the actual drink, and the waste and pollution associated with the production and discarding of the can. Final consumption thus immediately links the production and consumption dynamics of economy and ecology.

PERSPECTIVES ON CONSUMPTION

Adequate transformations of (final) consumption patterns that solve today's ecological problems are usually heavily predicated on specific ontological understandings of the nature and function of consumption. A wide variety of such idealized understandings exist, each taking a different position on the agency and structure of consumption. Disagreements about how consumption patterns arise and reproduce lead to different conclusions about how to transform them. Therefore, before we explain our theory of consumption lines, let us first take a look at the most common perspectives on consumption: the neoclassical, competitive, sentimental and productivist perspectives. None of these perspectives analytically account for the basic interdependence of the consumption and production sides of the economy and its effects on final consumption patterns and the environment.

The neoclassical perspective of consumption is likely the most influential. In it, autonomous and rational agents with consistent and independent preferences consume to fulfill their insatiable demand for goods and services (Varian, 1992). As Schor (1999) notes, in this view demand is only limited by individual budget constraints and by the prices of the desired products. Consumers signal their tastes and desires through the price mechanism in complete and competitive markets (at least when things are going according to the neoclassical ideal). Think of the consumer with a shopping cart (whether a material shopping cart or a 'shopping cart' on a website) grabbing items and heading for the checkout line. Producers observe consumers' demand, and adjust their prices and output in line with that demand. In this way, consumers' choices indirectly shape the quality and quantity of the produced goods. Consumer sovereignty over the economy is (allegedly) very high for, as the phrase goes, 'the customer is always right.' The neoclassical perspective gives little consideration to the significance of social context, networks and collective needs in consumption decisions. Rather, it centers on the assumption of rational calculation by atomized actors pursuing their own preferences, and implicitly equates public goods with private goods.

Almost as familiar is the competitive perspective of consumption. In his 1899 classic *The Theory of the Leisure Class*, Thorstein Veblen emphasizes the competitive and comparative character of modern consumption. Most of us living in affluent countries are long past direct subsistence needs in most of our consumption, says Veblen, especially the rich – whom Veblen called the 'leisure class.' The main motivation for consumption by the leisure class, and those who aspire to it, is the desire to indicate a lofty social position through what Veblen (1899) terms 'conspicuous consumption,' 'conspicuous waste' and 'conspicuous leisure.' Think of holidays in the Caribbean, Gucci sunglasses or red Ferraris. In Veblen's perspective, status goods are first adopted by the affluent and subsequently mimicked by lower income groups. In contrast to the neoclassical perspective of consumption, the competitive perspective places consumption decisions in a social context. But while it expands the motivation for consumption beyond purely atomistic and individual considerations to a social (and class) dimension, in essence the competitive perspective still rests on the alleged sovereignty of the consumer in pursuit of desires and preferences. Consumption per se occurs primarily because it serves the interests of consumers.

In the sentimental perspective of consumption, consumption is not necessarily rooted in self-interest as in the neoclassical perspective, but is more broadly and deeply embedded in the social context of specific moments of consumption. Sentimental consumption does not need to constitute a signal of social status, but provides a means for supporting feelings of social communion and to 'make and maintain social relationships' (Douglas and Isherwood, 1996). Think of giving flowers, putting on a yarmulke, eating a meal traditional to one's family or wearing a tee-shirt from your Tuesday night volleyball leagues. Goods can embody a feeling of the social presence of those who are not physically there, as in the special value of jewelry handed down from one's mother or the end-table made by one's father – what the Maori people call the *hau* of an object and what we might term, after Stiles et al. (2011) and Bell (1997), the 'ghosts of goods.' Goods consumption can also be a source of political action toward other-oriented ends, as in what Schor and Willis (2008) (see also Schor, 2010) call conscious consumers and what Micheletti and her colleagues (2006) call political consumerism. The consumption of goods, in short, can satisfy social needs by providing a symbolic language for the social communication that lies at the heart of the social world, and by providing a basis for political action, allowing consumers to seek, make and contest identity (Arnould and Thompson, 2005).

The productivist perspective of consumption is heavily predicated on Marx's theory of production. The 'treadmill of production' approach of Schnaiberg, Gould and colleagues (see, for example, Gould et al., 2004) is a leading example. It argues that if producers are making money with a good, other producers will try the same thing, increasing supply and thus forcing prices down, leading producers to either go out of business or try to produce and sell even more to make up the difference – which forces prices down even further, repeating the cycle ad infinitum. Think corn farmers, ever increasing output with bigger equipment, more chemicals and larger farms. The common solution to the treadmill that producers seek is to force feed their growing output to consumers, so that production comes to shape consumption. The Frankfurt School (Schor, 2007) more explicitly takes the view that capitalists essentially create and manipulate consumers' preferences and behavior at will, and in essence control and guide the direction of consumption patterns. Think corn farmers convincing politicians to subsidize (and in some cases require) the use of corn ethanol in automotive fuel. In such a case, consumption follows supply, regardless of demand, and the consumer is a sheep on the rope of capital. But the political economic need of capital to shape the consumer's context of decision making immediately implies the existence of contention and resistance. However, the traditional Marxist perspective of the unwilling worker and the willing consumer misses the presence of what Bell (2009) calls a double conflict in the economy, which spans the production and the consumption sides of the economy. The capitalist must equally struggle for the worker's labor and the consumer's cash, as we shall detail later.

Several points follow from these four perspectives of (end-) consumption:

- We suggest that each captures an important dimension of consumption. Preferences do matter, but so too do the competitive, sentimental, social and productive contexts in which preferences take form and direction.
- These perspectives are not mutually exclusive but end-consumption is a context-dependent configuration of all of them. One can have a rational preference for a sentimental connection that has competitive consequences as well – say, the purchase of a fancy new laptop for your child, which at once exhibits desire for function, status and family ties.
- The consumption decisions of rational, competitive, sentimental and unwilling consumers follow different logics than the production side of the economy, which does not care whether the preference, status, identity and sovereign concerns of consumers are actually met. All the production side cares about is that the consumer consumes. But, crucially, the worker and consumer are the same people. They are all worker-consumers with the two major points of conflict with capital and the owners of production (Bell, 2009) – which alerts us to some important political potentials, none of which are satisfyingly captured by the above perspectives of consumption, and to which we shall return later.
- None of the above perspectives on consumption captures the full ecological impact of the material lifecycle associated with any single consumption good.

For now, let us note that the conceptual question of how certain (final) consumption patterns arise, reproduce and change over time boils down to the empirical question of who does the reproducing and changing – worker-consumers, capitalists or both – and, more conceptually, how the interaction (and conflicts) between capitalists and worker-consumers shape consumption patterns and their environmental impacts. As we shall show, this interaction is essentially a political one.

CONVENTIONAL SOLUTIONS TO THE ECOLOGICAL CONSEQUENCES OF CONTEMPORARY CONSUMPTION

Contemporary strategies aimed at transforming existing consumption patterns and reducing their environmentally destructive impact are conceptually positioned at the two extremes of an ideal end-consumption sovereignty scale and are essentially rooted in the neoclassical perspective or the productivist perspective of (end-) consumption (Figure 5.1). Neoclassical, consumer-based strategies aim to change (final) consumption patterns by focusing on the transformation of consumption behavior at the individual level. Productivist strategies identify producers as the key agents of change and seek to change (final) consumption patterns by transforming production processes and structures. (For the sake of brevity, we largely bracket the temporal and spatial aspects of these two ideal strategies.) Neither of these transformative strategies explicitly incorporates the possibility of (end-) consumption perspectives' analytical conjunctures or the inherent conflicts between worker-consumers and producers and their importance for the shape and direction of final consumption patterns.

Consumer-based Solutions

Due to the globalized nature of many final consumption lifecycles, local consumption patterns usually have complex global ecological repercussions.

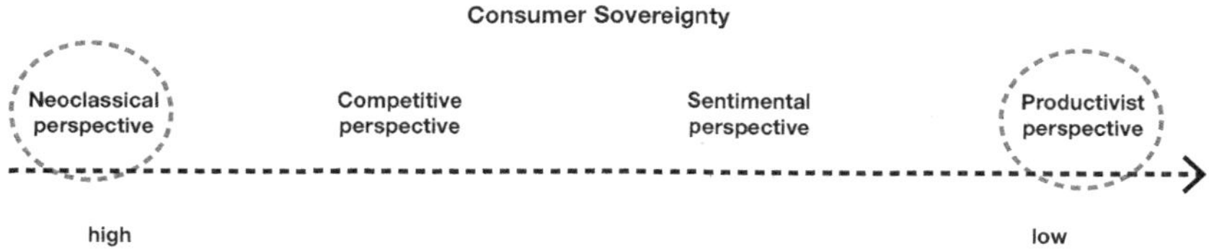

Figure 5.1 Degree of consumer sovereignty by perspective

Strategies aimed at transforming global consumption patterns recognize this feature. They identify autonomous individual end-consumption patterns as driving final consumption and thus as the root cause of ecological problems associated with the breaching of planetary boundaries, resource depletion and greenhouse gas emissions. Typically embedded in a neoclassical and thus highly sovereign notion of consumption, such solutions regard consumers' end-demand as driving the (aggregate) supply of goods and services and products' material lifecycles through flexible prices and free markets. From this perspective it is not end-consumption per se that is the problem, but the nature of the environmental impact of the products and services that are demanded, consumed, produced and ultimately discarded.

In short, the key transformative agents in this approach are end-consumers, who should spend their money on less harmful things: compact fluorescents, hybrid cars, organic food and the like. By increasing demand for less material- and energy-intensive products and services, end-consumers can reduce the profitability of environmentally harmful goods and induce capitalist-producers, via the power of the market, to switch to more sustainable and ecologically friendly production practices. The market place and flexible prices become mechanisms through which the consumer implements a transformative agenda through the *50 Simple Things You Can Do to Save the Earth*, to quote the title of a popular book of some years ago (Earthworks, 1989). The scaling up of more sustainable individual habits and strategies restructures material and waste lifecycles, while keeping the fundamental structure of consumption and capitalist market mechanisms and institutions in place. Greater individual environmental awareness and better-structured markets are deemed sufficient to transform ecologically harmful consumption patterns. The innovative capacity and the flexibility of capitalism can be maintained.

Producer-based Solutions

Producer-based approaches argue that consumer-based solutions will inevitably founder in the face of a simple fact: consumers can only buy what producers make. As Gould et al. (2004, p. 300) put it, 'although consumers can accept or reject these products, they have no influence over the allocation of capital to productive technologies.' In this view, the production side of the economy is the dominant driver of end-consumption, and as such, is also the main cause of global emissions and resource extraction.

Solutions proposed in the broad vein of green Keynesianism, for example, do not see the fundamental mechanisms of capitalism as responsible for ecologically unhealthy final consumption patterns, but instead fault the nature of specific, outdated institutions and resulting production (and by extension consumption) processes as causing environmental problems. Here, the state and producers are the crucial transformative agents. Green Keynesian strategies such as the New Economic Foundation's *A Green New Deal* (Elliot et al., 2008) or Van Jones's (2008) The *Green Collar Economy* take an approach that draws much from Roosevelt's New Deal faith in the progressive state and economy. They argue that by redirecting public and private investments toward sustainable ends, the state, as well as the corporate sector, can restructure the economy in a way that will shift final consumption patterns to ecologically sustainable pathways. The 'greening' of material throughput, increased resource efficiency and widely used renewable energy can all be achieved while simultaneously safeguarding, and indeed taking advantage of, the growth dynamics of capitalism. As a result, we can literally outgrow our environmental problems, while simultaneously restoring employment and reducing social injustice. Natural capitalism – a view closely related to green Keynesianism – takes a more bottom-up approach to producer-based strategies, arguing that it is in the individual interests of capitalists to green both their production processes and their products (Hawken, 1993, 1997, 2007; Friedman, 2008), while maintaining confidence in the potentially benign transformative power of capitalism.

This faith in the potential of sustainable growth to resolve emission and resource-extraction problems in turn is challenged by the proponents of 'no-growth' and 'degrowth' strategies by, for example, Tim Jackson, Herman Daly, Nicholas Georgescu-Roegen and Serge Latouche. Their transformative strategies question whether outgrowing our ecological problems is either desirable or feasible. For instance, Jackson (2009, p. 85) argues that it is too simplistic to assume that 'capitalism's propensity for efficiency will allow us to stabilize the climate or protect against resource scarcity.' Overall, the vision for no-growth or degrowth centers on an economy that is 'better not bigger,' in which qualitative not quantitative growth takes place, poverty is reduced by redistribution and inequality addressed by minimum and maximum income.

No-growth and degrowth strategies share with green Keynesianism and natural capitalism a production-based orientation and a limited view of the conflicts involved in capitalist relations. Their main focus is on the conflict between firms, how firms direct consumption patterns and the resulting effects on the environment. They are strikingly silent on the double conflict between firms and worker-consumers, a conflict that we shall see is central to the form and direction of final consumption's material and waste lifecycles.

The original UNEP concept of final consumption is essentially predicated on industrial ecological input-output perspectives that represent the metabolic circulation of materials and wastes through the economic system, but do not theorize interactions between capitalists and worker-consumers and their collective and interconnected political, economic and environmental processes that direct the circulation of what Mol and Spaargaren (2005) have called 'environmental flows.' Such environmental flows might more accurately be called 'socio-environmental flows' because they originate and reproduce in the social realm and specifically through the conflict between capitalists and worker-consumers. While the protection of the global environment is undoubtedly dependent on a major transformation of production, producers' ability to implement beneficial change will always be eroded unless they are embraced and implemented by worker-consumers who are close to the local consequences of change for ecology, economy and society.

We therefore claim that the transformations of global and local final consumption patterns will be successful in averting ecological crises only if they involve a combination of measures addressing both capitalist and worker-consumer behavior and their collective shaping of material and waste cycles. Inevitably, transformative agents' interests, the structure within which the collective shaping takes place, and actors' ontological understandings of the connections between consumption, production and the worsening environmental situation will significantly influence any such solution. In that respect, Radkau (2008) has convincingly argued that environmental policies historically have tended to become increasingly subject to the 'laws of power' and the preservation of authority as the management of environmental problems moves more to higher levels of social organization.

THE ECONOMIC POLITICS OF CONSUMPTION

Consumer-producer Interaction and Conflict

While the concept of end-consumption can be conceptualized as a context-dependent configuration of the individual consumption perspectives outlined above, it does not capture the full ecological impact of consumption. As discussed above, proposed solutions to environmental problems premised on such notions of end-consumption are inherently limited and are bound to be unsuccessful. By moving from a view of end- to final consumption we conceptualize consumption and production as one single near-decomposable metabolic cycle and explicitly take into account the entire ecological lifecycle or socio-environmental flows of consumption. Crucially, the outlined existing transformative strategies above neither take into account this entire lifecycle nor the inherent interconnection between consumption and production. In the remainder of this chapter we discuss how the consumption and production sides of the economy combine to shape the socio-environmental flows of final consumption and focus on how socio-technical organization of (end-) consumption makes possible those flows. By doing so we hope to provide a sounder conceptual basis for the search for consumption-focused solutions to the contemporary environmental crises.

We begin with a point made by Bell (2009): the capitalist economy's unrelenting need to expand arises not only from competitive pressures between producers but also out of worker-consumers' own expansionary cycles. Both capitalist and worker-consumer give away to get back more. The capitalist, as an owner of the means of production and employer of worker-consumers, invests money to expand production to maintain (or increase) the rate of profit. The worker-consumer, who sells labor to the capitalist in exchange for wages for consumption and savings, spends money on her own productive capacity both to maintain employment and likely also in the hope of earning more – what Schor (1998) terms the 'cycle of work and spend.' Competitive pressures and the desire to earn profits compel producers to push for low wages and high prices, while worker-consumers push for the exact opposite out of a desire to maximize consumption possibilities. Consequently, the economic interests of worker-consumers and capitalists are in direct conflict in both production and consumption realms. Both do, however, also require each other to fuel their individual expansionary cycles. The worker-consumer needs the capitalist to provide wages and goods, while the producer needs the worker-consumer to provide labor and sales. It is this conflicted codependence of worker-consumers and capitalists on each other that binds together the consumption and production realms of the economy – as well as constantly threatens to shred this binding.

In the context of the ecological impact of consumption, production cannot be understood in isolation of consumption, and consumption cannot be understood without production. While each side of the economy might have varying degrees of power to influence the other's behavior at any point in political history, in practice consumption will never be fully sovereign over production as the neoclassical consumption perspective contends, nor will the producers ever render consumers redundant in the reproduction of capitalism as implied by the productivist perspective of consumption. Rather, in a capitalist economic system, the direction and speed of final consumption patterns (and their ecological impacts) are the

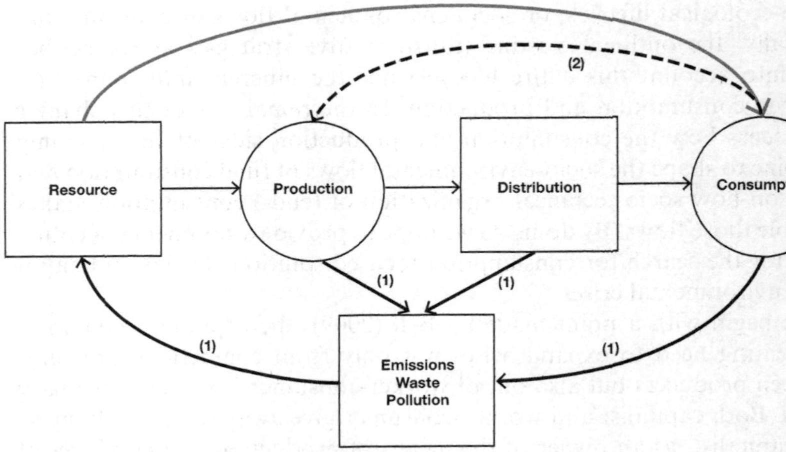

Figure 5.2 The material cycle of the economy

outcome of a continuous and multidimensional conflict and codependence between consumers and capitalists in the production and consumption realms.

Conceptually, final consumption's material and waste cycles 'start' with the extraction of resources. During the production stage, capitalists employ technologies, capital, energy and labor from the worker-consumers and transform raw materials or throughput into products and services, which are in turn distributed to consumers.

Every stage of this cycle (Figure 5.2) produces emissions, waste and pollution (1) that in aggregate stretch planetary boundaries and check the availability of underlying resources and environmental services for further production (and consumption). The flow of the material and waste cycle is controlled, reproduced and grown by contested and contradictory social structures and processes (2) that historically emerge from the (temporary and spatially limited) resolution of the inherent double conflict between worker-consumers and capitalists, as well as the 'problem of the original capitalist' that we shall describe in a moment. Resources are also directly consumed through consumption of many goods, as in the electricity and water required to operate a washing machine or the fuel required to run an automobile, which we indicate with the grey arrow directly from resources to consumption. The manner of the resolution both of the original capitalist's problem and its related double conflict are crucial in linking consumption to the productive side of the economy, in shaping the direction and speed of final consumption patterns and thus in controlling for (and solving) final consumption-related ecological pressures.

Let us now explain what that original capitalist's 'problem' is. In addition to the capitalist's double conflict for worker labor and consumer cash in both the production and consumption realms, every capitalist faces a dilemma of collective action that equally bridges the production and consumption sides of the economy, and that also has crucial implications for the original double conflict. The dilemma – which capitalists themselves scarcely recognize – is as follows: the incentive of the individual capitalist is to pay worker-consumers as little as possible in the production side of the economy and to get them to pay as much as possible for the goods produced in the consumption side of the economy. This is just straight buy low, sell high logic – buy labor low and sell the products of labor high. And it works out fine for the individual capitalist as long as other capitalists are paying their worker-consumers plenty. The individual capitalist can pay his or her worker-consumers little and still get products sold because other capitalists' worker-consumers can buy them. In effect, the individual capitalist treats his or her own employees as workers and the employees of other capitalists as consumers, in blindness to their analytical and practical unity as worker-consumers in the larger economy. But of course, as in the classic prisoner's dilemma of game theory, each capitalist is locked into the same logic, paying their own worker-consumers little and hoping other capitalists' worker-consumers will be able to buy their products. As a result, in aggregate, capitalists wind up paying worker-consumers less money than they need to buy everything that they have produced, which, in capitalism, capitalists must do: in order to make a profit, capitalists must pay out to worker-consumers less than they take in through sales. But worker-consumers cannot spend any more than what they get paid, leading to the ever-present gulf in capitalist economies that Bell (2009) calls the wage-price gap. The width and precise nature of the wage-price gap at any point in time embodies the balance of power between capitalists and worker-consumers in the double conflict over pay and working conditions in the production realm, and spending and living conditions in the consumption realm.

For consumers to be able to consume and for capitalist market economies to function, this wage-price gap needs to be temporarily bridged in a process that Bell (2009) terms 'stretching,' and which we here separate into 'financial stretching' and 'ecological stretching.' Financial stretching is the socio-technical means that allows capitalists to avoid having to confront their own aforementioned collective action problems of treating their own employees as workers and other capitalists' employees as consumers. Drawing on the work of David Harvey (2006), Bell argues that the failure to work out the means of financial stretching, and thus the failure to bridge the economy's wage-price gap, leads to recessions and depressions. Practically, financial stretching occurs through the expansion of credit, which, at least temporarily, allows worker-consumers to consume produced goods today in exchange for paying for them tomorrow – and, in fact, paying more for them tomorrow, considering interest. The specific socio-technical means by which financial stretching is achieved are the product of contested resolutions of the conflict of interests between worker-consumers and capitalists in a wide variety of contexts and scales on the production as well as the consumption side of the economy. The historic and context-specific configurations of those outcomes in turn shape the direction and speed of (final) consumption patterns and their ecological impact.

By doing so, financial stretching gives rise to ecological stretching, which essentially comprises the drawing down of tomorrow's natural capital to enable today's consumption, and the natural capital of someplace else – like, for example, the exploitation of fossil fuels, which borrows from the there and then for the here and now. Material flows and their associated ecological impacts associated with financial stretching, in turn, can be seen as the material embodiment of temporary resolutions to the double conflict between capitalists and worker-consumers, and the collective action problem among capitalists. In this sense, it is perhaps helpful to distinguish end- and final consumption from what we might term financial consumption – not the end-consumption of a good at a particular site (say, the dinner plate), not final consumption's full material lifecycle of the good (say, from the farm to the fork), but consumption as a solution to the financial problem faced by the capitalist with production to sell and the worker-consumer seeking to be paid. In the first instance, neither capitalist nor worker-consumer thinks about the ecological stretching of final consumption to provide end-consumption, for their conflicted relationship is defined financially, not ecologically. This avoidance of the recognition of ecological stretching deepens the political problem by submerging it from view.

Consumption Lines

Four central implications follow from the political-economic need for stretching:

- The necessity of economic growth to achieve financial stretching.
- The necessity of economic faith that the growth will happen and credit will be repaid.

- The necessity of financial consumption to stretch and grow ever more and buy all the merchandise.
- The necessity of ecological stretching of final consumption to provide the end-consumption that yields financial consumption.

But how is all this stretching accomplished? What are its socio-technical means, who employs them and how?

To get a better grasp on those questions, let us take a look at how the production side manages its own stretching. In industrial capitalist economies production is arranged by means of what have classically been called 'production lines' that we define as follows: the effort to organize the unruly masses of humanity to produce as many standardized products as possible for as little as possible. Likewise, we can think of consumption being organized along what we term consumption lines that we define in parallel: the effort to organize the unruly masses of humanity to consume as many standardized products as possible for as much as possible. The formation and reproduction of such production lines has been extensively studied, but that of consumption lines less so. In what follows we therefore focus on the means by which the organization of consumption lines achieves stretching.

In combination with existing knowledge concerning the stretching of production lines, we hope that a better understanding of the socio-technical processes that guide consumption lines will give greater insight into the dynamics of existing final consumption patterns and allow for the development of more successful transformative strategies to solve their negative environmental consequences. Significantly, consumption lines are far from being an exclusive domain of (end-) consumers, but instead can be conceptualized as near-stable yet continuously contested configurations of the physical, legal, cultural and economic relations of worker-consumers and capitalists. These relations structure and are structured by different moments of consumption that in turn emerge from the financial problems of capitalism's double conflict: labor cost reducing capitalists aim to steer unruly consumers into bridging the wage-price gap through financial consumption, and wage maximizing worker-consumers aim to expand their utility, status and sentimental gratification through end-consumption. Consumption lines, in summary, are the conceptual, socio-technical resolution of the consumption dimension of the problem of the original capitalist and the associated double conflict between worker-consumers and capitalists. In connection with production lines, consumption lines are thus the socio-technical means that enable stretching, shape final consumption patterns and give rise to the breaching of planetary boundaries.

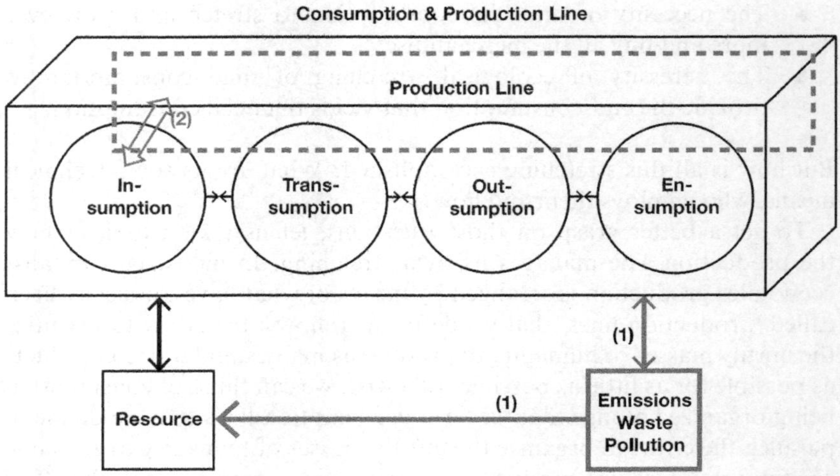

Figure 5.3 The moments of a consumption line

We distinguish four elemental, semi-distinct moments of consumption, each of which is linked to the production line by being a moment of conflict between worker-consumers and capitalists, as well as a moment of opportunity for change: in-sumption, trans-sumption, out-sumption and en-sumption (Figure 5.3).

In-sumption refers to the capitalist challenge of getting consumers into a consumption line and accounts for the kind of structural inducements for consumption that Juliet Schor (1998) described as the 'cycle of work and spend.' Central to in-sumption is advertising and competitive pricing, but it also more subtly entails social organization at the household, community and national levels that makes particular products necessary to the ordinary conduct of a person's day, encouraging people to enter a consumption line. We are reminded here of the story of the high school friend of the son of one us (Bell) who bought a car to get to his after-school job. When this middle-class boy was asked why he needed the job in the first place, he replied, with no trace of irony, 'why, to pay for my car.' In a society with poor public transit and enormous social prestige surrounding car ownership, such circular logic continues to make sense to many people. Advertising for cars represents in-sumption operating through ideas, and the paucity of alternative options represents material inducements to consume. Rather than cut prices and sell more for less, rather than cut production and sell less for more, rather than the truly desperate move of cutting prices and production and selling less for less, capitalists try to use in-sumption techniques to achieve the happy state of selling more for more, and connecting more consumption to more production. In-sumption thus critically links the production to the consumption side of the economy. Further, the degree of power capitalists have over consumer behavior (and vice versa) is, to a large degree, decided at the in-sumption stage of the consumption line.

Trans-sumption refers to the challenge of bringing the seller and the buyer into direct contact so that goods can actually be exchanged for money. Such an exchange requires formal and informal rules that can be monitored and enforced to minimize the risks of one party reneging on the exchange (for example, long-distance trade). It also requires different technologies that facilitate goods and service exchanges, such as automatic teller machines, and the support structures of those technologies, such as banking regulations. As such, trans-sumption operates at the level of the actual economic transaction, in which the seller presents the good and the buyer plunks down cash for it. Different forms of trans-sumption can differ vastly in their capacity to encourage or discourage consumption in one time or place. For example, the problem of a lack of effective consumption demand over the last 30 years was resolved not only by the introduction of cheap consumer credit, but also new technologies and financial re-regulation that obscured the consequences of cheap and easy credit – consequences that in time undermined what they were supposed to promote.

Out-sumption refers to the socio-technical challenge of getting people through a literal line and out of the door, headed to their sites of consumption, recognizing that the repeat consumer will take into account not only the money spent but also the time and hassle. Store layout, checkouts, line management, retail location, parking lots, transportation infrastructure are all familiar aspects of out-sumption. Much contemporary trans-sumption and out-sumption also takes place via the Internet and associated warehousing and shipping procedures.

En-sumption refers to the challenge of actually consuming a purchased good and employing it in social practice. Such challenges can range from a lack of knowledge of how to use a product (for example, software programs), how to assemble it (such as much modern furniture), to time and space constraints of consumption (resulting in spoilage and jam-packed refrigerators), to changes in taste (rendering goods obsolete), to difficulties of display (undermining the status use of a good), to means of disposing of the consumed good and its waste (filling garage shelves with half-used containers of various toxics such as paint and lawn chemicals, awaiting a garbage amnesty day), as the work of Elizabeth Shove (2003) and her colleagues (Shove et al., 2009) has alerted us. En-sumption easily slips into in-sumption, turning the consumption line into a circle, as the consumer reorganizes his or her life in ways that the good facilitates or that the good requires, resulting in still more waste, the impact of which can be seen in any of the myriad consumer-sponsored local sales of now unwanted items. The many terms for these sales indicate their ubiquity: yard sales, garage sales, tag sales, jumble sales, rummage sales, church sales and flea markets.

In short, the central struggle between consumer-workers and capitalists during in-sumption is over control, during trans-sumption over trust, during out-sumption over movement and during en-sumption over use. This struggle can take many forms. Although historically conditioned, the number of possible configurations of moments within a single consumption line, and the number of different consumption lines for a single good at any given moment, greatly varies. An individual consumer can, for example, obtain the bible by driving to her closest bookstore, buy the book there and then reading it in the armchair of her living room. Alternatively, she can also buy the bible by downloading it to her e-reader. Just as different consumption lines achieve different ways and degrees of financial stretching, so do they differ in their associated ecological stretching. The resources extracted and emissions produced by moving through the e-book consumption line, for example, will differ from the ones required by the production and transportation of the physical book. Further, consumption lines and their inherent worker-consumer and capitalist conflicts greatly differ through time and space just as do their environmental implications. The number and quality of existing consumption lines associated with the bible in New York City are much greater than they are in Khartoum, and likewise they are probably much greater today in Khartoum than they were in early twelfth-century Paris. Further, due to differences in technology, knowledge, production processes and distribution systems, bible consumption in twelfth-century Paris presumably resulted in a much smaller environmental footprint than contemporary bible production and consumption.

Context-specific configuration of consumption lines and their inherent moments of conflict and potential for change are historically embedded in and imperfectly reproduce four broader structural relations: infrastructure, laws and regulations, (consumer) culture and the monetary system (Figure 5.4).

Infrastructure comprises the human-made and used physical environment and technology that shapes all stages and scales of consumption lines. Infrastructure helps to move people into, through and out of consumption lines, and creates or modifies the physical space in which commodity exchange and actual consumption take place. The physical nature of infrastructure renders such spaces path dependent and creates

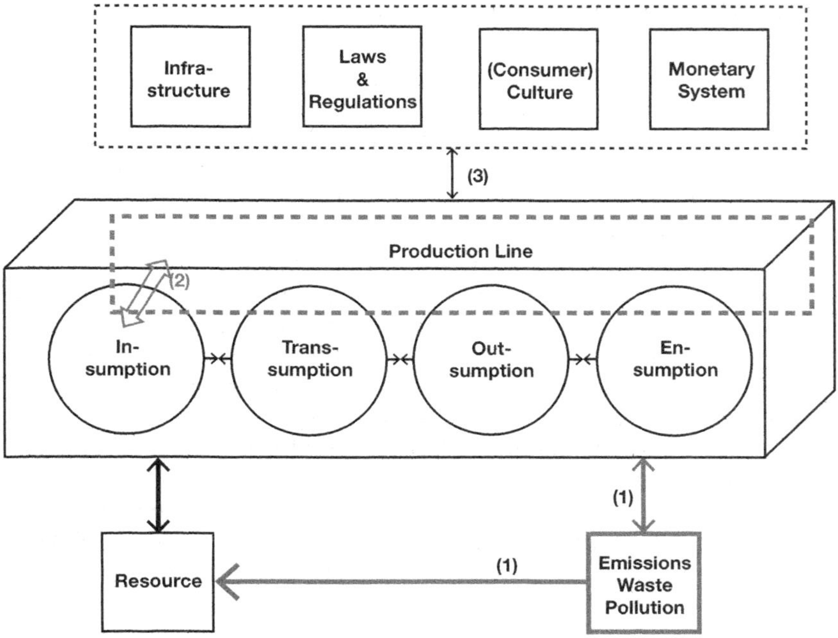

Figure 5.4 *The moments of a consumption line and their forms of social relations*

material boundaries within which moments of conflict between worker-consumers and capitalists can unfold. Infrastructure then channels the overall direction of consumption lines, the physical configuration of its moments, and the speed at which worker-consumers and materials can move through the different stages. The quicker they do, the more the economy grows but the harder worker-consumers have to work to close their wage-price gaps. As a result, it is the economic interests (often not conscious) of worker-consumers to create and maintain infrastructure that slows down the movement of people and materials, while capitalists will be interested in speeding up that movement. The decisive political and economic role of infrastructure, though, is to stabilize the balance of power in this conflict, giving advantage to one side or another. As we saw earlier, the consumption of shelter and mobility are both significant contributors to global greenhouse gas emissions and energy usage. Once the infrastructure of urban sprawl is in place, for example, it is difficult to change, encouraging en-sumption that in turn encourages in-sumption, as worker-consumers invest in cars and suburban residences to organize their daily lives, all the while encouraging further social investment in sprawl.

Laws and regulations further stabilize the balance of political and economic power and thus the speed with which goods and consumers flow through consumption lines. Laws that ban or severely restrict the distribution and consumption of certain goods, for example, will usually severely slow down the flow of those goods, and the environmental pressures associated with them. In contrast, regulations that establish standards for goods ensure their reliability, safety and conformability to handling and monitoring procedures. Whether agents adhere to laws and regulations or not is, among others factors, a function of existing monitoring (and enforcement) technologies, and the political will to enforce. These regulations, however, do not necessarily come from government. Under neoliberalism, economic government has increasingly morphed in economic governance, as corporate entities establish the rules of trade that formerly lay under more democratic control.

(Consumption) culture in the form of 'consumerism' comprises the categories and practices through which consumers make sense of their consumption contexts, including the meaning and nonmonetary value they attach to the goods and services they purchase. Consumption culture allows consumers to form subjective meanings around their consumption practices. As we have seen, the degree to which culture influences consumption behavior and channels people through consumption lines depends on the form and degree of the consumer's rationality, competitiveness and sentiments. Examples include the creation of niche consumerism and individualized lifestyles built around a postmodern style of urban consumerism. Compared to the infrastructure and legal relations, (consumption) culture changes more frequently and is generally more flexible in adapting to changes in the different moments of a consumption line.

The monetary system enables the circulation of money, which forms the basis of material exchanges along the consumption line. Besides enabling (or disabling) financial stretching via the credit system, money, in combination with culture, can also transform and fix the meaning of space and time in consumption lines. In modern financial systems, monetary flows are highly flexible and fast moving, and constitute the highest frequency behavior of all four structuring relations.

The physical and social reproduction of consumption lines and the resulting achievement of (financial) stretching is the result of daily negotiations of individual worker-consumers' and capitalists' interests within a given structural context. Individual worker-consumers reproduce existing configurations of consumption lines either by passively embracing or by actively maintaining those structures with variable coherence and effectiveness. Consumers, for example, consciously or unconsciously make daily decisions regarding whether or not to shop at their local store, whether to drink this brand of coffee or another one and so forth. But we should not confuse 'decisions' with 'choices,' for these decisions are not manifestations of economic free will, but rather of economic politics. It is here that we must look to discover both the prevention and the possibility of change. Cultural processes coproduce the ideological mechanisms that shape the subjectivities of worker-consumers, influencing whether they passively fall in or out of their consumption lines, or whether they challenge the way consumption is organized around them just as they do in their respective production lines. Worker-consumers can, for example, follow the laws and regulations that form the institutional rules that shape consumption lines (as well as production lines), or they can oppose and try to alter them. Likewise individual worker-consumers can reproduce or oppose coercive mechanisms that raise the costs of collective challenges to existing consumption lines. The monetary system ties the welfare of individuals to the effective functioning of the production side of the economy and translates from the political into the economic plane. The reproduction of, or challenge to, the infrastructure of consumption lines occurs at all levels, from state investments in roads and port facilities to corporate investments in retail locations and machinery to worker-consumer investment in housing, transportation and home computers.

Importantly, none of the processes of social and physical reproduction go uncontested. Due to their historic nature, each process in practice exhibits limits, gaps and contradictions that can give rise to unintended or intended changes and blockages to the socio-environmental flows through the consumption line. Contestations of the reproduction of consumption lines at the consumer level arise out of the opposing material interests of capitalists and worker-consumers and the ramification of their differing strategic intentionalities. Advertising, for example, stimulates both our dreams of utility and our suspicions that we are being conned. As well, consumption lines are never perfected. They are always unfinished and at risk of falling apart. Incoherences continually arise out of institutional and physical rigidities and ever-present conflict. Consumption lines are thus never immune from what Bell (2011) calls the 'strange music' of the unexpected. Because of such limits and gaps, existing consumption lines change over time – often in surprising and unintended ways that can lead to the slowing down or even blockage of consumption flows. Enduring consumption lines are those that have been able to 'correct' their unintended, gradual mutations, as well as to adapt to larger, unpredictable exogenous shocks such as natural disasters (see the chapter by David Hess in this volume). They persist through change. While there may be uncoordinated drift in a consumption line, deliberate intervention by collectivities takes place at different levels and in different guises – from appeals to the state by industry groups and worker-consumer movements, to corporate advertising campaigns and consumer boycotts, to direct conflict through bills sent to courtrooms and collection agencies and through protestors marching on corporate headquarters.

Consumption and Collective Organization

Negotiations over specific, intentional changes to the processes within consumption line moments, the configuration of the different moments and the structural context of consumption lines all involve a complex variety of social, economic and political actors at a wide range of different societal levels (Figure 5.5). Both worker-consumers and capitalists struggle to use their political or any other available clout (5) to shape government policies or any other form of collective decision making (4) that directly or indirectly affect the nature and configuration of the different relations (such as physical infrastructure, the monetary system and so forth) that structure consumption (as well as production) lines.

Consistent with their original collective action problem, capitalists, for example, can generally be expected to lobby for pro-business legislation

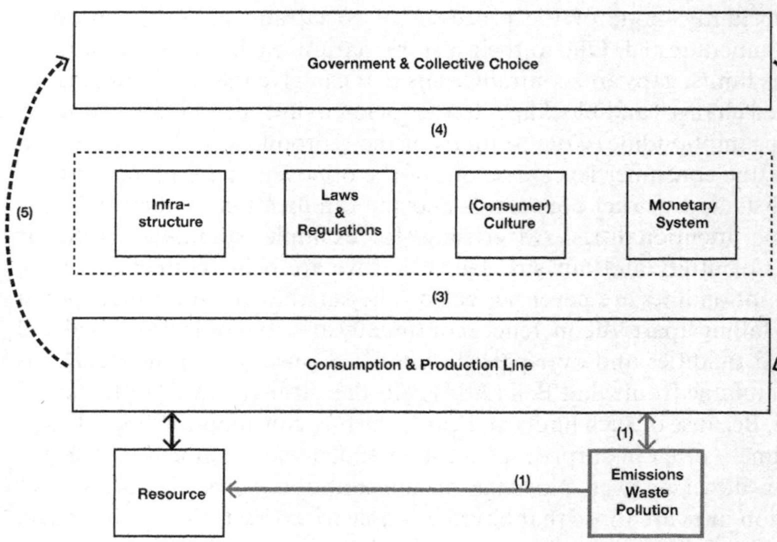

Figure 5.5 The collective organization of consumption and production lines

such as low minimum wages, weak social benefits and lax environmental regulations, while worker-consumers will press for an opposite agenda. Depending on the autonomy of the state, the compromises that are the outcome of those political conflicts between capitalists and worker-consumers will significantly affect the physical and socio-economic reality of consumption (and production) lines, final consumption patterns and resulting ecological stretching. At any moment in time, consumption (and production) lines and their pressures on the environment therefore can be viewed, at a first approximation, as the embodiment of power relations in society, and the lines' changes over time as a rough indicator of changes in those power relations.

As noted in Figure 5.5, the state or other collective organizations can use their resources to directly or indirectly bridge the private wage-price gap and stimulate the economy by engaging in or increasing public consumption (6). The transformation of private into public deficits through financial bailouts and public stimulus following the 2008 financial crisis in the United States, for example, highlights at least temporary capitalist power to induce the state to recatalyze the economy and, thereby, artificially stretch it, once existing consumption lines no longer managed to bridge the wage-price gap. But we would not like to imply here that economic interests are plain, even to those to whom they apply. Capitalists often disagree on both their individual and their collective interests, as do worker-consumers. So while some capitalists and worker-consumers have advocated financial stimulus as a response to the Great Recession, others have advocated austerity, seeking to balance lower sales with lower wages – likely, in our view, to the detriment of both sales and wages.

Barring the situation of a single, all-powerful, all-knowing dictator, not one party in the political and collective societal decision-making process will, however, ever be able to fully shape and control the structure of consumption lines. Political compromises, the providence of context and the unintended consequences of the interaction of consumers (and capitalists) with that structure will nearly always result in consumption (and production) lines that neither entirely block nor completely free up the flow of worker-consumers, goods and moneys through consumption lines.

CONCLUSION

Existing (final) consumption patterns are demonstrably associated with certain material and waste flows that cause significant and growing ecological problems that not only threaten the continuation of the very consumption patterns that cause them but also human civilization as we know it. Those patterns are neither the exclusive outcome of individual worker-consumer choices nor of isolated demand manipulation by capitalists. Instead, consumption and production are fundamentally interlinked through the material conflicts of worker-consumers and capitalists, and the resulting wage-price gaps in capitalist economies. The need to bridge those wage-price gaps translates into the partly intentional and partly unintentional organization of consumption (and production) lines. The structure of consumption lines (and their associated production lines) in turn shapes consumption patterns that, together with the associated production lines, give rise to the material and waste cycles at the heart of today's deepening environmental crisis. All of this is not a static process but unfolds dynamically. Worker-consumers and capitalists individually and collectively reproduce or challenge the manner that wage-price gaps are bridged and are subject to accidents and contradictions that lead to suboptimal and unintended changes to consumption lines over time. Due to the unpredictability of nature, this leads to even greater uncertainty regarding the impact of those changes on the environment.

How can those growth patterns be transformed to avoid ecological crisis? We view the conflict between worker-consumers and capitalists as the central driver of the emergence, reproduction and transformation of existing (final) consumption patterns and their associated ecological impacts. Once one accepts the existence of a wage-price gap and the need of stretching to bridge it, it becomes clear that consumer- or producer-driven solutions alone will not be enough to alter environmentally harmful consumption patterns. Even if consumers wanted to change their existing consumption habits, the infrastructure, legal, cultural and monetary barriers embodied in existing consumption line configurations, as well as production practices, would make it quite difficult to do so. Likewise, even a most radical greening of capitalist production processes would still not break its dependence on financial stretching to sustain itself, thus continuing to produce ecological stretching and the transgression of our ecological planetary boundaries. Instead, any environmentally sustainable transformative politics must connect consumption and production lines by permanently addressing the wage-price gap and the double conflict between worker-consumers and capitalists.

REFERENCES

Arnould, E. and C. Thompson (2005). 'Consumer culture theory (CCT): twenty years of research', *Journal of Consumption Research*, **31**(4), 868–82.

Bell, M. (1997). 'The ghosts of place', *Theory and Society*, **26**(6), 813–36.

Bell, M. (2009). 'The problem of the original capitalist', *Environment and Planning A*, **41**(6), 1276–82.
Bell, M. (2011). *The Strange Music of Social Life: A Dialogue on Dialogic Sociology*, Philadelphia, PA: Temple University Press.
Douglas, M. and B. Isherwood (1996). *The World of Goods: Towards an Anthropology of Consumption*, New York: Routledge.
Earthworks (1989). *50 Simple Things You Can Do to Save the Earth*, Ashland, OR: Bathroom Readers Press.
Elliott, L., C. Hines, T. Juniper et al. (2008). *A Green New Deal*, London: New Economics Foundation.
Friedman, T. (2008). *Hot, Flat, and Crowded: Why We Need a Green Revolution and How it Can Renew America*, New York: Farrar, Straus, and Giroux.
Gould, K., D. Pellow and A. Schnaiberg (2004). 'Interrogating the treadmill of production: everything you wanted to know about the treadmill but were afraid to ask', *Organization and Environment*, **17**(3), 296–316.
Harvey, D. (2006). *The Limits to Capita*, 2nd edn, London: Verso.
Hawken, P. (1993). *The Ecology of Commerce*, New York: Harper Collins.
Hawken, P. (1997). *Natural Capitalism: Creating the Next Industrial Revolution*, New York: Little Brown.
Hawken, P. (2007). *Blessed Unrest: How the Largest Social Movement in History is Restoring Grace, Justice, and Beauty to the World*, New York: Penguin.
Jackson, T. (2009). *Propserity Without Growth: Economics for a Finite Planet*, New York: Earthscan.
Jones, V. (2008). *The Green Collar Economy: How One Solution Can Fix Our Two Biggest Problems*, New York: HarperOne.
Marx, K. (1956). *Capital, Volume II*, trans. I. Laskar, Moscow: Progress Publishers.
Mehring, F. (1935). *Karl Marx: The Story of His Life*, trans. E. Fitzgerald, New York: Covici, Friede.
Micheletti, M., A. Føllesdaland D. Stolle (2006). *Politics, Products, and Markets: Exploring Political Consumerism Past and Present*, New Brunswick, NJ: Transaction Publishers.
Mol, A. and G. Spaargaren (2005). 'From additions and withdrawals to environmental flows: reframing debates in the environmental social sciences', *Organization and Environment*, **18**(1), 91–107.
Radkau, J. (2008). *Nature and Power: A Global History of the Environment*, trans. T. Dunlap, New York: Cambridge University Press.
Rockström, J., W. Steffen, K. Noone et al. (2009). 'Planetary boundaries: exploring the safe operating space for humanity', *Ecology and Society*, **14**(2), 32.
Schor, J. (1998). *The Overspent American: Why We Want What We Don't Need*, New York: Basic Books.
Schor, J. (1999). 'The new politics of consumption', *Boston Review*, **24**(3–4), 4–9, available at http://bostonreview.net/BR24.3/schor.html (accessed 14 October 2012).
Schor, J. (2007). 'In defense of consumer critique: revisiting the consumption debates of the twentieth century', *Annals of the American Academy of Political and Social Science*, **611**, 16–30.
Schor, J. (2010). 'Beyond business as usual', *The Nation*, 24 May, available at http://www.thenation.com/article/beyond-business-usual (accessed 14 October 2012).
Schor, J. and M. Willis (2008). 'Conscious consumption: results from a survey

of new dream members', *Center for a New American Dream*, available at http://205.153.117.210/consumption/survey.pdf (accessed 14 October 2012).
Shove, E. (2003). *Comfort, Cleanliness, and Convenience: The Social Organization of Normality*, New York: Berg.
Shove, E., F. Trentman and R. Wilk (eds) (2009). *Time, Consumption, and Everyday Life: Practice, Materiality, and Culture*, New York: Berg.
Stiles, K., O. Altiok and M. Bell (2011). 'The ghosts of taste: food and the cultural politics of authenticity', *Agriculture and Human Values*, **28**(2), 225–36.
UNEP (United Nations Environment Programme) (2010). *Assessing the Environmental Impacts of Consumption and Production: Priority Products and Materials: A Report of the Working Group on the Environmental Impacts of Products and Materials to the International Panel for Sustainable Resource Management*, Paris: UNEP.
Varian, H. (1992). *Microeconomic Analysis*, New York: W.W. Norton.
Veblen, T. (1899). *The Theory of the Leisure Class: An Economic Study of Institutions*, New York: Macmillan.

PART II

Socio-technical transitions

6. The dual challenge of sustainability transitions: different trajectories and criteria

René Kemp and Harro van Lente

INTRODUCTION

The notion of sustainability transition was introduced as a response to major socio-economic challenges including depletion of certain critical natural resources and global climate change.[1] The idea is that systems of transportation, agriculture and energy have to be superseded by other systems. Such encompassing transitions have occurred in the past, such as the shift from sailing boats to steamships during the nineteenth century, the shift toward individual, motorized mobility from 1890 to 1960/1970 and the change from coal to natural gas for space heating after World War II. And thus, the argument goes, they are likely to happen again.

Such systemic changes have been studied by evolutionary researchers, historians and other scholars in the fields of science, technology and society. Frameworks such as the multi-level perspective (MLP) and strategic niche management (SNM) highlight both the persistence of incumbent regimes, as well as their vulnerability. The guiding assumption is that it is possible – based on an understanding of the systemic and dynamic properties of existing and emerging systems – to guide or actively encourage a transition from the current to a new system (Rotmans et al., 2001; Rotmans and Loorbach, 2009). To do so will be a major challenge that goes well beyond the capability of governments and individual actors.

In this chapter, we argue that the issue of sustainability adds an additional challenge. The idea of sustainability transitions not only includes the challenge of orchestrating a change of systems of provision (for example, transportation, agriculture, energy), but also a change in criteria that actors use to judge the appropriateness of products, services and systems. In the transition from sailing ships to steamships fueled by coal, for instance, the criteria for choosing ships did not change dramatically. Both types of vessel competed in terms of tonnage, reliability and speed, as sailing ships had already done for decades or even centuries. Also, in the transition from coal to natural gas the basic aspects on which technologies had to compete did not change dramatically in terms of price, ease and reliability.

For sustainability transitions, however, criteria need to change sharply or else the transformation runs the risk of not being sustainable due to rebound effects and other adverse impacts. For instance, a possible sustainable transition from combustion engines to electric vehicles will require not only changes in the vehicles (powered by renewably generated electricity rather than gasoline), but also the way in which they are used (more selectively, in combination with other modes of transportation). This situation gets us into the topic of the dynamic relationship between needs and systems of provision. The structure of the chapter is as follows. The next section outlines the sustainability transition perspective. This is followed by a discussion of two transitions to modern sanitation and better waste management as transformations in which user benefits were co-optimized with societal benefits. We subsequently examine the dual challenge of the transition to sustainable mobility. The final section develops six themes relevant to the dual challenge including system-wide effects and cultural and social ambivalence.

SUSTAINABILITY TRANSITIONS AS PROCESSES OF CO-EVOLUTION

The term 'sustainability transition' is used by sustainability proponents to highlight the need for a fundamental change and the wide-ranging nature of such change. The Preface to this volume offers a clear illustration of this view.

> it is futile to think that households might be able to significantly advance sustainable consumption on their own. They are themselves deeply entrained in the dominant socio-technical systems that provision goods and services, the structure of daily life and the economics of work-and-leisure time. . . . the evolution of new, more sustainable lifestyles will require harmonized changes in several domains including civil society, political and economic institutions, culture and government policies.

The term transition suggests that a population-wide change in daily practices cannot occur overnight, but is rather a long, gradual (mostly evolutionary) process. Whereas political regimes may be voted away or overthrown through social revolt, socio-technical regimes of automobile-based mobility, agrofood provisioning and building construction cannot be changed from one day to another. Past changes in systems of production and consumption were the long-term outcomes of changes in technology, cultural aspirations, problem definitions and various processes of coordination in a changing landscape involving dissent and political struggle. For people living during particular past transitions, it may not have been apparent that a transition was going on because of the slow pace of change and the coexistence of different systems.

The dynamic aspects of interconnected processes of change are taken up in the literature about sustainability transitions and technological regime shifts (Kemp, 1994; Rip and Kemp, 1998; Geels, 2002, 2004; Elzen et al., 2004; Geels and Schot, 2007; Grin et al., 2010). The focal concern is not just with new artifacts, but with the structures, agents and processes that reproduce a 'socio-technical practice' and those that unsettle it.

The literature finds that 'some socio-technical systems are embedded more robustly than others, in the sense that they enjoy greater institutional support, larger economic significance, more supportive infrastructures, better integration with other social practices, and broader political legitimacy' (Smith and Stirling, 2010). These factors can help some systems to survive and even to expand – even when they impose a considerable cost upon society. A good example is automobile-based modes of mobility that give rise to carbon emissions, local air pollution, noise, congestion, traffic accidents and deaths, social exclusion, land fragmentation, oil dependence and energy insecurity (Cohen, 2006). Most of these problems have been around for a long time.

If we look at the response strategies to these issues, we observe that they have primarily been addressed in a partial and piecemeal manner. Examples include the requirement for seat belts to reduce injuries from collisions, unleaded gasoline to prevent neural damage from lead poisoning, road pricing to deal with congestion (a measure that has proved difficult to implement), fuel-injection systems to increase the efficiency of engines and emission-control systems. The solution is found within the system of automobility and not in alternative systems of mobility, a topic to which we shall return later in this chapter. Due to opposition from those who stand to lose, it is easier for governments to assist the creation of new technology and technology-based systems than to take apart those that exist (Steward, 2008). Creating new systems is not that easy either because it requires money and legitimization. For example, the British government was initially reluctant to invest in the construction of a highway system for motorcars because of the dominant role of railway engineers in setting transportation policy, the cost to the public budget and the absence of a constituency speaking forcefully in favor of road investment. Automotive interests remained in an economic and political backwater well into the

1950s when a Conservative government decided to build roads and to lead the government into the creation of a car regime (Dudley and Chatterjee, 2012).

More generally, the transition to automobility was a slow and gradual process, driven by cultural enthusiasm for cars and many other factors (for example, rising incomes, better roads, special highways and greater mobility of people). It illustrates that for a transition to occur different developments must come together (Rip and Kemp, 1998; Rotmans et al., 2001; Geels, 2002, 2004; Geels and Schot, 2007; Grin et al., 2010). The coming together of multiple developments, feeding on one another, is captured in the multi-level perspective of transition illustrated in Figure 6.1.

Figure 6.1 displays three levels: micro, meso and macro. At the micro level, we have local practices that are usually part of a regime and occur within a so-called macro-level landscape. At the micro level, there are local variations as well as global novelties. At the meso level, we have a number of regimes: in transportation a regime of individualized and motorized mobility, in power supply a regime of centralized electricity generation (based on fossil fuels in almost all nations), in food production a regime of intensive, high-throughput farming with distribution organized by transportation companies and large retailers. Novelties occur at the micro level, and spread out geographically and across users. They become elements of new or existing systems and are shaped by economic, social, cultural and technological factors. Transitions are viewed as the outcome of pressures on product regimes (cultural criticisms, regulations) and the (emergent) development of alternative systems, elements of which originate in product niches. Some products can break out of these niches as a result of learning economies and support from various actors (including incumbent companies, governments and consumers). The landscape of prices, values, associations and regulations exercises selection pressures, but the economic, political and social landscape is also undergoing change. Over time, a new regime may emerge due to processes of alignment, with new technologies and practices becoming the basis for development.

Some readers may see an element of technological determinism in this narrative, but the literature stresses the role of social actors and culture. It is in association with human agency and institutions ('rules of the game') that artifacts fulfill functions (Geels 2004; Berkhout, 2009; Smith and Stirling, 2010). We now describe two transitions, with special attention to the sustainability benefits achieved, as well as to the gains that have thus far been elusive.

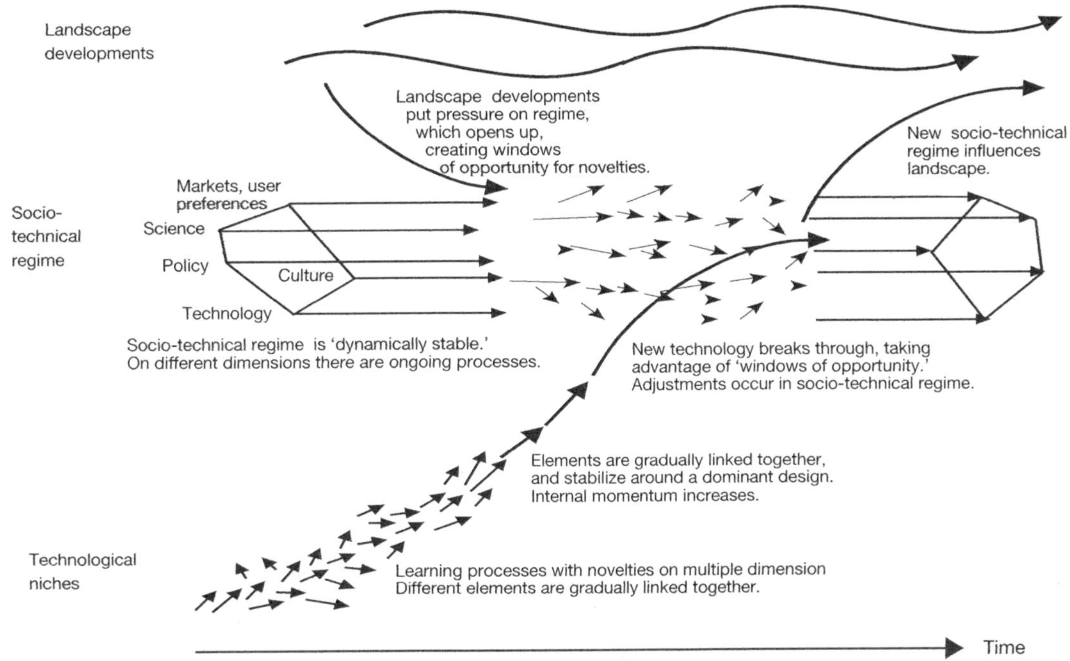

Note: For Canada, metro and other local rail services are included in the 'bus' category.

Source: Geels (2002).

Figure 6.1 A dynamic multi-level perspective on system innovations

THE TRANSITIONS TO MODERN SANITATION AND BETTER WASTE MANAGEMENT

Few transitions are driven by environmental problems and sustainability demands. Here we highlight the hygienic transition and the waste management transition as examples of socio-technical transitions in which criteria changed dramatically, in ways that align with sustainability concerns rather than with economic benefits.[2] The hygienic transition concerned a shift from cesspools to integrated sewer systems, motivated by sanitary concerns. In the Netherlands, the transition occurred over a period of 60 years (1870–1930). In the absence of toilets, most people relieved their bowels in public spaces, dumping urine and excrement on streets and in (urban) canals. The middle and upper classes had personal privies in-house, where excrement was collected in cesspools that were emptied a few times a year. The collected excrement was used as fertilizer.

The transition, involving major health and nuisance benefits, was a slow process. In the Netherlands, in contrast to the UK, Germany and France, the sewer option was not used before 1893 because of a battle between proponents of different systems (with sewers competing against a barrel-collection system and the Liernur pneumatic system).[3] By 1938, 47 percent of all municipalities in the Netherlands had sewers. Comfort and convenience were important drivers, as well as the new criteria of public hygiene. Costs at first counted against the sewer system, but with growing affluence this became less and less of an obstacle.

The transition from cesspools to sewerage was not an easy or obvious transformation. There were heated debates about the hygienic aspects of the various options and a long history of rejected plans for sewer systems (plans for sewerage systems were rejected in 1870, 1897 and 1902 in Amsterdam). The barrel system was not popular among the public as it involved stench, but it was popular with city authorities because it was cheap. The nuisances that this arrangement generated were more or less accepted. Having two engineering options (Liernur and sewerage systems) also worked against sewerage, with some engineers being in favor for the Liernur system. There were also expert concerns about whether the wet and sponge-like Dutch soil was suited for sewerage. Another problem was the flatness of the terrain that necessitated the use of special pumps. The transition to sewerage owed much to two unrelated factors: the diffusion of piped water and water closets in houses and the development of artificial fertilizers in the 1890s. Water closets stimulated sewerage in the sense that flushing became easier. The higher water content of waste streams also undermined both the Liernur and the barrel systems. Increasingly, municipalities decided to build sewer systems that were introduced first in new neighborhoods for wealthy residents and later in older parts of the cities. Recommendations from health specialists played an important role, but were not the deciding factor. Some people today criticize the sewer system on environmental grounds for using drinking water to flush toilets and the high energy consumption required for wastewater treatment.

The history of another transition in the Netherlands, the transformation that occurred around waste management from 1970 to 2000, also exemplifies a change in values, practices and criteria as an integral element of the process. Before 1970, waste management consisted primarily of landfilling, a task carried out by municipalities. Getting rid of waste was the primary concern, with waste material also being used to fill up ditches and create land for housing. This set of practices began to change during the 1970s: waste and the absence of effective waste management received increasing attention. Environmentalists criticized governments and business about how waste was being managed, while local resistance grew with regard to new landfill sites. The 1972 report to the Club of Rome about limits to growth, together with the oil crisis in 1973, drew attention to the scarcity of raw materials. The important change that we should emphasize is that waste disposal came increasingly to be reframed as a problem instead of a solution. Special legislation for waste was developed and responsibilities were assigned to provinces in the Netherlands to put an end to (uncontrolled) dumping in landfills and to benefit from economies of scale for incineration. An important cognitive institution was the famous 'waste hierarchy' proposed in the parliamentary motion of Ad Lansink in 1979, which came to be known as Lansink's Ladder. The waste management hierarchy went from prevention, through reuse (of products), recycling (of materials) and incineration (with energy production), to landfilling as the last option.

The new criteria for waste were further consolidated when the Dutch government opted for a differentiated waste stream approach in which certain types of waste (notably paper and glass) were singled out for recycling. Despite these intentions for upgrading waste practices, many improvements in the area of waste management were only implemented on a small scale and did not result in adequate environmental protection. Concerns about unsustainable waste management did not disappear and reached a peak in the 1980s, following the discovery of leaking landfills (*Vogelmeerpolder*) and contaminated land (*Lekkerkerk* and *Griftpark*).

Waste scandals often figured as news items during the 1980s. At the end of the decade, the Dutch waste management system was in a state of crisis because of capacity problems stemming from growing volumes and reduced capacities. The system was reviewed by a specially created committee (*Landelijke Coördinatie Commissie Afvalbeleid*), which concluded that the then-prevailing organization was too fragmented, dispersed and small scale. It argued for the creation of a national organization to oversee and manage waste streams and to keep disposal costs under control. This advice resulted in the creation of four waste regions in the country and establishment of the Waste Management Council (*Afval Overleg Orgaan* (AOO)) that would come to play an important role in the modernization of the waste system.

In response to a range of measures (such as a ban of 32 waste streams for landfilling, a packaging covenant and higher tariffs for landfill disposal), the amount of waste being sent to landfills fell from 14 million tons in 1990 to 5 million tons in 2002. Today, all landfills in the Netherlands have advanced systems of soil protection and facilities to extract methane. During the same period, the capacity of incineration increased gradually, from 2.2 million tons in 1980 to 4.9 million tons in 2000. The recycling of materials increased between 1985 and 2000 from 23.5 to 45.3 million tons.

The transformation of the waste management system is often viewed as the result of the implementation of effective policies. Such a view, however, overlooks how policy itself was the result of various changes: the growing volumes of waste, the waste scandals in the 1980s and early 1990s and, in particular, changes in perception in which waste became 'a waste of resources.' In addition, the waste scandals helped to close down old incinerators and build more environmentally sound ones.

The AOO as an institution of governance played an important role in the transformation process. Negotiations between different layers of government and with private waste companies took place within the AOO, with the actors agreeing on the general direction of creating a modern and efficient system of waste management with less waste being disposed in landfills. Although officially opposed to incineration, the Dutch environmental movement did not focus on this aspect because key figures understood the bigger picture – the high costs of advanced systems of incineration necessitated a high tax for the landfilling of burnable waste and these circumstances encouraged waste prevention and recycling. The waste companies were satisfied with the greater scale at which they could operate. The reorganization of the sector was seen as a blessing by the AOO, as major companies from North America including Waste Management and BFI took control of small operators. The large firms were committed to full compliance and had a strong incentive to respect the law.

In the case of this transformation, new 'sustainability' criteria were internalized formally in law and informally in the practices of waste management companies and consumers separating their trash. The reorganization of the waste market suited the interests of large waste companies and environmentalists were content with the incentives for prevention and recycling that were created through laws and taxes negotiated within the AOO. However, the system did not manage to radically alter product features in terms of design for disassembly and reuse. The final waste goal was therefore not achieved because of opposition from product manufacturers and because consumers did not seek products with second-life components.

THE DUAL CHALLENGE IN THE TRANSITION TO SUSTAINABLE MOBILITY

This section examines the transition to sustainable mobility.[4] During the last half-century, personal mobility has rapidly expanded in affluent countries around the world. Figure 6.2 describes the evolution of passenger kilometers per capita in eight industrialized countries – the USA, Canada, Sweden, France, Germany, the UK, Japan and Australia. In each country,

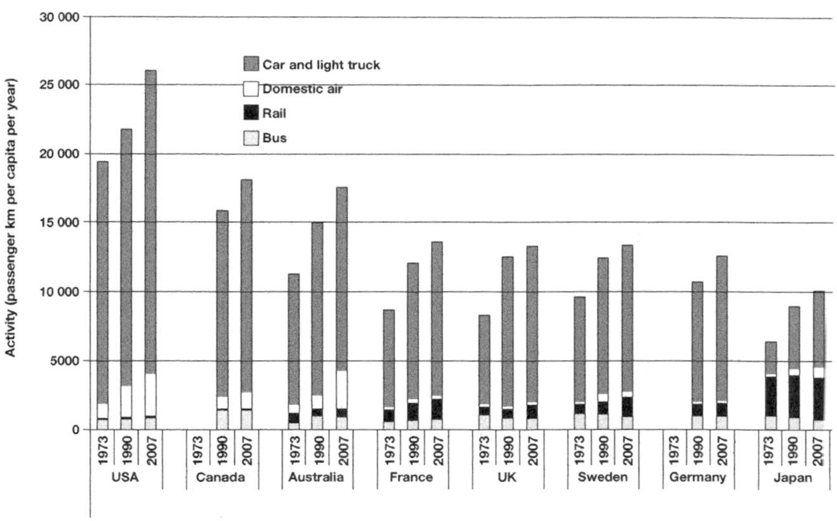

Note: Greenhouse gas emissions and share of road in transportation emissions, 1990 to 2006 (million tons of carbon dioxide equivalent and percent).

Source: Eurostat (2009).

Figure 6.2 Passenger travel per capita by mode for selected countries

personal mobility increased enormously between 1973 and 2007/2008. The greatest increase in passenger kilometers has been for cars, the dominant mode of transportation in virtually all affluent countries. The modal share for bus and rail has remained relatively constant or declined slightly, except for Japan where it fell significantly (Millard-Ball and Schipper, 2010). The long-term change in transportation modalities has coincided with the increasing adoption of private automobiles by consumers. In the Netherlands, car ownership increased from 165 per 1000 households in 1960 to 1005 in 2007 (Kemp et al., 2012). In the UK, 80 percent of households possessed a car in 2005, against 41 percent in 1965 (Dudley and Chatterjee, 2012).

The expansion of automobile-based transportation has, as described above, given rise to a range of persistent social problems (Cohen, 2006; see also Bassett et al., 2008). Some of these issues have been substantially reduced in the past few decades; for instance, traffic safety has generally improved. The fatalities per million inhabitants in the 27 European Union (EU) countries has fallen steadily, due to enhanced driver education, enhanced vehicle design, safety technologies (for example, seatbelts, air bags) and better road design. Still, about 40 000 Europeans die each year in fatal traffic accidents. In 2006, 42 950 persons lost their lives in road accidents: car drivers and passengers, occupants of buses, riders and passengers of powered two-wheelers, cyclists, pedestrians and commercial vehicle drivers (Eurostat, 2009).

In many places, problems of local air pollution have also diminished, especially due to catalytic converters, improved engine design and changes in fuel composition. The general pattern is quite different in, for example, Southeast Asia where cities suffer from extremely poor air quality as a result of motorized transportation. Carbon dioxide emissions per kilometer have fallen as a result of fuel-economy improvements and regulations, but in absolute terms, emissions from transportation have increased (Figure 6.3). Aviation and road transportation are the main contributors to the increase, with road transportation being responsible for more than 90 percent of the greenhouse gas emissions from transportation.

Both the EU and national governments are actively encouraging alternative fuel vehicles: fuel-efficient internal combustion vehicles, hybrid-electric vehicles, battery-electric vehicles and hydrogen fuel-cell vehicles. These innovations may be more environmentally friendly, but their introduction is unlikely to have significant effects on the numbers of vehicles on the road. They do not significantly address issues such as traffic congestion, road accidents and casualties and do little to ameliorate geographical and spatial problems such as the role and place of the car in the built and

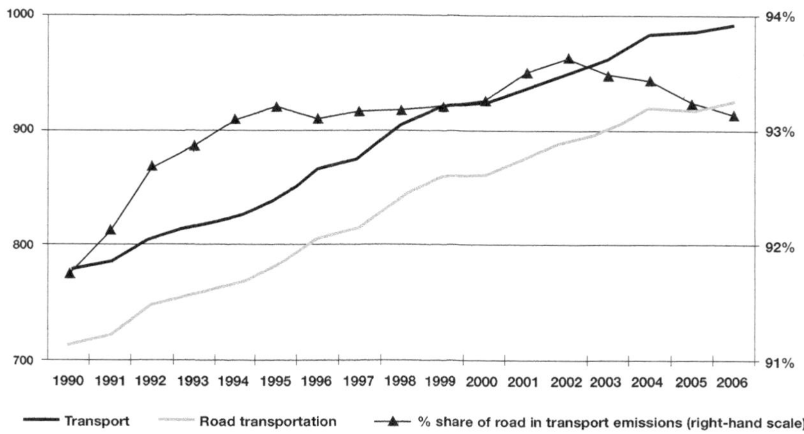

Figure 6.3 Total transportation and road transportation for EU-27 countries

natural environment. Broader visions of 'sustainable transportation' exist, including projections that entail a more modest role for automobiles such that car use is combined with the deployment of other modes of transportation (for example, public transit and the use of bikes). Other plans anticipate reducing the need for transportation through teleworking and the implementation of plans to enable people to live in closer proximity to work places, shopping facilities and schools, and facilitating mobility with robust public transit and bicycle infrastructure (Newman and Kenworthy, 1999; Henderson, 2009).

Problems of congestion can be reduced by integrating new information and communications technologies into highway systems, dynamic traffic management and automated vehicle guidance that allows cars to drive in tight convoys, thus improving the efficiency of road use (Mitchell et al., 2010). More effective use of the road infrastructure can also be achieved with the implmentaiton of road pricing. Each of these visions has its supporters. A common feature of all of these ideas is that they maintain the paradigm of individual, material-intensive mobility.

Cars are adopted today on the basis of speed, range, reliability and 'image.' It is normal in contemporary society to own a car and use it for almost every trip. In the USA, 200 meters is considered a drivable distance. Looking at alternatives, electric vehicles ameliorate two problems that stem from the intensive use of cars (noise and pollution), but they do not address dilemmas of congestion and safety, while the intensive use of electricity and batteries raises additional concerns. Moreover, an unanticipated effect of the development of batteries for cars is their use in bicycles. Unless electric bicycles are used for longer trips, more commonly made by cars, this process of vehicle electrification constitutes a negative development, especially if the bicycles are used to make more trips. Therefore the assumption of individualized and material-intensive mobility as something normal, acceptable and desirable has to be reframed.

Compared to the transitions of hygiene and waste, the transition to sustainable mobility can be expected to be much more difficult because the system of automobility based on the internal combustion engine is embedded much deeper. Car use is anchored in lifestyles (for example, bringing children to school or to sporting events, shopping, family visits, holidays), supported by cultural discourses (around freedom, individuality, adventure) and stabilized by positive feelings and emotions (Kemp et al., 2012). Given all this, we should not expect car use to disappear anytime soon As Mimi Sheller (2004, p. 236) writes,

> Cars will not easily be given up just (!) because they are dangerous to health and life, environmentally destructive, based on unsustainable energy consumption, and damaging to public life and civic space. Too many people find them too comfortable, enjoyable, exciting, even enthralling. They are deeply embedded in ways of life, networks of friends and sociality, and moral commitments to family and care for others.

The criterion of affordability – so important for users and governments – conflicts with sustainability because inexpensive mobility and energy will stimulate mobility and energy use. In this respect, the low operating costs of electric cars are an undesirable feature because of the stimulating effects of the technology.

THE DUAL CHALLENGE

In the final section of this chapter, we develop six themes that capture the dual challenge for sustainability transitions and examine the linkages with new economics and social practices (as well as social movements) that are at the heart of this volume.

First, in sustainability assessment the system-scale effects of various 'solutions' should be considered. There are many examples of negative effects in the overall system canceling positive outcomes. Transportation studies show that free and better public transportation will stimulate mobility. The building of park-and-ride stations around cities may actually encourage people to drive to the cities rather than to use a train for getting to another city. In Rotterdam, a transportation study at one such site revealed that 33 percent of current users previously traveled by public transportation or by bicycle (Mingardo, 2008). In three cities in the Netherlands (Amsterdam, Utrecht, Rotterdam), park-and-ride facilities were found to contribute to an overall increase in the supply of city-center parking and thus paradoxically acted as a facilitator of urban automobile traffic (Dijk, 2010).

Second, we urge reconsideration of wants and needs since these are not static conditions but change together with technological developments. The availability of clean water in Paris during the nineteenth century, for instance, considerably altered the criteria for hygiene (Graber, 2007). Similarly, mobility requirements in industrialized countries have changed dramatically during the last century. The endogenous nature of wants and needs has consequences for the analysis of sustainability transitions. Instead of taking wants and needs as given conditions to which technological systems should comply, a critical examination is necessary. From a sustainability perspective, practices of conspicuous consumption need to be addressed and reframed. It appears desirable, for instance, to recast car mobility as materially intensive and environmentally disruptive. Such a reframing will reduce the current status of the automobile. Such an initiative is, of course, a cultural matter and not something for government take up solely on its own. There are also deeper issues of individualism and responsibility. An interesting issue in this respect is our own inconsistency. As Cohen (2010, p. 466) notes, '[i]t is not unusual for someone to embrace the virtues of localism in the morning by shopping at a farmer's market, only to board an airplane for a distant city in the afternoon.'

Third, we need comprehensive visions of sustainable subsystems and special criteria or principles to guide policy, investment and individual choice. A useful attempt to define sustainable mobility is provided in an award-winning paper by David Banister (2008) in the journal *Transport Review*. Banister argues that sustainable mobility is based on the following elements: promoting reasonable travel time rather than travel-time minimization; limiting the need to travel (through distance reduction and homeworking); seeing transportation as a valued activity rather than derived demand; achieving a modal shift (especially in favor of walking and bicycling); lowering levels of pollution and noise from transportation; deriving greater energy efficiency and more effective use of infrastructures (through higher vehicle occupancy and demand management); and increasing the quality of places and spaces. Some of these elements are already used by transportation experts and planning authorities, others not so widely or not at all. The demands of car users often stand in the way of applying these principles, making planners ambivalent about using them, but it is nonetheless important to have them.

Fourth, sustainable mobility cannot be achieved through transportation policies alone. For electric vehicles we need carbon-free electricity and battery recycling. Green infrastructure in cities may stimulate urban recreation and reduce automobile-based transportation, but changes in economic frame conditions (for example, carbon taxes), and policies for resource efficiency are necessary. Scholars in the emergent field of new economics – and in ecological macroeconomics more specifically – have taken up the issue by arguing for green public investment and ecological tax reform (Harris, 2007, 2009; Victor, 2008; see also the chapters by Jonathan Harris and Inge Røpke in this volume).

Fifth, more attention should be given to developments that are moving in the wrong direction: outdoor patio heating (Hitchings, 2007) and preheated, self-cleaning toilets (Shove and Walker, 2007) and personal aeromobility (microjets) (Cohen, 2010). Sociologist Elizabeth Shove (2003) has analyzed increases in bathing and showering, laundering and diffusion of air conditioning. She makes visible the changing meaning and norms behind 'normal' practices and describes how they co-evolve with artifacts such as air conditioners and freezers. Users do not generally consider the resource implications of such technologies. A transition model of a change in practices has been developed by Gert Spaargaren and his colleagues (2007) that starts with de-routinization prompted by dissatisfaction and difficulties with existing routines. Under such circumstances, people learn about new practices that develop into new routines (re-routinization). By putting the focus on the meaning of normal practices and their evolution over time, practice theory offers a different perspective on behavioral change. Spaargaren focuses on 'consumption junctions' that are meeting points such as a gas station or an automobile showroom, as situated contexts in which decisions are being made. These venues have physical (material) elements and are culturally relevant.

Finally, we would be remiss if we did not raise here the issue of effective governance in a consumer society. During the nineteenth century, choices about the remaking of society were very much put into the hands of engineers and politicians who decided about needs and ways to meet them.[5] In a consumer society, it is consumer needs that count. The question then is: can we remake ourselves as part of a process of remaking society? Better technology does not produce better people and it is misguided to expect too much from this quarter. There is a role for self-imposed constraints to reduce the impacts on the environment and both proximate and distance others. This is the hardest part of the sustainability transition challenge, requiring political choice and personal restraint (Meadowcroft, 2009; Voss et al., 2009). It is difficult to forgo something that confers so many individual benefits to us. Efforts to facilitate sustainable mobility may need to be reconciled with rival societal aspirations such as the pursuit of faster and more convenient forms of travel (Cohen, 2010).

In contrast, there is cultural contestation in the sense that environmentally disruptive practices, and the processes undergirding them (for example, capitalism, population growth, special interests and resistance to policy action), become a source of cultural criticism. In the USA, the Hummer was labeled as a climate-destroying car and the tax break created for pick-up trucks became known as the Hummer tax loophole. The work on social movements is relevant here because it highlights how people become engaged in expressive, identity-oriented actions (Buechler, 2011). The chapter in this volume by Sabine Hielscher, Gill Seyfang and Adrian Smith examines the transformative power of community-innovation projects in sustainable energy in the UK, finding that the local niches studied do not really provide blueprints but rather constitute reservoirs of ideas and practices, requiring dedicated work to transfer lessons to other locations, scales and contexts. Politically, green values have been incorporated into practically every party program, but green issues compete with other demands for time and attention. Scholars such as Dobson (1995) have called for an ecocentered politics, but green concerns have not taken precedence over other issues and are unlikely to do so. Green technologies benefit from ecological modernization strategies, but green growth is simply another form of growth. We need to develop an ethos of moderation based on restraint, respect, empathy and self-actualization.

Sustainability has to be taken up in a more consequential way than it is at present. Catering to consumers' desires for comfort, convenience and low prices is unlikely to facilitate sustainability transitions. Transitions that are not accompanied by a shift in values, practices and consumer criteria, and that move away from material and conspicuous consumption, will not be sustainable and will disappoint in the end after a promising start. In other words, sustainability transitions are a dual challenge.

NOTES

1. The chapter is a further development of a short essay previously published in the journal *Environmental Innovation and Societal Transitions*. See Kemp and van Lente (2011).
2. Our description of the hygienic and waste management transitions is based on Geels and Kemp (2007) and the sources cited therein.
3. The barrel-collection system consisted of the collection of containers from households in which people had deposited their excrement. The barrels were transported to a central collection place where their contents were processed into compost and then sold to farmers as fertilizer. The barrels were then cleaned and reused. The Liernur system consisted of a toilet, a funnel and underground pipes that connected the house to main

conduits that ended in a collection reservoir. A steam pump was used to create a vacuum and collect faeces in the reservoir. Excrement was collected daily, processed and sold as fertilizer. A benefit of the system was its cleanliness. Faeces were collected without spillage and the process did not involve laborers carrying dirty barrels. Hygienists favored this system because it was sanitary and produced faeces for agriculture, but it was relatively complex and expensive.

4. The section draws from the introduction to the recently published book *Automoblity in Transition* (Geels et al., 2012).
5. See Graber (2007) for an illustrative analysis of public water supply proposals in Paris.

REFERENCES

Banister, D. (2008). 'The sustainable mobility paradigm', *Transport Policy*, **15**(2), 73–80.

Bassett, D., J. Pucher, R. Buehler, D. Thompson and C. Crouter (2008). 'Walking, cycling, and obesity rates in Europe, North America, and Australia', *Journal of Physical Activity and Health*, **5**(6), 795–814.

Berkhout, F. (2009). 'Innovation theory and socio-technical transitions', in J. van den Bergh and F. Bruinsma (eds), *Managing the Transition to Renewable Energy: Theory and Practice from Regional and Macro Perspectives*, Cheltenham, UK and Northampton, MA, USA: Edward Elgar, pp. 129–47.

Buechler, S. (2011). 'New social movement theory', in G. Ritzer (ed.), *The Concise Blackwell Encyclopedia of Sociology*, Malden, MA: Blackwell, pp. 423–4.

Cohen, M. (2006). 'A social problems framework for the critical appraisal of automobility and sustainable systems innovation', *Mobilities*, **1**(1), 23–38.

Cohen, M. (2010). 'Destination unknown: pursuing sustainable mobility in the face of rival societal aspirations', *Research Policy*, **39**(4), 459–70.

Dijk, M. (2010). *Innovation in Car Mobility: Coevolution of Demand and Supply Under Sustainability Pressures*, Maastricht: Universitaire Pers Maastricht.

Dobson, A. (1995). *Green Political Thought*, 2nd edn, London: Unwin Hyman.

Dudley, G. and K. Chatterjee (2012). 'The dynamics of regime strength and instability: policy challenges to the dominance of the private car in the UK', in F. Geels, R. Kemp, G. Dudley and G. Lyons (eds), *Automobility in Transition? A Sociotechnical Analysis of Sustainable Transport*, New York: Routledge, pp. 83–103.

Elzen, B., F. Geels and K. Green (eds) (2004). *System Innovation and the Transition to Sustainability: Theory, Evidence and Policy*, Cheltenham, UK and Northampton, MA, USA: Edward Elgar.

Eurostat (2009). *Panorama of Transport, 1990–2006*, Luxemburg, Eurostat, European Commission.

Geels, F. (2002). 'Technological transitions as evolutionary reconfiguration processes: a multi-level perspective and a case-study', *Research Policy*, **31**(8–9), 1257–74.

Geels, F. (2004). 'From sectoral systems of innovation to socio-technical systems: insights about dynamics and change from sociology and institutional theory', *Research Policy*, **33**(6–7), 897–920.

Geels, F. and R. Kemp (2007). 'Dynamics in socio-technical systems: typology of change processes and contrasting case studies', *Technology in Society*, **29**(4), 441–55.

Geels, F. and J. Schot (2007). 'Typology of sociotechnical transition pathways', *Research Policy*, **36**(3), 399–417.

Geels, F., R. Kemp, G. Dudley and G. Lyons (eds) (2012). *Automobility in Transition? A Sociotechnical Analysis of Sustainable Transport*, New York: Routledge.

Graber, F. (2007). 'Inventing needs: expertise and water supply in late eighteenth- and early nineteenth-century Paris', *British Journal for the History of Science*, **40**(3), 315–32.

Grin, J., J. Rotmans, J. Schot, F. Geels and D. Loorbach (2010). *Transitions to Sustainable Development: New Directions in the Study of Long Term Transformative Change*, New York: Routledge.

Harris, J. (2007). 'Reorienting macroeconomic theory towards environmental sustainability', in J. Gowdy and J. Erickson (eds), *Frontiers in Ecological Economic Theory and Application*, Cheltenham, UK and Northampton, MA, USA: Edward Elgar, pp. 36–52.

Harris, J. (2009). 'Ecological macroeconomics: consumption, investment, and climate change', in J. Harris and N. Goodwin (eds), *Twenty-first Century Macroeconomics: Responding to the Climate Challenge*, Cheltenham, UK and Northampton, MA, USA: Edward Elgar, pp. 169–86.

Henderson, J. (2009). 'The politics of mobility: de-essentializing automobility and contesting urban space', in J. Conley and A. McLaren (eds), *Car Troubles: Critical Studies of Automobility and Automobility*, Farnham, Surrey: Ashgate, pp. 147–63.

Hitchings, R. (2007). 'Geographies of embodied outdoor experience and the arrival of the patio heater', *Area*, **39**(3), 340–8.

Kemp, R. (1994). 'Technology and the transition to environmental sustainability: the problem of technological regime shifts', *Futures*, **26**(10), 1023–46.

Kemp, R. and H. van Lente (2011). 'The dual challenge of sustainability transitions', *Environmental Innovation and Societal Transitions*, **1**(1), 121–4.

Kemp, R, F. Geels and G. Dudley (2012). 'Introduction: sustainability transitions in the automobility regime and the need for a new perspective', in F. Geels, R. Kemp, G. Dudley and G. Lyons (eds), *Automobility in Transition? A Sociotechnical Analysis of Sustainable Transport*, New York: Routledge, pp. 3–28.

Meadowcroft, J. (2009). 'What about the politics? Sustainable development, transition management, and long term energy transitions', *Policy Sciences*, **42**(4), 323–40.

Millard-Ball, A. and L. Schipper (2010). 'Are we reaching peak travel? Trends in passenger transport in eight industrialized countries', *Transport Reviews*, **31**(3), 1–22.

Mingardo, G. (2008). 'Cities and innovative urban transport policies', *Innovation: Management, Policy, and Practice*, **10**(2–3), 269–81.

Mitchell, W., C. Borroni-Bird and L. Burns (2010). *Reinventing the Automobile: Personal Urban Mobility for the 21st Century*, Cambridge, MA: MIT Press.

Newman, P. and J. Kenworthy (1999). *Sustainability and Cities: Overcoming Automobile Dependence*, Washington, DC: Island Press.

Rip, A. and R. Kemp (1998). 'Technological change', in S. Rayner and E. Malone (eds), *Human Choice and Climate Change, Volume 2*. Washington, DC: Battelle Press, pp. 327–99.

Rotmans, J. and D. Loorbach (2009). 'Complexity and transition management', *Journal of Industrial Ecology*, **13**(2), 184–96.

Rotmans, J., R. Kemp and M. van Asselt (2001). 'More evolution than revolution: transition management in public policy', *Foresight*, **3**(1), 15–31.

Sheller, M. (2004). 'Automotive emotions: feeling the car', *Theory, Culture and Society*, **21**(4–5), 221–42.

Shove, E. (2003). *Comfort, Cleanliness and Convenience: The Social Organization of Normality*, New York: Berg.

Shove, E. and G. Walker (2007). 'CAUTION! Transitions ahead: politics, practice and sustainable transition management', *Environment and Planning A*, **39**(4), 763–70.

Smith, A. and A. Stirling (2010). 'The politics of social-ecological resilience and sustainable socio-technical transitions', *Ecology and Society*, **15**(1), 11, available at http://www.ecologyandsociety.org/vol15/iss1/art11 (accessed 17 October 2012).

Spaargaren, G., H Mommaas, S. van den Burg et al. (2007). *Duurzamer Leefstijlen en Consumptiepatronen: Een Theoretisch Perspectief voor de Analyse van Transitieprocessen binnen Consumptiedomeinen (Sustainable Lifestyles and Consumption Patterns: A Theoretical Perspective for the Analysis of Transition Processes in Consumption Domains)*, Wageningen: Environmental Policy Group. Wageningen Universiteit, Milieu Natuur Planbureau, Tilburg Universiteit Telos and Landbouw Economisch Instituut (in Dutch).

Steward, F. (2008). *Breaking the Boundaries: Transformative Innovation for the Global Good*, London: National Endowment for Science, Technology, and the Arts, available at http://www.nesta.org.uk/library/documents/Prov%20-%20BtB%20v8.pdf (accessed 17 October 2012).

Victor, P. (2008). *Managing Without Growth: Slower by Design, Not Disaster*, Cheltenham, UK and Northampton, MA, USA: Edward Elgar.

Voss J.-P., A. Smith and J. Grin (2009). 'Designing long-term policy: rethinking transition management', *Policy Sciences*, **42**(4), 275–302.

7. Grassroots innovations for sustainable energy: exploring niche-development processes among community-energy initiatives

Sabine Hielscher, Gill Seyfang and Adrian Smith

INTRODUCTION

Community-led sustainable energy projects have flourished lately in the UK. The most substantial research to date identified (in 2005) over 500 such initiatives (Walker et al., 2007). On the consumption side, community-energy demand projects are likely to be of a similar or larger order. In 2010, the UK government's Low Carbon Community Challenge attracted more than 500 expressions of interest. It joins a portfolio of policies (local to European) to help community projects and nurture local support for wider processes of low carbon energy transition (for example, HM Government, 2009; NESTA, 2009). Policy initiatives such as this suggest that governments have an instrumental interest in community energy, to help facilitate additional, larger-scale sustainable energy transitions. However, the rationales of community-energy participants are often broader in scope, covering community-development objectives, as well as perceiving that community-based projects deliver energy savings and behavior changes that top-down policy instruments cannot achieve. These very different perspectives on the role and potential of community energy suggest that policy support is not unproblematic.

Additionally, these values-based grassroots innovations are experimenting with new energy-related consumption practices with a view to the socio-technical transition to local, renewable or lower carbon energy systems. These practices are often based on alternative 'new economics' values that challenge mainstream growth-based conceptions of wealth and progress, and put forward alternative visions of a more radical political economy of consumption (Hargreaves et al., 2012; Seyfang and Haxeltine,

2012). However, previous research shows grassroots innovations face a series of critical challenges requiring support to overcome and to achieve their potential benefits more widely. This assistance includes developing 'niche' networks for mobilizing reforms both to highly centralized energy institutions and infrastructures (Seyfang and Smith, 2007), as well as making changes to deeply ingrained social practices[1] of 'normal' energy consumption and everyday life.[2]

Little is known about the processes and conditions required to successfully harness community-energy projects and to increase their influence on wider energy systems. Conceiving of these projects as niche innovations, or spaces where things are done differently, allows us to draw on relevant areas of coevolutionary socio-technical transitions theory that seeks to understand and explain systemic transitions and the role of radical niches in such transitions (Geels, 2002). Within this literature, effective niche formation is a necessary but not sufficient condition for influencing wider systems, but to date community-led innovative niches have been insufficiently researched (Grin et al., 2010).[3]

To address this knowledge gap, in this chapter we conduct a niche analysis of the community-energy sector. Specifically, we describe the community-energy sector in the UK and examine the extent to which it constitutes an effective niche.[4] However, while the sustainability transitions approach can be a useful tool for conceptualizing the emergence and development of community energy, there are a number of weaknesses within the model that become evident when applying it to the community-based context of grassroots innovations. One limitation that we aim to counter, by seeking evidence to test the theory in this new grassroots context, is the tendency to simplify accounts of interactions between niches and regimes, obscuring the complex plurality of socio-technical configurations (that is, community-led initiatives) into unrealistically homogeneous niches working against a similarly problematic homogeneous regime (Shove and Walker, 2007; Genus and Coles, 2008).

The next section briefly outlines a multi-level perspective of coevolutionary socio-technical change in the context of grassroots innovation to provide a theoretical background to the chapter. The third section describes the current state and character of community-energy innovations in the UK. We identify what precisely is unusual and interesting about these initiatives in terms of promoting more radical forms of sustainable consumption and where community-energy projects offer something distinctive to top-down or business-led solutions. The fourth section applies a niche analytical framework to this community-energy sector, to better understand how the sector is developing and to assess its potential to form an influential niche. We conclude by reflecting on the suitability of this niche framework for this context of innovation, identifying under-theorized elements, and suggest an emerging research agenda.

INTRODUCING GRASSROOTS INNOVATIONS

The combined pressures of global climate change, peak oil and threats to energy security are driving a policy agenda toward creation of a more sustainable energy system. Theories of socio-technical change have built on coevolutionary systems thinking to develop understanding of how radical system innovation occurs in complex industrial societies. They show that transforming complex, interdependent systems populated by multiple actors and interests, and embedded in every aspect of every-day life, requires more than merely reforming efficiency improvements. Where existing innovation paths are locked-in and path-dependent, radical changes are required to shift the entire system onto a more sustainable trajectory. Such sustainability-oriented innovations are the subject of the sustainable transitions literature that sees path-breaking, systems-transforming innovation as involving coevolutionary change processes encompassing technologies, institutions, infrastructures, producers, consumers, intermediaries and regulators. Interactions are complex, but patterns are observable (Geels, 2002). Incumbent 'regimes' develop incrementally and path-dependently. The centralized production of fossil-fueled electricity from private utility power stations has coevolved with markets, infrastructures, regulatory institutions and energy-related consumption practices. This electricity regime constitutes a form of structural power that disadvantages the diffusion of path-breaking socio-technical practices, such as many community-led energy initiatives (Smith et al., 2005).

Nevertheless, the transitions literature notes how historic regime transformations developed through an accumulation of projects in 'niche' spaces that were forgiving toward radical alternatives, and a body of work has emerged studying the nature and characteristics of successful transformative niches where new radical innovations are tested and developed.[5] These (temporarily) 'protective' spaces tolerate poor returns, accept uncertainty over the 'best' form and function, and provide supportive networks for experimentation and advocacy (Schot et al., 1994). We conceive the field of community-led sustainable energy projects as a niche supportive toward innovative local-scale sustainable energy solutions.

Case studies of these historical examples (see Schot and Geels, 2008 for a review) suggest that there are three characteristics of successful, influential niches: shared expectations; resourceful networks; and second-order and collective learning. In particular, (a) expectations contribute to successful niche-building when they are robust, specific and of high quality (substantiated by ongoing projects); (b) social networks contribute when their membership is broad (plural perspectives) and deep (substantial resource commitments by members); and (c) learning processes not only accumulate facts, data and first-order lessons, but also generate second-order learning about alternative cognitive frames and different ways of valuing and supporting the niche (Hoogma et al., 2001; Schot and Geels, 2008). Niche practices become influential to the extent that processes 'a' to 'c' become robust enough to influence wider institutional changes (Geels, 2002; Raven, 2006). The opportunity to affect wider systems emerges when tensions in mainstream energy regimes, such as security and environmental crises, cast niche solutions in a positive light, thereby attracting interest from policy makers and businesses in the regime.

Until recently this literature has concentrated on technological resource efficiency innovations in supply-side issues such as energy generation and infrastructure, focusing on technology producers and intermediaries, businesses and government actors. Yet this focus may be unwarranted: despite improvements in eco-efficiency, the rate of consumption growth is outweighing efficiency gains (Jackson, 2009). Production technologies alone will not meet the sustainability challenge: attention must turn to the factors that influence and might transform consumption – demand – at individual, household and community levels.

However, the sustainability transitions literature has hitherto largely neglected demand-side factors such as lifestyles, social practices and coevolutionary formulations of normal consumption, and has neither adequately conceptualized nor understood the role of civil society in contemporary transition processes. A recent review by some of the key contributors to transitions research concludes that 'we acknowledge that the role of consumers and grassroots initiatives in transitions is underrated and under-conceptualised, therefore we welcome new perspectives which theorise changes in demand-side practices as motors for transition' (Grin et al., 2010, p. 331). Thus, our contribution here is to apply a niche-analytical conceptual framework to the UK's community-energy sector.

CIVIL SOCIETY INNOVATORS AND SOCIAL INNOVATION

Echoing work by the National Endowment for Science, Technology, and the Arts (NESTA), the Young Foundation, Green Alliance and others internationally, the UK government has come to recognize that recent innovation thinking and policy is constrained by its historic focus on technology firms (HM Government, 2008). The customary emphasis underplays the value and potential of social innovation concepts, organizational forms and arrangements, and distributed innovation in other contexts (for example, civil society) and by other actors (for example, user-led). Innovation in local communities in particular is an insufficiently researched area that potentially offers ideas for sustainable, low carbon policy goals (Verheul and Vergragt, 1995; Hegger et al., 2007; Hess, 2007; Seyfang and Smith, 2007; Avelino and Kunze, 2009). In contrast to commercial innovation, community innovation operates in civil society arenas, in particular mobilizing the energies of voluntary and neighborhood groups, social enterprises and cooperatives, mutual societies and charities. It involves grassroots experiments in locally meaningful problem interpretations and social innovations, as well as more environmentally and socially benign technologies and results from high community involvement in both processes and outcomes (Seyfang and Smith, 2007).

This framing of community action for sustainability as 'innovative' allows us to make novel contributions to the sustainability transitions literature around 'grassroots innovations,' which are distinct from the existing literature in terms of: context (civil society rather than the market economy); driving force (social and/or environmental need rather than rent seeking); the nature of the niche (alternative values as opposed to incubation from market forces); organizational forms (diverse forms including voluntary organizations, cooperatives and community groups rather than firms); the resource base (grant funding, voluntary input, mutual exchange and reciprocal relations); and the distribution of possible profits (local and collective and based on notions of solidarity) (Seyfang and Smith, 2007). Little is known about the conditions under which community-led innovations do or do not diffuse into wider society and their potential to influence regimes or energy systems more generally. There is a tendency to treat community projects as marginal and parallel to mainstream energy systems rather than exploring how mutual adaptations may contribute to wider low carbon transitions.

We do know some of the intrinsic and extrinsic challenges facing community-led grassroots innovations (Seyfang and Smith, 2007). They often remain small scale and fail to grow because of a lack of institutional support and long-term funds, while technological innovations have an established infrastructure of support (Mulgan et al., 2007). Additionally, community values can clash with commercial priorities, inhibiting the translation of knowledge and practices, and requiring careful negotiation by intermediaries (for example, social entrepreneurs) (Smith, 2007; Seyfang, 2009). Mainstream marketing of narrower forms of the original community innovation can represent failure to originating activists, but facilitates a shallower-yet-wider greening to less active groups (Smith, 2006).

These challenges are not insurmountable. Community-led innovations have diffused in the past, when conditions permitted (Douthwaite, 2002; Hess, 2007). The Danish wind-turbine industry emerged from a community-energy niche (Kemp et al., 2001; Garud and Karnøe, 2003). Home-insulation policy for socially disadvantaged households in the UK built upon models pioneered by community activists in the 1970s (Smith, 2006). If renewed policy interest is to lead to effective institutional support (HM Government, 2009), then evidence is needed about the extent to which the community-energy sector in the UK constitutes an influential niche and its interactions with mainstream energy developments. To this end, we present our empirical subject below: community-led sustainability energy projects.

COMMUNITY-LED SUSTAINABLE ENERGY PROJECTS IN THE UK

In this section, we explain what 'community energy' means, and why it is an interesting sector, particularly in relation to radical initiatives to promote more sustainable practices based on alternative, 'new economics' values. Grassroots activists were relatively unnoticed by energy policies up to the 1990s, although they had been initiating community-based energy initiatives for over 30 years. During this time, grassroots endeavors to develop alternative energy technologies were informed by the literature on appropriate technology (see, for example, Dunn, 1987), small-scale development (Schumacher, 1973) and 'soft energy paths' (Lovins, 1977), later bolstered by moves to implement Local Agenda 21 plans for civil society participation in community-based sustainability projects (UNCED, 1992), and networks such as Local Governments for Sustainability (ICLEI).[6] Activists engaged in community-based initiatives without the assistance of public resources frequently were overlooked by mainstream energy suppliers. This disregard of local energy projects changed with the emergence of the rhetoric of 'new localism' and 'community' in the UK's energy policy in the late 1990s. For example, in the UK government's report on sustainable development, community initiatives are implied to have the following potential.

> Community groups can help tackle climate change, develop community energy and transport projects, help minimise waste, improve the quality of the local

environment, and promote fair trade and sustainable consumption and production. (HM Government, 2005, p. 27)

To this end, the UK's Low Carbon Transition Plan in 2009 encouraged local authorities and community groups to work in partnership to not only address carbon- and energy-related issues, but also advance wider policy needs (HM Government, 2009).[7]

However, although 'community energy' is now the subject of UK government-supported initiatives, research and competitions such as the 'Big Green Challenge,' the term 'community energy' is defined in different ways and used in a flexible manner by policy makers, academics, intermediaries and community participants.[8] It describes numerous types of energy initiatives with varying emphases on the degree of community involvement, the designation of geographical boundaries and the patterns of benefit for local residents.[9]

Project initiation, administration and construction can either develop out of grassroots actions, be grounded in partnerships between communities, nongovernmental organizations (NGOs) and local government, or be initiated by entrepreneurs and utilities that are willing to share some of the gains with the community. The involvement of communities in energy schemes can therefore take various forms from project initiation, administration, development, decision making and financial support (Rogers et al., 2008). We share the view advanced by Walker and colleagues (2007) that what makes community-energy initiatives distinct from other energy approaches is the local and collective character of the outcomes achieved and the open and participatory process employed.[10] These attributes are shown in the top right-hand quadrant of the matrix in Figure 7.1 that utilizes two dimensions representing 'outcome' and 'process.'

For instance, Walker and Devine-Wright (2008) position a 'utility company-developed wind farm' in the bottom left-hand corner of Figure 7.1. Such a renewable energy project might be compared with the governmental campaign 'Are you doing your bit' when thinking about behavior change and energy-efficiency projects. Both initiatives have minimal interactions with local communities and are implemented by 'distant and closed institutions.' Economic returns and the electricity produced benefits the developer in the renewables project and similarly the outcomes of the campaign might impact on national carbon reduction measures but do not facilitate social cohesion or create social capital. In the top right-hand corner Walker and Devine-Wright place projects that are being initiated and developed by civil society and where benefits (such as heat) are locally distributed. An example of such a renewable project is one of Walker and Devine-Wright's case studies in the North of England. The community

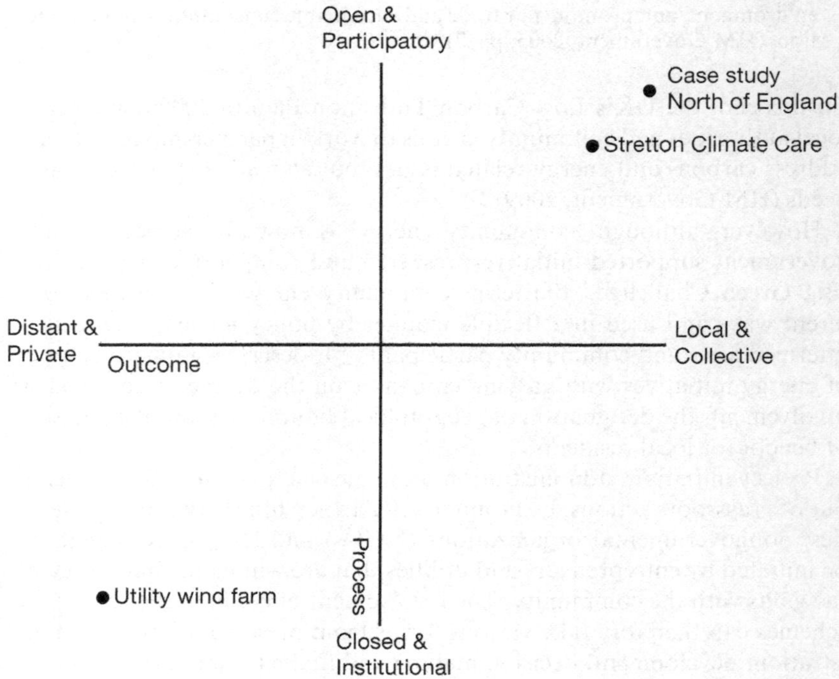

Source: Adapted from Walker and Devine-Wright (2008).

Figure 7.1 Illustration of the process and outcome dimension of community energy

installed a ground source heat pump when refurbishing its village hall. The energy efficiency and awareness-raising projects of the 'Stretton Climate Care' group could also be placed in this corner of Figure 7.1. Launched in September 2007, the organization conducts free energy checks in its local area and organizes talks about practical actions to reduce energy consumption. Everybody from the community is able to join and participate in the activities and group.

The local and collective character of the outcomes achieved, and the open and participatory process employed, make community-energy initiatives clearly different from top-down and business-led energy interventions. After reviewing the community-energy literature, three other areas where community-energy projects are distinctive became evident and can be directly attributed to the 'top-right quadrant' characteristics of openness and participation, locality and collectivity. They are: a multi-faceted approach; an ability to change contexts; and a focus on engagement. We discuss each aspect in turn while concluding the section with a reflection on the challenges that community-energy groups face.

Multi-faceted

Community-energy projects often aim to combine a variety of activities from providing information, conducting home-energy audits with follow-up progress meetings and retrofits to setting up voluntary initiatives and groups that measure their own personal change. An example of such groups is the Carbon Reduction Action Groups (CRAG) network. A CRAG is a group of local people that has an interest in reducing its collective and individual carbon footprints. They come together in regular meetings to set themselves an annual emission target, a carbon ration and to track their emissions throughout the year, measuring their progress against an agreed carbon allowance. The groups provide constant support and encouragement to their members to help them reduce their carbon footprints and also try to engage the wider community in doing so by raising awareness, promoting practical actions and providing knowledge and skills. Other initiatives share information and conduct workshops and community events that sometimes connect religious beliefs with practical actions or demonstrate different ways of living and consumption practices (SCR, 2006; Moloney et al., 2010). The attempt to focus on more than one approach and field of activity is further verified by the conclusion advanced by Steward and his colleagues (2009) that the applicants of the 'Big Green Challenge' made use of a range of interlinked carbon reduction measures.[11] The initiatives frequently aimed to develop holistic approaches that could potentially drive a more systemic change.

Changing Contexts

Proponents of community-energy initiatives and policy makers have both acknowledged the potential of such 'holistic approaches' in recent years, in particular when trying to find ways to change people's behaviors. For decades, attempts made by policy makers to alter energy-related behavior was individualistic, grounded in the assumption that people are decision makers who are in full control of their actions and – perhaps unsurprisingly – were of limited effectiveness (Wilhite et al., 2000). Nevertheless, research has demonstrated that behaviors are not mainly controlled by individuals but are shaped by socio-technical infrastructures and conventions (Shove, 2003). The UK Sustainable Development Commission's (SDC, 2011) recent report *Making Sustainable Lives Easier* concludes that with respect to sustainable consumption 'changing contexts' is more effective that 'changing minds.' Consequently, individuals often feel disempowered when faced with the enormity of the task of tackling, for example, climate change (Thøgersen, 2005).

With this in mind, we see that contexts – the socio-technical systems within which people operate – need to change in order to achieve more sustainable consumption outcomes; furthermore, individuals have very limited agency to change societal structures. Models of system change are required that engage with, and respond to, this challenge. Heiskanen et al. (2010) have argued that the structure and context of communities aids the process of reframing the issues associated with individual behavior-change programs. Community-led approaches assist the process of people changing their everyday practices together in a supportive environment, empowering others to do the same and increasing the visibility of the impacts of behaviors (Steward et al., 2009). Such initiatives can be holistic, making use of local knowledge and approaches that not only inform people of actions but also demonstrate them in real-life examples. A community-based approach can improve people's capacities to act through attempts to develop locally appropriate approaches to change (Walker, 2008; Capener, 2009; Houghton Research, 2010). Potentially, community-energy initiatives are therefore able to reach 'the parts other can't reach' (Steward et al., 2009), influencing conventions, shaping local infrastructures and affecting positively on socio-economic factors (such as increasing local income, skills and social cohesion). In policy, community projects are assumed to promote behavioral change, and embed social acceptability for larger sustainable energy technologies (HM Government, 2005).

A project that seeks to develop carbon reduction approaches on a street-by-street level is 'Transitions Streets' initiated by 'Transition Town Totnes.' The project strives to engage the local community in behavior change, energy-efficiency measures, renewable energy and community awareness (Lockyer, 2010) while providing emotional support and bringing people together in their local neighborhood. 'Transition Town Totnes' is part of a wider project known as 'Transition Networks.' Transition Initiatives that make up the network are groups of people that are keen to develop a community-led response to fossil fuel depletion and climate change. The aim is to organize local people to enhance the community to be more economically self-sufficient and resilient, embedding new energy-related consumption practices. These practices are directed toward anti-consumerism and anti-growth and try to influence the social, infrastructural and cultural context that gives meaning to actions. These initiatives therefore help to change contexts rather than minds, as proposed by the SDC (2011).

Engagement

A third key characteristic that differentiates community-energy initiatives such as Transitions Towns from other approaches that address energy-related consumption practices is the focus on participation (Hoffman and High-Pippert, 2009). The role of a project participant is only obtainable for members of the public in a community-based approach (Walker and Cass, 2007). Public utilities, households and business-energy developments are usually constituted for an exclusive group of people that are not accessible to the wider community. A predominantly participatory approach to the initiation of community-energy initiatives is often based on a strong sense of social cohesion and trust even before starting a project. These relationships sometimes go beyond specific interest groups, 'bridging' across numerous actors and creating influential and robust initiatives and networks (Putnam, 2000). Putnam (1993, p. 171) further regards interpersonal trust to be an elementary feature of civic participation and engagement; in his words, 'trust lubricates cooperation and cooperation builds trust.' Such feelings of trust become strengthened the longer people work on their projects. Community participation and interpersonal trust is not only what defines these initiatives; it is also what keeps them alive.

Members are keen to participate for various reasons: because of the potential benefits to the community; an appreciation of place or a sense of duty; and not predominantly because of self-interest. Indeed, previous research has shown that participation in such initiatives is often driven by a desire to create a space where alternative values may be lived out and practiced; to experiment with alternative ways of living and provisioning, and to demonstrate that alternatives are possible (Seyfang, 2009). The initiative brings together people from different backgrounds who might experience the community work in quite different ways. Community-energy initiatives therefore tend to counter 'what some argue is an era of declining civic engagement' (Hoffman and High-Pippert, 2009, p. 6). Such community-energy projects are potentially examples of Barber's (1984) participatory democracy in which community initiatives become part of innovative institutions of self-governance (Hoffman and High-Pippert, 2009). They entail debates over concerns that are not mutually shared, developments of shared agendas and statements of common interest. Although these community initiatives exist, Hoffman and High-Pippert (2009) have recognized that the number of schemes that practice participatory democracy is currently small.

Challenges

Although a growing interest in community-energy initiatives is apparent, the prevailing positive view among policy makers seems to suggest that they regard these projects as channels for carrying out government policies and maintain that these efforts can change the wider social structures that surround them. In addition, this interpretation presumes that these initiatives currently have the 'capacity' to alter their own and other people's actions. Middlemiss and Parrish (2010, p. 7559) have associated the term 'capacity' with 'the ability of the community in question and its members to make changes by drawing on the resources available to them individually and collectively.'

But community initiatives still often face various challenges to increase their capacity to act. The successful implementation and progression of these efforts cannot be taken for granted. Church (2005) has drawn attention to the fact that community-energy initiatives spend only 10 percent of their time on developing projects as the rest of their time is used trying to survive. Such obstacles are not regularly linked to technological problems, as technical features are often well developed; rather they relate to operational, legal or funding issues. In addition, community-energy initiatives rely on supportive contextual factors and their ability to quickly pick up a variety of skills necessary to persevere. One of the key concerns for community-energy initiatives is to create a steady income stream. Grant-funding packages are often only a short-term fix and are complicated to coordinate, as they regularly derive from more than one funding body – each imposing different obligations (Houghton Research, 2010).

DISCUSSION: COMMUNITY INNOVATION FOR SUSTAINABLE ENERGY?

In this section, we apply a niche analysis to these community-energy grassroots innovations. The aim is to better understand how this new sector is developing and to appreciate the kinds of support that are needed to help it achieve its potential and overcome current challenges. If the community-energy sector is to be able to influence mainstream energy systems, the transitions literature tells us that it must first constitute a robust niche, comprising certain characteristics and activities. Is this process of influential niche formation evident?

Identifying a Community-energy Niche

Viewed from the perspective of grassroots-innovations theory, we see the community-energy sector as a group of local projects that may or may not form a coherent niche. Our analytical task is therefore to assess the extent to which niche processes are occurring and to identify what the conceptual framework says the sector could do to overcome the challenges it currently faces. We can certainly identify a flourishing of community-energy projects, and we can say that they represent innovative energy systems, in relation to the regime, by virtue of their sustainability. But do they constitute a niche?

Raven et al. (2010) have illustrated how a collection of local, innovative projects, at first without any real connection, gradually develop into a niche (Figure 7.2). The projects start to network with each other and exchange learning, and then begin to develop a range of niche activities such as standardization, shared learning, conferences, networks and so forth, which then make it easier to set up subsequent projects, thereby growing the niche. They note that the literature of niche developments has gradually shifted in its focus and its understanding of niches from individual projects and initiatives, which are seen as 'carried by local networks and characterised by local variety' toward the 'global level.' This distinction allows for the assumption that instead of regarding individual community initiatives as numerous distinct niches, it is a number of them, or even the totality of groups, that create the 'global-level' niche. Specific

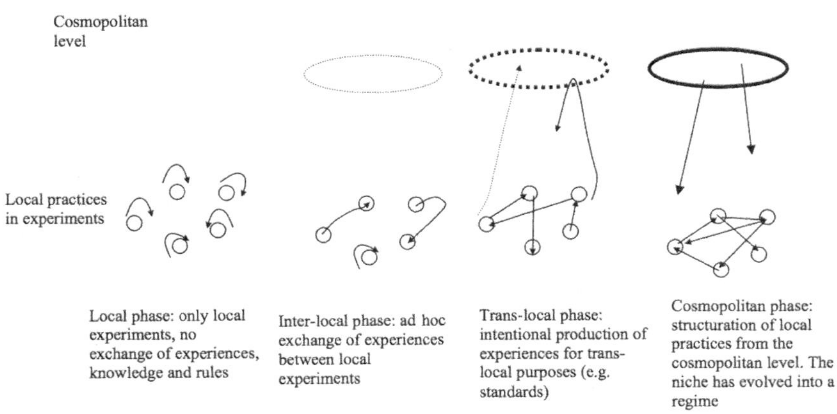

Source: From Raven (2005).

Figure 7.2 Emerging level of niches in relation to local practices

community-energy initiatives are therefore 'projects,' a smaller unit of analysis than the overall 'abstract' niche.

Given the diverse character of the field of community energy (Walker and Devine-Wright, 2008), determining the overall 'abstract' niche is not straightforward. Community-energy initiatives can be differentiated, for example, in relation to their focus for improving the energy system: renewable energy; energy efficiency; and behavior change. Even the community-led renewable energy projects can be subdivided into the different technologies applied such as solar, wind and hydro. Community-led solar projects could therefore be considered to constitute the 'abstract' niche or a subset of the community-energy niche. However, Raven et al. (2010) have pointed out that the distinction between local experiments, niche and regime and their boundaries are 'analytical, and not ontological.' Niches are not concrete entities that exist 'out there' to be discovered, but rather the niche concept provides a way of thinking through regime interactions and assessing the internal processes of niche development. Furthermore, the community-energy sector and its actors such as community-led energy initiatives, intermediaries and policy and funding bodies often do not create these 'artificial' boundaries. Community-energy initiatives typically focus on more than one field of activity and set of technologies (Capener, 2009; Steward et al., 2009). Projects are often interlinked, as groups aim to develop holistic approaches to climate change that could potentially drive a more systemic change. It might therefore make most sense to conceive of all the diverse community-led energy initiatives together as one niche, as they share a common focus on 'sustainable energy.'

Niche Processes: Networking, Learning and Visions

We therefore see a community-energy niche that consists of networks of community-energy projects distributed spatially and temporally and that enables participants to do a number of things: (1) help to mobilize resources for future initiatives through their networking activities; (2) shape expectations about the initiatives' role in a wider transition of energy systems in the future; and (3) learn from one another and make demands for facilitating policy and market reforms on the basis of those lessons.

How does the UK community-energy niche perform these tasks? One of the most important features of a niche is that it is something more (or other) than its constituent projects. Raven et al. (2010, p. 63) have argued that the 'circulation of knowledge and actors is important, to enable comparison between local practices and formulation of generic lessons. Conferences, workshops, technical journals, proceedings and newsletters play a major role therein.' They go on to suggest that these 'aggregation activities' occur in a niche and in the process reproduce and consolidate the niche. We therefore also ask: what evidence is there of such activities in the UK's community-energy niche?

Networking

In the UK over the last decade growing policy support and the increased role of intermediaries allowed for numerous 'aggregation activities' to occur, in particular in relation to networking.[12] Community-energy programs such as the 'Green Communities' that was run by the Energy Savings Trust distributed case-study reports about community-energy projects so that other initiatives could learn from their experiences. Similarly, the Local United 'diffusion packs' consist of individual reports that aim to inspire groups to pursue community-energy projects by providing 'how-to' guides and templates for various legal and financial documents needed to set up a project. Instead of providing written reports to community-energy initiatives, the 'PlanLoCal' resource, launched by the Centre for Sustainable Energy in 2011, consists of filmed stories of communities' experiences and learned lessons.

These 'intermediary' niche actors have generated commonalities between initiatives to develop resources for community-energy groups, aiding the process of gaining prominence and contributing to an upsurge of interest in the field within the UK. Intermediaries have not only played a key role in distributing best-practice reports but have also been involved in activities that lead to 'project-networking' and 'regime-interfacing.' Networking activities among community-energy initiatives can be informal through telephone contact or on networking website setup, for example, by an intermediary called 'Community Central.' Other networking 'aggregation activities' reveal themselves through conferences such as the 2011 event 'Communities and Climate Action' and the Carbon Leapfrog workshop 'Creating Low Carbon Communities' that bridged across and between specific community-energy initiatives. These venues provide project proponents with a space to exchange experiences and learning and to create shared expectations.

Visions and Expectations

However, Walker et al. (2006) have pointed out that shared, overriding visions are not in place. These authors contend that goals for community energy are based on short-term strategies that do not consider how the current energy system could be replaced by a more distributed and locally owned system and the sector envisages 'remaining firmly in its expanded but not transforming niche.' So, there is a diversity of goals, from system transformation to continuation of 'simple' niche (Seyfang and Smith, 2007). In addition, the diversity of the sector itself, covering energy supply and demand projects, different technologies and organizational forms, divergent visions and varying sets of actors, does not bode well for acting in concert in relation to the regime. For example, the Low Carbon Communities Network aims to act as a voice for community energy by providing evidence and advocacy to policy makers, fulfilling this 'regime-interfacing' role.

However, efforts to develop a shared voice are often not straightforward in such a diverse field. This difficulty is exemplified by a recent discussion involving different community-energy initiatives at the 'Communities and Climate Change' conference that we attended in 2010. Members of the different projects deliberated whether they should create a 'network of networks' to create a stronger and shared voice for community energy in the policy context – which is what the strategic niche-management literature suggests would be most effective in terms of building niche influence on the regime. Some of the initiatives argued that community-energy groups would have more impact on policy development if different voices were encouraged rather than one common voice. This lack of shared vision and goals, and an absence of perceived common interest, could lead to fragmentation and splintering among current participants of the community-energy niche.

Learning

In addition to networking activities and the shaping of expectations, learning processes, the third characteristic of successful niches, have occurred among initiatives through, for example, site visits and, of course, the shared best-practice reports mentioned above. But more systemic learning processes are not necessarily in place on a more strategic level. It seems that to date there is not a clearly identifiable set of common lessons that have been learned across community-energy projects in the UK. Instead, throughout the range of the diverse community-energy sector, each project is learning quite distinct sets of lessons specific to its local circumstances. Church (2005) indicates that consolidation is impossible in a context of short-term survival management and here an obvious policy recommendation would be to support the development of cross-project, strategic shared learning. The lack of strategic learning mechanisms potentially hinders the impact of community energy in the UK as an influential niche.

The Department of Energy and Climate Change (DECC) Community Energy Online (2010) website may aim to fulfill some of these functions, but at present it appears to be reliant on the energy projects themselves to supply information, and thereby fails to address the root problem which is that local projects do not have the capacity to build consolidated learning resources.[13] Further, such a resource mainly brings together facts and data (such as how-to manuals and good practice guides) but does not necessarily allow for reflexive learning processes (for example, questioning the course taken or the underlying assumptions for development of the sector). One of the key learning processes for the sector might involve consideration of how to maintain the distinctiveness of community-energy approaches (such as the emphasis on trust, supportive environment and emotional support) when moving from projects to niche, as these characteristics might be easily lost on the way. One of the greatest strengths of community-energy initiatives is their ability to respond to local needs and to create a strong sense of social cohesion and trust, but this also raises broader questions beyond the scope of this chapter about the importance of local contexts and the extent to which projects are able to transfer learning to new situations, as well as whether they might be able to learn collectively.

Understanding the Policy Context

While grassroots activists have long developed more sustainable energy initiatives, the recent wave of policy support and related interest in community energy has certainly enabled the sector to grow. Indeed, the DECC Low Carbon Communities Challenge highlights the need to seed experiments working toward a sustainable energy transition and to learn from them how to harness and scale up their ideas and practices to meet policy goals – in much the same way as the Dutch transition managers have done. The UK Energy White Paper (HM Government, 2009) summarized measures to support community-energy initiatives, many of which had been identified in previous policy documents, including the implementation of a smart grid, new funding strategies, licensing arrangements and performance indicators (Houghton, 2010). Grant programs, including the requirement to pay upfront for energy-efficiency measures and microgeneration technologies, have been replaced by 'clean energy cashback' – such as the Feed in Tariff (FiT)[14] and 'pay as you save' (HM Government, 2009) to financially support energy-efficiency and renewable energy initiatives. The UK government's 2011 Energy Act also paved the way for a Green Deal initiative, in which households receive home energy efficiency measures upfront, and then pay back the investment costs through a supplementary charge on their energy bills. Communities and local authorities have been exploring what roles they might play under this scheme, and how this might sit alongside the government's intent to create a 'market' in home energy-efficiency measures supplied by larger installation surveyors and companies.

The Low Carbon Communities Network claims that these developments bring certain challenges and opportunities to the community-energy sector. For example, the attempt by the government to ensure that local groups provide certain services corresponds with the aims of numerous community initiatives and would encourage new groups to form and old ones to grow. However, the delivery of such services might create a competitive environment between these groups and larger competitors in which the former would need to have a strong support structure to succeed. This observation points to the need for government to attend to the factors that enable successful niche emergence and consolidation if it is to harness niche innovations. For example, even small changes to this currently favorable selection environment (such as changing the terms of the FiT) might undermine a fragile and emergent niche. Introducing more competitive relations among projects, as in the example above, might be a disincentive for groups to share learning and network effectively and develop shared visions. Removing funding for intermediary organizations while simultaneously calling for civil society to step into the role of public service providers will almost certainly undo the good work that has recently been put in place to develop the niche through aggregative activities.

CONCLUSION

We have described the current state and character of community-led sustainable energy projects in the UK and sought to understand what makes this emerging sector interesting and distinct to scholars of sustainable consumption. We have shown that community-energy approaches are multi-faceted, bridging energy production and consumption in a variety of ways. In the first instance, they have the ability to move beyond simplistic attempts to modify behavior through individualistic mechanisms, by having the ability to change contexts. Moreover, they enable a far greater degree of engagement in processes of co-creating new energy systems than traditional top-down approaches. Not least of the benefits is the fact that participants in these projects often specifically seek the ability to put their 'new economics' values into practice, mutually planting potential seeds of change within wider systems and seeking to foster spaces where different rules apply (see the chapters in Part I of this volume). In doing so, such initiatives create opportunities where the political economy of consumption can be reconfigured through new social practices of consumption.

We applied a niche analytical framework to help us understand the emergence and potential trajectory of the sector and analyzed the extent to which the community-energy sector constitutes a niche – which the literature on transitions says is a necessary (but not sufficient) condition for exerting wider influence. There is good evidence that the community-energy sector is performing the sorts of activities that the literature predicts is required for successful niche-building, including networking (such as through convening workshops and conferences), collective organizing (such as the creation of a 'network of networks') and working with intermediaries (such as the production of the 'PlanLoCaL' resource), but there is more to be done, and in particular, the fragile emerging niche is vulnerable to changes in government policy and support.

While the transitions literature, and niche frameworks specifically, can be useful tools for conceptualizing the emergence and development of community energy, there are a number of weaknesses with the model related to the civil society context of grassroots innovations. These preliminary findings therefore suggest an emerging research agenda around several issues. The key item on this research agenda is to better understand the undertheorized relations between situated socio-technical projects and the emergence of an abstracted, niche-level identity and interest, based around stylized socio-technical practices (Smith, 2007; Raven et al., 2008; Seyfang, 2009). This is problematic for three reasons. First, in terms of niche development, how do community projects reinterpret and reinvent, yet reinforce, the generic, mobile lessons and norms constituting a niche? The niche-transitions literature is vague as to the precise roles of projects in niche-building. What dedicated intermediating work is needed, and by whom, for social learning to take place, expectations to develop and supportive networks to build (Raven et al., 2008)? Conversely, when is social learning ignored, when do expectations deflate and how do networks fragment? Our wider project seeks evidence for the hypotheses that niches grow through replication of projects in different locations; that strategic learning across replicated projects facilitates scaled-up adaptations; and that elements of these translate into new business models and markets. This suggests community niches do not provide blueprints, but rather reservoirs of ideas and practices, and that dedicated work is needed to transfer and adapt from across locations, scales and contexts (for example, into commercial prospects).

Second, in terms of niche influence: how do strategic niches press for institutional reform? While the literature argues that successful niches prompt facilitating institutional reforms within the wider energy regime (Geels and Schot, 2007), it is unclear why this would happen given path dependencies in the regime (see Shove and Walker, 2007). What political roles do community-energy niches need to play to influence these reform processes? This is where social movement theory might inform the transitions literature and reveal the political roles niches must adopt in sustainability transitions (Smith, 2005; Scrase and Smith, 2009). How do community-energy niches develop collective identities and interests; and what repertoires of activism press for reforms (Foweraker, 1995)? Where are the socio-technical (cf. political) 'opportunity structures' for pursuing community energy demands (Rootes, 1999; Van der Heijden, 1999)? On this latter point, we have to look at community energy the other way around, from the perspective of the regime. What appropriable solutions do community-energy niches suggest for businesses and policy makers in the regime? This speaks to the translation mode of diffusion: what niche practices can be adapted into more conventional business forms addressing pressures, say, to cut demand. The appeal of community energy to energy business and policy will depend upon how the former's performance is perceived and valued and the context in which regime actors are operating into the future.

Finally, there is more empirical work to be done to explore whether and how these experiments in sustainable energy are able to reconfigure everyday life practices and express a more radical political economy of consumption than the mainstream norm. What do more sustainable energy-consuming practices look like; how are they configured and how are unsustainable practices dismantled? Can these practices survive and evolve through translation, interpretation and capture (the policy-instrumental 'harnessing') by regime-affiliated policy interests? How should the niche and transitions literature adapt to better consider this aspect of civil society engagement and everyday life?

The research presented here has demonstrated a potential role for grassroots innovations in sustainable energy, in the transition to a more sustainable energy system, while also opening up further agendas for research. These are crucial questions that need to be addressed to better understand, support and nurture this potentially exciting and untapped resource for change.

ACKNOWLEDGMENTS

This chapter forms part of our Community Innovation for Sustainable Energy (CISE) research project that has been funded by the UK

Engineering and Physical Science Research Council (EPSRC) and the European Centre Laboratories for Energy Efficiency Research (ECLEER) of EdF Energy. We are grateful to our CISE colleagues Tom Hargreaves, Mari Martiskainen, Isabelle Moussaoui, Dominique Osso, Jin Park and Jim Watson for their contributions to the development of the ideas in this chapter, to the participants of the SCORAI workshop in Princeton for feedback and discussion on an earlier version and to the editors of this volume for helpful suggestions that have strengthened the chapter.

NOTES

1. Social practice theorists, from Giddens (1984) and Bourdieu (1977, 1990), to more recent work by Schatzki (1996, 2002), Reckwitz (2002), Warde (2005) and Shove (2010), regard practice itself, rather than the individuals who perform them or the social structures that surround them, as the core unit of analysis. Social practice theory deals therefore with a middle level between agency and structure (see the chapters in Part III of this volume).
2. Consideration of the development of new social practices is beyond the scope of this chapter. For a related discussion, see Seyfang et al. (2010) and Hargreaves et al. (2012).
3. In addition to historical, post hoc studies of system transitions, an applied branch of the literature centers on transition management and strategic niche management (see the chapter by René Kemp and Harro van Lente in this volume). Both of these topics highlight policy interventions developed in the Netherlands with the aim of triggering and directing societal transitions to sustainability.
4. This chapter draws on early findings from the Community Innovation for Sustainable Energy (CISE) research project. CISE applies a multi-level framework of socio-technical transitions to the field of radical community-led innovations for sustainability to assess the potential of community energy to diffuse innovative ideas and practices, and so influence wider energy systems. For further details, see http://www.grassroots innovations.org (accessed 17 October 2012).
5. Other civil society sources of radical systems change are described in the literature. See, for example, Narberhaus (2011) and Smith (2012), which identify opportunities to influence landscape and regime levels as well as niches. For current purposes attention focuses only on the role of radical niches.
6. The organization was originally established in 1990 as the International Council for Local Environmental Initiatives. See http://www.iclei.org (accessed 17 October 2012).
7. The White Paper details a strategy to achieve an 80 percent reduction in greenhouse gas emissions by 2050. One of the key strategies is to reduce emissions from homes to near to zero by this target year through energy efficiency and low carbon energy measures.
8. Intermediaries are organizations and networks that build links between specific community energy groups and which exist to share experience, good practice, expertise and advice. In some cases, intermediaries also act as a voice for community energy by providing evidence and advocacy to policy makers.
9. It is not only the term 'community energy' that is used in a flexible manner but also the term 'community' itself. There have been numerous definitions of what should be regarded as a community that have derived from the sociological literature. But the concept still represents 'an elusive and somewhat intractable term with regards to its actual definition and meaning' (Peters and Jackson, 2008). Themes that recur in this literature are social capital, community capacity, social learning, social norms and social networks (Peters, 2010) as they play key roles in characterizing communities.

10. Methodological considerations of how to sample community-energy projects in accordance with Walker and Devine-Wright's (2008) distinction is beyond the scope of this chapter.
11. Community projects that entered the 'Big Green Challenge' were able to reduce their carbon dioxide emissions by between 10 and 32 percent over a period of one year. When considering these reductions against UK targets of achieving an overall reduction of 34 percent by 2020, these community projects have been able to achieve a considerable cut (Houghton, 2010).
12. While transitions theory assumes a smooth diffusion of niche ideas into regime settings, grassroots innovations display oppositional values to the incumbent regime and so this process of translation is difficult. Community values can clash with commercial priorities and policy developments, inhibiting the translation of knowledge and practices between initiatives but also between the community-energy niche and the incumbent regime. This translation between niche and regime requires careful negotiation by intermediaries conducting 'regime-interfacing' activities (Smith, 2007).
13. For details on the Community Energy Online website, see http://ceo.decc.gov.uk (accessed 17 October 2012).
14. FiTs constitute a 'Clean Energy Cashback' scheme. Under this program, energy suppliers are required to make fixed payments above the market rate to householders and communities that generate their own electricity from renewable or low carbon sources. The tariffs were introduced by the government to help increase the level of smaller-scale renewable energy in the UK. Although the coalition government initially agreed not to review FiTs until 2012, Chris Huhne, the former Secretary of State for Energy and Climate Change, launched a comprehensive review of the scheme in February 2011. Among the changes, the review cut tariff rates for solar photovoltaic electricity generation by up to half, and limited the maximum size of installation to 50 kilowatts. The reason for this review was based on the government's concern that the scheme was being used for large-scale solar farms rather than for community projects. However, these changes have had detrimental implications for community-based cooperatives that make use of solar technologies. Projects such as the Brighton Energy Cooperative have had to shelve their plans as a result.

REFERENCES

Avelino, F. and I. Kunze (2009). 'Exploring the transition potential of the ecovillage movement', Paper presented at the KSI European Conference on Sustainability Transitions, Amsterdam, 4–5 June.

Barber, B. (1984). *Strong Democracy: Participatory Politics for a New Age*, Berkeley, CA: University of California Press.

Bourdieu, P. (1977). *Outline of a Theory of Practice*, New York: Cambridge University Press.

Bourdieu, P. (1990). *The Logic of Practice*, Palo Alto, CA: Stanford University Press.

Capener, P. (2009). *People-powered Response to Climate Change: Research Summary for NESTA's Big Green Challenge*, London: National Endowment for Science, Technology and the Arts.

Church, C. (2005). 'Sustainability: the importance of grassroots initiatives', Paper presented at the Grassroots Innovations for Sustainable Development Conference, University College London, 10 June.

DECC (Department of Energy and Climate Change) (2010). *The Low Carbon Communities Challenge*, London: DECC.

Douthwaite, R. (2002). *Enabling Innovation: A Practical Guide to Understanding and Fostering Change*, London: Zed Books.

Dunn, P. (1987). *Appropriate Technology: Technology with a Human Face*, New York: Macmillan.

Foweraker, J. (1995). *Theorizing Social Movements*, London: Pluto Press.

Garud, R. and P. Karnøe (2003). 'Bricolage versus breakthrough: distributed and embedded agency in technology entrepreneurship', *Research Policy*, **32**(2), 277–300.

Geels, F. (2002). 'Technological transitions as evolutionary reconfiguration processes: a multi-level perspective and a case-study', *Research Policy*, **31**(8–9), 1257–74.

Geels, F. and J. Schot (2007). 'Typology of sociotechnical transition pathways', *Research Policy*, **36**(3), 399–417.

Genus, A. and A.-M. Coles (2008). 'Rethinking the multi-level perspective of technological transitions', *Research Policy*, **37**(9), 1436–45.

Giddens, A. (1984). *The Constitution of Society: Outline of the Theory of Structuration*, Berkeley, CA: University of California Press.

Grin, J., J. Rotmans and J. Schot (2010). *Transitions to Sustainable Development: New Directions in the Study of Long Term Transformative Change*, New York: Routledge.

Hargreaves, T., N. Longhurst and G. Seyfang (2012). 'Up, down, round and round: connecting regimes and practices in innovation for sustainability', *Environment and Planning A*, in press.

Hegger, D., J. van Vliet and B. van Vliet (2007). 'Niche management and its contribution to regime change: the case of innovation in sanitation', *Technological Analysis and Strategic Management*, **19**(6), 729–46.

Heiskanen, E., M. Johnson, S. Robinson, E. Vadovics and M. Saastamoinen (2010). 'Low-carbon communities as a context for individual behavioural change', *Energy Policy*, **38**(12), 7586–95.

Hess, D. (2007). *Alternative Pathways in Science and Industry: Activism, Innovation, and the Environment in an Era of Globalization*, Cambridge, MA: MIT Press.

HM Government (2005). *Securing the Future: The UK Government Sustainable Development Strategy*, London: HM Government.

HM Government (2008). *Building a Low Carbon Economy: Unlocking Innovation and Skills*, London: HM Government.

HM Government (2009). *The UK Low Carbon Transition Plan*, Norwich: Stationery Office.

Hoffman, S. and A. High-Pippert (2009). 'From private lives to collective action: recruitment and participation incentives for a community energy program', *Energy Policy*, **38**(12), 7567–74.

Hoogma, R., M. Weber and B. Elzen (2001). 'Integrated long-term strategies to induce regime shifts to sustainability: the approach of strategic niche management', Paper presented at the Towards Environmental Innovation Systems Conference, Eibsee, Germany, 27–29 September.

Houghton Research (2010). *Galvanising Community-led Responses to Climate Change*, London: NESTA.

Jackson, T. (2009). *Prosperity Without Growth: Economics for a Finite Planet*, London: Earthscan.

Kemp, R., A. Rip and J. Schot (2001). 'Constructing transition paths through the

management of niches', in R. Garud and P. Karnøe (eds), *Path Dependence and Creation*, Mahwah, NJ: Lawrence Erlbaum Associates, pp. 269–99.
Lockyer, J. (2010). 'Intentional community carbon reduction and climate change action: from ecovillages to transition towns', in M. Peters, S. Fudge and T. Jackson (eds), *Low Carbon Communities*, Cheltenham, UK and Northampton, MA, USA: Edward Elgar, pp. 47–60.
Lovins, A. (1977). *Soft Energy Paths*, New York: Penguin.
Middlemiss, L. and B. Parrish (2010). 'Building capacity for low-carbon communities: the role of grassroots initiatives', *Energy Policy*, **38**(12), 7559–66.
Moloney, S., R. Horne and J. Fien (2010). 'Transitioning to low carbon communities: from behaviour change to systemic change: lessons from Australia', *Energy Policy*, **38**(12), 7614–23.
Mulgan, G. with R. Ali, R. Halkett and B. Sanders (2007). *In and Out of Sync: The Challenge of Growing Social Innovations*, London: NESTA.
Narberhaus, M. (2011). 'Smart CSOs report: effective change strategies for the great transition, five leverage points for civil society organisations', available at http://www.smart-csos.org (accessed 17 October 2012).
NESTA (National Endowment for Science, Technology and the Arts) (2009). *People-powered Responses to Climate Change: Mapping Community-led Proposals to NESTA's Big Green Challenge*, London: NESTA.
Peters, M. (2010). 'Community engagement and social organization: introducing concepts, policy and practical applications', in M. Peters, S. Fudge and T. Jackson (eds), *Low Carbon Communities*, Cheltenham, UK and Northampton, MA, USA: Edward Elgar, pp. 47–60.
Peters, M. and T. Jackson (2008). 'Community action: a force for social change? Some conceptual observations', RESOLVE Working Paper 01–08, Research Group on Lifestyles, Values, and Environment, University of Surrey.
Putnam, R. (1993). *Making Democracy Work: Civic Traditions in Modern Italy*, Princeton, NJ: Princeton University Press.
Putnam, R. (2000). *Bowling Alone: The Collapse and Revival of American Communities*, New York: Simon and Schuster.
Raven, R. (2005). *Strategic Niche Management for Biomass: A Comparative Study on the Experimental Introduction of Bioenergy Technologies in the Netherlands and Denmark*, Eindhoven: Eindhoven University Press.
Raven, R. (2006). 'Towards alternative trajectories? Reconfigurations in the Dutch electricity regime', *Research Policy*, **35**(4), 581–95.
Raven, R., E. Heiskanen, R. Lovio, M. Hodson and B. Brohmann (2008). 'The contribution of local experiments and negotiation processes to field-level learning in emerging (niche) technologies: meta-analysis of 27 new energy projects', *Bulletin of Science, Technology Society*, **28**(6), 464–77.
Raven, R., S. van den Bosch and R. Weterings (2010). 'Transitions and strategic niche management: towards a competence kit for practitioners', *International Journal of Technology Management*, **51**(1), 57–74.
Reckwitz, A. (2002). 'Towards a theory of social practice', *European Journal of Social Theory*, **5**(2), 243–63.
Rogers, J., E. Simmons, I. Convery and A. Weatherall (2008). 'Public perceptions of opportunities for community-based renewable energy projects', *Energy Policy*, **36**(11), 4217–26.
Rootes, C. (1999). 'Acting globally, thinking locally? Prospects for a global environmental movement', *Environmental Politics*, **8**(1), 290–310.

Schatzki, T. (1996). *Social Practices: A Wittgensteinian Approach to Human Activity and the Social*, New York: Cambridge University Press.
Schatzki, T. (2002). *The Site of the Social: A Philosophical Account of the Constitution of Social Life and Change*, University Park, PA: Pennsylvania State University Press.
Schot, J. and F. Geels (2008). 'Strategic niche management and sustainable innovation journeys: theory, findings, research agenda, and policy', *Technology Analysis and Strategic Management*, **20**(5), 537–54.
Schot, J., R. Hoogma and B. Elzen (1994). 'Strategies for shifting technological systems: the case of the automobile system', *Futures*, **26**(10), 1060–76.
Schumacher, E. (1973). *Small is Beautiful: A Study of Economics as if People Mattered. Sphere*, New York: Harper and Row.
SCR (Sustainable Consumption Roundtable) (2006). *Communities of Interest – and Action?* London: SCR.
Scrase, J. and A. Smith (2009). 'The (non-)politics of managing low carbon socio-technical transitions', *Environmental Politics*, **18**(5), 707–26.
SDC (Sustainable Development Commission) (2011). *Making Sustainable Lives Easier*, London: SDC.
Seyfang, G. (2009). *The New Economics of Sustainable Consumption: Seeds of Change*, New York: Palgrave Macmillan.
Seyfang, G. and A. Haxeltine (2012). 'Growing grassroots innovations: exploring the role of community-based social movements for sustainable energy transitions', *Environment and Planning C: Government and Policy*, **30**(3), 381–400.
Seyfang, G. and A. Smith (2007). 'Grassroots innovations for sustainable development: towards a new research and policy agenda', *Environmental Politics*, **16**(4), 584–603.
Seyfang, G., A. Haxeltine, T. Hargreaves and N. Longhurst (2010). 'Energy and communities in transition: towards a new research agenda on agency and civil society in sustainability transitions', CSERGE Working Paper, EDM 2010–13, Centre for Social and Economic Research on the Global Environment, University of East Anglia, Norwich.
Shove, E. (2003). *Comfort, Cleanliness, and Convenience: The Social Organisation of Normality*, New York: Berg.
Shove, E. (2010). 'Beyond the ABC: climate change policy and theories of social change', *Environment and Planning A*, **42**(6), 1273–85.
Shove, E. and G. Walker (2007). 'CAUTION! Transitions ahead: politics, practices, and sustainable transition management', *Environment and Planning A*, **39**(4), 763–70.
Smith, A. (2005). 'The alternative technology movement: an analysis of its framing and negotiation of technology development', *Human Ecology Review*, **12**(2), 106–19.
Smith, A. (2006). *Supporting and Harnessing Diversity? Experiments in Alternative Technology*, ESRC End of Award Report, Reference No. RES-332-25-0005, Science Policy Research Unit, University of Sussex.
Smith, A. (2007). 'Translating sustainabilities between green niche and socio-technical regimes', *Technology Analysis and Strategic Management*, **19**(4), 427–50.
Smith, A. (2012). 'Civil society in sustainable energy transitions', in G. Verbong and D. Loorbach (eds), *Governing the Energy Transition: Reality, Illusion or Necessity?* New York: Routledge, pp. 180–202.

Smith, A., A. Stirling and F. Berkhout (2005). 'The governance of sustainable socio-technical transitions', *Research Policy*, **34**(10), 1491–510.
Steward, F., S. Liff and M. Dunkelman (2009). *Mapping the Big Green Challenge*, London: NESTA.
Thøgersen, J. (2005). 'How may consumer policy empower consumers for sustainable lifestyles?', *Journal of Consumer Policy*, **28**(2), 143–77.
UNCED (United Nations Conference on Environment and Development) (1992). *Agenda 21: The United Nations Program of Action From Rio*, New York: United Nations Publications.
Van der Heijden, H. (1999). 'Environmental movements, ecological modernization and political opportunity structures', *Environmental Politics*, **8**(1), 199–221.
Verheul, H. and P. Vergragt (1995). 'Social experiments in the development of environmental technology: a bottom-up perspective', *Technological Analysis and Strategic Management*, **7**(3), 315–26.
Walker, G. (2008). 'What are the barriers and incentives for community-owned means of energy production and use?', *Energy Policy*, **36**(12), 4401–5.
Walker, G. and N. Cass (2007). 'Carbon reduction, "the public" and renewable energy: engaging with socio-technical configurations', *Area*, **39**(4), 458–69.
Walker, G. and P. Devine-Wright (2008), 'Community renewable energy: what should it mean?', *Energy Policy*, **36**(2), 497–500.
Walker, G., P. Devine-Wright and B. Evans (2006). 'Embedding socio-technical innovation? Niche management and community-based localism in renewable energy policy in the UK', *SPRU Proceedings of the Future of Science, Technology and Innovation Policy Conference*, Brighton, 11–13 September.
Walker, G., S. Hunter, P. Devine-Wright, B. Evans and H. Fay (2007). 'Harnessing community energies: explaining and evaluating community-based localism in renewable energy policy in the UK', *Global Environmental Politics*, **7**(2), 64–82.
Warde, A. (2005). 'Consumption and theories of practice', *Journal of Consumer Culture*, **5**(2), 131–53.
Wilhite, H., E. Shove, L. Lutzenhiser and W. Kempton (2000). 'The legacy of twenty years of energy demand management: we know more about individual behaviour but next to nothing about demand', in E. Jochem (ed.), *Society, Behaviour, and Climate Change Mitigation*, Dordrecht: Kluwer, pp. 109–26.

8. Sustainable consumption, energy and failed transitions: the problem of adaptation

David J. Hess

INTRODUCTION

Theories of socio-technical transitions provide two principle advantages for the analysis of sustainable consumption: a multidecade, multiscale approach that enables long-term, systemic thinking in a comparative perspective; and an integrated analysis, in the tradition of technology studies, of the social and technical aspects of the design and development of large-scale technological systems, including infrastructures (for example, Hughes, 1987). The approach has been used to study how to manage long-term changes in socio-technical systems to make them more sustainable (for example, Jørgensen and Sorensen, 1999; Smith et al., 2010; Geels, 2011). However, there is growing recognition that sustainability transitions are occurring at a pace that is too slow to stop or reverse the worst effects of human societies on natural systems. As a result, there is a need to analyze more carefully not only the problem of how to achieve a sustainability transition but also the implications of transition failure. This study will examine the thesis that the failure to address significant global environmental problems in a timely way has resulted in an ensuing shift toward an adaptation transition. The emergence of an adaptation transition has significant policy implications for the management of the sustainability transition, including sustainable consumption.

The rise of severe weather events associated with climate change has forced societies into investing growing resources into disaster response and adaptation strategies for climate change. In many countries, subnational governments such as cities and states now have adaptation plans in addition to sustainability plans. In effect, the failure of the sustainability transition has forced governments to engage in an adaptation transition. Because resources are limited, the allocation of funds to adaptation can occur in a zero-sum relationship with potential investments in sustainability such as the greening of electricity systems, buildings and transportation. However, there are also new opportunities that emerge in the design of technological systems that can address both adaptational and sustainability concerns. By doing so, it becomes possible to rethink sustainable consumption by exploring policies associated with sustainable consumption in relationship to adaptation goals.

The argument is made in three sections: an introduction to the concept of a failed sustainability transition and its implications for studies of socio-technical transitions; an analysis of the concept of resilience as central to the study of adaptation transitions; and a demonstration of how adaptation and sustainability goals can be brought into alignment in the case of policies governing energy efficiency and distributed renewable energy generation. The goal is to show not only the potential for the alignment of adaptation and sustainability goals in the design of socio-technical systems but also how concerns with adaptation and resilience may also inform and improve research and policy on sustainable consumption.

TRANSITION STUDIES, LANDSCAPES AND THE FAILURE OF THE SUSTAINABILITY TRANSITION

Before discussing the relationship between the adaptation transition and sustainable consumption, it is first necessary to discuss differing approaches to sustainability and some features of multi-level analysis of sustainability transitions (see the chapter by René Kemp and Harro van Lente in this volume). Sustainable consumption researchers have tended to work with a concept of sustainability that is based on the tradition of intergenerational equity in the Brundtland Report (WCED, 1987). For example, the European Environmental Agency (EEA) defines sustainable consumption as 'the use of services and related products which respond to basic needs and bring a better quality of life while minimizing the use of natural resources and toxic materials as well as the emissions of waste and pollutants over the life cycle of the service or product so as not to jeopardize the needs of future generations' (EEA, 2010; for a review of the literature, see Cohen and Murphy, 2001; Jackson, 2006). Unfortunately, the approach to sustainability in the Brundtland tradition does not draw attention to the relationship between societal change and ecosystem adaptation. For that reason, the approach to sustainability developed by ecological economist Herman Daly (1990, 1996) is more appropriate to the problem of the failure of the sustainability transition and the emergence of the adaptation problem. He defined sustainability in terms of the capacity of an ecosystem to replenish consumed resources and process wastes.

Although the definition lacks the intergenerational equity perspective of the United Nations' approach, it draws attention much more to the ecological limits of a society and the overall problem of the adaptation of society to its ecosystem (including at a global scale).

The Daly approach to sustainability can be used to expand on the multi-level analysis of transition studies by providing the basis for modifications of the concept of the 'landscape.'[1] Although the landscape can include society-environment relationships, the implications of those relationships are central to the study of sustainability transitions. To understand the implications of the failure, one must disaggregate the category of 'landscape' that is commonly used in transition studies, because there is an important feedback loop between human systems and environmental degradation. The slow pace, and in some regions even outright failure, of the sustainability transition has created environmental changes that have political and economic repercussions, because increasing levels of resources must be devoted to environmentally related disaster management and adaptation measures. Thus, there is potential for a negative feedback loop to develop. In other words, the failed sustainability transition could force societies to devote increasing resources to adaptation measures, which can come at the expense of additional investments in the sustainability of infrastructures and other socio-technical systems.

Unlike historical comparison cases of other transitions in large-scale socio-technical systems, in the case of the sustainability transition the relationship between the society and the ecosystem changes as a result of the success or failure of the transition. For example, a delay of 50 years in the transition from steam-powered ships and trains to diesel power would have had societal consequences, but the society-ecosystem implications would probably have been negligible in terms of issues such as greenhouse gases, because of the relatively low levels of steam-energy consumption in transportation during that time period. However, a delay of 50 years today in the transition from fossil fuels to low-carbon energy will have dramatic effects on global warming and other environment-society feedback loops. Although the economic and technical outcome of a failed green energy transition may be business as usual (in the sense of continuing growth in energy consumption and ongoing use of fossil fuels), the landscape and ecosystem relations are transformed by the slow, and in some cases blocked, transition to low carbon energy and other technologies associated with reduced environmental impact.

The failure of the sustainability transition implies that governments throughout the world will be turning increasingly to the problem of climate adaptation rather than climate mitigation and sustainable consumption. (One can focus on climate, but it should be understood that there are many other issues of environmental degradation, such as the depletion of aquifers, that result from failures to transition a society to a more sustainable relationship with the ecosystem.) Although something approximating a green energy transition that goes beyond a reduction in carbon intensity will continue to be found in some countries, even in some North American states and provinces, those changes will coincide with the adaptation of socio-technical systems to increasing ecosystem stressors caused by climate change and general ecosystem degradation. For example, in the United States several state governments have already put in place a climate adaptation planning process (Cruce, 2009). Governments will not have a choice to defer investments in adaptation, because climate change will increase the frequency of weather-related disturbances such as severe droughts, floods, ice storms and snowfall that will require an immediate response. Likewise, general resource and food shortages due to land-use policies, economic growth and population growth will create related crises of adaptation. Where resources are not drained in immediate-response mode, preventative resources will be oriented increasingly toward short-term adaptational needs. In many areas of the world, water management and associated land-use politics will become pressing issues, because governments will need to respond to issues of water shortages and floods that have emerged from the interaction of climate change and land-use patterns. In short, alongside the uneven, mitigation transition toward more sustainable systems, there will be another, also uneven, transition toward adaptation to climate change and other ecosystem stressors.

The second major conceptual modification in transition studies for the concept of the landscape involves the need to understand macrosocial political change or stasis not as an exogenous variable but as a dynamic field of interactions characterized by relationships of cooperation and conflict across different levels of government and policy arenas (Fligstein and McAdam, 2011). For example, in the United States, some state governments have developed renewable electricity standards, building-efficiency standards, and various tax credits and financing mechanisms to support the retrofitting and solarization of buildings, but the federal government has failed to enact a basic policy framework such as a renewable electricity standard and a cap on carbon emissions. It has also failed to utilize its position of global economic and political power to develop international agreements to reduce greenhouse gas emissions and to bring the aggregate levels of consumption of the world down to the level of planetary carrying capacity. Instead, within the country a well-funded industry network has fanned skepticism about climate-change science and hostility to green-transition policies, and on the international stage the government has worked to block reforms proposed by other countries. Thus, one finds that the sustainability transition is not only a failure in an ecological sense (in terms of moving at a rapid-enough pace to bring the world's consumption into a Daly-type condition of sustainability), but also uneven (across policy fields governing different technologies and across scales of government).

Case studies of transitions have recognized the emergence of resistance and industrial opposition as part of the transition process (for example, Geels, 2002, 2005). However, historical cases do not always provide a good sense of political conflicts that characterize the sustainability transition in the twenty-first century. The level of sophistication in the resistance to the sustainability transition is considerably higher than in cases such as the transition from horse-drawn vehicles to automobiles. In the United States, the fossil fuel industries have effectively utilized conservative foundations and conservative political organizations to mobilize a broad movement that has reframed the green energy transition as without scientific basis, socialistic and too expensive in a time of economic hardship (Dunlap and McCright, 2011). The rapid and effective counter-mobilization to the green-jobs programs of the first two years of the Obama administration has all but ended any hope of reform on the part of the federal government. The 2010 elections brought to power a wave of anti-green legislators at both the national and state levels. Although reforms have continued in a few states where Democratic Party majorities were retained and governors backed green energy, the overall progress of a green energy transition in the United States is blocked (Hess, 2012).

Furthermore, counter-mobilizations have altered the political culture of sustainability politics by embedding them in ongoing ideological contestations over neoliberalism and social liberalism. In contrast with other socio-technical transitions (such as the shift to internal combustion engines), the sustainability transition requires complex government intervention and planning, because of the problem of impending ecosystem destruction and the need to coordinate the transition of multiple socio-technical systems. The kinds of engagement are more complex and more time-sensitive than the rule-making of regimes associated with, for example, the creation of roads for automobiles or licenses for electricity-transmission lines, in which maturing entrepreneurial organizations and market-driven investments could play a more substantial role. However, the need for government intervention and planning itself has become a central area of contestation in the sustainability transition, thus embedding sustainability politics in ongoing political tensions and debates involving political ideology.[2]

Even in countries where industrial control of the political field and ideological debate is more limited, the situation is only superficially more positive. For example, China has a clear national plan to increase renewable energy and nuclear energy, but it is within the context of overall energy growth. Goals are framed in terms of energy intensity (consumption per unit of gross domestic product) rather than absolute reductions in energy consumption. Consequently, although headlines point to increases in renewable energy production, the current five-year plan allows coal-based energy output to increase as well (Seligsohn and Hsu, 2011). The pattern for China also extends globally; research by sociologist Richard York has shown that although renewable energy production has increased, each unit of growth in nonfossil fuel sources of electricity generation has only displaced one-quarter unit of fossil fuel consumption. Like the Jevons paradox, which shows that efficiency gains can lead to increases in consumption, York's research suggests that an increase in renewable energy does not lead to a one-to-one decrease in fossil fuel consumption (York, 2006, 2010, 2011; see also Herring, 2009).

In summary, the sustainability transition is a political and historical event in which the 'landscape' (in the sense of the long-term, macrosocial processes and changes in society-ecology relations) is itself changed fundamentally by the pace of the socio-technical transition. To develop social science research that can effectively guide policy, it is necessary to have a conception of the landscape as including the dynamic interaction of human and natural systems and as comprised of a contested political field in which power and ideology are central features. The transition to more sustainable socio-technical systems, and corresponding levels and forms of consumption, is also different from many other prior transitions because it requires significant government planning, has a very sophisticated machinery of industrial opposition and is in a state of failure. There are some positive examples of national and subnational governments that are making progress, but the aggregate level of fossil fuel and energy consumption is increasing. In turn, the failure of the transition creates feedback loops that provoke a forced adaptation transition. Because budgets are limited, there is potential for a zero-sum relationship to emerge between the adaptation transition and the sustainability transition. In the long term of a half-century or more, there may be significant progress toward a green energy transition and the decarbonization of the global economy. But in the short term of the first half of the twenty-first century, overall growth in consumption is likely to swamp the slow pace of the sustainability transition. As a result, governments and other organizations will be increasingly forced to respond to problems of adaptation. Research on sustainable consumption will need to incorporate the broader landscape changes involving adaptational pressures to develop policy guidance that is effective in contested political fields.

ADAPTATION, SUSTAINABILITY AND RESILIENCE

The initial configuration of the relationship between climate adaptation and mitigation policies may likely be zero-sum because of limited budgets, but is that the only possible relationship? In other words, can a design perspective on socio-technical systems enable policy makers to develop a positive-sum relationship between adaptation and mitigation? Certainly, the forced transition toward more well-adapted technological systems creates a new political opportunity structure that may be restrictive for advocates of policy reforms for green energy and sustainable consumption. However, it may be possible to design socio-technical systems that integrate the goals of climate adaptation and mitigation. For example, a region that has an urban waterfront on a flood plain may need to expend significant resources to build floodgates, canals and dikes, but it can also explore land-use patterns upstream that both enhance water retention and reduce atmospheric carbon dioxide (CO_2), such as reforestation, more dense development patterns, rain gardens and green roofs. Likewise, in some cases cities that have faced the prospect of rebuilding after a disaster have used the opportunity to construct more sustainable infrastructure (Postgate, 2009).

Just as the primary theoretical concept for thinking about climate change mitigation strategies is sustainability, the primary theoretical concept to date for thinking about ecological adaptation and socio-technical systems is resilience. Resilience is the topic of a substantial literature, including in engineering, security, corporate strategy and socio-ecological systems (see, for example, Berkes et al., 2002; Walker et al., 2004; Sheffi, 2005; Peters, 2008; Cascio, 2009). The common ground that is the basis for the use of the term here is the capacity of a system to maintain essential functions when faced with disruptive perturbations. Increasingly, the literature has also explored issues of resilience with respect to urban policy and design (for example, Newman et al., 2009), and much of the work on resilience and cities is concerned with responsiveness to disasters (for example, Tobin, 1999; Godschalk, 2003; Vale and Campanella, 2005; Rose 2007). Although disaster planning and sustainability are very distinct topics, they come together as a result of climate-related weather instability and general environmental decision making, such as land-use regulations, that affect water flow and quality.[3]

This section focuses on the design of socio-technical systems and its implications for making consumption more sustainable. Decisions by households and organizations about their consumption patterns take place within broader industries and socio-technical systems such as electricity, buildings, transportation and food. The design of those systems establishes frameworks that shape consumer decisions and options, just as consumer decisions also shape the changes that occur in technological systems (Rohracher, 2003; Van Vliet et al., 2005). Thus, the focus on the design of socio-technical systems – in the broad sense of the design of technical features and of organizational, legal and user-technology relationships – is an important aspect of sustainable consumption.

In general, whereas a mitigation perspective seeks design changes that modify socio-technical systems in a sustainability direction, an adaptation perspective modifies socio-technical systems to increase their resilience. For example, in the case of energy supplies, a system is more resilient if it has multiple sources of energy, backup energy sources and local storage. In the case of transportation, the perspective would open political opportunities for the use of alternative fuels, but it might close opportunities for the complete greening of a fleet that is reliant on a single type of energy source (such as electricity from grid-based renewable energy to power both consumer vehicles and public transit fleets). Likewise, for building-energy systems, a resilience perspective would open opportunities for distributed renewable energy because it increases the diversity of energy generation, but it would also recognize the importance of energy storage, multiple types of energy sources (including fossil fuels and renewable energy) and the mixture of both centralized and distributed energy production. In the case of food, a resilience perspective would open opportunities for some localization, but it would balk at complete localization, which would create risks for supply disruption in the event of disasters.

The adaptation transition can potentially open opportunities for the greening of socio-technical systems, but it can also pose limits on the extent and configuration of the greening of a system. To the extent that the greening of a socio-technical system narrows the sources of energy (such as to all solar or renewable energy), it increases the exposure of the system to supply disruptions and decreases the system's resilience. Here, a resilience perspective suggests a change in its pathway of transition toward reconfiguration in the direction of diversity. Conversely, from a sustainability perspective, it may appear to be undesirable to increase the resilience of a system that is based on less sustainable technologies such as fossil fuels. Instead, a sustainability advocate may wish to see lower resilience in older systems to hasten their demise.

The greatest zone of compatibility between resilience and sustainability perspectives in systems design is with the reduction of consumption; reduction both eliminates a drain on resources and the need for resources in the event of a challenge to system resilience. The greatest zone of potential conflict is with highly efficient technologies that are reliant on a single source of inputs and can reduce storage capability, because the reduction of diversity and storage can lead to a reduction in resilience, and an increase in resilience may result in a larger ecological footprint. For example, in the cases of fuels and electricity, a resilience perspective could include a continuing role for fossil fuels, at least as a backup stream of energy sources that improves overall system robustness and flexibility.

The analysis to this point remains focused on the technical issues of system design, or what I term 'material' resilience. A fully sociological approach to the understanding of the relationship between adaptation and sustainability transitions must also include an economic form of resilience. At the household level, material resilience refers to the capacity of a domestic unit to maintain its physical state of resource use, whereas economic resilience refers to its capacity to withstand economic shocks and the economic dimensions of material shocks such as natural disasters (Hess, 2010). Various strategies can increase the economic resilience of a household, such as savings, multiple jobs and social networks. In a similar way, one can also think about the economic resilience of a city or metropolitan area.

The concept of economic resilience is not widely discussed in the literature on cities, and where it has been raised, the focus has been on the capacity of an economy to replenish capital stock in the event of a disaster (for example, Rose, 2007). Although the literature does discuss the economic implications of natural disasters at a city or local level (for example, Cohen 1996; Hallegatte et al., 2011), it has mostly focused on material resilience as a strategy of adaptation, such as changes in land use, zoning in flood plains and infrastructure for stormwater. Economic resilience also should be included as part of the adaptation strategy. Economic resilience can be enhanced by putting in place policies that increase household-level economic resilience, such as by encouraging savings and providing resources for part-time and second jobs. However, an urban or regional resilience approach could also include strategies that make the regional economy as resilient as possible, that is, as capable of withstanding economic shocks as possible. One strategy is to develop a regional innovation system that is capable of creating new technologies and products that can adapt quickly to global market conditions (Cooke, 2008) (see the chapter by Jennie C. Stephens and Stephen M. McCauley in this volume). For example, the economy of Silicon Valley is resilient in the sense that it has been able to develop new industries in response to global economic change. Another strategy is to increase locally owned, independent businesses, because they are unlikely to leave the region and are more likely to purchase from other local businesses (Hess, 2009). Although this point cannot be developed here, a resilient regional economy requires both a regional innovation system and a strong sector of locally owned, independent businesses. That economy can also be made consistent with the development of green businesses (Hess, 2012).

With this background discussion of the concept of resilience in mind, it is now possible to analyze how the politics and design of adaptive systems can be brought into alignment with a sustainability approach. The next section will show that when one brings questions of adaptation and resilience into socio-technical system design (which governs the limits and possibilities of consumption), a much deeper analysis of design is made possible than one purely focused on sustainability criteria. Thus, it may be possible to use the perspective developed here to formulate sustainable consumption policies that are more effective both technically and politically.

ENERGY EFFICIENCY AND DISTRIBUTED RENEWABLE ENERGY GENERATION

Because the transition to a green energy or low carbon economy is central to the sustainability transition, the sector of buildings and energy is a good choice for the study of the relationship between resilience and sustainability. The sustainability transition ideally involves both the reduction of energy consumption and the greening of the type of energy consumed. For example, the transition to sustainable consumption for a building entails increased levels of energy efficiency (EE) and increased levels of renewable energy (RE) consumption. From a sustainability perspective, the main way to analyze the relationship between the strategies is to look at net reductions in a building's ecological footprint (such as how much carbon is saved by an EE or RE shift) and compare them with cost. From a carbon-accounting perspective, it matters little if the RE is supplied over the grid or if it produced on a rooftop; likewise, it matters little where the EE gain is achieved (in an air conditioner versus a refrigerator), provided that lifecycle gains and rebound effects are equivalent. Even the tradeoff of an EE and RE gain can be analyzed in terms of the net reduction of carbon emissions caused by either. Because the focus of attention is on the ecological footprint of a building (for example, operationalized as a reduction of net carbon emissions), many kinds of design choices become technically neutral or black boxed. In other words, an orientation based purely on carbon mitigation or a similar framework is neutral with respect to choices such as rooftop versus grid energy, savings in air conditioners versus refrigerators and so forth, provided that the savings bring about equivalent net reductions in carbon footprints without differential rebound effects. There is a *ceteris paribus* aspect to a purely mitigational perspective that offers little additional guidance on many system-design choices.

However, from an adaptation perspective, other issues become important. In a cold climate, an EE improvement to the heating system is arguably the most important among possible EE changes, because it reduces demand on backup systems in the event of a power failure. Likewise, insulation and weatherization provide temporary resilience in the event of a disruption of energy flow to the building. Distributed renewable energy (DRE, defined as on-site energy generation that is connected with the electricity grid) that has localized storage and a grid connection provides a much higher level of resilience than grid-supplied renewable energy, because the building is prepared to obtain power both from the grid in the event of a system failure of the DRE and from the local system in the event of a failure of the grid. Furthermore, the relationship between EE and DRE is not neutral. Because no amount of EE will be helpful in the event of a power outage, DRE is arguably preferable to EE from an adaptation perspective. In summary, with respect to the consumption of energy by buildings, the adaptation transition will tend to open political opportunities for DRE relative to EE, and it will also alter the preferences within DRE and EE. Thus, an adaptation perspective reconfigures the decision-making criteria for EE and DRE interventions, many of which might otherwise be seen as relatively neutral tradeoffs when the goal is reducing net greenhouse gas emissions from a building.

DRE generation is of general interest for the study of the relationship between the adaptation and sustainability transitions because it has the capacity to serve as a boundary object, that is, as a vague area of convergence that enables political coalitions to form and policies to be built with respect to both mitigation-sustainability and adaptation-resilience transitions (Star and Griesemer, 1989; Hess, 2007). Some forms of DRE and EE can enhance the material resilience of a building but also achieve sustainability goals. Furthermore, to the extent that installation and construction businesses are locally owned, economic resilience for a regional economy (as defined above) can also be enhanced, because expenditures going out of the regional economy for nonlocal energy are captured for recirculation in the local economy (Hess, 2009, 2012). To the extent that the markets for DRE and EE are connected to local technology innovation and manufacturing, they could also be part of a system of regional innovation that increases the resilience of a regional economy.

The following will compare policies for encouraging the financing of DRE and EE at the state and local government level in the United States. Although the suite of policies involving net metering, grid-interconnect standards and licensing of DRE and EE contractors is important, the section will focus only on the policies that provide the financing and other support for building owners who seek to add DRE and EE. To clarify, the policies operate at the interface of a sustainability and adaptation transition; hence, they can be understood as policies that affect sustainable consumption as well as the material resilience of buildings and the economic resilience of building owners. Although there are many barriers to the successful implementation of building-level EE and DRE policies, this analysis will focus on the financial and ownership structure of the programs, because that aspect is where the resilience issues become especially salient.[4]

There are two standard ways to finance DRE and EE improvements. First, third-party agreements rely on private sector investment to fund and maintain DRE such as rooftop solar. The installation is owned by the company rather than the building owner, but the building owner usually receives the benefit of reduced energy costs based on the cost of producing the distributed energy. At the end of the agreement period of 6 to 25 years, the building owner may renew the arrangement, purchase the installation or allow the company to retrieve the equipment. Third-party agreements have the advantage of passing installation and maintenance responsibility over to another party and of stabilizing long-term electricity rates based on DRE, but they achieve the advantages at the loss of local ownership. At the end of the lease, the building owner has nothing other than potential accumulated savings, and economic resilience for the owner has not improved. The service provider generally does not pay for the cost of onsite DRE storage, such as batteries, and consequently there may be few opportunities to increase the material resilience of the building.

A second standard approach is a government-sponsored incentive for DRE and/or EE in the form of tax credits, rebates and loans. The programs are often funded by a system-benefits charge and administered through a state-government agency in partnership with a nonprofit organization and electricity utilities. In effect, the programs represent a transfer from all ratepayers to those who take advantage of DRE and EE potential. The transfer is potentially regressive (a point not lost on conservative opponents) unless it is accompanied by a low-income energy program. The building owner (either a homeowner or commercial building owner) must contract for the energy audit, arrange for the contractor to do the work and set up the financing arrangement if a loan is used. Rebates and credits also require an up-front investment of capital, and loans increase the debt load that can affect the credit of a household or business.

Government-sponsored programs have several advantages over third-party agreements. First, these initiatives often combine DRE and EE incentives, and consequently they are broader in scope. Second, the programs result in a transfer of ownership of electricity generation to the building owner, either in the form of DRE generation or in the more implicit form of energy not consumed because of conservation. Over time, the building owner achieves a positive return on investment (a potential increase in economic resilience) but also has increased material resilience in the form of improvements to the building. Finally, the programs are open with respect to the building owner's preference to include on-site storage and direct generation for the building.

In comparison with third-party agreements, the rebate and loan programs offer greater leeway for enhancing resilience. Economic resilience is increased because the building owner eventually owns a greater portion of the electricity consumed, and the owner is less subject to exogenous price shocks. Furthermore, because the building owner also owns the DRE, it is easier to connect the DRE with on-site storage. That consideration plus the energy-conservation benefits of EE incentives result in lower material dependence on grid-supplied electricity. Thus, there is a valence in local ownership toward increased economic and material resilience for the building.

Although government incentives have been successful, they have several drawbacks that a new generation of DRE and EE financing policies has attempted to address. If a building owner wishes to sell the building, the long-term horizon of the return on investment makes the investment illiquid, and it may not be possible to recoup the investment with an increase in the selling price for the building. The reduced liquidity of the building owner is, in the terminology used here, a factor that reduces economic resilience. Another drawback is the transaction cost associated with finding a contractor and supervising either a DRE or EE building-improvement project. In general, the programs require a fairly knowledgeable person who is willing to work through the maze of government requirements and to supervise a contractor on a building.

For a short period of time, residential property-assessed clean energy (PACE) bonds represented a financial innovation that solved the problems of long-term liquidity. The basic innovation of PACE financing is that the long-term payment on the DRE or EE improvement becomes part of the property tax of the building, so that it can be passed on to new owners. In some cities in the United States, PACE programs for a time provided an 'energy concierge' who helped to reduce transaction costs by guiding building owners through the bureaucratic process. In terms of an adaptation perspective, PACE financing increased economic resilience by making the building investment more liquid in the event that the owner decided to sell the building.

PACE programs grew at a rapid rate after they were first introduced in 2008. Within two years, such initiatives had been approved in half of the states, often with bipartisan support, in 2010 the federal Department of Energy awarded hundreds of millions of dollars to the programs. The

California program was especially large, with over 100 cities poised to participate. However, in May 2010, the Federal Housing Finance Agency (FHFA) ended residential PACE programs because it was concerned that a city's lien was senior to the mortgage instruments that federal agencies held. Although it is commonly assumed that PACE programs died with the FHFA decision, the decision did not apply to commercial buildings. Some holders of commercial mortgages allowed PACE financing, and some banks saw the program as a financial opportunity for new, credit-worthy loans (IBE, 2010). PACE financing for commercial buildings was potentially very large, with estimates as high as $2.5 billion annually by 2015 (Pike Research, 2010). Another option that has emerged is the state of Maine's 'junior lien' arrangement for property-based financing for residential homes. Legal under the FHFA ruling, over 100 cities had adopted ordinances to enable the new PACE loans by the end of 2011 (Efficiency Maine, 2011). Cities were also developing commercial PACE programs, and some states were developing 'on-bill financing,' which refers to programs that allow borrowers to pay back a loan for DRE or EE projects as a line on their utility bill. The loan can be attached either to the property, therefore staying with the building when it is sold, or to the owner, who must pay off the loan when the building is sold. The former approach is most similar to PACE, because it provides the desired liquidity in the event of an unplanned sale.[5]

Because PACE-type programs and on-bill financing recoup investments so that new loans can be made with repaid loans, the economic resilience of the program is greater than for rebate schemes, which simply expend funds on a one-time basis. Furthermore, the programs enhance the economic resilience of a building owner, because they increase liquidity in the event of a forced sale but do not require up-front investment. Moreover, the building owner can sell surplus electricity back to the grid. The programs have a valence toward increased material resilience over third-party agreements because the localization of ownership provides building owners with increased leeway to build the systems in ways that are connected to on-site storage.

DISCUSSION

In summary, an adaptation-resilience perspective creates distinctions that would appear to be neutral or unimportant from a purely sustainability perspective. Those differentiations emerge both in the technical design of system features (choices between and within EE and RE design improvements) and in the design of financial policies that are intended to increase sustainable energy consumption by building owners. Although there are many ways in which adaptation and mitigation policies can be in tension, the example discussed here shows that they can also be brought into fruitful synthesis.

From the perspective of enhancing the sustainability of energy consumption of building owners, there is general recognition of the distinction between two main approaches to energy consumption: energy conservation and greener forms of energy consumed. Policies that favor the installation of DRE replace grid-based household consumption with local solar energy, but they do not necessarily reduce the overall level of energy consumed per household or commercial building. In contrast, EE programs can result in a reduction of household energy consumption, such as fewer kilowatt hours or therms consumed per month for the same household, but they do not address the emissions levels of the remaining electricity that is consumed. Together, DRE and EE approaches to a building could result in positive synergies that reduce the building's overall carbon footprint, provided that rebound effects are controlled.

In contrast, from the perspective of increasing the building's resilience in the face of adaptational stressors, new questions emerge that make the analysis of DRE and EE policies more complex. For example, EE installations do not provide the same level of improvement in material resilience as do DRE installations. If the DRE is connected with local energy storage, such as in the case of rooftop solar with battery storage, then it provides strong material resilience in the event of an electricity outage, whereas EE installations do not help much because they only reduce the need for electricity. However, with respect to the economic resilience of the building owner, EE installations tend to provide a more rapid return on investment, and they are often considered the low-hanging fruit of the greening of buildings. As a result, it is possible that EE would be favored over DRE from an economic resilience perspective even if it would not be favored from a material resilience perspective. There are also differences in the resilience implications within EE or DRE installations. DRE installations that lead to long-term local ownership provide the building owner with greater long-term economic resilience because an asset is acquired over the long term, whereas third-party agreements do not provide the same benefit. Likewise, DRE installations that are financed through a PACE bond or on-bill financing that is tied to the building also increase economic resilience because they allow the building owner to have a better chance at recovering the investment in the event that the property must be sold.

A combination of sustainability and resilience perspectives provides a more holistic analysis of DRE and EE policies. It also may provide a source of hypotheses to test when studying problems of program implementation.

For example, the often-discussed problem of conversion of audits into implemented improvements may be better understood if the effects on economic and material resilience for the household or business are added to the analytical framework. There may also be intangible, noneconomic benefits associated with local ownership and control over the systems that a concept of material and economic resilience helps to articulate.

CONCLUSION

The multiscale, long-term, socio-technical approach to sustainable consumption found in transition studies has enormous benefits. However, the difficult problems of the unevenness and, from a global ecosystem perspective, failure of the sustainability transition draw attention to ways in which transition studies of sustainability can be modified and improved. The ecological ramifications of a slow, uneven and in some cases outright failure to engage in a sustainability transition requires a complex assessment of the ecology-landscape relationship, which in turn benefits from a concept of sustainability that is closer to the Daly approach than the Brundtland approach. As the failure of the sustainability transition deepens, adaptational demands will increase on political and economic systems as well as on consumers. A forced transition, the 'adaptation' transition, will require immediate resources that will potentially drain away resources for investment in sustainable technological systems.

Although the sustainability and adaptation transitions are potentially on a collision course, the relationship is not necessarily zero-sum. A more complex relationship is possible, because the politics of adaptation both open and reconfigure the political opportunity structure for the politics of sustainability. Likewise, the rather modest and uneven progress of the sustainability transition creates opportunities to design more resilient socio-technical systems. In the specific case of energy consumption for buildings such as households and businesses, resilience concerns pose different questions that reconfigure the range of policy interventions to make the energy-consumption patterns of buildings more sustainable. Furthermore, by pushing the conceptualization of resilience further to include both material and economic resilience, it becomes possible to identify new ways in which sustainability interventions might be made more effective.

This analysis is not intended to cover over the rather gloomy prognosis that the transition to a more sustainable society and economy at a global level is occurring too slowly to halt the worst effects of human societies on climate change and environmental degradation. Rather, it is meant to point to a way of assessing the changing politics of the political and economic landscape that has created an alternative adaptation transition and reconfigured the political opportunity structure for the politics of sustainable consumption.

ACKNOWLEDGMENTS

The chapter is based partly on research funded by the Science and Technology Studies Program of the National Science Foundation for the grant titled 'The Greening of Economic Development' (SES-0947429, Grant Number 1156187). Any opinions, findings, conclusions or recommendations expressed here are my own and do not necessarily reflect the views of the National Science Foundation or others who are acknowledged.

NOTES

1. The multi-level perspective of the Dutch school of transition studies includes niches, where new technologies are incubated; stabilized, large-scale socio-technical systems and governing regimes; and broader landscapes of socio-cultural change (see the chapter by René Kemp and Harro van Lente in this volume). Transition studies researchers have recognized the lacunae of a relatively undertheorized landscape and underdeveloped concept of power as areas for which further theoretical development and empirical research is needed (for example, Geels, 2002, 2007, 2011; Avelino and Rotmans, 2009).
2. Naomi Klein (2011) has also made the general argument that the problem of addressing climate change requires government intervention and therefore has, in itself, ideological and political implications.
3. Smith and Sterling (2008) also see potential for thinking about socio-technical systems and sustainability from a resilience perspective. My approach focuses more on contrasts and tensions between resilience and sustainability goals.
4. This section is based partly on research conducted during the summer of 2010 on DRE and EE financing policies at state and local government levels (Hess et al., 2010). The research project involved eight graduate students who developed case studies of green jobs and green economic development policies in approximately two dozen states and cities in the United States. Their work included some interviews about DRE and EE policies, as well as attendance at conferences and analysis of government documents and policy reports. The discussion that follows builds on the empirical base of these interviews and analyses by examining in more detail the financing policies for DRE and EE at state and local government levels. For a review of the policies, see Fuller et al. (2010).
5. More detailed discussions of the different financing approaches are in Farrell (2010a, 2010b), Hess (2012) and Van Nostrand (2011).

REFERENCES

Avelino, F. and J. Rotmans (2009). 'Power in transition: an interdisciplinary framework to study power in relation to structural change', *European Journal of Sociology*, **12**(4), 543–69.

Berkes, F., J. Colding and C. Folke (2002). *Navigating Socio-ecological Systems: Building Resilience for Complexity and Change*, New York: Cambridge University Press.
Cascio, J. (2009). 'The next big thing: resilience', *Foreign Policy*, May/June, available at http://www.foreignpolicy.com/story/cms.php?story_id=4851 (accessed 11 October 2012).
Cohen, M. (1996). 'Economic dimensions of environmental and technological risks: toward a tenable taxonomy', *Industrial Crisis Quarterly*, **9**(4), 448–81.
Cohen, M. and J. Murphy (eds) (2001). *Exploring Sustainable Consumption: Environmental Policy and the Social Sciences*, New York: Pergamon.
Cooke, P. (2008). 'Regional innovation systems, clean technology, and Jacobian cluster-platform policies', *Regional Science, Policy, and Practice*, **1**(1), 23–45.
Cruce, T. (2009). *Adaptation Planning: What U.S. States and Localities are Doing*, Washington, DC: Pew Center on Global Climate Change.
Daly, H. (1990). 'Toward some operational principles of sustainable development', *Ecological Economics*, **2**(1), 1–6.
Daly, H. (1996). *Beyond Growth: The Economics of Sustainable Development*, Boston, MA: Beacon Press.
Dunlap, R. and A. McCright (2011). 'Organized climate change denial', in J. Dryzek, R. Norgaard and D. Schlosberg (eds), *The Oxford Handbook of Climate Change*, New York: Oxford University Press, pp. 144–60.
EEA (European Environmental Agency) (2010). *Household Consumption and the Environment*, EFA Report No. 11/2005, Copenhagen: EEA, available at http://www.eea.europa.eu/publications/eea_report_2005_11 (accessed 11 October 2012).
Efficiency Maine (2011). *Maine PACE Loans*, Augusta, ME: Efficiency Maine, available at http://www.efficiencymaine.com/pace (accessed 11 October 2012).
Farrell, J. (2010a). 'Municipal energy financing', Paper presented at the Southwest Renewable Energy Conference, Santa, Fe, New Mexico, 14–16 September.
Farrell, J. (2010b). 'Municipal energy financing: lesson learned', Institute for Local Self-Reliance, Washington, DC, available at http://www.newrules.org/energy/publications/municipal-energy-financing-lessons-learned (accessed 11 October 2012).
Fligstein, N. and D. McAdam (2011). 'Toward a general theory of strategic action fields', *Sociological Theory*, **29**(1), 1–26.
Fuller, M., C. Kunkel, M. Zimring, I. Hoffman, K. Soroye and C. Goldman (2010). *Driving Demand for Home Energy Improvements: Motivating Residential Customers to Invest in Comprehensive Upgrades that Eliminate Energy Waste, Avoid High Bills, and Spur the Economy*, Berkeley, CA: Lawrence Berkeley National Laboratory.
Geels, F. (2002). 'Technological transitions as evolutional reconfiguration processes: a multi-level perspective and a case study', *Research Policy*, **31**(8–9), 1257–74.
Geels, F. (2005). 'Dynamics of transitions in sociotechnical systems: a multi-level analysis of the transition pathway from horse-drawn carriages to automobiles (1860–1930)', *Technology Analysis and Strategic Management*, **17**(4), 445–76.
Geels, F. (2007). 'Feelings of discontent and the promise of middle range theory for STS: examples from technology dynamics', *Science, Technology, and Human Values*, **32**(6), 627–51.
Geels, F. (2011). 'The multi-level perspective on sustainability transitions:

responses to seven criticisms', *Environmental Innovation and Societal Transitions*, **1**(1), 24–40.
Godschalk, D. (2003). 'Urban hazard mitigation: creating resilient cities', *Natural Hazards Review*, **4**(3), 136–43.
Hallegatte, S., F. Henriet and J. Corfee-Morlot (2011). 'The economics of climate-change impacts and policy benefits at a city scale: a conceptual framework', *Climatic Change*, **104**(1), 51–87.
Herring, H. (ed.) (2009). *Energy Efficiency and Sustainable Consumption: The Rebound Effect*, New York: Palgrave Macmillan.
Hess, D. (2007). 'What is a clean bus? Object conflicts in the greening of urban transit', *Sustainability: Science, Practice, and Policy*, **3**(1), 1–14.
Hess, D. (2009). *Localist Movements in a Global Economy*, Cambridge, MA: MIT Press.
Hess, D. (2010). 'Sustainable consumption and the problem of resilience', *Sustainability: Science, Practice, and Policy*, **6**(2), 1–12.
Hess, D. (2012). *Good Green Jobs in a Global Economy*, Cambridge, MA: MIT Press.
Hess, D., D. Banks, B. Darrow et al. (2010). 'Building clean-energy industries and green jobs: policy innovations at the state and local government level', Science and Technology Studies Department, Rensselaer Polytechnic Institute, Troy, New York, available at http://www.davidjhess.org (accessed 11 October 2012).
Hughes, T. (1987). 'The evolution of large technological systems', in W. Bijker, T. Hughes and T. Pinch (eds), *The Social Construction of Technological Systems*, Cambridge, MA: MIT Press, pp. 51–82.
IBE (Institute for Building Efficiency) (2010). *Property-assessed Clean Energy Bonds: Alive and Well in the Commercial Sector*, IBE, Washington, DC, available at http://www.institutebe.com/clean-energy-finance/pace-finance-commercial-sector.aspx (accessed 11 October 2012).
Jackson, T. (ed.) (2006). *The Earthscan Reader in Sustainable Consumption*, London: Earthscan.
Jørgensen, U. and O. Sorensen (1999). 'Arenas of development: a space populated by actor worlds, artifacts, and surprises', *Technological Analysis and Strategic Forecasting*, **11**(3), 409–29.
Klein, N. (2011). Keynote Lecture at the Annual Conference of the Business Alliance for Local Living Economies, Bellingham, WA, available at http://vimeo.com/25839058 (accessed 11 October 2012).
Newman, P., T. Beatley and H. Boyer (2009). *Resilient Cities: Responding to Peak Oil and Climate Change*, Washington, DC: Island Press.
Peters, K. (2008). 'Government urged to focus on resilience in homeland security', GovernmentExecutive.com, 1 October, available at http://www.govexec.com/federal-news/2008/10/government-urged-to-focus-on-resilience-in-homeland-security/27796/ (accessed 11 October 2012).
Pike Research (2010). *PACE Financing for Commercial Buildings to Reach $2.5 Billion by 2015*, Washington, DC: Pike Research, available at http://www.pikeresearch.com/newsroom/pace-financing-for-commercial-buildings-to-reach-2-5-billion-annually-by-2015 (accessed 11 October 2012).
Postgate, A. (2009). 'A greener Greensburg two years after tornado', *Washington Post*, 7 May.
Rohracher, H. (2003). 'The role of users in the social shaping of environmental technologies', *European Journal of the Social Sciences*, **16**(2), 177–92.

Rose, A. (2007). 'Economic resilience to natural and man-made disasters: multi-disciplinary origins and contextual dimensions', *Environmental Hazards*, **7**(4), 383–98.

Seligsohn, D. and A. Hsu (2011). 'How does China's 12th Five-Year Plan address energy and environment?', Washington, DC: World Resources Institute, available at http://www.wri.org/stories/2011/03/how-does-chinas-12th-five-year-plan-address-energy-and-environment (accessed 11 October 2012).

Sheffi, Y. (2005). *The Resilient Enterprise: Overcoming Vulnerability for Competitive Enterprise*, Cambridge, MA: MIT Press.

Smith, A. and A. Sterling (2008). 'Socio-ecological resilience and socio-technical transitions: critical issues for sustainability governance', STEPS Working Paper No. 8, Centre for Social, Technological, and Environmental Pathways to Sustainability, Sussex University, Brighton.

Smith, A., J.-P. Voss and J. Grin (2010). 'Innovation studies and sustainability transitions: the allure of the multi-level perspective and its challenges', *Research Policy*, **39**(4), 435–48.

Star, S. and J. Griesemer (1989). 'Institutional ecology, "translations," and boundary objects', *Social Studies of Science*, **19**(3), 387–420.

Tobin, G. (1999). 'Sustainability and community resilience: the holy grail of hazards planning?', *Global Environmental Change Part B (Environmental Hazards)*, **1**(1), 13–25.

Vale, L. and T. Campanella (2005). *The Resilient City: How Modern Cities Recover from Disaster*, New York: Oxford University Press.

Van Nostrand, J. (2011). 'Legal issues in financing energy efficiency: creative solutions for funding the initial capital costs of investments in energy efficiency measures', *Journal of Energy and Environmental Law*, **2**(3), 1–16.

Van Vliet, B., H. Chappells and E. Shove (2005). *Infrastructures of Consumption: Environmental Innovation in the Utility Industries*, New York: Routledge.

Walker, B., C. Holling, S. Carpenter and A. Kinzig (2004). 'Resilience, adaptability, and transformability in socio-ecological systems', *Ecology and Society*, **9**(2), 5, available at http://www.ecologyandsociety.org/vol9/iss2/art5 (accessed 11 October 2012).

WCED (World Commission on Environment and Development) (1987). *Our Common Future*, New York: Oxford University Press.

York, R. (2006). 'Ecological paradoxes: William Stanley Jevons and the paperless office', *Human Ecology Review*, **13**(2), 143–7.

York, R. (2010). 'Three lessons from trends in CO_2 emissions in the United States', *Society and Natural Resources*, **23**(12), 1244–52.

York, R. (2011). 'Do alternative energy sources displace fossil fuels?', *Nature Climate Change*, **2**(6), 441–3.

9. Clusters in transition: analysis of a sustainable energy-cluster initiative in Worcester, Massachusetts, USA

Jennie C. Stephens and Stephen M. McCauley

INTRODUCTION

The need to transition to less fossil fuel-reliant energy systems is increasingly recognized throughout the world (Vaitheeswaran, 2003; Holdren, 2006; IPCC, 2011). As powerful social and political forces restrict the shift away from entrenched fossil fuel-based systems at the national and global scales, some cities and municipalities are leading transition efforts.[1] At the scale of individual cities or towns, energy transitions include a myriad of strategies and practices including both promoting renewable methods of energy production and reducing energy consumption through social and technological changes related to energy conservation and efficiency. At the municipal level, implementing change in energy systems requires engagement, mobilization and coordination among a diverse set of organizations, individuals and urban energy consumers, including homeowners, renters, business owners, local governments and other local institutions (see the chapter by Sabine Hielscher, Gill Seyfang and Adrian Smith in this volume). Catalyzing an urban energy transition therefore involves enabling and empowering these stakeholders to make choices that support renewable energy and reduce energy consumption. Emerging work on energy use and consumption demonstrates that these individual and organizational choices are most likely to occur in the context of broader changes in values, lifestyles and cultural norms (Seyfang et al., 2010).

Conceptual work on sustainability transitions has increasingly recognized the importance of cultural change in the transition process. The earliest research on socio-technical transitions expanded the notion of technological change by locating innovation not only within firms but in the broader social and institutional contexts that coevolved with large technical systems. The multi-level perspective (MLP) emerged as a central conceptual model for understanding these transitions (see, for example,

Genus and Coles, 2008; Smith et al., 2010). In this framework, transitions occur when entrenched regimes experience significant pressures simultaneously from different levels, including competition from innovative niche technologies and social practices, shifts in the larger social and technical landscape and internal contradictions or challenges within the existing regime. As these pressures align, alternative socio-technical configurations can compete with and potentially displace entrenched regimes (Geels, 2005; Smith et al., 2005; Loorbach, 2007).

The socio-technical transitions framework was developed on the basis of historical analyses of prior transformations. As the framework has increasingly been applied to understanding and informing emerging sustainability transitions, with the goal of supporting these shifts, it has revealed a richer set of actors and social dynamics involved in the transition process, including community-led initiatives, grassroots innovations, social networks and collective learning processes. These developments are seen as critical for creating the broader cultural conditions in which changes in behaviors and social practices can take place. In the context of sustainable energy transitions, reducing energy demand through technological change and the advent of new social practices and social values are seen as critical first steps in initiating an energy transition. Consumer behavior also plays a key role in supporting novel energy-production technologies that provide potential alternatives to the entrenched fossil fuel regime.

As the social and economic benefits of an energy transition have come to be increasingly recognized, the potential of creating 'green jobs' through various green economic development initiatives has also attracted considerable attention (see the chapter by David J. Hess in this volume). One regional approach to promoting green jobs and developing a local green economy involves applying the cluster strategy of economic development to the sustainable energy sector. Based on the long-established notion that geographic clustering of related economic activities promotes innovation and other positive externalities among firms (Marshall, 1920), many cities, regions and countries around the world are actively pursuing sustainable energy-cluster initiatives (Benzaken, 2011; McCauley and Stephens, 2012). These cluster approaches generally focus on attracting innovative firms, promoting interactions between firms and other supporting institutions such as government agencies and universities, and generally facilitating supply-side dynamics with the intent to generate creative learning regions that can compete in global markets.

The sustainable energy sector, however, challenges conventional assumptions embedded in the cluster strategy. While the cluster strategy is founded on a growth-based economic paradigm concerned with supporting globally competitive firms, energy transition involves a broad-based cultural change that relies on the empowerment and participation of a diverse group of regional stakeholders. Many initiatives aimed at achieving energy transition at the community or city level are in fact based on alternative 'new economy' values that disavow growth as the singular goal of development (see the chapters in Part I of this volume). Sustainable energy clusters thus embody conflicting values and approaches to sustainability transitions. Are they simply extensions of the growth-based paradigm, albeit one oriented around ecological modernization? Or do they present an avenue through which alternative energy values and practices can reshape and possibly displace the existing energy regime? Resolving these questions can inform and expand both cluster theory and our understanding of transition dynamics.

This chapter explores these questions through a case study of a regional sustainable energy-cluster initiative in Worcester, Massachusetts in the northeastern United States. We examine the emerging form and structure of the green energy cluster and ask how the cluster initiative is contributing to mobilizing social and technical change in energy consumption and production in the area. We also explore how the application of a cluster strategy in the sustainable energy sector challenges and broadens conventional notions of clusters. In particular, we are interested in the extent to which community-based initiatives that rely on the empowerment of locally embedded energy users are engaging with the business-led, growth-based cluster initiative and the implications of this engagement on the evolution of the cluster.

The aims of this chapter are to understand the development of one regional sustainable energy-cluster initiative and to use the empirical details of the case to provide a context for exploring connections, synergies and tensions between economic development cluster initiatives and socio-technical transitions for sustainability. We first provide overviews of cluster theory and socio-technical transitions, focusing on the role of community-based initiatives in the transition process and then describe an integrated framework that considers the dynamics and intersections between a sustainable energy cluster and socio-technical transitions. We subsequently discuss the empirical details of the sustainable energy-cluster initiative in Worcester. The development of the case study is based on insights accumulated from multiple sources including interviews with key actors, an observer-participant-researcher role involving the researchers and review of secondary documents including formal reports, minutes of meetings and news articles. Respondents included participants from public sector agencies, private sector organizations, universities and citizens groups, as well as politicians and citizens. The final section of the chapter considers the ways in which sustainable energy clusters both challenge cluster theory and expand sustainability transition frameworks.

GREEN CLUSTERS AND SUSTAINABLE ENERGY TRANSITIONS

The Cluster Strategy for Regional Economic Development

Over the last decade, the public policy strategy of stimulating the development of industrial clusters has emerged as a primary objective in regional economic development (Porter, 2000; Martin and Sunley, 2003). The strategy is based on the assumption that firms experience positive externalities, or agglomeration economies, associated with their geographic proximity to related firms – either horizontally linked firms engaging in cooperation or competition or vertically linked suppliers and producers – and that the competitive advantages for clustering firms generate spillover effects for the regional economy (Bethelt et al., 2004; Deutz and Gibbs, 2008). While some clusters have emerged independent of public support (Atherton, 2003), many recent cluster initiatives have been proactively encouraged through engagement by local governments that strive to build on existing regional strengths to foster growth in a specific sector. Hundreds of cluster initiatives have recently been developed around the world seeking to create the conditions that allow cluster advantages to emerge and invigorate local, regional or national economies (Solvell et al., 2003).

Cluster initiatives generally focus on technology-intensive sectors that are seen to have high growth potential and to benefit particularly from spatial clustering among firms. Knowledge-based theories of clustering emphasize how the geographic proximity of firms in these sectors promotes collaborative learning, innovation and growth. In particular, interactive learning occurs through observational and interactive knowledge building (Vincente and Soire, 2007), labor mobility (Saxenian, 1994) and formal and informal interactions among private sector actors in a region (Gertler, 2003; Bethelt et al., 2004; Casper, 2007), as well as contact among institutions, including universities, that provide critical institutional 'thickness' (Amin and Thrift, 1995). In addition, externalities are derived from shared cultural traditions and habits within a specific industrial cluster, the development of social norms and routines in a region and the quality of local institutions (Saxenian, 1994; Amin, 1999). Face-to-face engagement and trust-building are also seen as important externalities (Malmberg and Maskell, 2005). Ultimately, learning regions emerge when a 'buzz' of activity and information exchange is created around innovative sectors (Bethelt et al., 2004).

The application of cluster theory to the sustainable energy sector derives from the same principles that have guided cluster developments in other sectors. Sustainable energy clusters have the primary aim of stimulating local and regional economic development by creating the conditions that attract and promote innovative firms in the area of sustainable, renewables-based energy systems (KanEnergi, 2007; Porter et al., 2008). Firms engaged in renewable energy technologies, smart-grid technologies and transportation solutions are particularly sought, as these are seen as high growth sectors with potential to address critical sustainability challenges and to solidify and advance a region's knowledge-based economy. It is expected that sustainable energy firms will benefit from the same agglomeration economies that have long benefited clustering firms, and that the advantages accrued by individual firms will generate economic spillovers that will promote dynamism in the local and regional economy.

In addition to the economic imperatives that motivate other cluster initiatives, sustainable energy clusters seek to catalyze a transformation in regional energy systems by harnessing the innovations of local firms. This objective rests on the expectation that locally embedded firms will establish proof-of-concept enterprises in the region and thus transform the region into a living laboratory in which new technologies and market innovations will provide the foundations of a local green economy. The same strategies that have been utilized in conventional cluster initiatives to promote agglomeration economies among firms, such as fostering networks, promoting education and expertise, and aligning regional policies and institutions to support the clustering industry, are also critical for coordinating efforts to transform regional energy systems.

Socio-technical Transitions

The dynamics through which complex socio-technical systems transition to new configurations have been widely explored. The MLP has become the central conceptual framework for framing and analyzing socio-technical transitions (Rip and Kemp, 1998; Geels, 2002, 2010; Smith et al., 2005). Strategic niche management has emerged as a policy agenda explicitly based on the notion of supporting niche experimental activities as 'protective spaces' in which alternative projects and initiatives, and related social processes such as knowledge, experience and resource transfer, can develop (Smith et al., 2005). Specific efforts have also focused on destabilizing entrenched regimes and supporting larger societal pressures that could foment a sustainability transition. Much research has focused on elaborating and expanding the basic MLP model to reveal the complex social dynamics involved in the transition process. Learning and innovation at the niche level have been explored (Smith, 2007; Brown and Vergragt, 2008), as has the role of different transition contexts in terms of the level of proactive coordination and the presence of resources from within or outside the system (Smith et al., 2005) (see the chapter by René Kemp and Harro van Lente in this volume).

Considerations of space and the benefits of geographic proximity have been integrated into some work on socio-technical transitions (Truffer, 2008; Coenen et al., 2010; Spath and Rohracher, 2010). But the need for more attention to geography within the MLP literature has been recently acknowledged (Smith et al., 2010). Considering the potential for clusters to contribute to and interact with socio-technical transitions provides one approach to integrating space and geography into the MLP literature.

Recent research has turned toward the cultural dimensions of sustainability transitions. This work recognizes that the behaviors and practices of resource users are critical to a sustainability transition. However, simple rational actor models of decision making are rejected in favor of a more socialized account of how individual consumers transform their practices. Seyfang et al. (2010), for example, argue that decision making and behavior changes at the individual and organizational levels are most likely to occur in the context of broader changes in values, lifestyles and cultural norms. Seyfang and Smith (2007) expand the MLP model with a grassroots-innovation model that describes how grassroots organizations and social movements promote the critical cultural shifts that are necessary for enabling and empowering individuals to make behavioral changes regarding recourse use. The chapter in this volume by Sabine Hielscher, Gill Seyfang and Adrian Smith similarly shows how bottom-up, community-based projects can facilitate energy transitions by supporting engagement, empowerment and exchange of social capital and trust among local actors. Still, the MLP framework remains largely a supply-side perspective on socio-technical transitions, thus leaving the integration of consumption patterns as a significant challenge.

Recent work on the importance of cultural change, social practice and consumer values in transition processes raises concerns that are far outside the scope of economic-cluster initiatives. Whereas cluster initiatives emphasize the importance of supply-side dynamics in generating vibrant, innovative regions with high economic growth potential, socio-technical transition frameworks increasingly point to the importance of behaviors, practices and cultural expectations related to energy consumption. Perhaps most importantly, much of this research on sustainability transitions points to the emergence of new economic values inherent in transition movements such as the Transition Towns in the UK. These social values, which favor a locally resourced, exchange-balanced economy and a wider set of social concerns – including health, security and equality – compete with the firm competitiveness strategy that undergirds conventional cluster initiatives.

Expanding and Integrating Clusters and Transition Frameworks

Theories of both economic clustering and socio-technical transitions have been used to inform local and regional sustainable development policies. While integration of these different notions of social change is occurring in practice, theoretical perspectives related to these approaches have been largely considered separately. Bringing these concepts together highlights the potential for synergistic alignment of multiple social priorities. Sustainable energy-cluster initiatives can be conceptualized as a coordinated effort to facilitate a collection of niche activities within a region by supporting the development and implementation of new technologies and social practices. Niche activities within a sustainable energy cluster have potential to influence change in both local and global energy regimes. Furthermore, sustainable energy clusters have undoubtedly developed in response to landscape-level concerns related to climate change and the need to reduce fossil fuel dependence and regime instability associated with the price of energy. Despite potential for synergies, uncertainty exists about whether and how economic clusters are capable of supporting socio-technical transitions. On the one hand, to the extent that sustainability transition requires a broad-based development agenda that is not accommodated by the growth-oriented approach, the cluster strategy may work against the long-run goal of a sustainable energy transition (see the chapter by David J. Hess in this volume). On the other hand, the locally embedded social networks and institutional coordination resulting from a cluster initiative could help catalyze an expansive sustainable energy movement with capacity to trigger changes in values, lifestyles and practices required to achieve energy sustainability. Reconciling tensions and highlighting synergies between these two notions may provide some useful insights.

The sustainable energy sector differs significantly from other knowledge-based sectors (for example, biotechnology, information technology) and requires attention to local energy cultures and social practices. Whereas cluster initiatives in other knowledge-based sectors typically seek to compete in global markets, the market for products and services of the sustainable energy sector has greater local potential due to the possibility for deployment within the region. The market for sustainable energy technologies and services, particularly those related to efficiency, requires diffusion of practices throughout a community and therefore relies significantly on social norms and societal contexts. Technological solutions for reducing energy consumption and improving energy efficiency also often entail low-tech interventions that are unlikely to generate the rapid profits that attract significant investment and firm growth. Furthermore, as increasing numbers of localities pursue sustainable energy development, the notion of clusters as unique growth poles may be replaced by a view of sustainable energy systems as a widely shared goal subject to specific local constraints. This embeddedness of energy systems requires and/or welcomes a broader conceptualization of clusters that explicitly acknowledges engagement and mobilization of a broad array of stakeholders with power to influence energy-consumption patterns and practices.

While recognizing the incompatibilities between conventional approaches to economic clusters and the imperatives of a sustainability transition, some components of the cluster strategy may nonetheless be valuable in promoting a sustainability transition. The geographic proximity of sustainable energy activities and the 'institutional thickness' that develops when interests align to support the sector could have great influence on a sustainable energy transition. The creation of local or regional buzz, and the ability for local social innovation involving people communicating directly and personally, may be critical in linking different stakeholders and expanding multi-sectoral interactions and social learning. For a cluster initiative to contribute to a sustainability transition, it must move beyond business-centered objectives to stimulate a broad sustainable energy movement in the region. Such a strategy would likely require participatory decision making that involves a wide range of stakeholders and forums that support open dialogue among them, and perhaps new or different intermediary organizations to facilitate communication and interaction. While conflicts and tensions will certainly arise in such an initiative, particularly around economic development values, the cluster strategy may help mobilize a sustainability transition.

THE SUSTAINABLE ENERGY-CLUSTER INITIATIVE IN WORCESTER, MASSACHUSETTS

The sustainable energy-cluster initiative in Worcester officially began in 2008 when a Massachusetts politician, Congressman Jim McGovern, approached the presidents of two of the city's private universities, Clark University and Worcester Polytechnic Institute (WPI), and asked them to assess their institutional strengths related to sustainable energy and to identify potential opportunities for a sustainable energy-cluster initiative in the region. A multi-sectoral steering committee was established to develop an organizational structure to facilitate what was envisioned as a center for economic revival based on the emerging 'green economy' in Worcester and Central Massachusetts. An intermediary organization, the Institute for Energy and Sustainability (IES), was created and supported with funds from the Massachusetts Clean Energy Center and with logistical support from the universities, and an executive director for IES was hired in November 2009. While IES assumed the mandate to lead the cluster initiative, several other multi-stakeholder groups were concurrently emerging in the area with a particular focus on reducing energy consumption from buildings.

This section explores the empirical details of the sustainable energy-cluster initiative in Worcester. First, background on the region and its experiences with a previous cluster initiative in the biotechnology sector are described. A summary of the region's sustainable energy-transition context is then provided, based on the three-level framework of the MLP model.[2] The landscape-level pressures influencing the region are reviewed first, followed by descriptions of the existing entrenched energy regime and the emerging niche-level sustainable energy activities, technologies and practices. With this context firmly established, we offer an in-depth description of the region's sustainable energy-cluster initiative.

Background on Worcester and the Region's Previous Cluster Initiative

Central Massachusetts is generally considered to be the area of the state located west of metropolitan Boston and east of Amherst and the Berkshire Mountains. The largest urban area in the region is Worcester, a mid-sized city with a population close to 185 000 people that lies approximately 45 miles (72 kilometers) west of Boston. Similar to other post-industrial cities, Worcester faces the challenge of generating new sources of economic vitality. The city grew and prospered in the years between the Industrial Revolution and World War II with a focus on metalworking and machine tools, but faced economic decline through the second half of the twentieth century. More recently, from 2001 to 2007, Worcester lost more than 2200 jobs, 2 percent of its total employment. Along with a shrinking labor force, the city's labor force participation rate has been declining. Also over the past several years, the weakening economy and the slowdown in the housing market have negatively affected property values, reducing municipal tax revenues. At the same time, city expenditures, primarily salaries and benefits, have been increasing. In spite of these challenges, a robust knowledge-based sector has developed in Worcester over the last several decades, led by the biomedical/life sciences, health services and higher education sectors. The city has experienced growth within each of these sectors over the last few years (City of Worcester, 2004; WMRB, 2008). The greater Worcester area is home to 13 colleges and universities that combine to serve 30 000 students and employ 11 000 people.

The recent development of a sustainable energy-cluster initiative in Worcester has been motivated in large part by the city's successful biotechnology-cluster initiative which, since its inception in the early 1980s, has been a key driver of regional growth. The biotechnology-cluster initiative grew out of the committed engagement of a group of civic-minded business leaders and the strong support of city and state governments and local universities. An intermediary organization, the Massachusetts Biotechnology Research Institute (MBRI), was created with the mission of incubating new biotechnology companies and promoting industry-academic partnerships. An associated biotechnology park has expanded over the years and attracted various high-profile tenants and an incubator initiative has over time transformed into a for-profit venture capital entity. The biotechnology cluster has become an increasingly important anchor in the regional economy, and a key component in the state's economic development initiatives. Recent biotechnology developments at the University of Massachusetts Medical School, WPI, the Massachusetts Biomedical Research Park and elsewhere in the region have resulted in thousands of new jobs. This development has shifted the employment structure of the city such that the leading employers are currently the hospitals and the associated medical service organizations.

Massachusetts has long been recognized as a state with a highly educated and skilled knowledge-based workforce. During the 1990s, the state became a leader in information and innovation-based industries, technology and entrepreneurialism, and Massachusetts has consistently ranked very highly as a state with an economy that matches the ideal structure of the new economy (Atkinson and Andes, 2008). The success of the biotechnology-cluster initiative in Central Massachusetts reflects a number of factors, one of which is the high collaborative disposition among sectors in the region. This attribute of cross-sectoral engagement is frequently mentioned by people in the region, including politicians, university administrators and actors from the private sector. As a second-tier city situated in the shadow of Boston and Cambridge, many in Worcester openly express a need for cooperation among different sectors.

Despite the current economic challenges in Worcester and Central Massachusetts, a sense of optimism and untapped potential is common in the region. As one stakeholder we interviewed described, 'Worcester today is just a very different place from what it was 20, 25 years ago. There's life, there's confidence, there are people as a residential center, it's kind of coming back.' The sustainable energy-cluster initiative comes in the context of a now mature local knowledge-based economy, and increased growth in knowledge-based industries nationally and globally.

The Landscape-level Context for Green Energy in Central Massachusetts

Sustainable energy activities in Worcester reflect the broader landscape of energy transition, including climate and energy policy at the national and international levels. Policy formation at both levels currently faces significant hurdles and uncertainties. At the international level, the global impact of the Kyoto Protocol, which has been extended until 2017, is questionable and confidence in the ability of the international negotiations process to develop effective policy is waning. The United States, the world's largest economy and one of the largest generators of greenhouse gases, plays an important role in international climate negotiations, yet the American political system has been an obstacle to the formation of national climate policy.

While the failure of the United States to formulate a national climate policy is inhibiting both global climate policy and the creation of incentives that would speed deployment of nonfossil fuel energy options domestically, cities and states across the country are taking a lead role in advancing climate action via a bottom-up strategy (see the chapter by David J. Hess in this volume). Massachusetts is a state with relatively high public climate change awareness and concern compared to other parts of the country. Along with nine other northeastern states, Massachusetts established the nation's first cap-and-trade regime for large power plants through the Regional Greenhouse Gas Initiative (RGGI), and has been ranked second only to California among leading clean energy states in terms of regulatory and financial incentives, knowledge capital and economic and workforce development (Clean Edge, 2010). In 2008, the state passed comprehensive energy reform legislation through the Green Communities Act (GCA) that promotes the production of renewable energy in the state by requiring utilities to enter into financing partnerships with renewable energy developers, promoting net metering and allowing utilities to own solar installations on residential rooftops. It also established the Green Communities Program (GCP) that provides up to $10 million per year to municipalities to implement efficiency and renewable energy technologies.

The landscape of energy transition in Central Massachusetts has also been shaped significantly by the Great Recession and its aftermath. Massachusetts was not as heavily affected by the post-2008 financial crisis as other states due to its industrial mix, relatively small share of overall economic activity based on housing production, virtually no automobile-related manufacturing, and high concentration of technology and science-based goods and services (Clayton-Matthews, 2009). Still, the availability of private capital for development projects has been significantly tightened as the cost of borrowing has risen and the terms on which money is being lent have become more conservative. The response to the financial crisis in the United States was the American Recovery and Reinvestment Act of 2009, an economic stimulus package that aimed to create jobs and promote investment. Particular areas targeted for increased federal spending included education, healthcare and infrastructure, including the energy sector. The sectors that have benefited from these funds in Massachusetts include 120 companies in the green energy sector and 114 additional solar projects that produce 20.7 megawatts of power in the state, including solar installations at public facilities. In Worcester County (the political jurisdiction in which the city is located), the majority of clean energy and environment funds were awarded to the city's anti-poverty group, Worcester Community Action Council (WCAC) that, through its fuel and energy programs, provides energy-audit services and appliance upgrades (Simon, 2010).

In addition to basic improvements in household energy efficiency, the energy upgrades have begun to increase opportunities for service providers in the Worcester region. However, while stimulus-supported energy-efficiency activities will likely continue for several years, there is concern that the increase in energy-related economic activities will reverse when the one-time influx of the stimulus funds is exhausted.

The Entrenched Energy Regime in Central Massachusetts

The entrenched socio-technical regime is understood to be the relatively stable, reinforcing configuration of technologies and infrastructures, as well as the institutions, rules, practices and networks that define the system (Rip and Kemp, 1998). The circumstances in Central Massachusetts reflect the region's development around fossil fuel energy for electricity, heating and transportation, with a small but growing renewable energy sector.

Massachusetts is a net electricity importer, meaning that electricity production in-state is less than electricity demand and consumption. Massachusetts residential customers pay substantially more for electricity than the national average, and prices have risen markedly since 2004 due largely to the increased price of natural gas which is the dominant fuel for electricity generation within the state. In 2009, the electricity-generation mix in Massachusetts included 43.6 percent from natural gas, 22.8 percent from petroleum, 12.2 percent from coal, 5 percent from nuclear, 4.1 percent from renewables and 12.3 percent from pumped storage. The state does not have any known coal or oil deposits and has one operating nuclear plant, the 690 megawatt capacity Pilgrim Nuclear Generating Station on Cape Cod Bay, about 75 miles (120 kilometers) from Worcester. Massachusetts has a deregulated, competitive market for electric power.

With regard to heating, Massachusetts is heavily reliant on oil, with close to 50 percent of its home heating provided by oil with natural gas, electricity and wood also used. The region experiences a cool climate with a long and severe heating season. The Worcester housing stock is comprised largely of older wooden structures, particularly the characteristic triple-deckers that were built to accommodate factory workers in the early twentieth century.

The transportation system in Worcester reflects the general structures of suburbanization and automobile dependency characteristic of metropolitan areas throughout the United States. Transportation, accounting for 31 percent of all energy consumption in Massachusetts, is almost entirely fossil fuel based. The region has some public transportation, including a municipal bus system operated by the Worcester Regional Transit Authority and a commuter rail line to Boston, but schedules and routes are limited and most residents use automobiles. Changes in the transportation sector face the daunting challenges of overcoming path dependency in interdependent infrastructural systems such as refueling stations, parking arrangements and highway networks.

Niche-level Green Energy Activities in the Region

A variety of niche-level activities associated with sustainable energy have emerged in the Worcester region over recent decades, many of which have evolved from grassroots and community-based organizations. The region's tradition of quasi-rural, small town autonomy, its conservation-oriented environmental ethos, and its high density of universities and innovative research centers have supported the emergence of multiple experimental sustainable energy activities. The Holy Name Central Catholic Junior/Senior High School installed the first wind turbine in Worcester with technical assistance from WPI students, while a local community development corporation installed solar panels on ten affordable housing units in the city. Private sector initiatives in the renewable energy sector have increased substantially in the last decade. One business leader who was interviewed described the Central Massachusetts region as a 'hotbed' of activity with respect to renewable energy.

These niche activities have been supported and encouraged by a range of institutions. The nonprofit sector's involvement in sustainable energy is increasing, and includes the Regional Environmental Council (REC), a grassroots organization with a focus on environmental justice and sustainability, as well WCAC and the Worcester Green Jobs Coalition (WGJC). State-funded programs, particularly the Massachusetts Technology Collaborative (MTC), also support niche-level sustainable energy activities in the city. Moreover, the region's universities have increasingly embraced a leadership role in responding to sustainability challenges (Stephens et al., 2009). In 2007, the municipal government approved a climate action plan that committed the city to ambitious reduction targets for greenhouse gas emissions, and the city created a new position of energy manager to facilitate ongoing energy improvements. Under the energy manager, Worcester has greatly expanded it activities supporting energy efficiency and renewable energy production. While niche-level activities continue to emerge, the need for enhanced communication and coordination to achieve the synergistic potential of these different initiatives was acknowledged by some key actors.

The Worcester Sustainable Energy-cluster Initiative

The establishment of IES is seen by many people in Worcester as a critical milestone in the development of the region's cluster initiative. The mission of IES has been described in different ways, but it generally includes benefiting the city and the surrounding area by creating green jobs, increasing energy efficiency and reducing greenhouse gas emissions, supporting the establishment of Worcester as a national leader in sustainability and facilitating research in the science of sustainability and sustainable technologies. Key strategies to accomplish these objectives include branding the region as a nationally competitive green business zone and attracting, growing and retaining green businesses through zoning, permitting and tax incentives. In addition, supporting research at the universities (including hydrogen fuel-cell research at WPI and socio-technical transitions research at Clark University) and supporting and coordinating workforce development, training and outreach to increase energy efficiency within the community have been articulated as key strategies (IES, 2010, 2011). While the central goals focus more on supply-side dynamics, the objective associated with increasing energy efficiency has resonated strongly with several grassroots organizations and some of the university stakeholders. The IES quickly recognized the importance of demand-side factors, as can be seen in their coordination of a multi-stakeholder weatherization roundtable in November 2010 focused on economic opportunities related to weatherization (that is, enhancing building energy efficiency) and its involvement throughout 2011 in bringing electric car charging stations to several communities in the region.

A strong network of grassroots and community-based organizations, university actors and initiatives, and others engaged in citywide sustainability efforts has been growing since the sustainable energy-cluster initiative began in 2008. The degree to which the expansion of these initiatives has been encouraged by or is connected with the official state-funded sustainable energy-cluster initiative is questionable, but the parallel progress being made in multiple sectors within the city and region is undeniable. The REC is an active agent of sustainability in the community through such programs as its YouthGROW urban farming and environmental justice programs. The organization has recently expanded its engagement in energy issues by facilitating the access of homeowners to a state-funded home energy assessment program. The WGJC works for resources to create green jobs that are supportive of the local community, culture and individual needs. Among its activities, it has supported the formation of the EMPOWER Energy Coop, a grassroots initiative in which former prisoners in the Worcester area produce biodiesel fuel from waste vegetable oil. The group has provided a space for a wide range of actors and organizations committed to facilitating green business creation and development and a healthy and just community. The Worcester Energy Barnraisers (WEB) is an all-volunteer effort that promotes environmental sustainability and social and economic justice through collaborative home 'energy barnraising' projects that allow participants to learn and implement efficiency upgrade skills. The WCAC has coordinated most of the federal stimulus funds that the city has received through its energy-efficiency program for low-income residents.

These grassroots initiatives have played a critical role in representing and advancing the interests of energy consumers in the city. Several of these organizations seek to forge linkages between consumers and support programs, and in doing so they help facilitate the emergence of a market for energy-efficiency upgrades and the diffusion of knowledge about energy sustainability. For example, even when incentives are available, residents are often unaware of the programs or have difficulty navigating their requirements. These groups also ensure that the operative discourse of energy transition in the context of the cluster initiative includes consideration of consumer needs and interests. The mission and activities of these groups include a central focus on inclusive decision making and access for low-income and other marginalized communities, and these concerns are regularly expressed in the context of multi-stakeholder forums. Many of these actors collaboratively hosted a Green Solidarity Economy

Conference in 2011 that brought together individuals and organizations in the city working toward progressive social, environmental and economic goals to share resources and skills, strengthen inter-organizational relationships and advance community sustainability.

The municipal government has also been a key player in recent energy-related developments in the region. The city's sustainable energy activities are coordinated through the City of Worcester's Executive Office of Economic Development and its Department of Administration and Finance through the jointly appointed energy manager. Economic development officials in the city are charged with implementation of the city's climate action plan that establishes a set of climate-response goals and a series of activities that result from them. Primary initiatives on this front include outreach for energy efficiency, managing stimulus funds related to residential energy-efficiency upgrades and implementing several solar and other renewable energy projects from the general capital fund. The city has contracted with the private sector to support its efforts by hiring a large international consulting company to manage aspects of its energy-efficiency outreach and a Minnesota-based firm to provide significant energy-efficiency upgrades to over 80 municipal and school buildings by using projected savings to finance municipal bonds.

In May 2010, Worcester was designated as one of the state's 53 Green Communities, a significant feat given the city's size and substantial industrial legacy. The designation was achieved by satisfying five criteria: as-of-right siting for renewable energy projects; expedited permitting for eligible energy companies; design of a 20 percent municipal energy reduction plan; formulation of a policy for the purchase of fuel-efficient vehicles; and adoption of an enhanced energy-efficient building code. Upon being selected, the municipal government released a statement saying that the Green Communities designation will 'enable the City to market itself on a regional, national and global basis as a City that is attractive to companies in the green energy sector, thus boosting our economic development, business attraction and expansion activities' (City of Worcester, 2004). While this language reflects the familiar, production-side goals of cluster initiatives in other sectors, the activities in which the city is engaged and that have positioned the city as a Green Community have much more to do with supporting demand-side initiatives and transitioning local energy systems.

The region's universities have played a key role in the cluster initiative since its inception. In addition to providing logistical support to the establishment of IES, both Clark University and WPI are involved in multiple niche-level green energy initiatives ranging from developing institutional climate action plans, to building energy-efficient buildings (several of them certified under Leadership in Energy and Environmental Design or LEED), to faculty and student research in areas of green energy. Machflow Energy, based in the physics department at Clark University, is developing a green air-conditioning technology and received support from the federal Department of Energy through Recovery Act funds. The fuel-cell center at WPI is an industry-university alliance that seeks to advance fuel-cell technologies and revolutionize the generation of power. Quinsigamond Community College, one of the region's community colleges, is also actively engaged in providing renewable energy training programs. Moreover, several colleges and universities in the area have built certified sustainable buildings, and students and faculty from these institutions have been engaged in multiple regional green energy projects and initiatives.

The private sector is of critical importance in the expansion of regional sustainable energy activities. The clean energy sector recently overtook textiles as the tenth largest industry in the state and there is some shared perception among the business community that Central Massachusetts already hosts a burgeoning cluster of clean energy companies (LeClaire, 2008). Firms identify the supportive role of city and state government, as well as the region's strong manufacturing tradition that has shifted toward more complex, technical manufacturing, as strengths of the sector. By contrast, some actors from other sectors in the city perceive a decline in the civic leadership role of the business community as the regional economy has shifted away from the large manufacturing companies that previously played this role. The corporate conference organized by IES in March 2010, however, attracted over 100 community leaders, many from the business community, and demonstrated considerable support from the private sector. A preliminary survey of clean energy firms in the region conducted by IES identified 63 companies in Worcester County that were in some way connected to clean energy activities. Of the major utility companies, National Grid has been particularly involved in green cluster developments, providing financial support for IES and developing an ambitious smart-grid pilot project that awaits state approval. The Worcester Chamber of Commerce has also recently engaged in supporting activities in the sustainable energy sector.

The overall sustainable energy initiative in Worcester is characterized by multi-sectoral breadth and increasing integration among networks. The degree to which this integration is due to efforts by IES to facilitate cluster development is uncertain, as multiple innovative forums are emerging to bring together actors from very different sectors within the region. One such forum, Worcester Housing, Energy, and Community (WoHEC), was created in 2009 by actors at Clark University to bring together community groups, business leaders, local government officials and university researchers to explore a large-scale strategy to enhance energy sustainability in the city's residential housing (Vergragt and Brown, 2010). The group has been meeting monthly under a broad agenda of exploring ways that energy retrofits could promote economic benefits, social justice and energy sustainability, and it continues to attract participants and generate research, knowledge-sharing and implementation practices.

A similar collaboration was formed initially around requests for proposals for a community-development grant issued by a federal agency. Coordinated by Clark University faculty in conjunction with IES, this group includes many of the participants in WoHEC, along with several university vice-presidents, planners from other municipalities in the region, staff from the regional planning commission, representatives from WCAC and students. The process of drafting the proposal strengthened connections among the universities, community organizations and municipal government. While IES, the intermediary organization established to stimulate initial cluster activities, remains an identifiable center point, in practice the cluster initiative has come to comprise a broad collection of horizontally related organizations and actors, including those representing energy consumers.

DISCUSSION

This review of the evolving Worcester sustainable energy cluster provides insights on both the conflicting and synergistic potential of applying the economic-cluster strategy to the sustainable energy sector. The emerging form and structure of this cluster initiative demonstrates a complex array of stakeholders with a spectrum of different visions as to the potential direction for regional change. While the cluster initiative seems to be contributing to mobilizing both social and technical change in energy consumption and production in the region, the initiative is nascent and assessment of its success to date is difficult. Still, analysis of this case demonstrates how the application of a cluster strategy to the sustainable energy sector challenges and expands conventional notions of clusters. This case also highlights both tensions and potential synergies between community-based initiatives with a focus on justice and local jobs and the business-oriented, growth-based conventional cluster vision that some stakeholders maintain. The extent to which the sustainable energy cluster might contribute to a socio-technical sustainability transition will depend on multiple factors including how well the cluster focus aligns with and contributes to new cultural sensibilities surrounding energy and changes in lifestyle practices.

Moving from a Supply-side Focus to Integration of Demand-side Practices

The cluster strategy for regional economic development rests on almost a century of analysis of the agglomeration tendencies of firms in related industries. Cluster initiatives, as a policy strategy, aim to cultivate the conditions that promote agglomeration economies in a city or region, but when applied to the sustainable energy sector the potential for the cluster notion to expand to integrate demand-side practices becomes evident. The developing sustainable energy cluster in Worcester demonstrates an important shift from the conventional supply-side focus of cluster initiatives toward the integration of demand-side dynamics.

IES (the state-supported intermediary organization spearheading energy-cluster implementation) defines itself primarily as a 'green business zone' and most of its efforts have followed the conventional model of clusters, focusing on attracting and supporting firms involved in energy production. While some stakeholders are disappointed that IES has not significantly embraced or supported community-level energy consumption and cultural change, the organization has incorporated multiple demand-side initiatives. The weatherization roundtable and the work it has done bringing electric car charging stations to the region are examples of initiatives that move beyond a production orientation and instead focus on initiatives that support change in energy-consumption patterns. Meanwhile, the multi-sectoral forums comprising nonprofit agencies, university actors and other stakeholders have advanced numerous initiatives aimed at supporting shifts in energy-consumption patterns. Specific strategies include offering home energy audits, devising innovative funding mechanisms that allow individual home and business owners to invest in energy upgrades and supporting social networks that facilitate social and behavioral changes related to energy practices.

The Worcester case demonstrates the great potential of wide-ranging community engagement, communication and stakeholder participation in a sustainable energy cluster. This is in contrast to much of the cluster literature in which local consumption is largely absent from economic theories of agglomeration and from the policy interventions derived from them. Much of the economic activity associated with an energy transition involves relatively rudimentary solutions and services aimed at enhancing energy efficiency at the scale of individual buildings, including homes, schools and businesses. Even where new low carbon technologies are developed, their uptake relies on diffusion among a diverse community of individual decision makers. In this context, green energy sector development must include cultivating a market of local consumers for energy-efficiency upgrades and small-scale energy-production technologies.

Expanding Cluster Leadership and Membership

A central objective of economic cluster initiatives is to cultivate the institutional base supporting cluster activities. These efforts have typically focused on connecting development agencies and autonomous political actors to business organizations and firms (Amin, 1999). This case of a sustainable energy cluster points to a reorganizing of relationships among actors and organizations involved in the cluster, and suggests a need for participation and engagement by a much broader constituency than other clusters. While some actors within the Worcester sustainable energy cluster still view the initiative primarily as a business-development endeavor, firms and business leaders are not the sole actors or even the primary decision makers, as other actors have assumed strong leadership positions. In the Worcester case, educational institutions have played a particularly strong role. They have spearheaded the cluster initiative, provided space for multi-sectoral forums and are increasingly emerging as possible lead developers in real estate development projects associated with cluster activities. While universities have long been recognized as key actors in cluster formation, an expanded role in this case is related to several factors. Universities nationwide, as well as globally, have shifted toward greater engagement in community-development activities as they have become more entrepreneurial. In the context of current economic volatility, universities are also acting as critical anchor organizations providing a stable institutional and economic presence that can support local and regional economic activity. As nonprofit, public interest institutions, they also have a stronger mandate to address noneconomic aspects of cluster development, including social justice and environmental concerns.

Grassroots and community groups have also played a key role in shaping the sustainable energy-cluster initiative, and activity in this sector plays a critical role in creating the larger social change required for a transition. Numerous nonprofit organizations have been active participants in cluster activities organized by IES, including roundtable events and networking opportunities, and in numerous other forums and events. Through both formal and informal channels, the values and rationales of the community groups, some of which are in direct opposition to the premises of the business-development initiative, come to influence the cluster's evolution. For example, several community groups have advanced a vision of energy transition centered on environmental justice and local autonomy in resource decisions. While this position conflicts with the growth-oriented perspective of the business community, the effect has been a widening of the discourse around energy transition such that business leaders in the community and representatives from IES now increasingly include in their framing of energy transition notions of local sustainability and inclusive access to decision making.

Creative Tensions

The Worcester case demonstrates how a sustainable energy cluster challenges conventional assumptions embedded in the cluster strategy and highlights the potential for conflicting missions. While the cluster strategy is founded on a growth-based economic paradigm concerned with supporting regional competitiveness, the notion of a sustainable energy transition requires broad cultural change that relies on the empowerment and participation of diverse group of regional stakeholders. The details of this case do not provide a definitive answer to the question of whether a sustainable energy cluster is simply an extension of the growth-based paradigm or whether sustainable energy clusters may provide a mechanism for change to alternative energy values and practices that could reshape, and possibly displace, the existing energy regime. This case does highlight, however, the complexity of coordinating different visions of green economic development.

While IES is the official organization designated to encourage cluster development, multiple other forces well beyond this intermediary organization are influencing the evolution of the cluster. In several interviews skepticism, distrust and even resentment from some stakeholders toward IES and its 'business orientation' were evident. During the first two years of IES's development and the evolution of the sustainable energy-cluster initiative, a constant challenge has been effectively ensuring a sense of participation and engagement from a diverse set of stakeholders. Some individuals associated with these organizations are unfamiliar with the IES initiative and others are knowledgeable but do not feel they have a place or mechanism for participating in and contributing to the initiative. This sense has been expressed by actors from local environmental nongovernmental organizations (NGOs) as well as people associated with the academic communities. In contrast, other stakeholders have expressed appreciation for what IES has accomplished so far, as well as optimism for its potential to influence change in the future.

The tensions between different visions of sustainability in the region are expressed as both specific conflicts around process and representation and as more general issues of mistrust related to differing values and agendas.

Some stakeholders have perceived an institutional emphasis on connecting with corporate leaders and potential new business opportunities to the neglect of community outreach, engagement and implementation activities. The top-down approach from state political leaders and IES's focus on national competitiveness leaves some grassroots activists feeling excluded and reinforces the belief that other important sustainability concerns are secondary to economic growth. Meanwhile, certain actors from grassroots organizations have expressed reluctance to engage at all with the private sector out of frustration from past experiences and an assumption that their values are irreconcilable. Just as trust is routinely cited as the most important factor in stimulating firm-to-firm interaction in conventional economic clusters, overcoming these tensions and establishing inter-sectoral trust is critical to creating the 'buzz' required to achieve a sustainable energy transition.

CONCLUSION

This integrated consideration of clusters and transitions in the Worcester sustainable energy-cluster case contributes a different approach and some new depth on the importance of local context, community and geography in socio-technical transitions. This case illustrates that the potential of a cluster initiative to advance a sustainable energy transition and the influence it can have beyond economic development depends on whether it can align with – and contribute meaningfully to – cultural change around energy consumption and production practices. Integrating the theoretical and practical elements of clusters and sustainability transitions in the analysis of this case suggests opportunities for more intentional synergies. Those involved in advancing the sustainable energy cluster could benefit from a broader perspective that includes the goal of stimulating a socio-technical transition. The unique nature of the sustainable energy sector, notably the active and important role played by community groups and the critical convening role of educational institutions, suggests that the evolution of Worcester's sustainable energy cluster will be quite different from other economic cluster initiatives.

The goals of the nonbusiness organizations differ significantly from the original business development goals of IES. To the extent that these organizations contribute to and help define the cluster, they shift or broaden the priorities of the initiative. Where conventional clusters generally aim to enhance the locality's competitiveness in the globally integrated high-technology economy, a sustainable energy-cluster initiative also aims to cultivate a local market for sustainable energy technologies and services, both sophisticated and rudimentary. Contributions from grassroots and community organizations and local higher education institutions have reframed the energy-transition process to include other urban development concerns such as community health, school quality, access to jobs with livable wages, and their involvement has expanded participation in decision making pertaining to cluster development and enhancing the local economy. These efforts have contributed to shifting the goal of the cluster initiative to include not only regional competitiveness and local jobs, but also consumption patterns, lifestyles and sustainability.

While IES and some other actors remain primarily focused on business development, the larger sustainable energy movement in the Worcester area encompasses a wider set of actors with a diversity of values and rationales. A shared goal of these individuals and organizations is to transform the city's socio-technical systems related to energy and housing. While we do not seek to downplay the tensions between different visions of sustainability in the region, the case suggests that there is room for synergy between business-oriented green energy initiatives and grassroots and other community-based efforts. Our initial research into the cluster initiative in Worcester showed two distinct pathways toward a sustainable energy transition – a business-oriented vision based on attracting new firms and achieving competitiveness in national and global green technology markets and a community-based vision that emphasizes local actors and institutions, developmental goals beyond economic growth and a diverse sustainable energy economy spanning multiple sectors. The case study moreover reveals the high degree of interaction and interdependence among stakeholders supporting these different visions, with a synthetic discourse and the beginnings of a policy agenda. Ultimately, a sustainable energy transition is most likely to occur if all sectors within the city embrace the challenge of an energy transition and, whether working collaboratively or in creative competition, contribute to a regional buzz around sustainable energy.

This exploration of Worcester's sustainable energy-cluster initiative demonstrates that a cluster strategy can have a positive motivating and encouraging influence on existing community-based initiatives to work toward a socio-technical transition. New multi-stakeholder collaborations and new mechanisms for communication among sustainable energy stakeholders have emerged in response to the official creation of the cluster as represented by the establishment of IES. With regard to the breadth of sectoral participation in the overall initiative, it is clear that there is a diversity of actors and organizations actively engaged and involved, including individuals and organizations from both private and public sectors, as well as higher education and NGOs. Some of these participants are more focused on the conventional cluster notion of attracting new firms and creating economic development through sustainable energy businesses, while others are focused on reducing energy consumption by supporting a combination of technical and social change. This breadth, conjoined with the diversity of focus within the cluster, offers opportunities for systemic social and cultural change, but also provides challenges for communication, leadership and implementation.

ACKNOWLEDGMENTS

The authors thank the Mosakowski Institute for Public Enterprise at Clark University for financial support for this research. In addition research collaborators Mary-Ellen Boyle, Jing Zhang, Lisa Kwiatkowski, Angela Marshall and Hila Benzaken are gratefully acknowledged for their contributions to this work. Thanks also to the editors of this book and the anonymous peer reviewers for valuable feedback and direction that greatly improved this chapter. We finally extend our appreciation to all of the people who gave their time to be interviewed and our university and community partners in the Worcester region.

NOTES

1. For a useful overview, see the website of Sustainable Cities International at http://sustainablecities.net/citiesnetwork (accessed 10 January 2012).
2. Here we have used the MLP to describe the local dynamics of one place – Worcester, Massachusetts. The cluster analysis describes innovative activities within the region as niche-level and explains how the existing energy regime and landscape-level influences are experienced in that location.

REFERENCES

Amin, A. (1999). 'An institutionalist perspective on regional economic development', *International Journal of Urban and Regional Research*, **23**(2), 365–78.

Amin, A. and N. Thrift (1995). 'Institutional issues for the European regions: from markets and plans to socioeconomics and powers of association', *Economy and Society*, **24**(1), 41–66.

Atherton, A. (2003). 'Examining clusters formation from the 'bottom-up': an analysis of four cases in the north of England', *Environmental and Plannning C*, **21**(1), 21–35.

Atkinson, R. and S. Andes (2008). *The 2008 State New Economy Index: Benchmarking Economic Transformation in the States,* Washington, DC: Information Technology and Innovation Foundation.

Benzaken, H. (2011). 'Developing a green economy in Worcester, Massachusetts', Unpublished Master's thesis, Department of International Development, Community, and Environment, Clark University.

Bethelt, H., A. Malmberg and P. Maskell (2004). 'Clusters and knowledge: local buzz, global pipelines and the process of knowledge creation', *Progress in Human Geography*, **28**(1), 31–56.

Brown, H. and P. Vergragt (2008). 'Bounded socio-technical experiments as agents as systemic change: the case of a zero-energy residential building', *Technological Forecasting and Social Change*, **75**(1), 107–30.

Casper, S. (2007). 'How do technology clusters emerge and become sustainable? Social network formation and inter-firm mobility within the San Diego biotechnology cluster', *Research Policy*, **36**(4), 438–55.

City of Worcester (2004). *Utilizing Worcester's Colleges and Universities to Promote Economic Development and Expansion of the Tax Base*, Worcester, MA: City of Worcester.

Clayton-Matthews, A. (2009). 'The plunging Massachusetts economy', Presentation at the Mccormack Graduate School of Policy Studies, University of Massachusetts-Boston, 23 January.

Clean Edge (2010). *A Future of Innovation and Growth: Advancing Massachusetts' Clean-energy Leadership*, Portland, OR: Clean Edge.

Coenen, L., R. Raven and G. Verbong (2010). 'Local niche experimentation in energy transitions: a theoretical and empirical exploration of proximity advantages and disadvantages', *Technology in Society*, **32**(4), 295–302.

Deutz, P. and D. Gibbs (2008). 'Industrial ecology and regional development: eco-industrial development as cluster policy', *Regional Studies*, **42**(10), 1313–28.

Geels, F.W. (2002). 'Technological transitions as evolutionary reconfiguration processes: a multi-level perspective and a case-study', *Research Policy*, **31**(8–9), 1257–74.

Geels, F. (2005). 'The dynamics of transitions in socio-technical systems: a multi-level analysis of the transition pathway from horse-drawn carriages to automobiles (1860–1930)', *Technology Analysis and Strategic Management*, **17**(4), 445–76.

Geels, F. (2010). 'Ontologies, socio-technical transitions (to sustainability), and the multi-level perspective', *Research Policy*, **39**(4), 495–510.

Genus, A. and A.-M. Coles (2008). 'Rethinking the multi-level perspective of technological transitions', *Research Policy*, **37**(9), 1436–45.

Gertler, M. (2003). 'Tacit knowledge and the economic geography of context, or the undefinable tacitness of being (there)', *Journal of Economic Geography*, **3**(1), 75–99.

Holdren, J. (2006). 'The energy innovation imperative: addressing oil dependence, climate change, and other 21st century energy challenges', *Innovations, Technology, Governance and Globalization*, **1**(2), 3–23.

IES (Institute for Energy and Sustainability) (2010). *2010 Interim Report: Focusing on Jobs, Energy and Science*, Worcester, MA: IES.

IES (Institute for Energy and Sustainability) (2011). *IES's 2011 Strategic Plan: Jobs, Energy and Science*, Worcester, MA: IES.

IPCC (Intergovernmental Panel on Climate Change) (2011). *Summary for Policymakers: IPCC Special Report on Renewable Energy Sources and Climate ChangeMmitigation*, New York: Cambridge University Press.

KanEnergi (2007). *Green Energy Clusters: Stimulation of Renewable Energy*

Markets through the Establishment of Regional Clusters, Skara, Sweden, available at http://www.kanenergy.com (accessed 7 June 2010).
LeClaire, J. (2008). 'Sustainable Boston: green-tech's rise spurs competition among its advocates', *Boston Business Journal*, 24 November, available at http://www.bizjournals.com/boston/stories/2008/11/24/focus12.html (accessed 7 June 2012).
Loorbach, D. (2007). *Transition Management: New Mode of Governance for Sustainable Development*, Utrecht: International Books.
Malmberg, A. and P. Maskell (2005). 'Localized learning revisited', *Growth and Change*, **37**(1), 1–18.
Marshall, A. (1920). *Principles of Economics*, New York: Macmillan.
Martin, R. and P. Sunley (2003). 'Deconstructing clusters: chaotic concept or policy panacea?', *Journal of Economic Geography*, **3**(1), 5–35.
McCauley, S. and J. Stephens (2012). 'Green energy clusters and socio-technical transitions: analysis of a sustainable energy cluster for regional economic development in Central Massachusetts, USA', *Sustainability Science*, **7**(2), 213–25.
Porter, M. (2000). 'Location, competition and economic development: local clusters in a global economy', *Economic Development Quarterly*, **14**(1), 15–34.
Porter, M., J.-H. Kwek, C. O'Neil, A. Satchcroft and T. Vogt (2008). 'The Australian renewable energy cluster: microeconomics of competitiveness', available at http://www.isc.hbs.edu/pdf/student_projects/australian_renewable_energy_2008.pdf (accessed 6 June 2011).
Rip, A. and R. Kemp (1998). 'Technological change', in S. Raynor and E. Malone (eds), *Human Choice and Climate Change*, Columbus, OH: Battelle Press, pp. 327–99.
Saxenian, A. (1994). *Regional Advantages: Culture and Competition in Silicon Valley and Route 128*, Cambridge, MA: Harvard University Press.
Seyfang, G. and A. Smith (2007). 'Grassroots innovations for sustainable development: towards a new research and policy agenda', *Environmental Politics*, **16**(4), 584–603.
Seyfang, G., A. Smith and N. Longhurst (2010). 'Grassroots innovations for sustainable development', *Economic Sociology*, **12**(1), 67–71.
Simon, J. (2010). 'Commonwealth conversations: Engage! Recovery and reinvestment', Worcester Community Action Council, Worcester, available at http://www.wcac.net/spotlight.html (accessed 5 June 2011).
Smith, A. (2007). 'Governance lessons from green niches: the case of eco-housing', in J. Murphy (ed.), *Framing the Present, Shaping the Future: Contemporary Governance of Sustainable Technologies*, London: Earthscan, pp. 89–109.
Smith, A., A. Stirling and F. Berkhout (2005). 'The governance of sustainable socio-technical transitions', *Research Policy*, **34**(10), 1491–510.
Smith, A., J.-P. Voβ and J. Grin (2010). 'Innovation studies and sustainability transitions: the allure of the multi-level perspective and its challenges', *Research Policy,* **39**(4), 435–48.
Solvell, O., G. Lindquist and C. Ketels (2003). *The Cluster Initiative Greenbook*, Stockholm: Bromma tryck ab, available at http://www.cluster-research.org (accessed 10 January 2012).
Spath, P. and H. Rohracher (2010). '"Energy regions": the transformative power of regional discourses on socio-technical futures', *Research Policy*, **39**(4), 449–58.
Stephens, J., M. Hernandez and M.-E. Boyle (2009). 'Learning from university-community partnerships (past and present) for sustainable development',

Working Paper No. 2009–04, George Perkins Marsh Institute, Clark University, Worcester, Massachusetts, available at http://www.clarku.edu/departments/marsh/news/workingpapers.cfm (accessed 5 June 2011).

Truffer, B. (2008). 'Society, technology, and region: contributions from the social study of technology to economic geography', *Environment and Planning A*, **40**(4), 966–85.

Vaitheeswaran, V. (2003). *Power to the People: How the Coming Energy Revolution will Transform Industry, Change Our Lives, and Maybe Even Save the Planet*, New York: Farrar, Straus and Giroux.

Vergragt, P. and H. Brown (2010). 'Managing urban transitions: visioning and stakeholder collaboration – a case study in transforming residential housing in Worcester, MA', Working Paper No. 2010–10, George Perkins Marsh Institute, Clark University, Worcester, Massachusetts.

Vincente, J. and R. Soire (2007). 'Informational cascades versus network externalities in locational choice: evidence of "ICT" clusters' formation and stability', *Regional Studies*, **41**(2), 173–84.

WMRB (Worcester Municipal Research Bureau) (2008). *Benchmarking Economic Development in Worcester*, Worcester, MA: WMRB.

PART III

Social practice theories

10. Sustainable lifestyles in a new economy: a practice theoretical perspective on change behavior campaigns and sustainability issues

Bente Halkier

INTRODUCTION

The mainstream policy agenda on environmental issues has changed since the end of the 1980s. In most developed countries, the focus has shifted away from an emphasis on pollution problems with technical solutions and an imposition of responsibility on public authorities toward recognition of complex global problems in need of a variety of governance strategies, including the active involvement of citizens. Accordingly, to improve sustainability, public policies, private organizations and businesses have called upon ordinary consumers to contribute to the process (Seyfang, 2006; Tukker et al., 2008; Rumpala, 2011).

One of the dominant ways in which this ascription of responsibility to citizens as individual consumers has occurred has been through the application of change behavior campaigns through various types of media (Kolandai-Matchett, 2009; Shove and Walker, 2010; Hargreaves, 2011). Such efforts have entailed the formulation of strategic communication initiatives (for example, newspaper and television advertisements, posters, websites and postings on electronic social networks) in which the intent is to persuade members of a so-called target group to alter their routines (Windahl et al., 1998; Dervin, 2003). In other words, mediated communication is being used to regulate ordinary consumer's everyday lives (Halkier, 2010).

These behavior change campaigns are frequently constructed on the basis of assumptions developed from traditional models for target-group analysis (McQuail, 1998; Craig, 2007). Several types of target-group models have been deployed in sustainability change behavior campaigns, but the two most frequently used approaches are the deficit model (Hansen et al., 2003; Eden, 2011) and the segmentation model (Dahl, 2005; Rokka and Uusitalo, 2008). Despite their differences, the traditional models for target-group analysis share a blind spot in how they conceptualize consumption in everyday life. Most notably, these approaches both fail to recognize the complexities of everyday life as a context of consumption. Thus, the deployment of these models in public campaigns implies several potential consequences for sustainability policies, as well as for everyday life. Sustainability policies run the risk of applying inefficient instruments and everyday life is in danger of becoming disempowered and disciplined (Jacobsen and Dulsrud, 2007).

A practice theoretical perspective on consumption (Shove, 2003; Warde, 2005) holds more potential for grasping the complexities of everyday life agency, change and reproduction. Recent conceptual syntheses of practice theoretical concepts in relation to consumption research offer a framework that is sensitive to the multiplicity of social conditioning and the dynamism of everyday life. At the core of this work is an understanding of social life as performativity. This means that social life consists of activities people have to do – to carry out, to perform and to get done. Compared with the two most frequently used models in target-group analysis, there are several analytical benefits that accrue from using practice theories to study how consumers engage with change behavior campaigns motivated by sustainability objectives (Halkier and Jensen, 2011).

This chapter proceeds as follows. First, I present and discuss the traditional models of target-group analysis in relation to change behavior campaigns and highlight specifically how they have been applied in the field of sustainable consumption. Second, I outline some of the foundations of practice theories. Third, I describe several of the key contributions in consumption research that have emerged on the basis of practice theories and assess their relevance for how consumers respond to change behavior campaigns on sustainability issues. Fourth, the chapter outlines two analytical challenges for the use of practice theories in research on sustainable consumption. Finally, I discuss some possible implications for understanding everyday agency in relation to sustainability issues and planned communication.

TARGET-GROUP MODELS, CONSUMPTION AND SUSTAINABILITY

As mentioned above, target-group models comprise the most frequent way to understand consumption within the context of change behavior communication campaigns. Target-group analysis, or at least target-group models as assumptions about communication users, is an integral part of formulating so-called planned communication by public and private organizations (Windahl et al., 1998; Dervin, 2003). There are numerous target-group models, but the two that are most commonly used in the field of sustainable consumption are the deficit model and the segmentation model.[1]

The deficit model typically entails quantitatively mapping the consumer characteristics of single individuals to measure how they influence one another. The variables of interest are generally knowledge, attitude and behavior and the emphasis is on assessing the relationships and gaps among these different dimensions. It is assumed that there are (or at least ought to be) strong correlations between, for example, consumers' familiarity with sustainability issues, their attitudes toward sustainability and their everyday decisions and actions (for example, Thøgersen, 2006; Vermeir and Verbeke, 2006; Fraj and Martinez, 2007; Whitmarsh, 2009). The model is referred to as the deficit model because it is assumed that citizens and consumers are deficient in something – be that knowledge, the correct attitudes or other resources (Eden, 2011). In terms of concrete change behavior campaigns, a fictional example on climate change would focus on supplying the individual consumer with correct and sufficient information about the climate effects from meat consumption and give directions about how to cut down on the use of meat in household meals.

The deficit model, as well as other similar models for target groups and change behavior campaigns, is widely used not only in actual public campaigns but is also prominent in research on sustainable consumption (Jacobsen and Dulsrud, 2007). The prevalence of this approach is attributable to its ostensible ability to measure and quantitatively compare factors in relation to planned communication and behavior change.

However, the main problem with the deficit model is its presumption of rational action (Gronow and Holm, 2008). Consumption patterns are understood to be consequences of cognitive motivations and rational choices, which leaves little room for including other dimensions of consumption in everyday life, especially their cultural, social and contextual elements. In the fictional example about climate change and meat consumption, the cultural, social and contextual significance and use of meat are not taken into consideration. Meat is not only consumed or avoided to work against or facilitate a sustainability agenda. More probably, meat is eaten or not as a part of taste patterns, negotiated relations within the household, logistics of everyday practicalities and numerous other tacit considerations.

The segmentation model covers types of analysis and campaigns where evidence of the expression of consumer lifestyles is mapped and the individual consumer is categorized according to a typology and placed in a particular lifestyle segment. There is in this approach often a focus on consumption as reproduced patterns of taste and social status that are related to the location of the individual consumer in larger social structures of class and culture (see also the chapter by Emily Kennedy, Harvey Krahn and Naomi Krogman in this volume). In this kind of model of target-group analysis, it is assumed that there are strong relations between social belonging, cultural frames of reference and habituated routines, and it is furthermore supposed that an individual can be placed unambiguously as a member of one segment (for example, Sanjuan et al., 2003; Didier and Sirieix, 2008; Rokka and Uusitalo, 2008; Zia and Todd, 2010). Going back to the fictional example of a climate change campaign, the 'consume less meat' message would be constructed to appeal to tastes and status values belonging to a particular segment of the consumer population. This could be a segment that has already been mapped and identified to express tastes for meals with less meat and for valuing environmental protection as a sign of social status (so-called 'locavore' or LOHAS (lifestyles of health and sustainability) consumers, see Campbell et al., 2010). Alternatively, a survey could map, on the basis of questions regarding tastes and values about food and climate, and geared to a segment of highly educated urban women who would be more prone to respond positively to such a campaign (Lawson and Todd, 2002).

Segmentation models are also often a prominent part of planned communication campaigns and in the literature on sustainable consumption (see, for example, Boström and Klintman, 2008). Part of the explanation for this uptake could be that these approaches offer a conceptualization of collectively shared patterns of consumer lifestyles. Lifestyles, and more particularly changing of lifestyle patterns, have been important facets of debates about sustainable consumption because the strength of the concept comes from its ability to take into account the socially and culturally structured conditions of routines. Segmentation models recognize that there can be collectively shared lifestyle patterns that hinder transitions to novel routines or render such changes more difficult. For example, scaled back meat consumption clashes with social norms of what men are expected to eat in distinct social groups.

However, there are two main problems with these types of models. The first is that these general approaches assume a fairly high degree of stability in the social and cultural conditions for consumption patterns and leave little room for consumer agency and more complex relations between reproduction and change. Turning back to the fictional climate change example, it is not certain that members of the ecofriendly consumer segment reduce their meat consumption every week as there is often a difference between general characteristics of a social group and actual specific performances. The second problem is that proponents of such models assume that an individual can be placed in a specific segment, but such a designation is likely to ignore variations in expressions and behaviors across different situations, contexts and social relationships. In the fictional example, an alleged ecofriendly consumer may eat new Nordic porridge on Wednesday and then have steak on Saturday.

Other models of target-group analysis for change behavior campaigns attempt to correct for some of the problems discussed above in relation to the deficit and segmentation models. Some of these approaches are based on social network communication (for example, Rogers, 1995) and on communities of practice understandings (Lave and Wenger, 1991). The social network communication models presuppose that behavior is more easily changed if social interaction among consumers' network relations supports such changes. Communities of practice models assume that behavior is more easily adapted if such adjustments form an integral part of a practice already shared with others, such as colleagues or families. Thus, both of these types of models for target groups include the importance of social dynamics.

I now turn to a discussion of a theoretical framework for consumption that is capable of understanding the complexities of social dynamics in reproduction and change in everyday life, namely practice theories. This theoretical framework could potentially be combined with network communication models or communities of practice models, thus providing more realistic and meaningful perspectives on changes of consumption habits in everyday life.

PRACTICE THEORIES

Practice theories revolve around the concept of social practices. Regardless of other theoretical differences, most practice theories focus on the processes of carrying out social life. It is the details and conditions in how ordinary activities are socially done that practice theories are intended to conceptualize. This way the debates about practice theories and their uses in empirical research can be seen in light of continuing social scientific discussions about actor-structure relations. Such considerations are also often at the center of analyses and discussions about sustainable lifestyles.

The (re)turn toward social practices as a central concept in social and cultural theorizing has not produced a coherent practice theory. Rather, there are multiple theories of practices that are part of classic social and cultural theories (for example, Foucault, 1978; Giddens, 1984; Bourdieu,

1990; Turner, 1994), contemporary attempts to synthesize these elements (Reckwitz, 2002; Schatzki, 2002) and work to develop syntheses in different academic subfields (Swidler, 2001; Thevenot, 2001; Couldry, 2004; Warde, 2005; Gherardi, 2009; Røpke, 2009). In relation to sustainability, practice theories have, for example, been developed in the context of ecological economics (Røpke, 2009), technological and social change (Shove, 2003) and consumption routines (Nye and Hargreaves, 2010). This theoretical multiplicity is not necessarily an analytical disadvantage for the study of sustainable lifestyles. Instead of seeking to apply theory in completely consistent and coherent ways, this pluralism opens up possibilities to explore the complexities of a particular field and to combine them with other relevant approaches that dovetail with practice theoretical assumptions (see, for example, Truninger, 2011).

The theoretical roots of current syntheses of practice theories are usually ascribed to a composite of concepts and ideas about social action from the work of Pierre Bourdieu (1990), Anthony Giddens (1984), Michel Foucault (1978), Judith Butler (1990) and Bruno Latour (1993). It is of course impossible to do justice here to five complicated sets of theoretical work, so this discussion points to the central elements upon which recent syntheses in practice theories draw. First, current practice theories draw heavily on the concepts of habitus and field articulated by the French sociologist Pierre Bourdieu. Habitus denotes people's embodied and tacit dispositions for understanding and acting, learned through their experiences over time and across different activities. Fields constitute the limits and conditions for such experiences, but with room for action. Second, the work of the British sociologist Anthony Giddens, and particularly his structuration theory, is an important element of current practice theories. With structuration theory, Giddens attempted to redefine the relationship between actors and structures toward a relation between flows of acting and structures that are both resources and conditions for acting. Third, current practice theory draws on the writings of the French historian and philosopher Michel Foucault with special attention devoted to his post-structural understanding of the relations between people's bodies, societal discourses and social regulation of practices. Fourth, Judith Butler emphasizes the performative character of people's activities by which she means how activities are carried out and understood is a continuous practical and discursive accomplishment. Finally, current practice theories are inspired by Bruno Latour's conception of actor-network theory (ANT) that articulates the interdependence between materiality and social life.

The most cited and debated current syntheses of practice theories is Andreas Reckwitz's (2002) sociological effort to locate practice theories in relation to other cultural theories and Theodore Schatzki's (1996, 2001,

2002) social philosophical development of concepts in the constitution of social life (see the chapter by Gert Spaargaren in this volume).[2]

Reckwitz (2002) positions practice theories in relation to two other grand conceptual approaches within sociology and cultural theory. Practice theories are understood as different from what he refers to as 'cultural mentalism,' which is meant to cover, for example, such well-known and otherwise quite distinct theoretical understandings as rational choice (for example, Ajzen, 1991) and phenomenology (for example, Luckmann, 1989). Reckwitz argues that in cultural mentalism, the social is placed in mental repertoires of actors' consciousness and in mental activities such as common understandings and assumptions. Social life is treated as primarily tied up with sense-making processes, and the focus in empirical analysis is primarily on social actors. By contrast, practice theories constitute 'cultural textualism,' which covers well-known and otherwise different theoretical approaches such as discourse analysis (for example, Laclau, 1996) and systems theory (for example, Luhmann, 1995). Reckwitz claims that in cultural textualism the social is located outside of actors in larger chains of signs, symbols, language and discourses. Moreover, social life is understood as primarily tied up with structures of meaning external to the social actors and the focus of empirical analysis is primarily on social structures.

Reckwitz (2002, pp. 249–50) thus defines practice theories as placing the social in practices, so that empirical analysis centers on the organization and playing out of practices. His frequently quoted definition is:

> A practice . . . is a routinised type of behaviour which consists of several elements, interconnected to one other: forms of bodily activities, forms of mental activities, things and their use, a background knowledge in the form of understanding, know-how, states of emotion and motivational knowledge. A practice – a way of cooking, of consuming, of working, of investigating, of taking care of oneself or of other etc. – forms so to speak a 'block' whose existence necessarily depends on the existence and specific interconnectedness of these elements, and which cannot be reduced to any one of these single elements.

Apart from the content of the definition of a practice, there are two specific elements of it that are worth considering. First, a practice is organized through a configuration of multiple dynamics. Accordingly, there are multiple analytical 'units' to cover when analyzing practices in everyday life – a practice is not 'just' something consumers do. Second, the configuration of a practice consists of equally important and interdependent dynamics. This means that none of the dynamics should be analytically privileged at the expense of others as the starting point – their relative importance is an empirical question.

Theodore Schatzki (2002, p. 77) defines a practice within his social philosophy in a more or less parallel manner, and the two points identified above with respect to Reckwitz also apply here, namely that a practice is organized as a block of different elements, and that these elements are equally important for holding practices together.

> As indicated, practices are organized nexuses of actions. This means that the doings and sayings composing them hang together. More specifically, the doings and sayings that compose a given practice are linked through 1) practical understandings, 2) rules, 3) a teleoaffective structure, and 4) general understandings. Together, the understandings, rules and teleoaffective structure that link the doings and sayings of a practice, form its organization.[3]

Where Reckwitz focuses on locating practice theories in relation to other grand theories, Schatzki (2002) is more occupied with developing micro-level concepts about practices. In addition to defining what a practice consists of, he defines how to distinguish one type of practice from another, outlines different levels in which practices are done and distinguishes between integrative practices and dispersed practices.

According to Schatzki, the boundaries of one practice – for example, eating – are constituted by the elements in the organizing nexus in the quote above, and the practical understandings and rules of eating are different from the practical understandings and rules of parenting (although there are certain doings and sayings in common within these two types of practices). In other words, distinct practices are carried out at different levels. The concrete doings and sayings can form groups that he calls 'tasks.' One of the usual tasks in eating practices is to participate in sharing a meal. Combinations of tasks within the same practice can form a project. In the case of eating practices, one project can be to attempt to eat as many sustainable meals as possible. Eating is defined as a classical example of the complex integrative practices with which practice theories are more preoccupied, and that are organized in the multi-relational configurations highlighted above. But Schatzki argues that there are also dispersed practices that cover only one type of action that is part of many different integrative practices, for example, describing, sitting, moving things and so forth.

Especially in relation to research on consumption and communication, there has been some debate about whether these two kinds of activities – consumption and communication – can in fact be seen as integrative practices, or should be seen as dispersed practices, or elements in all practices (Couldry, 2004; Warde, 2005). I shall return to this point later in the chapter. Before doing so, the next section considers the application of practice theories in consumption and sustainability research.

PRACTICE THEORIES, CONSUMPTION AND SUSTAINABILITY

Practice theories began to receive active attention in consumption research after the publication of an article by Alan Warde (2005) in the *Journal of Consumer Culture*. In this work, Warde presented Schatzki's main concepts and discussed them in relation to classical practice theoretical concepts from Bourdieu and Giddens. He highlighted this perspective by considering private car-driving practices. Furthermore, Warde suggested an analytical 'translation' of Schatzki's key elements of a practice into slightly more operative terms, namely understandings, procedures and engagements, and he added moments of consumption to the configuration.

This theoretical interpretation of consumption as an element in almost any kind of practice turns upside-down a key assumption of many other kinds of consumption, consumer culture and social marketing research, namely that motives, wishes and choices are preludes to consumption activities (for example, Ratneshwar and Mick, 2005; Ventakesh and Meamber, 2008; Peattie and Peattie, 2009). In Warde's (2005, p. 140) conceptualization, it is the practices that generate wishes and occasions for choice: 'The principal implication of a theory of practice is that the sources of changed behavior lie in the development of practices themselves. The concept of practice inherently combines a capacity to account for both reproduction and innovation.'

Relating back to the discussion of the two traditional models for target-group analysis, the implication is that sustainable consumption is dependent neither on individual consumer choices nor socialized structures of motivating lifestyle values for consumption. Rather, sustainable consumption patterns are predicated on the organization and conditions of the various relevant practices in people's everyday lives. For example, in a Danish qualitative study of how young consumers managed the environmental dimensions of their daily routines, a noticeable number of more sustainable activities were not systematically related to either environmental knowledge or high engagement in environmental issues (see Halkier, 2010). Rather, environmentally friendly everyday activities were carried out when they could become part of embodied routines (for example, shopping in a proximate market with local vegetables), supported by structural conditions (for example, waste-sorting systems) and accomplished as appropriate conduct through negotiations in social networks (for example, eating organic food).

Another important element in Warde's (2005) contribution that transcends, on the one hand, individualistic actors and, on the other hand, decisive cultural structures is his use of Reckwitz's insight about the individual being a crossing point for the intersecting of multiple practices. In other words, each individual participates in many different intersecting practices in his or her everyday contexts, for example, job practices, parenting practices, transportation practices, food practices, hygiene practices, socializing practices and so forth. When looking at instances of multiple practices, it becomes apparent that several of them are overlapping. If one lives in a family with children, it will oftentimes be necessary to carry out parenting practices and food practices at the same time. Thus, people often enact more than one practice at a time or shift between them and negotiate different practices on a recurring basis.

Relating back to the discussion about the two traditional models for target-group analysis, there are analytical implications that emerge from conceptualizing the individual as a crossing point for multiple practices.

First, when practitioners practice several things concurrently, and therefore draw upon several sets of expectation for proper behavior, questions arise regarding the assumption about the significance of individual cognition for action in the deficit model. A climate-friendly meal, for example, is organized not only through understandings, procedures and engagements related to 'doing climate-friendly,' but also through understandings, procedures and engagements in cooking practices, eating practices, parenting practices, relationship practices and socializing practices. The concrete ways of eating a climate-friendly meal entail routine juggling and negotiation of the different sets of conduct.

Second, the notion that the individual is a crossing point for multiple practices calls into question the segmentation models in terms of the assumption that individuals can be readily placed in a particular lifestyle segment with a major or minor cultural propensity to carry out more sustainable consumption. When practitioners practice several things simultaneously, which clusters of behavior should predominate?

It is likely that the ability to use practice theories to argue against both individualist and structuralist accounts of everyday life, and to give more complex accounts of social change and reproduction, have made them attractive to consumption researchers interested in sustainability issues. Sociologist Elizabeth Shove's contributions are a prominent example of this analytical alliance. In her book *Comfort, Cleanliness, and Convenience*, she analyzes the organization of normality with respect to cleanliness on the basis of practice theoretical assumptions. The main empirical argument is that in the course of a relatively short time span, major changes in cleanliness practices became apparent among ordinary consumers. As an example, Shove points out the different environmental consequences associated with whether people shower every morning or take one bath every week. In parallel with Warde, Schatzki and Reckwitz, she draws on a practice theoretical understanding where practices are organized as multi-relational configurations (Gram-Hanssen, 2011); see also Shove et al., 2012.

One of Shove's (2003) important contributions is her concept of integration processes. By this term she means integrations between practices at the micro level of everyday life and material and discursive conditions at the societal macro level. Her argument is that such integrations between small practices and larger conditions are used as both practical guides for specific conduct as well as ways for legitimizing particular conduct as normal and acceptable.

Parallel practice theoretical ways of understanding consumption can be found in a growing number of research publications about sustainability, change of routines and consumption (for example, Spaargaren, 2003; Bartiaux, 2007; Connolly and Prothero, 2008; Røpke, 2009; Halkier, 2010; Shove and Walker, 2010; Gram-Hanssen, 2011; Hargreaves, 2011). The works listed here are, of course, only a few examples out of a much larger body of literature. They cover a variety of practices from hygiene to energy use and office habits to food, and they have a slightly different conceptual focus in the sense that some concentrate more on systems of provision and technologies as part of practices (for example, Spaargaren, 2003; Shove and Walker, 2010; Gram-Hanssen, 2011) and some devote more attention to social performance of conduct as part of practices (for example, Connolly and Prothero, 2008; Halkier, 2010; Hargreaves, 2011). However, they have in common an understanding of consumption in relation to sustainability whereby working toward more sustainable lifestyles has to do with analyzing and discussing different types of doable sustainable practices and the institutional, technological and social preconditions of such activities. A practice theoretical 'take' on consumption underscores the practical, routinized, conventional and collective character of consumption rather than concentrating on neat cognitive dispositions for sustainable values or heroic green segments of consumer lifestyles.

My own perspective on practice theories is that they provide an effective device that enables me to better analyze the details of consumption processes in everyday life and how people handle communication campaigns and media messages that call their daily routines into question – for example, in the area of sustainability.

My work focuses in particular on the performative aspect of practice theories, that practices are constructed through social conduct. Practices come into being in the processes of activities in everyday life that are carried out in front of others, together with others and in relation to others. Everyday life practices are characterized by recurring performances and accomplishments. For example, how eating is practically and relationally done, redone and slightly differently done, even in the most habitual ways of avoiding meat or using local products. Therefore, the practice theoretical roots that come from Judith Butler's intersectionality theory are as important as the initial insights of Giddens's concept of agency and Bourdieu's notion of practical sense. To me, practice theories hold two analytical affordances for empirically investigating consumption in everyday life in light of sustainability challenges.

In the first instance, practice theories enable the researcher to analyze various ways of consuming and to see how these ways of consuming are entangled in webs of social change and reproduction in everyday life. This approach stands in contrast to individual consumer choices as understood by the deficit model. In addition, practice theories allow the researcher to understand ways of consuming as continuous dynamic and relational accomplishments in the intersecting of multiple practices. Such a perspective goes some distance beyond the analysis of consumption as fixed types as suggested by the segmentation model.

CHALLENGES FOR USING PRACTICE THEORIES ON CONSUMPTION AND SUSTAINABILITY

Despite their promise and potential to generate new insights, practice theoretical understandings, like other theoretical perspectives, have certain notable weaknesses. In this section, I highlight two of the challenges associated with the use of these frameworks in empirical research on sustainable consumption.

The first obstacle is related to Alan Warde's (2005) otherwise important and influential conceptualization that consumption is not an integrative practice, and maybe not even a dispersed one. As explained above with respect to Schatzki's contribution to practice theories, he distinguishes between integrative practices that are complex multi-relationally organized practices and dispersed practices constituting a type of action that is part of many different integrative practices, such as arguing and moving things. Bringing food consumption and sustainability issues together illustrates the conceptual challenge. Not all types of food consumption are necessarily only an aspect of food practices. When people perform ecofriendly consumption, particular bundles of consumption activities, such as buying organic products, eating local and cooking with less meat, can become highly noticeable as a 'package' of consumption that is recognizable to other consumers as, for instance, 'green consumption.' In Denmark, this is indeed the case for 'ecofriendly food consumption.' Other consumers refer to this assemblage as a mode of consumption and as a consumer type in their everyday understandings. Such 'packages' of specific consumption can even amount to – to borrow Schatzki's terminology – a practice project where the consumption entity is recognized and reacted upon by other food practitioners as such.

The socially recognizable 'packaging' of ecofriendly food consumption activities has probably become manifest by the mainstreaming of organic food in the retail sector in Denmark and the Danish normalization of the discourses on individual consumer responsibility in public policies and debates (Christensen et al., 2007; Halkier et al., 2007). However, qualitative studies of 'green consumption' and identification in everyday life from other national contexts seem to suggest similar rudiments of socially recognizable 'packages' of doing green consumption (see, for example, Lockie et al., 2002; Horton, 2003; Conolly and Prothero, 2008; Evans and Jackson, 2008).

So, we can question whether all consumption types should be treated alike in practice theoretical perspectives, namely as moments in integrative practices. In contrast, if some types of consumption activities amount to socially recognizable 'packages' – like ecofriendly food consumption – should they be conceptualized in a manner different from ordinary consumption?

The second challenge is related to the lack of explicit conceptualization of social interaction in practice theories. There is no doubt that the use of practice theories in consumption research presupposes social interaction as a part of the collective organization of practices. Following Schatzki, Warde (2005) underlines that practices are not just organized patterns of activities, but are also constantly performed to exist as organized patterns. Following Schatzki and Reckwitz, Shove and Pantzar (2005) stress that by carrying out a set of activities that relate materials, associated meanings and competences, practitioners reproduce a certain practice. I find it theoretically unlikely that social performances and reproduction take place without building on at least some processes of social interaction.

Although the importance of social interaction seems to be a working assumption in some of the key writings on the use of practice theories in consumption research (Shove, 2003, 2009; Shove and Pantzar, 2005; Warde, 2005), social interaction tends to be treated implicitly, 'dressed' conceptually as recognition or coordination. Although recognition and coordination surely implies social interaction, interaction is not made conceptually operative, in contrast to some of the other key concepts such as 'understandings' or 'routines.' Røpke (2009) notices the same tendency in her overview article on practice theories and consumption in relation to ecological economics. Likewise, Hargreaves (2011) concludes there is a need to conceptualize social interaction within practice theoretical approaches to consumption on the basis of his analysis of an empirical case study on environmental behavior change.

It seems necessary to me to conceptualize social interaction explicitly in relation to practice theoretical perspectives on sustainable consumption because of the contestation of routines that is embedded in sustainability initiatives – be they practical, material or discursive (Shove, 2003). When routines become subject to societal challenges through media communication and peer pressure, processes of normative contestation are likely to be used in everyday life as what Shove calls 'integration with the carrying out of practices.' I would add that this normative contestation is also likely to become part of the means through which mutual social negotiation takes place and appropriate conduct is regulated. Thus, to be able to analyze how and why people in their everyday lives arrive at particular 'sustainable' patterns of conduct, the conceptual piece of the practice theoretical puzzle called social interaction has to be more clearly defined. Or practice theories should perhaps be supplemented with other theories and methods that are better able to capture social interaction.

CONCLUSION: EVERYDAY AGENCY, COMMUNICATION AND SUSTAINABILITY

Efforts to involve people in sustainability transitions take different forms, but one of the dominant approaches is through the use of behavior change campaigns delivered by different media that address how and why we all should use public transportation, produce less food waste, more adequately insulate our houses, eat less meat and so forth. Often, such campaigns 'frame' citizens as consumers and do so on the basis of traditional models for target-group analysis in planned communication. These customary models – the deficit model and the segmentation model – are not only used in the communication business, but also derive from theoretical models and are applied in empirical research. Each of these traditional models has its analytic and communicative strengths, but they also suffer from the same shortcoming, namely both models fail to take into account the complexities of everyday life as a context for consumption. The deficit model treats consumption in terms of individual choices and the segmentation model regards consumption as being steered by stable cultural structures. Under such circumstances, the involvement of ordinary people in initiatives to address the range of contemporary sustainability problems becomes, in perhaps brutal terms, a matter of either individual choice or cultural determinism.

In comparison to the deficit and segmentation models, practice theories offer a more subtle perspective, where doing something about sustainability in everyday life is seen as a matter of complex agency. In general, the concept of agency is usually defined as capacity to act and as a mediating notion that resides between choosing and determining action (Wilk, 2009). In practice theories, it is often Giddens's (1984) understanding of structuration theory that informs the concept of agency: the capacity to perform flows of acting on the basis of structures that are both enabling and restraining. Thus, through the lenses of practice theories, everyday agency consists of flows that enact a plurality of practices, conditioned by the collective organization of the practices but also continuously (re) producing these practices through small adaptations, negotiations and improvisations. Translated into slightly more customary language, everyday life is crammed with all sorts of different activities that routinely have to be done, redone and differently done, and what actually occurs is happening both due to, and in spite of, the ways in which daily life is organized in combination with relevant others. Seen from a practice theoretical perspective, this kind of everyday agency is what policy makers and communication campaign organizers face when they are involving citizens as consumers in sustainability initiatives.

This kind of everyday agency is not only different from the traditional target-group models on which change behavior campaigns are based. Such agency also differs from both pessimistic and optimistic understandings of agency and political change in academic discussions about political consumption and citizen-consumers (for example, Micheletti, 2003; Holzer, 2006; Jubas, 2007; Trentmann, 2007; Boström and Klintman, 2008; Spaargaren and Mol, 2008). In the optimistic version, it is assumed that political consumerism (in support of more sustainable activities) improves the space available to citizens in a context that is readily available to them, namely everyday life. By contrast, in the pessimistic version, there is skepticism about this alleged space for action and it is assumed that everyday life becomes more socially controlled and disciplined through political consumption, without much impact on sustainability problems.

Instead, a practice theoretical (or theoretically inspired) understanding of everyday agency takes both space for action and conditions for action into account. There is a focus on what is 'doable' in everyday life: what is practically possible to get done and what is socially acceptable to do. But given the critique of methodological individualism that is inherent in practice theories, such an understanding goes one step further and suggests that we abandon the concept of 'the active consumer' that is an essential part of both the segmentation and deficit models (Jacobsen and Dulsrud, 2007). Academic discussions, as well as policy making about citizen involvement in sustainable consumption, could benefit from focusing more on practically and socially 'doable' sustainable activities and what their social and institutional preconditions (in terms of social innovation and forms of public regulation) might be. The capacity for communication campaigns on their own to initiate changes of routines and other regulations of everyday life have long been overestimated.

NOTES

1. Other target-group models are the network communication model (for example, Rogers, 1995) and the models based on communities of practice (Lave and Wenger, 1991).
2. There is an explicit critical realism discussion about practice theories that contributes to the heterogeneity of practice theories, but I do not take this up here. Examples of this approach include Archer (2002) and Gronow (2008).
3. Teleoaffective structures are emotional and normative orientations for doings/sayings.

REFERENCES

Ajzen, A. (1991). 'The theory of planned behaviour', *Organizational Behaviour and Human Decision Processes*, **50**(2), 179–211.

Archer, M. (2002). 'Realism and the problem of agency', *Journal of Critical Realism*, **5**(1), 11–20.

Bartiaux, F. (2007). 'Does environmental information overcome practice compartmentalisation and change consumers' behaviours?', *Journal of Cleaner Production*, **16**(11), 1170–80.

Boström, M. and M. Klintman (2008). *Eco-standards, Product Labelling, and Green Consumerism*, New York: Palgrave Macmillan.

Bourdieu, P. (1990). *The Logic of Practice*, Palo Alto, CA: Stanford University Press.

Butler, J. (1990). *Gender Trouble: Feminism and the Subversion of Identity*, New York: Routledge.

Campbell, B., I. Lesschaeve, A. Bowen and S. Onufrey (2010). 'Purchase drivers of Canadian consumers of local and organic produce', *Hortscience*, **45**(10), 1480–8.

Christensen, T., M. Godskesen, K. Gram-Hanssen, M. Quitzay and I. Røpke (2007). 'Greening the Danes? Experience with consumption and environment policies', *Journal of Consumer Policy*, **30**(2), 91–116.

Connolly, J. and A. Prothero (2008). 'Green consumption: life-politics, risks and contradictions', *Journal of Consumer Culture*, **8**(1), 117–45.

Couldry, N. (2004). 'Theorising media as practice', *Social Semiotics*, **14**(2), 115–32.

Craig, R. (2007). 'Communication theory as a field', in R. Craig and H. Muller (eds), *Theorizing Communication: Readings across Traditions*, Thousand Oaks, CA: Sage, pp. 63–98.

Dahl, H. (2005). *Hvis din nabo var en bil: En bog om livsstil (If Your Neighbor was a Car: A Book about Lifestyle)*, Copenhagen: Akademisk Forlag (in Danish).

Dervin, B. (2003). 'Sense-making's journey from metatheory to methodology to

method: an example using information seeking and use as research focus', in B. Dervin and L. Foreman-Wernet (eds), *Sense-making Methodology Reader: Selected Writings of Brenda Dervin*, Cresskill, NJ: Hampton Press, pp. 133–63.
Didier, T. and L. Sirieix (2008). 'Measuring consumers' willingness to pay for organic and fair trade products', *International Journal of Consumer Studies*, **32**(5), 479–90.
Eden, S. (2011). 'Food labels as boundary objects: how consumers make sense of organic and functional foods', *Public Understanding of Science*, **20**(2), 1–16.
Evans, D. and T. Jackson (2008). 'Sustainable consumption: perspectives from social and cultural theory', RESOLVE Working Paper 05–08, Research Group on Lifestyles, Values, and the Environment, University of Surrey.
Fraj, E. and E. Martinez (2007). 'Ecological consumer behaviour: an empirical analysis', *International Journal of Consumer Studies*, **31**(1), 26–33.
Foucault, M. (1978). *The History of Sexuality, Volume 1*, New York: Penguin.
Gherardi, S. (2009). 'Practice? It's a matter of taste!', *Management Learning*, **40**(5), 535–50.
Giddens, A. (1984). *The Constitution of Society: Outline of the Theory of Structuration*, Berkeley, CA: University of California Press.
Gram-Hanssen, K. (2011). 'Understanding change and continuity in residential energy consumption', *Journal of Consumer Culture*, **11**(1), 61–78.
Gronow, A. (2008). 'The over- or the undersocialized conception of man? Practice theory and the problem of intersubjectivity', *Sociology*, **42**(2), 243–59.
Gronow, J. and L. Holm (2008). 'The perpetual concept of choice: reflections on a dominant theoretical construct in the field of food consumption', Paper presented at the European Sociological Association, Research Network on Sociology of Consumption Interim Workshop, Helsinki, 27–30 August.
Halkier, B. (2010). *Consumption Challenged: Food in Medialised Everyday Lives*, Farnham, Surrey: Ashgate.
Halkier, B. and I. Jensen (2011). 'Methodological challenges in using practice theory in consumption research: examples from a study on handling nutritional contestations of food consumption', *Journal of Consumer Culture*, **11**(1), 101–23.
Halkier, B., L. Holm, M. Domingues, P. Magaudda, A. Nielsen and L. Terragni (2007). 'Trusting, complex, quality conscious or unprotected? Constructing the food consumer in different European national contexts', *Journal of Consumer Culture*, **7**(3), 379–402.
Hansen, J., L. Holm, L. Frewer, P. Robinson and P. Sandoe (2003). 'Beyond the knowledge deficit: recent research into lay and expert attitudes to food risks', *Appetite*, **41**(2), 111–21.
Hargreaves, T. (2011). 'Practice-ing behaviour change: applying social practice theory to pro-environmental change', *Journal of Consumer Culture*, **11**(1), 79–100.
Holzer, B. (2006). 'Political consumerism between individual choice and collective action: social movements, role mobilization, and signalling', *International Journal of Consumer Studies*, **30**(5), 405–15.
Horton, D. (2003). 'Green distinctions: the performance of identity among environmental activists', *Sociological Review*, **51**(S2), 63–77.
Jacobsen, E. and A. Dulsrud (2007). 'Will consumers save the world? The framing of political consumerism', *Journal of Agricultural and Environmental Ethics*, **20**(5), 469–82.

Jubas, K. (2007). 'Conceptual con/fusion in democratic societies: understandings and limitations of consumer-citizenship', *Journal of Consumer Culture*, **7**(2), 231–54.

Kolandai-Matchett, K. (2009). 'Mediated communication of "sustainable consumption" in the alternative media: a case study exploring a message framing strategy', *International Journal of Consumer Studies*, **33**(2), 113–25.

Laclau, E. (1996). 'Deconstruction, pragmatism, hegemony', in S. Critchley and C. Mouffe (eds), *Deconstruction and Pragmatism*, New York: Routledge, pp. 45–67.

Latour, B. (1993). *We Have Never Been Modern*, Cambridge, MA: Harvard University Press.

Lave, J. and E. Wenger (1991). *Situated Learning: Legitimate Peripheral Participation*, New York: Cambridge University Press.

Lawson, R. and S. Todd (2002). 'Consumer lifestyles: a social stratification perspective', *Marketing Theory*, **2**(2), 295–307.

Lockie, S., K. Lyons, G. Lawrence and K. Mummery (2002). 'Eating "green": motivations behind organic food consumption in Australia', *Sociologia Ruralis*, **42**(1), 23–40.

Luckmann, T. (1989). 'On meaning in everyday life and sociology', *Current Sociology*, **37**(1), 17–30.

Luhmann, N. (1995). *Social Systems*, Palo Alto, CA: Stanford University Press.

McQuail, D. (1998). *Audience Analysis*, Thousand Oaks, CA: Sage.

Micheletti, M. (2003). *Political Virtue and Shopping: Individuals, Consumerism, and Collective Action*, New York: Palgrave.

Nye, M. and T. Hargreaves (2010). 'Exploring the social dynamics of pro-environmental behavior for change', *Journal of Industrial Ecology*, **14**(1), 137–49.

Peattie, K. and S. Peattie (2009). 'Social marketing: a pathway to consumption reduction?', *Journal of Business Research*, **62**(2), 260–8.

Ratneshwar, S. and D. Mick (2005). *Inside Consumption: Consumer Motives, Goals, and Desires*, New York: Routledge.

Reckwitz, A. (2002). 'Toward a theory of social practices: a development in culturalist theorizing', *European Journal of Social Theory*, **5**(2), 243–63.

Rogers, E. (1995). *Diffusion of Innovations*, 3rd edn, New York: Free Press.

Rokka, J. and L. Uusitalo (2008). 'Preference for green packaging in consumer product choices: do consumers care?', *International Journal of Consumer Studies*, **32**(5), 516–25.

Røpke, I. (2009). 'Theories of practice: new inspiration for ecological economic studies on consumption', *Ecological Economics*, **68**(10), 2490–7.

Rumpala, Y. (2011). 'Sustainable consumption as a new phase in a governmantalization of consumption', *Theory and Society*, **40**(6), 669–99.

Sanjuan, A., M. Sanchez, J. Gil, A. Gracia and F. Soler (2003). 'Brakes to organic market enlargement in Spain: consumers' and retailers' attitudes and willingness to pay', *International Journal of Consumer Studies*, **27**(2), 134–44.

Schatzki, T. (1996). *Social Practices: A Wittgensteinian Approach to Human Activity and the Social*, New York: Cambridge University Press.

Schatzki, T. (2001). 'Practice minded orders', in T. Schatzki, K. Knorr-Cetina and E. von Savigny (eds), *The Practice Turn in Contemporary Theory*, New York: Routledge, pp. 42–55.

Schatzki, T. (2002). *The Site of the Social: A Philosophical Account of the*

Constitution of Social Life and Change, University Park, PA: Pennsylvania State University Press.
Seyfang, G. (2006). 'Ecological citizenship and sustainable consumption: examining local organic food networks', *Journal of Rural Studies*, **22**(4), 383–95.
Shove, E. (2003). *Comfort, Cleanliness, and Convenience: The Social Organisation of Normality*, New York: Berg.
Shove, E. (2009). 'Everyday practice and the production and consumption of time', in E. Shove, F. Trentmann and R. Wilk (eds), *Time, Consumption, and Everyday Life: Practice, Materiality and Culture*, New York: Berg, pp. 17–33.
Shove, E. and M. Pantzar (2005). 'Consumers, producers and practices: understanding the invention and reinvention of Nordic walking', *Journal of Consumer Culture*, **5**(1), 43–64.
Shove, E., M. Pantzar and M. Watson (2012). *The Dynamics of Social Practice*, Thousand Oaks, CA: Sage.
Shove, E. and G. Walker (2010). 'Governing transitions in the sustainability of everyday life', *Research Policy*, **39**(4), 471–6.
Spaargaren, G. (2003). 'Sustainable consumption: a theoretical and environmental policy perspective', *Society and Natural Resources*, **16**(8), 687–701.
Spaargaren, G. and A. Mol (2008). 'Greening global consumption: redefining politics and authority', *Global Environmental Change*, **18**(3), 350–9.
Swidler, A. (2001). 'What anchors cultural practices', in T. Schatzki, K. Knorr-Cetina and E. von Savigny (eds), *The Practice Turn in Contemporary Theory*, New York: Routledge, pp. 74–92.
Thevenot, L. (2001). 'Pragmatic regimes governing the engagement with the world', in T. Schatzki, K. Knorr-Cetina and E. von Savigny (eds), *The Practice Turn in Contemporary Theory*, New York: Routledge, pp. 56–73.
Thøgersen, J. (2006). 'Norms for environmentally responsible behaviour: an extended taxonomy', *Journal of Environmental Psychology*, **26**(4), 247–61.
Trentmann, F. (2007). 'Citizenship and consumption', *Journal of Consumer Culture*, **7**(2), 147–58.
Truninger, M. (2011). 'Cooking with Bimby in a moment of recruitment: exploring conventions and practice perspectives', *Journal of Consumer Culture*, **11**(1), 37–59.
Tukker, A., E. Stö and C. Vezzoli (2008). 'The governance and practice of change of sustainable consumption and production: editorial', *Journal of Cleaner Production*, **16**(11), 1143–5.
Turner, S. (1994). *The Social Theory of Practices: Tradition, Tacit Knowledge, and Presuppositions*, Malden, MA: Polity.
Ventakesh, A. and L. Meamber (2008). 'The aesthetics of consumption and the consumer as aesthetic subject', *Consumption, Markets, and Culture*, **11**(1), 45–70.
Vermeir, I. and W. Verbeke (2006). 'Sustainable food consumption: exploring the consumer "attitude-behavioral intention" gap', *Journal of Agricultural and Environmental Ethics*, **19**(2), 169–94.
Warde, A. (2005). 'Consumption and theories of practice', *Journal of Consumer Culture*, **5**(2), 131–53.
Whitmarsh, L. (2009). 'What's in a name? Commonalities and differences in public understanding of "climate change" and "global warming"', *Public Understanding of Science*, **18**(4), 401–20.
Wilk, R. (2009). 'The edge of agency: routines, habits and volition', in E. Shove,

F. Trentmann and R. Wilk (eds), *Time, Consumption, and Everyday Life: Practice, Materiality, and Culture*, New York: Berg, pp. 143–54.
Windahl, S., B. Signitzer and J. Olson (1998). *Using Communication Theory: An Introduction to Planned Communication*, Thousand Oaks, CA: Sage.
Zia, A. and A. Todd (2010). 'Evaluating the effects of ideology on public understanding of climate change science: how to improve communication across ideological divides?', *Public Understanding of Science*, **19**(6), 743–61.

11. The cultural dimension of sustainable consumption practices: an exploration in theory and policy

Gert Spaargaren[1]

INTRODUCTION

Environmental social scientists have long been concerned with how to conceptualize 'environmental behaviors' and 'environmental awareness and norms.' From a scientific viewpoint, the question relates to how people in their everyday lives become engaged with issues such as climate change, water scarcity, biodiversity, waste generation and renewable energy. In other words, how do ordinary people get to grips with environmental issues and how do they perceive, comprehend, evaluate and manage the connections that their personal lifestyles and routine consumption practices have in terms of global environmental change (Cohen and Murphy, 2001; Southerton et al., 2004; Jackson, 2006)? From a policy perspective, there is the need to develop a better understanding of everyday consumption practices since how we dwell in our houses, drive our cars and participate in leisure activities are significant when it comes to achieving substantial reductions in overall carbon dioxide (CO_2) emissions and other environmental improvements (Dietz et al., 2009).

In many European countries, the policy debate on behavior change and sustainable consumption continues to be dominated by social psychologists and economists working primarily from an individualist standpoint (see the chapter by Bente Halkier in this volume). Theories of practice make possible a nonindividualist understanding of environmental behaviors while opening up new approaches for global environmental governance. When (re)conceptualized along the lines of practice theories, new issues are exposed and give rise to innovative questions and strategies for social science research. First, recasting the agency-structure dualism enables routine practices to be seen as new cornerstones with which to build environmental governance arrangements. Second, making conceptual room for the co-structuring role of objects, technologies and infrastructures in the reproduction of social practices makes it possible to analyze the crucial role of technology in environmental change without lapsing into technological determinism. Finally, when approached from the perspective of practice theories, the role of perception, norms and personal commitments to environmental change can be handled in a non-individualist way while simultaneously making room for cultural analysis of the activities of citizen-consumers as positive, energizing commitments.

Consideration of the cultural dimension of practices is especially relevant as a way to transcend dominant frames on sustainable consumption, particularly in terms of how they are used in the formulation of environmental policies. Frames that emphasize the risk-inducing, negative side of unsustainable consumption (Dauvergne, 2008) tend to neglect the encouraging, enabling and motivating functions of new, green actions connected to participation in more sustainable consumption practices. The final section summarizes the main ingredients for a practice-based research agenda on sustainable consumption.

EXISTING PARADIGMS FOR THE GOVERNANCE OF ENVIRONMENTAL CHANGE

Since the 1970s, two approaches have been dominant for studying and organizing research on the social dimensions of environment and climate change: the individualist paradigm and the systemic (or structural) paradigm. As Table 11.1 indicates, each of these archetypes is configured around its own theoretical assumptions and preferred policy strategies.

When policies are proposed to promote more sustainable consumption behaviors, the individualist paradigm tends to be invoked as the framework for organizing concrete programs of action (Jackson, 2005; DEFRA, 2008). The so-called model of the four Es – enable, engage, encourage and exemplify – is used to summarize and specify the mix of instruments for changing consumer practices (Jackson, 2006; DEFRA, 2008).[2] For example, nongovernmental organizations (NGOs) deploy the individualist model when working with the emerging business of 'footprinting' individuals while appealing to the moral responsibility of citizen-consumers to bring their consumption behaviors within the biophysical limits set by ecologists and other natural scientists (Wackernagel and Rees, 1996; Hobson, 2002; Middlemiss, 2010).

Among the main achievements of the four Es is a significant increase in public environmental awareness that has become manifest in recent decades. However, the primary consequence of this development is that attentiveness has proved to be a weak precursor of pro-environmental

Table 11.1 Two primary paradigms for the governance of environmental change

Individualist paradigm (Social psychology/economics)	Systemic paradigm (sociology/science studies)
Individuals and their attitudes are key units of analysis and policy	Producers/states and their strategies are key units of analysis and policy
Behavior change of individuals is decisive for environmental change	Technological innovation within the production sphere is decisive for change
Individual choices are the key intervention targets (micro level)	Socio-technical systems are the key intervention targets (macro level)
End-users/consumers determine the fate of green products and ideas	Technologies and markets determine the fate of green products and ideas
Key policy instruments and approaches: social (soft) instruments (persuasion through information provision)	Key policy instruments and approaches: the use of direct regulation targeting providers (laws, market-based interventions)

behaviors. Most people do not live up to the promises that they make in the surveys. Because of inadequate outcomes, policy makers in countries such as the Netherlands have quite modest expectations of the improvements that can accrue from national information campaigns and other strategies premised on the individualist paradigm (Beckers et al., 2000).

Partly because of disappointing experiences with the individualist model, policy makers in Europe have resorted in recent years to assumptions and strategies associated with the systemic paradigm. In the systemic paradigm, individuals no longer really matter. The focus is primarily on institutional actors: companies, branch organizations, municipalities, labor unions and NGOs. While working with producers and other experts involved in the greening of consumption, initiatives can best be organized, so it is thought, more or less 'behind the backs' of ordinary citizen-consumers. The basic assumption about behavior change is that new activities and purchasing preferences can and will be effectively enforced on citizen-consumers sooner or later. Citizen-consumers will have no choice but to conduct themselves in a sustainable manner once the required technologies, infrastructures and products are put into place as the result of strict regulations. In short, 'fit and forget' becomes the slogan with which to achieve sustainable consumption (Van Vliet et al., 2005).

Now people, of course, do not just develop ideas and ways of doing things 'from within' and all by themselves. Their thinking and doing are co-shaped by others and by the objects and situational factors that form an integral part of the contexts of their behaviors. When restricting themselves to strategies only from the individualist paradigm, policy makers are being sociologically naïve and disregarding the profound influences that wider chains of interaction have on systems of provision, prefiguring and co-evolving the range of choices available to individual citizen-consumers. As a result, far too much responsibility for change is put on the shoulders of citizen-consumers themselves.

A critique of the systemic paradigm highlights the converse problem. When resorting to institutionalized producer-led initiatives organized around new technologies and infrastructures, policy makers are failing to acknowledge the crucial role of human agents. In this top-down, structuralist approach, citizen-consumers are hardly offered possibilities to participate in and to democratically control processes integral to their own lives. As studies on failed technological innovations convincingly demonstrate (Schot, 2001; Heiskanen et al., 2005), it is a difficult challenge to realize the environmental benefits of eco-designed products when they are conceived and implemented without reference to the user practices that they help to constitute.

Because of these criticisms, there is a need for a balanced approach that pays attention to aspects of both agency and structure, that makes room for joining both bottom-up and top-down dynamics of change and that recognizes the mutual influencing and co-shaping of human actors and technologies. Practice-based approaches, as developed by sociologists since the 1970s, can provide this more balanced approach (Shove, 2003, 2006; Spaargaren, 2003; Southerton et al., 2004). The sections that follow discuss the practice paradigm from both theoretical and governance perspectives and point to how conceptual innovations with respect to agency, technology and culture can contribute to renewal of the policy agenda for encouraging more sustainable consumption.

PRACTICE THEORIES AND THE AGENCY-STRUCTURE DEBATE

At the time that social theorists Pierre Bourdieu (1977, 1979) and Anthony Giddens (1984) advanced their respective theories of practice, the main emphasis was on overcoming the agency-structure dualism (Knorr-Cetina and Cicourel, 1981). By introducing concepts such as practice, habitus and field (Bourdieu) and reformulating the notions of agency, system and structure (Giddens), both scholars tried to contribute conceptually to a synthesis between structuralist and interpretative schools of thinking in the social sciences.

What is generally regarded to be the lasting value of their work is the understanding of social life as a series of recursive practices carried out by knowledgeable and capable agents who draw on sets of virtual rules and resources connected to situated social practices. Agents reproduce practices within designated fields of social life by using specific sets of rules and resources that are constitutive of those practices. Because of the emphasis on practices as 'shared behavioral routines,' the individual is no longer in the center of the analysis. Practices instead of individuals become the most important units of analysis. It is practices that 'produce' and co-constitute individuals and their values, knowledge and capabilities, and not the other way around (Collins, 2004).

Looking 'beyond the individual,' however, does not imply reverting to the systemic, structuralist perspective that tends to discount – or at times forget altogether – agency and subjectivity. Both Giddens and Bourdieu made convincing cases about the need to investigate and organize changes in practices in direct connection with 'agency performed,' 'powers enacted' and 'interests pursued' by human agents. Practice theories go beyond individuals, but emphasize the fact that human subjectivity is at the heart of processes of structuration, reproduction and (also) environmental change.

Let us shift here to consider the role of environmental governance, which is about attempts to steer the reproduction of practices, systems and networks from the standpoint of sustainable development. Practices come in all kinds of different types. There are the routine consumption practices of everyday life, as well as practices that are part of the reproduction of markets, politics and civil society. Practices associated with corporate social responsibility can be the focus of environmental governance in much the same way as practices of consumption. Furthermore, practices can be situated at all segments or nodes of production-consumption chains and networks. When the focus is on the ecological modernization of practices, such as mining, processing, warehousing, transporting, retailing and distributing, this is known in the literature as 'upstream' processes and dynamics as enacted by providers of (green) products, services and infrastructures. In contrast, when attention is devoted to practices of buying, storing, consuming, (re)using and recycling as enacted by citizen-consumers as the end-users of (green) products and services, this is referred to as 'downstream' processes and dynamics (Spaargaren and van Koppen, 2009). In the discussion that follows, the downstream practices of consumption will be used to illustrate the relevance of a practice approach for environmental governance.

In principle, a virtually unlimited number of downstream consumption practices are relevant for environmental governance. Three criteria seem to be especially relevant for the selection of specific sets of practices that are central to the environmental governance of consumption. First, the focus should be on practices that have relevance from a citizen-consumer's (or practitioner's) point of view. This means the practices should be situated in everyday life and governed to a significant degree by life-world rationalities. They should moreover be recognizable to citizen-consumers, a condition that implies lay people have unconditional opportunities to gain first-hand knowledge about these practices.[3] For example, when studying 'shopping for food in a supermarket' it is presupposed that almost all citizen-consumers possess first-hand knowledge about the rules and resources implied in the practice.

Second, the consumption practices should be relevant for environmental governance. This caveat does not mean that only practices with large ecological impacts are selected, since practices with high eco-innovative potential can still be important. Also 'new,' not yet common or mainstream practices could nonetheless be of strategic interest to policy makers. Within the environmental sciences, the biophysical impacts of consumption practices, such as dwelling in a home or driving a car, are by now well understood in technical terms.

Finally, to prevent the fragmentation and 'horizontalization' of consumption policies (Fine and Leopold, 1993), researchers and policy makers should focus on clusters or sets of consumption practices situated within a limited number of 'domains' spanning everyday life. Within one domain – or field, as Bourdieu would have it – practices are reproduced under the influence of a shared 'regime' (Geels, 2005) since they are connected to similar chains and networks that contribute to the provisioning of the practices. Because of these shared subsets of rules and resources, practices within one domain can be said to be embedded in the specific, as well as historical, dynamics of this particular domain (Warde, 2004). When speaking of food, the sustainability criteria and frames demonstrate specific, customary elements tied to the consumption of food (for example, freshness, land use, animal welfare), but when compared to the domain of housing, a different set of criteria (for example, CO_2 emissions, water use) would become relevant.

To provide an impression of the sets and domains that are relevant for the governance of sustainable consumption, Table 11.2 displays several practices for six different domains. This selection is partly based on the CONTRAST research project that explored transitions toward sustainable consumption practices in the Netherlands (Spaargaren et al., 2007). This work demonstrated that the dynamics of environmental change are significantly different across consumption domains and varying levels of improvement have thus far been realized. The domains of 'housing' and 'food' have experienced the greatest degree of ecological modernization,

Table 11.2 Domains and practices relevant for the governance of sustainable consumption

Food	Leisure and tourism	Dwelling in the home	Being mobile	Clothing and personal care	Hobbies and sports
Dining out	Alpine holiday	Gardening	Business travel	Shopping for clothing	Fishing
Shopping for food	City trips	Redecorating the kitchen/ Bathroom	City biking	Jacuzzi/fitness	Playing ball
Cooking for friends	Beach holidays	Indoor climate control	Commuting	Showering	Horseback riding
Food on the move	Leisure parks	Moving house	Slow travel	Clothes laundering	Dogs and pets
Eating in a canteen	Backpacking	Handling domestic wastes	Buying a car	Sewing and mending	Running/biking
Kitchen-gardening	Outdoor recreation	Refurnishing the house	Leisure travel	Collecting old clothing	Do-it-yourself renovations/ repairs

while 'leisure and tourism' and 'clothing and personal care' lag behind. The 'mobility' domain occupies a middle position (Verbeek, 2010). Interestingly, the consumption domains in Table 11.2 are similar to the main categories used by Global Action Plan (GAP) (Staats et al., 2004) and are consistent with the international policy agenda for sustainable consumption and production (SCP) as it has developed since 2002 around the so-called Marrakech Process (Spaargaren and Cohen, 2009). Accordingly, when studying the greening of global consumption, some practices will be more relevant than others and will depend on the particular geographical region under investigation. It also warrants keeping in mind that the influence of national policies on consumption domains will vary. For example, state power in the domain of housing will generally be greater than in the domain of food or clothing.

Key questions for social scientists interested in the governance of sustainable consumption are related to the factors and dynamics of transitioning to future social practices with substantially lower ecological impacts. The challenge is to substantially reduce the ecological footprints of practices instead of only focusing on the footprints of individuals. This shift is realizable by, on the one hand, introducing more sustainable objects, products and technologies into the practices and, on the other hand, integrating into the practices new green images, norms and ideas. Stated differently, the ecological modernization of practices refers to incorporating and anchoring into practices novel 'ways of doing and saying' that are important for monitoring, assessing, valuing and improving the environmental performance of the practice. The technological and cultural dimensions of innovating consumption practices are respectively considered in the next two sections.

PRACTICE THEORIES AND THE AGENCY-TECHNOLOGY DEBATE

When environmental social scientists first took up practice theories during the late 1980s, the household provision of energy, water and waste services was an important field of empirical research. Sociological contributions to the debate on demand-side management emphasized that the interaction between demand and supply, between end-users and goods/services providers could be studied as a mutual process of 'serving and being served' (Otnes, 1988). When making tea or boiling an egg for breakfast, householders are 'being served' by utility companies with water and energy. However, at the very moment of turning on the tap, householders, in turn, are 'serving' the relevant systems by reproducing the socio-technical regimes for provisioning water and energy. The image of mutuality and interdependency between end-users and goods/services suppliers provided an alternative to the individualist and systemic explanations of domestic consumption.

On the one hand, the individualist paradigm was shown to be inappropriate because householders 'have to' use the social and material infrastructures set forth by the provisioning systems. The behavior of householders cannot be correctly understood as just resulting from the free, independent, isolated choices and preferences of individuals. Behaviors are preconfigured by socio-material infrastructures and the relevant regimes for heating, cooling and lighting the home, as well as for washing dishes and clothes, showering and collecting wastes (Shove, 2003).

The systemic paradigm, on the other hand, was demonstrated to be shortsighted because householders do not 'just' incorporate preconfigured technologies and rules into their domestic practices without consideration and reflection, as well as protest and conflict. At specific moments in time especially when domestic routines are interrupted or temporarily out of order – the process of serving and being served becomes the basis for political debates, and perhaps the restructuring of producer-consumer relationships (Southerton et al., 2004; Van Vliet et al., 2005).[4]

Because of the application of practice theories to utility-service provision, it is not difficult to understand why perspectives from the sociology of science and technology (and work from the more general field of science and technology studies) had a major impact on this branch of environmental social science research. Technological innovation, lock-in (and lock-out) effects, sunk costs, socio-technical regimes and similar concepts became quite useful in analyzing development of extensive and powerful socio-material infrastructures for provisioning households with water, energy, sanitation and solid-waste services (Graham and Marvin, 2001; Guy et al., 2001; Van Vliet, 2002). In addition, actor-network theory (ANT), in particular as developed by Bruno Latour (2005), was introduced in this context and challenged notions of agency that tended to overlook the crucial role of objectives and socio-material hybrids in the (co-)structuring of practices.

Nonetheless, this first generation of practice theories had little to offer for analyzing objects, technological systems and hybrids in more general ways. During the 1990s, several authors began to address this inadequacy by reformulating practice theories without discarding their core premises regarding the agency-(technological) structure relationship (see the chapter by Bente Halkier in this volume).

Theodore Schatzki (1996, 2002), Andreas Reckwitz (2002a, 2002b) and, in a different way, John Urry (2000) began to engage the issues of agency, structure and technology in greater depth and against the backdrop of both structuration theories and ANT. Reckwitz (2002a) especially contributed to the incorporation of technology into theories of practices. He argued for the need to reconcile a strong emphasis on the (autonomous impact of the) role of technology with structurationists' key assumption of human agency as the ultimate factor for making a difference in the world. The impact of things in the social order must be fully recognized and conceptualized, not just in terms of representations or as objects that are assigned and attributed meaning by human agents. The effects of the objects themselves, the role of inter-objectivity next to inter-subjectivity and the idea of objects being 'constitutive' with social practices all came to be conceptualized in more detail.

Reckwitz sought to complement Schatzki's work with Latour's idea of the equally important constitutive role of things for social practices. He argues that 'things handled' are as important for theories of social practices as 'minds/bodies performing.' Reckwitz (2002a, p. 249) characterizes the crucial role of things and their use for social practices in one of the most elaborate definitions of the concept articulated to date. Social practices are 'a routinized type of behaviour which consist of several elements, interconnected to one other: forms of bodily activities, forms of mental activities, '*things and their use,*' a background knowledge in the form of understanding, know-how, states of emotion and motivational knowledge' (emphasis added).

This formulation of the material dimension of social practices is the closest one can come to ANT without violating the key assumption of practice theories, namely the crucial importance of the role of knowledgeable and capable agents in shaping social life. In comparison to Giddens, Reckwitz assigns greater analytical power to objects and technology without embracing the ANT-based idea that objects and things 'act' in ways that are similar to the way humans act.

When translated for purposes of empirical research, a number of consequences follow. First, things or objects as crucial elements of practices do not figure in isolation but – to use a seminal phrase from the work of Schatzki – they 'hang together' in specific ways. This means that lock-in mechanisms and other sources of inertia usually ascribed to existing technologies and infrastructures can, and must, be analyzed in terms of both the inter- and intra-dependencies between human agents and physical, material objects. These 'prefigurational relationships' are particularly interesting when studying environmental change because they refer to the kinds of future figurations that are feasible given the existing state of affairs. For example, when new objects or technologies enter into social practices, they can display a different level of 'fit' or 'misfit' with regard to the existing order of things. The successful introduction of new products thereby comes to depend not just on their 'mental appropriation' by human agents, but equally on the levels of fit or misfit they show with respect to the existing portfolios of objects, bodies and meanings that are involved in the practice. As a result, the portfolios of the actors involved in the reproduction of the practice enable and constrain specific forms of appropriation, normalization, cultivation and naturalization of new objects and technologies (Schot and Albert de la Bruhèze, 2003; Wilk, 2009).

Elizabeth Shove has been one of the few sociologists who has to date explored the impact of technologies in everyday life from a practice-informed perspective. In her path-breaking book, *Comfort, Cleanliness and Convenience*, and a series of related articles (Shove, 2006; Shove and Walker, 2007), she discusses the co-evolution of practices, norms and technologies. She illustrates the sometimes pervasive and autonomous influence of technologies on social practices by analyzing innovations pertaining to laundering, showering, cooling and heating. Building upon this 'technology and everyday life' research tradition, she demonstrates how it is possible to elevate the analysis of agency and technology beyond, on the one hand, deterministic interpretations and, on the other hand, voluntarist theories on the 'adoption of innovations.'

PRACTICE THEORIES AND THE AGENCY-CULTURE DEBATE

Over the past quarter-century, both the quantity and the quality of more sustainable products, services and technologies available for domestic consumption have increased significantly. For the ecological modernization of consumption practices in the areas of food and housing in particular, the availability of more sustainable technological alternatives can no longer be regarded as the major constraining factor. In most wealthy countries, household provisioning with respect to energy, water, sanitation and solid waste has gone through a process of ecological modernization and in ordinary supermarkets green, eco-labeled products are no longer uncommon (Oosterveer et al., 2007; Mol et al., 2009).

Now that in ever more domains of social life the ability to live more sustainable lifestyles is available, the challenging question is why more sustainable consumption patterns have not yet become mainstream and why they are generally restricted to a small minority of the population. Some authors explain the lack of success in terms of the so-called 'value-action gap,' while others point to the need for more effective and stringent policies (Hobson, 2002; Rief, 2008). In the practice paradigm, the constraining and enabling roles of technological factors and dynamics have been extensively explored by authors from the field of transition studies (see, for example, Geels, 2005; Geels and Schot, 2007; Grin et al., 2010). For example, Frank Geels and Johan Schot argue that specific forms of (strategic) niche management are necessary for environmental innovations to more successfully challenge existing socio-technical regimes.

Perhaps because of a desire to steer clear of the value-based agenda and approaches of the individualist paradigm, authors have tended to undertheorize the cultural dimension of green lifestyles and consumption routines. This is an unfortunate development because the cultural dimension of (green) practices or performances deserves full analytical attention (Szerszynski et al., 2003), especially by environmental social scientists working in the practice tradition.

A cultural approach to environmental change should, first, be applicable at the level of situated consumption practices. Second, by focusing attention on culture it would be possible to conduct a thorough analysis of the role of objects and symbols in the reproduction of practices. Finally, to complement existing emphasis on the negative aspects of (un) sustainable consumption, a cultural approach would create conceptual space for simultaneously considering the positive aspects of sustainable consumption.[5] To realize this objective, we need to formulate a conceptual framework that allows not just for analysis of the 'negative logics' of environmental risks (Beck, 1992, 2009), but for grasping as well the countervailing 'positive logics' of improved environmental quality and performance. Since we are engaging with practices of consumption, dreams, fantasies, excitement and enjoyments should be considered as constitutive elements of the very kind of practices under study (Campbell, 2006; Sassatelli, 2007).

Randall Collins's theory of interaction ritual (IR) chains seems to satisfy all of these prerequisites. Although he does not explicitly label his approach a theory of practices, the core assumptions are very much in line with them. Collins is well known for his in-depth knowledge about both classical and contemporary sociology, and for his accessible way of writing about the field (see, for example, Collins and Makowsky, 1998). When summarized in one sentence, he claims to provide a 're-reading of Emile Durkheim through the eyes of Erving Goffman.' This endeavor is necessary because Durkheim's analysis of the reproduction of norms, moral sentiments and solidarities in society has been given a specific twist by post-Durkheim functionalists who interpreted the reproduction of norms and values primarily in terms of macro-scale system categories and phenomena. What has been lost then is an emphasis on the situational characteristics and mechanisms implied in the reproduction of culture. With the help of Goffman's micro version of Durkheim, it is possible to formulate a more adequate contemporary version of a theory on interaction rituals.

Collins's treatment is a 'radical micro-sociology' that shows in concrete detail how norms and solidarities are produced by situated actors in everyday life. When enacting their daily lives, human agents move through chains of interaction rituals, reproducing along the route forms of solidarity and (also material) symbols of group membership while, in turn, being charged up with sentiments, beliefs and emotional energy (EE) that result from situated IRs. By putting Durkheim's ritual analyses on Goffmanian feet, Collins (2004, p. 8) is able to show that 'what often appears to be a fixed global culture is in fact a situational generated flux of imputed rules and meanings.' Especially when in reflexive modernity, everyday life experiences become less tightly coupled with the fixed macro categories of family, church, union and class, the dynamics of situated practices or 'situations' gain strategic importance for sociology.

These situations form the core of Collins's theory. Paraphrasing Goffman (1969, 1974), he argues that his theory is 'not about individuals and their interactions, but interactions and their individuals; not persons and their passions, but passions and their persons' (Collins, 2004, p. 5). A conceptual framework emerges for analyzing IRs (Figure 11.1). On the left side are the necessary ingredients for an IR to take place: bodily

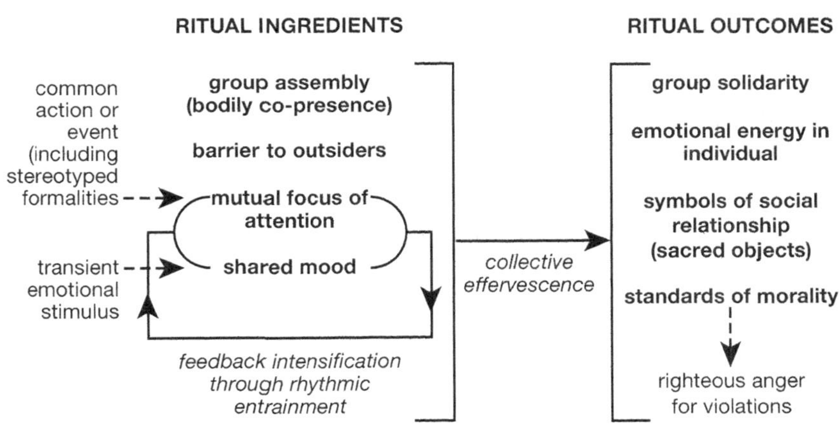

Source: Collins (2004).

Figure 11.1 The conceptual model of interaction ritual theory

(co-)presence, group boundaries, a shared mood and a mutual focus of attention. These ingredients feed back upon each other and result in a process of what Durkheim labeled 'collective effervescence'; people get excited, become mutually entrained, something is happening. As a result, the ritual produces group solidarity, symbols and objects of social relations, standards of morality and EE in the individual. With respect to the agency-structure theme, Collins contends that the classical micro-macro distinction is not as obsolete and confusing as Giddens or Bourdieu would have it. He defines agency in terms of the flows of EE that appear in human bodies during interactions and that travel along IR chains.

In IR theory, energy (or agency) is primarily 'local' or 'micro' in origin since it emerges from situated IRs enacted on a face-to face basis by individuals who set themselves apart from nonparticipants. Agency, however, is not restricted to the micro level since the flows of EE also travel along wider chains of IRs in society. These flows are embodied in and carried along by individuals – they are, however, not 'individualist' in nature. In line with practice theories, Collins argues that not individuals but 'EE flows running through interaction chains' are more interesting topics for sociological theorizing and research. For that reason, EE can be regarded as the single most important concept to emerge from this line of inquiry.

Collins's IR theory also advances an interesting perspective on the agency-technology interactions discussed above. The IRs that produce EE can take the form of either formal rituals (for example, divine services, funerals, championship games) or 'natural rituals' (most of our everyday life interactions). The role of sacred objects in formal IRs (for example, Christian cross in the church ceremony, coffin at the funeral, ball in the championship game) is well established and has been extensively studied by anthropologists and sociologists ever since Durkheim. As sacred objects, they are co-constitutive for the ritual interaction in a direct and visible way. Without such tokens, formal rituals could hardly be imaginable. As sacred objects they are 'necessary' for the production of these events as specific kinds of social practices. At the same time, symbols depend on the rituals being enacted on them, since without the ritual interactions they would just be 'dead symbols.'

What counts for formal rituals, however, is also true for ordinary practices that Collins refers to in terms of natural rituals. They also depend on and help to produce material objects and infrastructures that serve as symbols representing social relations and are important for the participants in the IR. Rituals are about doing honor to what is socially valued (Douglas and Isherwood, 1979; Douglas and Wildavsky, 1982; Collins, 2004). The mechanism of 'doing honor to objects' applies to ordinary artifacts that are given special significance in the context of natural rituals as much as it applies to the divine objects used in a religious ceremony. What is at stake is the mutually constitutive relationship between physical items and human actors: actors acting on things, and things triggering action and 'producing' agency or, as Collins would have it, EE.

For Collins, the relationship between actors and objects should best be analyzed in terms of the amount of EE being stored in, and released from, objects as a result of IRs. Objects can be said to 'act' during the IR by focusing the attention of participants and by getting them entrained. Human actors bestow material objects with special values, and get excited and energized by these objects in return. Consumers are keen to use objects and symbols in the context of practices that they expect to add to their existing stocks of EE. The ownership and use of products are not ends in themselves for citizen-consumers, but are rather objects to be desired, fantasized about, bought, maintained and divested since the consumption rituals are expected to deliver an increase in EE.

Instead of just being regarded as the 'users of goods,' citizen-consumers, according to Collins, are best understood as EE seekers. They do not just 'handle' things or consider their (mis)fits in relation to existing portfolios and values belonging to the practices. They get excited or disappointed, enthusiastic or sad, energized or bored with the objects that co-constitute the practice, and these forms of heightened inter-subjectivity between agents and material objects are what impel consumption practices and what gives them their (cultural) dynamics. The EE from (green) symbols, objects, technologies and infrastructures is what drives environmental changes in everyday practices of consumption.

The EE gets stored in bodies, objects and symbols and in this way it is prevented from fading away prematurely once the IR ends. By circulating through IR chains, bodies, objects and symbols keep the flows of EE from rapidly dissipating. This circulatory flow can be regarded as representing the meso and macro forms of agency. When EE flows decrease, objects and symbols lose their original attractiveness or emotional loading. Once this occurs, the practices that they helped to organize will 'fade away' or disappear altogether. In a similar way we can study how new practices and their symbols and EE flows originate and develop.

At this point, Collins suggests making an analytical distinction between the first-, second- and third-order circulation of symbols and objects. The first-order circuit is the face-to-face IR or practice responsible for initially producing the symbol or loading the objects and technologies. Once the meanings of the objects are established, the symbols can be taken up by participants in other practices and by the media, resulting in secondary processes of circulation. Local symbols start being used in national, regional or global chains of IRs. Finally, the symbols and objects can circulate in tertiary circuits of individual human actors, performing rituals with objects and symbols outside the presence of others. A person talking to her refrigerator, bicycle or personal computer is an exemplary case of such a 'third-order circulation' of symbols and objects.

For social scientists interested in the cultural dimension of consumption, Collins advises considering a number of well-defined, concrete methodological steps. First, examine the symbolic item or material object itself. What does the thing or the idea look like? Does it have a positive or negative social loading? Is it widely shared or restricted to certain groups? Second, seek out the practices that initially produced the symbol. What kinds of practices are typically attached to it? Are they traditional or modern, old or new, cool or out of fashion. Third, analyze the circulation of the symbols or objects outside their primary circuits of origin. Through what kind of IR chains – or nexus of practices as Schatzki would argue – do the objects and symbols circulate or travel? What kinds of impacts do they have when spilling over into secondary circuits? Finally, investigate the tertiary circulation of the symbols, when sacred symbols or objects are being used by actors outside the presence of other people.

This methodology for developing a cultural approach to sustainable consumption is innovative and relevant for two reasons. First, it shows how norms, morals and awareness result from situated interactions in which (green) symbols, objects and morals are used by individuals to gain energy and to 'produce' sustainability. Second, this approach offers useful opportunities to display the positive logics implied in sustainable consumption. This second point is worth considering in more detail.

Most environmental debates, as well as appeals for sustainable consumption, are about avoiding particular objects, breaking problematic habits, limiting energy and material throughput, reducing impacts and dealing with the shadow side of consumption (Dauvergne, 2008). An overriding number of green symbols and practices associated with sustainable consumption have a 'negative' valence in the sense of representing a kind of logics and dynamics that run counter to the established, positive logics of consumption. For example, the behavioral alternatives advanced by climate change policies most of the time refer to not doing things or doing things that require extra or special effort. The so-called top ten things one can do to 'save' the environment – the most significant actions to shrink an individual's ecological footprint – always include calls 'to eat less meat,' 'to reduce car use' and 'to fly less frequently.' To 'do your bit' means withdrawing from established behavioral routines that are fairly central to the everyday lives of major segments of the population in wealthy countries.

While a small group of frontrunners are building their green identities by participating in novel and more sustainable or 'low impact' practices

(Horton, 2003; Etzioni, 2006), most people are not yet able to connect the use of green products, objects and symbols with processes of display and identity formation in a positive manner. In Collins's terminology, most citizen-consumers cannot imagine how the use of green goods in their everyday lives might increase their levels of EE. In other words, they do not yet know how to frame the EE they get from subscribing, for example, to green energy schemes.

The 'energizing' part of sustainable consumption is hardly considered by environmental social scientists when developing research on sustainable consumption. How does it feel to vacuum the house with electricity generated by one's own solar panels, to run an elaborate set of divestment practices in the home, to prepare a meal with organic ingredients?

With Collins's analysis in mind, it is possible to reframe the issue of green commitment, excitement and awareness in a nonindividualistic and positive manner. The more frequent, intense and dense the enrollment of individuals in sustainability-related IRs, the greater the chance that their resolve and levels of awareness will increase over time. This elevated engagement can be researched for the kinds of IRs at play and the particular green symbols and objects used to develop and carry along green EE. When green goods start to perform well across a range of different IRs they can be said to have strategic (or policy) significance for the gradual greening of IR chains within specific consumption domains.

With respect to food, housing or mobility, different items can carry along the flows of EE attached to sustainable consumption. Farmers markets can be shown to attract people who also tend to subscribe to local agrofood networks, who enjoy growing vegetables in their home gardens and who dine in restaurants that offer a rich variety of local food items. The flows of foodstuffs, eating habits, production methods and recipes traveling through the food IR chain can be specified in empirical research and assessed for their EE-enhancing capacities (Mol and Spaargaren, 2005). Instead of 'spill-over' being a characteristic of individual lifestyles only (Thøgerson, 1999), this methodology offers a new way to study 'green contagion' at the level of chains of practices. As such, we can start to answer some of the outstanding questions that pertain to the cultural dimension of sustainable consumption while keeping in line with the main tenets of practice theories. Such a redefined, post-Brundtland agenda emphasizing the positive, EE-enhancing logics of the greening of consumption could supplement existing policies for sustainable consumption in crucial ways (Spaargaren and Cohen, 2009). It is this renewed, global policy agenda for sustainable consumption practices that is considered in the conclusion.

CONCLUSION: TOWARD A PRACTICE-BASED RESEARCH AGENDA

To bring a more sustainable modernity into closer view, existing patterns of consumption must be reconsidered and transformed from an environmental perspective. Because the two paradigms presently used to frame and organize policy interventions for sustainable consumption are subject to major biases and fall short of analytical precision, there is a strong rationale for considering a new practice-based approach. This conceptualization makes it possible, on the one hand, to simultaneously analyze and assess the crucial influences of socio-technical dynamics at higher levels of system reproduction and, on the other hand, to engage with lifestyle and life-world dynamics. In a practice paradigm, sustainable consumption patterns are treated as resulting from innovations in (chains of) practices situated within distinct consumption domains such as food, housing, mobility, leisure, clothing and personal care. Innovations in consumption practices refer to the introduction of novel and more sustainable ways of 'doing,' 'saying,' 'knowing' and 'thinking' from the perspective of practitioners. To achieve an in-depth understanding of these dynamics of change, a combined focus on the technological and cultural dimensions of innovation in consumption practices is required. The practice theories surveyed above, as well as work within science and technology studies and ANT, are well suited for analyzing the technologies, infrastructures, objects and products that (co-)shape everyday consumption routines. Collins's theory of IR chains in particular offers useful insights for assessing the cultural dimension of innovation in consumption. This work helps to avoid a narrow, technological focus on sustainable consumption, while at the same time it creates space for more positive, emergent cultural perspectives.

It also merits noting that although the practice approach has been developed most extensively in Europe and the United States, it is relevant beyond these regions. The globalization of lifestyles, practices and systems of provision adds a new dimension to efforts to develop sustainable consumption patterns at an international scale. The policy agenda formulated in the context of the Marrakech Process has struggled to overcome a European outlook embodied by calls for more sustainable consumption (Cohen, 2001; Spaargaren and Cohen, 2009). Many commentators recognize the need for a global approach to the greening of consumption, but there is little evidence of progress along these lines (Spaargaren and Mol, 2008). Three elements for a future research agenda on sustainable consumption practices are detailed below.

First, when developing a global perspective on sustainable consumption, the analysis of transitions in consumption practices under the influence of technological and cultural innovations has been shown to provide a useful point of departure (Oosterveer et al., 2007). As outlined above, a practice approach is not restricted to local or national levels of analysis and can offer an alternative to contemporary geographically delimited consumption studies. Such a perspective lends itself to an investigation of the globalization of both lifestyles and systems of provision in relation to selected practices within a limited number of consumption domains. Housing, food and mobility are key units of analysis for consumption policies throughout the world system. International and local dynamics in these domains work out differently in specific regions of the global network society. For example, sustainable housing practices in rural India or East Africa are different from the climate-proofing of houses in the Netherlands or the United Kingdom.

Second, there is a need to move away from the Eurocentric bias of present approaches to sustainable consumption. The debate on making available more sustainable products, services and technologies to citizen-consumers at the so-called 'base of the pyramid' (Kandachar and Halme, 2008) might help to illustrate the fact that companies, governments and NGOs have started to recognize the need to develop more internationalized strategies. By connecting to this discourse, the policy agenda could be extended in a more globally inclusive way without losing sight of the specificities of local practices.

Finally, for such a policy agenda to be legitimate and effective, new forms of environmental authority that transcend governments and states will have to be developed, relying to a considerable extent on the inputs of actors and institutions in the global civil sphere (Anheier et al., 2001; Newell, 2005; see also Sassen, 2006). In addition to transnational companies and global-scale retail chains, NGOs and (organized) groups of citizen-consumers must become active in bringing about effective forms of global governance for sustainable consumption.

NOTES

1. This chapter is an adapted version of an article that originally appeared in 2011 in *Global Environmental Change*, **21**(3) under the title 'Theories of practices: agency, technology, and culture.'
2. Tim Jackson's (2006) discussion of sustainable consumption policy in the United Kingdom can be regarded as one of the most sophisticated treatments with respect to the 'science-policy interface' written from a social psychological perspective. His approach has been taken up by DEFRA (2008) in the United Kingdom and in other European countries.
3. 'Backstage performances' such as cooking in a restaurant kitchen or repairing cars in

a garage cannot be known first hand because backstage practices are regulated and restricted from the perspective of the general public (Goffman, 1969).

4. In the 1990s, this methodology was used to investigate the impact of liberalization and privatization on the domestic consumption of energy, water and waste services. Since the turn of the century, it has been applied to new provider-consumer relations implied in the emergence of so-called smart grids (Charles, 2009).
5. Arguing for a stronger focus on the upside of sustainable consumption does not, of course, imply closing one's eyes to the downside. As Buttel (2000) observed, the phenomena of greenwashing, free-riding behavior, rebound and Jevons effects are too real to be ignored in any serious empirical research design.

REFERENCES

Anheier M., M. Kaldor and H. Anheier (eds) (2001). *Global Civil Sphere*, New York: Oxford University Press.

Beck, U. (1992). *Risk Society: Towards a New Modernity*, Newbury Park, CA: Sage.

Beck, U. (2009). *World at Risk*, Malden, MA: Polity Press.

Beckers, T., G. Spaargaren and B. Bargeman (2000). *Van Gedragspraktijk naar Beleidspraktijk: een Analytisch Instrument voor een Consument-georiënteerd Milieubeleid (From Behavioral Practices to Policy Practices: An Analytical Tool for Consumer-oriented Politics)*, The Hague: Ministry of Housing, Spatial Planning, and Environment (in Dutch).

Bourdieu, P. (1977). *Outline of a Theory of Practice*, New York: Cambridge University Press.

Bourdieu, P. (1979). *Distinction; A Social Critique of the Judgment of Taste*, New York: Routledge.

Buttel F. (2000). 'Globalization, environmental reform, and U.S. hegemony', in G. Spaargaren, A. Mol and F. Buttel (eds), *Governing Environmental Flows: Global Challenges to Social Theory*, Cambridge, MA: MIT Press.

Charles, D. (2009). 'Renewables test IQ of the grid', *Science*, **324**(5924), 172–5.

Campbell, C. (2006). 'Consuming goods and the good of consuming', in T. Jackson (ed.), *The Earthscan Reader in Sustainable Consumption*, London: Earthscan, pp. 278–90.

Charles, D. (2009). 'Renewables test IQ of the grid', *Science*, **324**(5924), 172–5.

Cohen, M. (2001). 'The emergent environmental policy discourse on sustainable consumption', in M. Cohen and J. Murphy (eds), *Exploring Sustainable Consumption: Environmental Policy and the Social Sciences*, New York: Elsevier, pp. 21–37.

Cohen M. and J. Murphy (eds) (2001). *Exploring Sustainable Consumption: Environmental Policy and the Social Sciences*, New York: Elsevier.

Collins R. (2004). *Interaction Ritual Chains*, Princeton, NJ: Princeton University Press.

Collins, R. and M. Makowsky (1998). *The Discovery of Society*, 7th edn, Boston, MA: McGraw-Hill.

Dauvergne, P. (2008). *The Shadows of Consumption: Consequences for the Global Environment*, Cambridge, MA: MIT Press.

DEFRA (Department of Environment, Food, and Rural Affairs) (2008). *A Framework for Pro-environmental Behaviours*, London: HMSO.

Dietz, T., G. Gardner, J. Gilligan, P. Stern and M. Vandenbergh (2009). 'Household actions can provide a behavioral wedge to rapidly reduce U.S. carbon emissions', *Proceedings of the National Academy of Sciences USA*, **106**(44), 18452–6.

Douglas, M. and B. Isherwood (1979). *The World of Goods; Towards an Anthropology of Consumption*, London: Allen Lane.

Douglas, M. and A. Wildavsky (1982). *Risk and Culture: The Selection of Technological and Environmental Dangers*, Berkeley, CA: University of California Press.

Etzioni A. (2006). 'Voluntary simplicity: characterization, select psychological implications and societal consequences', in T. Jackson (ed.), *The Earthscan Reader in Sustainable Consumption*, London: Earthscan, pp. 159–78.

Fine, B. and E. Leopold (1993). *The World of Consumption*, New York: Routledge.

Geels, F. (2005). *Technological Transitions and System Innovation: A Co-evolutionary and Socio-technical Analysis*, Cheltenham, UK and Northampton, MA, USA: Edward Elgar.

Geels, F. and J. Schot (2007). 'Typology of sociotechnical transition pathways', *Research Policy*, **36** (3), 99–417.

Giddens A. (1984). *The Constitution of Society: Outline of the Theory of Structuration*, Palo Alto, CA: Stanford University Press.

Goffman, E. (1969). *The Presentation of Self in Everyday Life*, New York: Penguin.

Goffman, E. (1974). *Frame Analysis*, New York: Harper and Row.

Graham, S. and S. Marvin (2001). *Splintering Urbanism: Networked Infrastuctures, Technological Mobilities, and the Urban Condition*, New York: Routledge.

Grin J., J. Rotmans and J. Schot (2010). *Transitions to Sustainable Development: New Directions in the Study of Long Term Transformative Change*, New York: Routledge.

Guy, S., S. Marvin and T. Moss (eds) (2001). *Urban Infrastructure in Transition: Networks, Buildings, and Plans*, London: Earthscan.

Heiskanen, E., P. Kasanen and P. Timonen (2005). 'Consumer participation in sustainable technology development', *International Journal of Consumer Studies*, **29**(2), 98–107.

Hobson, K. (2002). 'Competing discourses of sustainable consumption: does the "rationalisation of lifestyles" make sense?', *Environmental Politics*, **11**(2), 95–120.

Horton, D. (2003). 'Green distinctions: the performance of identity among environmental activists', in B. Szerszynski, W. Heim and C. Waterton (eds), *Nature Performed: Environment, Culture, and Performance*, Malden, MA: Blackwell, pp. 63–78.

Jackson, T. (2005). *Motivating Sustainable Consumption; A Report to the Sustainable Development Research Network*, London: Sustainable Development Research Network.

Jackson, T. (2006). 'Challenges for sustainable consumption policy', in T. Jackson (ed.), *The Earthscan Reader in Sustainable Consumption*, London: Earthscan, pp. 109–29.

Kandachar, P. and M. Halme (eds) (2008). *Sustainability Challenges and Solutions at the Base of the Pyramid: Business, Technology, and the Poor*, Sheffield: Greenleaf.

Knorr-Cetina, K. and A. Cicourel (1981). *Advances in Social Theory and*

Methodology: Toward an Integration of Micro- and Macro-sociologies, New York: Routledge.
Latour, B. (2005). *Reassembling the Social: An Introduction to Actor-network Theory*, New York: Oxford University Press.
Middlemiss, L. (2010). 'Reframing individual responsibility for sustainable consumption: lessons from environmental justice and ecological citizenship', *Environmental Values*, **19**(2), 147–67.
Mol, A. and G. Spaargaren (2005). 'From additions and withdrawals to environmental flows: reframing debates in the environmental social sciences', *Organization and Environment*, **18**(1), 91–107.
Mol, A., D. Sonnenfeld and G. Spaargaren (eds) (2009). *The Ecological Modernization Reader: Environmental Reform in Theory and Practice*, New York: Routledge.
Newell, P. (2005). 'Climate for change? Civil society and the politics of global warming', in M. Glasius, M. Kaldor and H. Anheier (eds), *Global Civil Society 2005/2006*, Thousand Oaks, CA: Sage, pp. 1–31.
Oosterveer, P., J. Guivant and G. Spaargaren (2007). 'Shopping for green food in globalizing supermarkets: sustainability at the consumption junction', in J. Pretty, A. Ball, T. Benton et al. (eds), *Sage Handbook on Environment and Society*, Thousand Oaks, CA: Sage, pp. 411–28.
Otnes, P. (ed.) (1988). *The Sociology of Consumption: A New Research Agenda*, Atlantic Highlands, NJ: Humanities Press.
Reckwitz, A. (2002a). 'Toward a theory of social practices; a development in culturalist theorizing', *European Journal of Social Theory*, **5**(2), 243–63.
Reckwitz, A. (2002b). 'The status of the "material" in theories of culture: from "social structure" to "artifacts"', *Journal for the Theory of Social Behaviour*, **32**(2), 195–217.
Rief, S. (2008). 'Outlines of a critical sociology of consumption: beyond moralism and celebration', *Sociology Compass*, **2**(2), 560–77.
Sassatelli, R. (2007). *Consumer Culture: History, Theory, and Politics*, Thousand Oaks, CA: Sage.
Sassen, S. (2006). *Territory-authority-Rights: From Medieval to Global Assemblages*, Princeton, NJ: Princeton University Press.
Schatzki, T. (1996). *Social Practices: A Wittgensteinian Approach to Human Activity and the Social*, New York: Cambridge University Press.
Schatzki, T. (2002). *The Site of the Social: A Philosophical Account of the Constitution of Social Life and Change*, University Park, PA: Pennsylvania State University Press.
Schot, J. (2001). 'Towards new forms of participatory technology development', *Technology Analysis and Strategic Management*, **13**(1), 39–52.
Schot, J. and A. Albert de la Bruhèze (2003). 'The mediated design of products, consumption and consumers in the twentieth century', in N. Oudshoorn and T. Pinch (eds), *How Users Matter: The Co-construction of Users and Technology*, Cambridge, MA: MIT Press, pp. 229–45.
Shove, E. (2003). *Comfort, Cleanliness, and Convenience: The Social Organization of Normality*, New York: Berg.
Shove, E. (2006). 'Efficiency and consumption: technology and practice', in T. Jackson (ed.), *The Earthscan Reader in Sustainable Consumption*, London: Earthscan, pp. 293–305.
Shove, E. and G. Walker (2007). 'CAUTION! Transitions ahead: politics,

practice, and sustainable transition management', *Environmental Planning A*, **39**(4), 763–70.

Southerton, D., H. Chappells and B. van Vliet (eds) (2004). *Sustainable Consumption: The Implications of Changing Infrastructures of Provision*, Cheltenham, UK and Northampton, MA, USA: Edward Elgar.

Spaargaren, G. (2003). 'Sustainable consumption: a theoretical and environmental policy perspective', *Society and Natural Resources*, **16**(8), 1–15.

Spaargaren, G. and M. Cohen (2009). 'Greening lifecycles and lifestyles: sociotechnical innovations in consumption and production as core concerns of ecological modernization theory', in A. Mol, D. Sonnenfeld and G. Spaargaren (eds), *The Ecological Modernization Reader: Environmental Reform in Theory and Practice*, New York: Routledge, pp. 257–75.

Spaargaren, G. and A. Mol (2008). 'Greening global consumption: politics and authority', *Global Environmental Change*, **18**(3), 350–9.

Spaargaren, G. and C. van Koppen (2009). 'Provider strategies and the greening of consumption', in H. Lange and L. Meier (eds), *Globalizing Lifestyles, Consumerism, and Environmental Concern: The Case of the New Middle Classes*, Dordrecht: Springer, pp. 81–100.

Spaargaren, G., H. Mommaas, S. van den Burg et al. (2007). *More Sustainable Lifestyles and Consumption Patterns: A Theoretical Perspective for the Analysis of Transition Processes within Consumption Domains*, Wageningen: WUR, Telos, MNP and LEI.

Staats, H., P. Harland and H. Wilke (2004). 'Effecting durable change: a team approach to improve environmental behaviour in the household', *Environment and Behavior*, **36**(3), 341–67.

Szerszynski, B., W. Heim and C. Waterton (eds) (2003). *Nature Performed: Environment, Culture, and Performance*, Malden, MA: Blackwell.

Thøgerson, J. (1999). 'Spillover processes in the development of a sustainable consumption pattern', *Journal of Economic Psychology*, **20**(1), 53–81.

Urry, J. (2000). *Sociology Beyond Societies: Mobilities for the Twenty-first Century*, New York: Routledge.

Van Vliet, B.J.M. (2002). 'Greening the grid', PhD thesis,. Wageningen University, Wageningen.

Van Vliet, B., H. Chappells and E. Shove (2005). *Infrastructures of Consumption: Environmental Innovation in the Utility Industries*, London: Earthscan.

Verbeek, D. (2010). *Sustainable Tourism Mobilities: A Practice Approach*, The Hague: SCP.

Wackernagel, M. and W. Rees (1996). *Our Ecological Footprint: Reducing Human Impact on the Earth*, Gabriola Island, BC: New Society.

Warde, A. (2004). 'Practice and field: revising Bourdieusian concepts', CRIC Discussion Paper No. 65, Manchester: Centre for Research on Innovation and Competition, University of Manchester.

Wilk, R. (2009). 'The edge of agency: routines, habits, and volition', in E. Shove, F. Trentmann and R. Wilk (eds), *Time, Consumption, and Everyday Life*, New York: Berg, pp. 143–56.

12. Taking social practice theories on the road: a mixed-methods case study of sustainable transportation

Emily Kennedy, Harvey Krahn and Naomi T. Krogman

INTRODUCTION

A carbon tax, a levy on plastic bags and public education about littering are all strategies for encouraging sustainable consumption practices – and tend to focus on a few individual behaviors. However, given the urgency of climate change and related pollution, changing a society's consumption patterns on a behavior-by-behavior basis is too slow. Further, shifting individual consumption in one area (for example, of light bulbs to more energy-efficient types) has been found not to lead to a reduction in material use in other domains; instead, savings in one area lead to higher consumption in the same or other domains (Sorrell, 2009). In addition, some existing policy (and theoretical) approaches erroneously assume autonomous and rational individuals are unaffected by and have minimal impact on others (Burgess et al., 2003). Clearly, approaches that look beyond the individual are required to understand the structure-agency nexus and conditions under which more rapid social change around consumption can occur (see the chapters by Bente Halkier and Gert Spaargaren in this volume).

Social practice theories represent one such alternative (Røpke, 2009). This general set of approaches is premised on a duality of structure and agency; distinguishes between resources, norms and infrastructure; and deploys user practices – not individuals – as the central unit of analysis (Hargreaves, 2011). Notable contributions to this literature include Andreas Reckwitz's (2002) detailed comparison of social practice theories to other social science theories; Elizabeth Shove and colleagues' wide ranging empirical work with social practice theories (Shove, 2003; Shove and Pantzar, 2005; Shove et al., 2007); Gert Spaargaren's (2003) application of social practice theories to ecological modernization theory to understand household energy consumption; and Alan Warde's (2005) theoretical exploration of how social practice theories could be applied to the study of consumption behavior. More recently, a special issue in the *Journal of Consumer Culture* (2011) provided qualitative empirical examples of social practice theory in relation to consumption behavior.

Given these highly promising beginnings, we believe there is a need for further empirical work (including both qualitative and quantitative studies) to explore the theoretical assumptions of social practice theories and what they can offer to our understanding of sustainable consumption behaviors. In this chapter, we analyze both qualitative and quantitative data on sustainable transportation practices collected in Edmonton, Alberta, Canada between 2009 and 2010. We use the former to explore how neighborhood location and design can influence the resources, norms and infrastructure that help to shape sustainable consumption practices. We then use our quantitative survey data to build a multiple regression model to refine our description of neighborhood and sustainable transportation practices. Despite our focus on neighborhood in this chapter, it is worth acknowledging that neighborhood is not simply 'Point A' in an analysis of sustainable transportation practices. Where people choose to live is shaped by other practices, such as raising children (for example, education, recreation, social life) and personal care (for example, staying safe). As we discuss elsewhere (Kennedy et al., 2012), neighborhood choice is contingent on many other factors.

SOCIAL PRACTICE THEORIES

As described in the chapters by Bente Halkier and Gert Spaargaren in this volume, social practice theories have an illustrious heritage. Prior to their explicit development, the routinized nature of practices was theorized in Giddens's (1984) distinction between practical consciousness and discursive consciousness, or tacit knowledge of behavior versus interpreted, annotated behavior (Middlemiss, 2009). Also, Bourdieu's concepts of habitus and field stress the fact that practices are slow to change, rarely questioned and strongly connected to one's personal and cultural history (Kasper, 2009). The centrality of practices as an organizing feature of social order is fundamental in the ontology of these approaches. As Inge Røpke (2009) has written, '[s]ocial systems are . . . relations between actors, organized as repeated social practices and reproduced and transformed by the actors . . . The structural properties involve elements of meaning and communication, control and power relations, and legitimacy.' Individuals, in this context, are seen as carriers of practices, rather than as completely autonomous agents. As Røpke (2009, p. 2491) further explains, 'practices recruit practitioners.' In short, practices influence individuals, resources, norms, and infrastructure, but these elements also influence practices, in a reciprocal and dialectical relationship.

Exactly what constitutes a 'practice' is widely debated in the literature. While some reject entirely the association between 'behavior' and 'practice' (Shove, 2010), others are more accepting of the view that a practice can encompass a number of different behaviors (Warde, 2005). Across this body of work, there is general agreement that practices are routinized and connected to largely unexamined cultural norms. There is also consensus that a focus on domains (for example, mobility, eating) is generally viewed as the most effective way to examine bundles of practices (Hargreaves, 2011) (see the chapter by Gert Spaargaren in this volume). Research on social practice theory within the context of sustainable consumption typically requires action that has a material dimension; that is, a direct link to material resources as needed to sustain a particular practice (Røpke, 2009).

Spaargaren (2003) and Southerton et al. (2004) argue that the elements that hold a practice together include resources (for example, economic, social, cultural), norms and infrastructure. For our purposes, among other social practices frameworks (Schatzki, 2002; Warde, 2005), those developed by Spaargaren (2003) and Southerton et al. (2004) offer useful concepts for examining sustainable transportation practices. Of greatest interest to us are their concepts of resources, norms and infrastructure. 'Resources' is a broad term that accounts for, as Southerton et al. (2004) explain, the choices that are available to individuals that shape the establishment of routines. Much of the work on resources is drawn from the work of Bourdieu (1977) who delineates between cultural, social and economic resources. More explicitly, '[t]ogether, economic, cultural, and social capital constrain the choices available to individuals. Money, cultural orientations, and networks influence access to, judgment of, and the satisfactions received by engaging in different forms of consumption' (Southerton et al., 2004, p. 38). As an example, in another contribution originating from our research, we discuss the role of having access to a social network of sustainable consumers within one's neighborhood, explaining that those whose mobility, eating and energy practices are less materially intensive are more likely to be those who have access to a network of others interested in reducing consumption (Kennedy, 2011).

'Norms' are also highly influential. Southerton et al. (2004, p. 38) note that 'how people consume is shaped by their capacity to read and comply with the norms and expected competencies of any given context.' Without recourse to an alternative normative framework, individuals are left to rely on mainstream norms, where reducing consumption is a marginal practice, at best (Seyfang, 2009; Hargreaves, 2011).

Finally, 'infrastructure' has obvious impacts on delineating social practices. When Shove (2003) describes changes in bathing practices in the UK, she stresses that in addition to norms and resources, technological developments such as household electricity, domestic plumbing and power showers prompted the dominance of the personal shower. In our research, we examined two neighborhood types to explore how access to services (including public transit) and distance to the city core (where many residents work) influence the extent to (and manner in) which households avoid single-occupancy vehicles (Kennedy et al., 2012). As Southerton et al. (2004, p. 39) conclude, 'any radical change to lifestyles requires similar changes to an individual's volume of resources, and to infrastructural and material arrangements that constrain consumption.'

Empirical work to date on social practices is largely qualitative (for example, Shove and Pantzar, 2005; Middlemiss, 2009; Hargreaves, 2011), and these studies have added much to the understanding in various domains. The lack of quantitative research involving social practice theories may reflect the relative infancy of these perspectives. Nonetheless, the broader sampling and potentially higher external validity of quantitative research may provide greater explanatory power and generalizability to complement existing qualitative research. Social practice theories do present measurement challenges, of course, but so too do other leading sociological theories linking agency and structure (that is, approaches developed by Giddens and Bourdieu).

Beyond general epistemological differences between qualitative and quantitative approaches to scientific research, which we do not discuss here (see Johnson et al., 2007 for a more thorough discussion), there are also important differences in the unit of measurement. The methodological individualism of so much empirical environmental social science (for example, environmental social psychology) is clearly at odds with the ontological and epistemological premises of social practice theory (see the other chapters in Part III of this volume). For instance, measurement within quantitative research tends to be at the level of the individual or household, while social practice theories call on researchers to conduct measurements at the level of practice. Thus, individuals or households must be quantified as carriers of practice, rather than as individuals in and of themselves. While we do not resolve these methodological challenges, we do focus our attention on the performance of sustainable transportation practices, relying on individual and household data to do so.

SUSTAINABLE TRANSPORTATION

Transportation has a significant impact on a society's consumption of natural resources and is highly relevant for climate change due to the association between vehicle emissions and greenhouse gases (Boyd, 2003; Dietz et al., 2009). Furthermore, there is considerable room for innovation in sustainable transportation, including improved public transit service, more fuel-efficient vehicles (or vehicles that use renewable fuel) and development (or reintroduction) of rail travel in lieu of automobile or air travel.

As a practice, sustainable transportation may actually be better described as a moment in a variety of practices – recreating (for example, exercise and shopping), working (for example, commuting), facilitating children's education (for example, commuting to school and activities) and eating (for example, grocery shopping). Nonetheless, as transportation is environmentally significant and habitual, we have chosen to use this simplified practice to begin to examine social practice theories using quantitative methods.[1] In the qualitative phase of our study (described below), we allowed participants to describe their transportation practices and adopted their definitions of when such practices are sustainable, or less resource-intensive. In the quantitative phase, we operationalize sustainable transportation as the sum of bicycling, walking, using public transit and leaving one's vehicle at home to avoid driving (explained in more detail below).

In our study, therefore, the practice of sustainable transportation may involve different meanings to different participants. For example, avoiding air travel may constitute 'sustainable transportation' in a suburban community, while walking to work might connote sustainable transportation in an urban neighborhood. However, based on interviews with participants in the qualitative phase of our study, the means by which households reduce consumption are strongly connected to daily choices. Still, one of the most frequently mentioned differences our qualitative respondents noted between themselves and the 'mainstream' is in their emphasis on decisions that shape daily life, including where to work, how much to work, where to live and how to educate their children. At a daily level, meanings of sustainable transportation may refer to exercising in one's neighborhood rather than driving to a gym, walking, bicycling, or using public transit to get children to school or taking the bus to work, among others.

Resources, norms and infrastructure affect the frequency of sustainable transportation practice across a landscape. The economic resources required for sustainable transportation are likely less than for vehicle use, though large incomes may discourage sustainable transportation. Social resources include interpersonal networks that foster talking to others about environmental issues, and influencing and being influenced by them.

Norms in our study refer to the routine, everyday transportation practices of residents who live in close proximity to each other. The culturally dominant mode of transportation in our study context is the single-occupancy vehicle. Vehicle ownership is certainly the norm in Alberta; in fact, Alberta leads Canada in the percentage of households owning a vehicle (86.6 percent) and gas consumption per person (estimated at 1667 liters annually) (Birrell, 2009). Furthermore, using data from 2005, a Statistics Canada report comparing major Canadian cities found that Edmonton residents were the most likely to have made all their trips on the reference day exclusively by car as either the driver or a passenger (75 and 77 percent, respectively) (Turcotte, 2008). Thus, those who partake in sustainable transportation in Edmonton are often challenging the norms of their neighborhood, and also setting an example for others.

Finally, infrastructure related to sustainable transportation could include having access to bicycle trails and public transit, and living within walking/bicycling distance of work, schools, shops and other services.

METHODS

Study Area

Both our qualitative and quantitative data were collected in Edmonton. In many ways, Alberta is similar to other Canadian provinces, but it is also unique in several important respects. Its economy relies much more heavily on resource-extraction industries, particularly natural gas, conventionally drilled oil and heavy oil from the Athabasca oil sands (centered in Fort McMurray, 280 miles (450 kilometers) north of Edmonton). Alberta has had the same political party (a right-leaning conservative party) in power for roughly four decades, while other Canadian jurisdictions see shifts in power much more frequently. It is a wealthy province – average earnings in 2005 (US$42 290) were the highest in Canada and considerably higher than the national average (US$35 546). Household expenditures are also among the highest in Canada (Statistics Canada, 2006). Compared to the rest of the country, Alberta has a similar proportion of residents with university degrees, a comparable proportion of residents who are members of a visible minority group and a similar distribution of the population across urban and rural areas.

Our sampling approach was not limited geographically for the qualitative phase – participants were selected from around the city, with an attempt to have roughly equal numbers of respondents from central areas as from outlying neighborhoods. However, we took note of the kind of neighborhood in which each of our interviewees lived. Each participant can be described as either living in a walkable, public transit-oriented community or in suburban neighborhood. By noting this distinction, we were able to identify patterns of choices and daily routines that were linked to infrastructure.

Based on typical access to services for these two groups, we selected two neighborhoods for the quantitative phase that best represented the structural features of an urban and a suburban residence (for example, access to employment, recreation and other services) while offering similar levels of income and home value. The areas chosen have similar average incomes, and are populated predominantly by single-detached dwellings with few apartment buildings. Homes in Terwillegar Towne (the suburban area) are considerably newer and somewhat larger, on average, than homes in Millcreek (the central neighborhood). Both neighborhoods have average incomes that are on par with the rest of Alberta but higher than the Canadian average.

Qualitative and Quantitative Data

Overview

The overall aim of the research program of which this chapter forms a part was twofold: (1) to describe the heightened efficacy of a network of households in reducing consumption and removing barriers for others to do so and (2) to explore the role of urban context in fostering household-level sustainable consumption. Addressing the research questions associated with these two goals led us to collect both qualitative and quantitative data. Our qualitative data focused on the motivations, daily activities and well-being of families that sought to reduce their material consumption, and concentrated our attention on the impact of physical place on sustainable practices (for example, within the domains of eating, mobility, household maintenance and recreation). Participants in this initial phase of the study were recommended to the research team by individuals who knew the family in question as leaders in reducing material consumption.

Interviews

From June to November 2009, members of the research team conducted 26 interviews (two interviews each with 13 families). All families were two-parent households with children living at home. The first round of (semi-structured) interviews asked questions about how to incorporate a commitment to reducing consumption into daily practices, the challenges involved and the benefits to quality of life from doing so. The second (unstructured) round was designed to elaborate on themes of interest from the first round. For most, the second interview was connected to the issue of bringing about change as an individual. Due to the focus of this chapter, we draw almost solely on data from the first round of interviews. This first round of interviews was conducted at participants' homes and many of the second round interviews were conducted in the home of the first author of this chapter. Interviews ranged in length from 35 to 95 minutes. All interviews were recorded and professionally transcribed.[2] The means by which qualitative participants reduced material consumption included: opting for sustainable modes of transportation; reorienting household purchasing to focus on used goods and high-quality goods; reducing waste by composting, recycling, reusing and avoiding products that are poorly made or heavily packaged; retrofitting homes to reduce energy consumption; purchasing locally produced food and/or growing food; and interacting with others to share knowledge and resources.

Survey

Key qualitative findings included: the identification of the means by which low-consumption families significantly reduced material consumption; the need for engaging with others to sustain a commitment to lowering material consumption; and the relevance of neighborhood of residence for affecting sustainable social practices, including engaging with like-minded others (Kennedy, 2011). Using findings from the interviews, we administered a survey in the summer of 2010.

Together with four hired undergraduate students, the first author of this chapter dropped off and picked up questionnaires door-to-door. A total of 712 questionnaires were left at homes in two neighborhoods, one urban and one suburban. In Terwillegar Towne (the suburban neighborhood), 237 complete questionnaires were picked up, along with 254 in Millcreek (the urban neighborhood), resulting in a 69 percent response rate. The survey questions used in the following analysis are drawn from the sustainable transportation section that read: 'In 2009, *to avoid driving*, how often did members of your household . . . (a) Leave your vehicle at home when you went out? (b) Walk? (c) Bike? (d) Use public transit?' Other questions are drawn from the section called 'Influencing others.' These four items read, 'In 2009, how often did your household . . . (a) Talk about environmental issues among yourselves? (b) Talk to others about environmental issues? (c) Behave in ways that show others how they could reduce their consumption? (d) Actively encourage others to reduce their consumption?'

We also asked participants to indicate why they selected to live in their chosen neighborhood. We found suburban residents ascribed significantly more importance to low crime rates and having a large home, while central residents placed a greater priority on living in proximity to work and shops and services. In other work, we include a broader discussion of differences in choosing where to live (Kennedy et al., 2012).

Qualitative and Quantitative Analyses

The qualitative data were entered and coded in NVivo 8 qualitative software. Our interviews focused on the practices and norms of a specific subculture – people reducing material consumption. We followed principles of ethnographic coding, including using informants' own definitions of values and practices. Some of the themes relevant to the findings presented in this chapter include norms, resisting the mainstream, practices associated with reducing material consumption and influencing others. These themes shaped our questionnaire items in the survey instrument.

With our quantitative data, we first conducted descriptive analyses to examine the distributions of our variables of interest and correlation analyses to explore the possibility of constructing indices from multi-item questions. Building on social practice theories, multiple regression analysis was then employed to analyze the socio-demographic, structural and normative correlates of the practice of sustainable transportation. The final model controls on gender, age, educational qualifications, presence of children in the home and household income. In this model, we use neighborhood of residence (suburban or urban) as a proxy for structural constraints. To justify this decision, we call attention to the unique resources, norms and infrastructure germane to these two types of neighborhood (for a more thorough description, see Kennedy et al., 2012).

RESULTS

Interview Findings

Neighborhood of residence affects sustainable transportation practice in several ways. Drawing from previous discussions of social practices (Spaargaren, 2003; Southerton et al., 2004), we begin by using qualitative data to illustrate the unique resources (including social networks and skills), norms and infrastructure (including access to public transit and proximity to hubs of commercial and recreational activity) for our interviewees in each of the two neighborhood types.

The resources available to an established neighborhood near a city center compared with a newly constructed neighborhood at the periphery of a city differ significantly. Residents in suburban areas described feeling frustrated that they did not know their neighbors. One woman said she and her family had lived in the same house for 14 years and knew no one on their street – she saw neighbors pull out of the garage in the morning and pull back into the garage in the evening. Another woman became involved in building a community garden in her suburban neighborhood. She expected that one fringe benefit would be meeting others with similar interests. After four months of gardening, she and her daughters had yet to meet another family. While the economic resources of the qualitative participants varied somewhat, more relevant to sustainable transportation practice were social resources. Those who had a source of inspiration – another family who mirrored their own choice to use sustainable transportation practices – motivated them to also avoid single-occupancy vehicle use (Kennedy, 2011).

We include a dimension of skills under our qualitative account of resources. There are many skills required to incorporate sustainable transportation practice into everyday habits. A familiarity with bus routes and schedules, perhaps knowing others with whom to ride-share and knowing how to ride a bicycle (often with traffic) are a few of the many competencies needed. The following excerpt from Eleanor's interview demonstrates the importance of skill transfer and normalizing a behavior that is outside the mainstream; in the excerpt, she connects skills to social resources, such as the ability to teach others.

> My husband loves bicycles and he can fix bicycles. He works on his bike on our front porch. We had so many neighbors come by and say, 'Oh, can you help me with this?' So now we do free bike repairs once a year and get so many people coming. If we just show how much we love bicycles and how easy they are to maintain, we're going to get more people to ride.

By making an alternative practice visible, Eleanor's family's commitment to cycling builds social resources around sustainable transportation while transferring important skills. These elements are also connected to norms and their influence on transportation.

We found that norms differed by neighborhood and affected sustainable transportation practice. The lack of visible alternatives to the vehicle in suburban neighborhoods made those choosing sustainable transportation practices feel marginalized. In fact, Julie moved from a suburb to a central neighborhood over the course of our study. Below, she relates an experience that made clear to her the dominance of unsustainable transportation practice.

> I bike my daughter to school and it often feels really unsafe. There are Porsche Cayennes going 80 kilometers an hour past me to get to school, with maybe one kid and a nanny getting out . . . I expected to find some high consumers but it is completely the norm here.

While some found strength in choosing a practice outside the norm, these people tended to have access to a strong social network of support. Those without such a network expressed a sense of futility in transportation practices that differ from those around them. While participants could refer to the ways in which norms they used to justify their driving behavior were at odds with their stated commitment to reduce consumption, they invoked a feeling of time pressure (convenience), a cultural preference for vehicle travel, a perception that driving a large vehicle is safer and a lack of awareness about alternatives to driving to explain their continued dependence on personal vehicle travel. In the following excerpts, Elaine, who has access to a strong network of support, expresses a sense of excitement when she challenges unquestioned norms that lead to unsustainable transportation practices. She provides two examples.

(1) I find it's fun to meet people who find the way I live completely bizarre. I can make it pretty clear that I use my bike to get there [to business school] without trying to convince anyone of anything. I also try to show that I don't have to fit the stereotype of a granola. I can just go with my bike helmet and still dress business casual. It's kind of fun to show that I can play a bit of the game but still, you know, do my thing.

(2) One example of seeing some things changing would be riding our bicycles with Liam to all his soccer games. He'd be on the tag-along [bike attachment] and all the other kids would drive. We would arrive on our bike and the other kids thought that that was really fun. I could hear them [say], 'Mom, can we do that?'

In contrast, without access to social resources premised on alternative normative foundations, the distance from a destination and a desire for convenience can routinize transportation behavior that is unsustainable, from the perspective of the participant. For example, a father with two sons, living in the suburbs, knows it is more consumptive to drive, but relies on norms of convenience and efficiency to justify his decision to own two vehicles and avoid sustainable transportation.

> I sometimes worry about the degree to which we drive but I really enjoy the freedom it gives me versus imagining trying to do it by public transit which in our neck of the woods would be . . . well, that to me would kind of turn our whole world upside down . . . It's all well and good to say, 'Well you should take public transit whenever and however you can.' But when the reality is that it can double, triple, quadruple your travel time, it leaves a lot to be desired.

> And so I don't see at this point any resolution between the buses and personal vehicle ownership that really is going to work at this point.

The above excerpt connects norms to infrastructure: the final element of our qualitative analysis.

Infrastructure is the final component of neighborhoods that has a potent effect on sustainable transportation practice. For participants living in suburbs, their neighborhoods offered little in the way of grocery stores, services (such as hospitals and recreation centers) and proximity to workplaces. One participant built a home in a suburb and later decided to move to a central neighborhood. In the following excerpt, she alludes to a lack of social resources and physical infrastructure, demonstrating how these elements are interrelated. She explicates the contrast in her transportation practices through differences in social resources and infrastructure.

> Building [in the suburbs] seemed like a good idea at the time. We moved in August of 1998 and our daughter was born in February of 2000. It was okay before she was born: we only had one vehicle so we drove or bussed in downtown for my husband's work and I was doing school. When [our daughter] was born, suddenly I found myself at home, by myself. I did have a vehicle because [my husband] bussed to work but most people out there had two cars. I was unbelievably isolated. I couldn't even walk to get groceries. So I had to drive to the grocery store and [the baby] just screamed in the car. Now we still have our car but we almost never use it and we walk or bike everywhere.

Despite the fact that those participants who lived in suburban areas expressed similar levels of commitment to sustainability in many domains of practice (for example, eating, dwelling in the house), neighborhood of residence had a large impact on sustainable transportation practice in our small qualitative sample. For example, there were no suburban residents who lived without a vehicle, while this was the most frequently cited mechanism for reducing material impact among residents of central neighborhoods. For suburban residents, choosing fuel-efficient vehicles and trying to institute 'car-free' days were the only examples of daily sustainable transportation. In contrast, another way that centrally located families reduced use of a personal vehicle was to share vehicles with others. We were unable to locate participants living in suburban neighborhoods who participated in vehicle-sharing arrangements.

Survey Findings

Since neighborhood emerged as such a powerful explanation of the use of sustainable transportation in our qualitative study, we chose to use it as a structural independent variable in our regression models of sustainable transportation practices. As noted earlier, the dependent variable in the following analysis is a sustainable transportation practices index created from responses to four questions about how frequently (never, rarely, sometimes, often, always) survey respondents chose alternatives to driving an automobile. Scores on this scale, which has an acceptable level of inter-item reliability (Alpha = 0.721) range from 0 to 16 (see Carmines and Zeller, 1979 for a discussion of measurement reliability and validity). There is a large, statistically significant difference ($p < 0.001$) in sustainable transportation practices between the two neighborhoods: the average index score for central Millcreek (8.14) is almost twice as large as in suburban Terwillegar Towne (4.93).

Selection of variables

Based on the social practices models developed in Spaargaren (2003) and Southerton et al. (2004), we use multiple regression to explore the impact of agency and structure-related variables on sustainable transportation practices. Socio-demographic variables that have been previously found to be correlated with some types of sustainable practices include gender (Stoddart and Tindall, 2011), age (Pickett-Baker and Ozaki, 2008), household income (Stern, 2000) and education (Steg and Vlek, 2009). While there is little to suggest that there might be gender differences in avoiding vehicle use, gender is nevertheless often deployed as an independent variable in models of pro-environmental practices. With respect to age, older people are typically less environmentally concerned than youth, attributed in part to higher incomes and different values. Also, youth are likely more physically fit and thus better able to commute by walking or bicycling. Those with higher incomes (often older) are more likely to be able to afford the purchase and maintenance of a vehicle. Typically, people with more education tend to adopt pro-environmental practices that deviate from the mainstream. We also include the presence of children in the household as a predictor variable, because our interview participants used this example as a reason for why sustainable transportation is more appealing, and why it is also more challenging.

We include two cultural/normative measures in our regression models. Our normative behavior index (with a range of 0 to 16) sums responses (never, rarely, sometimes, often, always) to four statements: 'I try to model sustainable consumption behavior for others'; 'I actively encourage others to reduce their consumption'; 'I talk to others about environmental issues'; and 'We talk about environmental issues in our household.' The index has an excellent level of reliability (Alpha = 0.827). We chose to construct this index because our interviewees revealed that serving as an example for others was an important way of questioning dominant cultural norms that encourage material consumption. Also, interviewees drew inspiration from talking with others about the environment and sustainable living. In our survey, we included open-ended questions, inviting participants to comment on their reasons for not engaging in sustainable transportation practices. Though the relatively few responses to these questions do not allow us to use them in our regression analysis, we provide a brief summary of the barriers to sustainable transportation and how these differ across the two neighborhoods in the subsequent section.

Our travel attitude measure consists of responses on a five-point scale (strongly disagree to strongly agree) to the statement, 'I chose to live close to the places I need to travel to in order to minimize my impact on the environment.' We included this statement in our survey because our earlier interviews showed that people who had considered the impact of where they lived in relation to work, school and services found it much easier to walk, bicycle and use public transit. Though Shove (2010) questions the notion that individuals have much choice in relation to their practices, we feel it is important to take into account survey participants' earlier preferences for neighborhoods that might allow sustainable transportation practices.

While we cannot directly measure resources, norms and infrastructure, we use the decision to live close to amenities as illustrative of resources (following our qualitative findings that there are like-minded others in central neighborhoods), normative behavior to account for skills and competencies, and neighborhood of residence to measure infrastructure (since the suburb and the central neighborhood have such contrasting access to shops and services and hubs of employment and recreation). The socio-demographic variables help to refine the measurement of norms and resources, given the influence of education, income and family structure on the cultural profile of an area.

Barriers to sustainable means of transportation

In the questionnaire, we asked participants, 'if you "never" or "rarely" leave your vehicle at home (or walk, bicycle or use transit), could you indicate why?' After coding responses, we found that the majority of people who never or rarely leave their vehicle at home live in the suburbs, and credit lack of convenience and distance as the two most significant barriers. In Millcreek, more participants said that doing so requires too much time. When opting to walk, those in Terwillegar Towne said they do so for exercise, not as a mode of transportation and that this is mostly because of distance. Few in Millcreek never walk. Across both neighborhoods, bicycling is less common than walking. In Terwillegar Towne, this is because many do not own a bicycle, and in Millcreek, it is because of concerns with safety. Finally, there are also many residents who never use public transit in both neighborhoods. For most people, this is because transit is perceived as inconvenient. We present this information solely to provide a clearer picture of the different reasons why sustainable modes of transportation may not be used across the two neighborhoods.

Multiple regression models

Working from a social practices perspective, we first examine the impact of neighborhood on sustainable transportation practice (Table 12.1, Model 1). We then add demographic and socio-economic status measures to the equation (Model 2). Model 3 includes the normative behavior index, while Model 4 introduces the travel attitude measure.

Table 12.1 shows that neighborhood (infrastructure) alone (Model 1) accounts for 22.7 percent of the variation in sustainable transportation practice in our sample. As already noted in our earlier bivariate analysis, Millcreek residents are much more likely to engage in sustainable transportation practices. When we add the socio-demographic characteristics

Table 12.1 A social practices model of sustainable transportation: stepwise regression

Model	1	2	3	4
Neighborhood (Millcreek = 1)	0.479***	0.543***	0.525***	0.449***
Gender (female = 1)	–	−0.010	−0.005	0.019
Age (years)	–	−0.141**	−0.139**	−0.137**
Children (number)	–	0.156**	0.144**	0.132**
Household income ($)	–	−0.122**	−0.118**	−0.100**
Holds a university degree (yes = 1)	–	0.109*	0.102*	0.081
Normative behavior index	–	–	0.161***	0.108**
Chose to live close to amenities (1 to 5)	–	–	–	0.215***
N	394	394	394	394
Adjusted R^2	0.227	0.279	0.304	0.338
F	116.76	26.47	25.55	26.14
Significance (*p*) of equation	0.000	0.000	0.000	0.000

Note: Standardized multiple regression coefficients (β) displayed in table. * Slope is significantly different from zero ($p < 0.05$); ** slope is significantly different from zero ($p < 0.01$); *** slope is significantly different from zero ($p < 0.001$).

to the multiple regression equation, the net effect of neighborhood actually increases (the suppressed effect suggests some possible interaction effects that we explore later in Table 12.2). In addition, all of the socio-demographic variables except gender have small but statistically significant net effects. They together explain an additional 5 percent of the variation in the dependent variable. We see that older (β = −0.141) and wealthier (β = −0.122) members of the population are less likely to incorporate sustainable transportation into their lives. Having children is positively associated (β = 0.156) with sustainable transportation practices, which could be explained by the fact that, even in suburban areas, many children attend a neighborhood school that is accessible by walking, bicycling or school bus. Having a university education is also positively associated with sustainable transportation (β = 0.109).

Models 3 and 4 add the normative index and travel attitude measure, respectively. The effects of neighborhood are weakened slightly, suggesting that a small part of the 'Millcreek effect' is a function of the cultural/normative differences between residents of the two neighborhoods. Even so, neighborhood remains the strongest predictor of sustainable transportation practice and the direction and strength of the socio-demographic variables change little. The index of normative behavior is positively associated (β = 0.161) with sustainable transportation and explains an additional 2.5 percent variation in sustainable transportation practice (Model 3). Finally, in Model 4, the addition of the travel attitude (resources) measure (β = 0.215) explains another 3.5 percent of the variation in sustainable transportation practices. The effects of the socio-demographic predictors change little when the cultural/normative predictors are added to the multiple regression equation. As we might expect, the travel attitude measure has a considerably stronger net effect than does the normative behavior index. In other words, personal attitudes about travel choices influence sustainable travel practices more than trying to set an example for others.

The models in Table 12.1 focus on the main effects of neighborhood, socio-demographic variables and normative/cultural measures. However, as we observed when discussing Model 2, there appear to be some interaction effects at play as well. In other words, the effects of some of the predictor variables added in Models 2 through 4 may differ, depending on the neighborhood in which survey participants lived. To explore this possibility, in Table 12.2 we split our sample by neighborhood and compare the effects of the socio-demographic and normative/cultural variables across the two subsamples. In this analysis, we shift our focus from the standardized regression coefficients (β) to the unstandardized coefficients (*b*s) and ask whether the slopes for the same variables are significantly different across the two subsamples.[3]

Table 12.2 Regression Model 4 compared across neighborhood

	Terwillegar Towne	Millcreek
Gender (female = 1)	0.023 (0.136)	0.037 (0.218)
Age (years) #	0.015 (0.005)	−0.223 (−0.047)***
Children (number)	0.123 (0.319)	0.158 (0.461)**
Household income ($)	−0.143 (−7.993E − 6)*	−0.132 (−6.296E − 6)*
Holds a university degree (yes = 1) #	−0.099 (−0.548)	0.270 (1.650)***
Normative behavior index	0.160 (0.134)**	0.076 (0.074)
Chose to live close to amenities (1 to 5)	0.129 (0.408)	0.251 (0.705)***
N	195	199
Adjusted R^2	0.071	0.269
F	3.106	11.471
Significance (*p*) of equation	0.004	0.000

Note: Both standardized (β) and unstandardized (*b*) multiple regression coefficients are displayed, the latter in parentheses. * Slope is significantly different from zero ($p < 0.05$); **slope is significantly different from zero ($p < 0.01$); ***slope is significantly different from zero ($p < 0.001$); # difference between slopes is significantly different ($p < 0.05$).

Table 12.2 shows that our social practices model is much more effective at explaining sustainable transportation practices in Millcreek (Adjusted R^2 = 0.269) than in Terwillegar Towne (Adjusted R^2 = 0.071). This very large difference is primarily a result of age and education having much more powerful effects in Millcreek. Age has almost no effect on sustainable transportation practices in Terwillegar Towne, but a moderately strong negative effect in Millcreek – the difference between the two slopes is significant ($p < 0.05$). In other words, in the suburban neighborhood, older and younger residents have very similar transportation practices, but in Millcreek, the older the resident, the less likely he or she is to engage in sustainable travel practices. Equally interesting, in Terwillegar Towne, more educated residents are slightly less likely to engage in sustainable practices while, in sharp contrast, more educated Millcreek residents are more likely to do so. Table 12.2 also shows that the normative behavior index has a stronger effect in the suburban subsample while transportation attitudes (chose to live close to amenities) matter more in Millcreek, but the differences between these two sets of slopes are not significant.

Summing up these quantitative analyses, we have demonstrated (in Table 12.1) how socio-demographic variables such as age, the presence of children in the household, education and household income affect sustainable transportation practices, as do normative/cultural factors. In addition, and much more strongly than these other two types of predictors, neighborhood itself has a pronounced net effect. Residents of Millcreek, the central urban neighborhood in our study, are much more likely to engage in sustainable transportation practices, less so due to differences in their socio-demographic characteristics and attitudes (the multivariate analyses in Table 12.1 take these into account) as due to the physical characteristics of their neighborhood (for example, street design, access to public transit, availability of amenities).

Furthermore, the effects of some socio-demographic and cultural/normative predictors can differ substantially, depending on neighborhood. In Table 12.2, we observed that age had virtually no effect on sustainable transportation practices in Terwillegar Towne, but a moderately strong negative effect in Millcreek. This might mean that, over time, Millcreek has attracted young individuals and families with a preference for sustainable transportation practices quite different from that of older, long-term residents. The same pattern is not present in Terwillegar Towne, perhaps because there are few long-term residents but more likely because young families that chose to live there did so because of housing (cost and size) preferences rather than the central city benefits offered by a neighborhood like Millcreek. Similarly, Millcreek may have attracted a higher proportion of well-educated individuals and families who tend toward sustainable practices (in transportation and in other life spheres) in contrast to equally well-educated individuals and families with different attitudes and lifestyles who were more inclined to Terwillegar Towne (Kennedy et al., 2011).

DISCUSSION

Methodological Approach

Regardless of one's epistemological stance, subjecting theoretical work to empirical analysis presents the disadvantage of reducing complexity of theorized work. As Røpke (2009, p. 2491) warns, 'the sociological and empirically applicable insights [of social practice theories] are emphasized at the expense of philosophical subtleties.' In many respects, our empirical analyses can be seen as simplifying the nuanced features of this perspective that make it so attractive to students of sustainable consumption. Hargreaves (2011, p. 84) clarifies the empirical challenge at stake.

> The focus is no longer on individuals' attitudes, behaviours and choices, but instead on how practices form, how they are reproduced, maintained,

> stabilized, challenged and ultimately killed-off; on how practices recruit practitioners to maintain and strengthen them through continued performance, and on how such practitioners may be encouraged to defect to more sustainable practices.

However, there are also important advantages of empirical study. Social practice theories are attractive in part because one can simultaneously consider lifestyle and the social (political and economic) dynamics of system reproduction (see the chapter by Gert Spaargaren in this volume). In operationalizing lifestyle and an overarching system, empirical research calls attention to particular factors that influence daily practices. Elsewhere, we have examined the impact of having a network of support for challenging mainstream, high-consumptive practices (Kennedy, 2011). Here, we have demonstrated the importance of considering the effects of place of residence on daily behavior, and called attention to the reciprocity between place of residence and social support systems for reducing consumption. We maintain that, ultimately, social practice theories will need more rigorous empirical (both qualitative and quantitative) testing to explore critical questions around when individuals begin to serve as carriers of particular practices, when marginalized practices become prevalent in the mainstream, and which practices are identified as 'sustainable' and how. We found subjecting the notion of social practice to quantitative analysis to be fraught with challenges and compromises. We would recommend, therefore, that some attention be paid to how best to design and analyze quantitative research along these lines.

Our focus on neighborhood type in this study emerged from qualitative data suggesting that neighborhoods and sustainable practices exist in a reciprocal, dialectical relationship. Residents interested in sustainability were drawn to neighborhoods that appeared to pose few barriers to reducing material consumption. Once situated, residents of central neighborhoods were able to form networks that altered the visible norms of the area, making the neighborhood more appealing to potential carriers of sustainable practices and better situated to allow access to systems of provision that facilitate reducing material consumption. However, as we have acknowledged elsewhere (Kennedy et al., 2012), the relationship between practice and neighborhood is bidirectional and reciprocal. Furthermore, where one chooses to live is intricately woven into other practices. Those who have children may seek a residence that offers them the opportunity to play safely in the street; living comfortably may appear to be easier with a newer home as opposed to an older home; and those who like to escape the city at weekends may feel that this is easier to accomplish when living at the edge of an urban center.

This study is a starting point in this theoretical and methodological journey and through this work we have begun to imagine other methods by which to examine social practices. Most quantitative work on sustainable consumption practices focuses on the individual and is administered at a single point in time. To follow a practice (using individuals or households as carriers of practices), future surveys should employ longitudinal designs (for example, to see how norms and practices emerge over time). Alternative approaches to measuring social practices might include time-use journals or similar surveys designed to capture the daily routines of a given population and points at which unquestioned unsustainable practices become discursive, and then also taken for granted.

Interpretation of Results

Social practice theories propose that practices arise as a function of resources, norms and infrastructure – elements that draw together agency and structure. We have shown that individuals have a degree of control in shaping social and cultural resources when deciding where to live, but that once situated in a neighborhood, infrastructural constraints have the greatest influence on sustainable transportation practice. An important caveat, however, is that neighborhood, as operationalized in our quantitative study, includes both an infrastructural and a cultural component. The cultural component arises from the fact that families and individuals looking for places that reflect their values are drawn to different forms of physical spaces. Linking why people choose to live in certain places with infrastructure, we argue that norms have the potential to transmute some of the rules and resources of a given location. We begin the interpretation of results by commenting on the importance of resources, norms and infrastructure, in turn.

Resources, norms and infrastructure are not mutually exclusive concepts; they are interdependent and reciprocally related, as evidenced by our qualitative and quantitative studies. In the qualitative phase, participants in suburban neighborhoods made clear that not knowing their neighbors – not knowing if there were other families committed to reducing material consumption – limited the social and cultural resources of their areas. In this example, infrastructure is strongly tied to resources: with no points of interest within walking distance, no cafes, parks or grocery stores, neighbors had little chance to get to know one another. The physical layout of the neighborhoods precluded the formation of social networks. We saw that sentiment reflected in the quantitative study: those who had chosen their neighborhood based on a desire for car-free access to points of interest were much more likely to engage in sustainable transportation practices.

In this way, while practices do 'recruit practitioners,' as Røpke (2009) explains, this process is – at least in part – mediated through physical place in our study. In Millcreek, the central neighborhood, the presence of shops and services, and the proximity to downtown and to forested recreation areas, attracted residents interested in sustainable practices, broadly speaking, and also served to lessen barriers to sustainable practices for other residents. Consequently, these residents altered the profile of the neighborhood and introduced practices that continued to define it as abiding to a set of more sustainable practices. For example, participants from the qualitative phase, who moved to Millcreek over 15 years ago, noted that the neighborhood has begun to attract more families with young children in the past decade and that there is now a strong presence of households growing their own food, bicycling and participating in and organizing community events.

The normative standards of a neighborhood also affect practices. In the vehicle-dependent suburbs, walking, bicycling and using public transit were considered inconceivable for several of our qualitative informants and most quantitative participants. As a result, the mainstream, or dominant normative, display was one of vehicle use. The following comment from Southerton et al. (2004, p. 32) mirrors our findings about the importance of norms.

> [Social practice theories describe] a society where individuals have little option but to consume in unsustainable ways if they are to participate fully in that society. Cars are necessary to reach work, to obtain food, to deliver children to school; owning a variety of clothes is required to enter diverse social contexts without 'sticking out'; there is no alternative to having a highly mechanized kitchen. All are consequences of the socio-technical and normative ordering of daily life.

Nonetheless, the comments from those respondents in central neighborhoods who felt they were able to influence others to adopt less resource-intensive modes of transportation suggest that there is room for changing normative standards. This relationship also explains how practices can become 'contagious' in a given area. In places where sustainable practices can be made visible (for example, repairing one's bicycle on a front porch), normative practices begin to be challenged and redefined, affecting the culture of a neighborhood. Again, there is a connection to infrastructure: without places to see one another (for example, parks, shops), there is little opportunity for conveying alternative transportation practices. Interestingly, we found that in our quantitative comparison of the suburb and central neighborhoods, normative behavior was strongly related to sustainable transportation practice in the suburb and not in the central area. As Randles and Warde (2006, p. 229) explain, '[p]ractices do not float free of technological, institutional, and infrastructural contexts.' This is indeed what we found in both the qualitative and quantitative phases.

Infrastructure emerged as a strong pressure on sustainable transportation practices in the qualitative and quantitative phases. Interviewees in the suburbs stressed that the need to drive trumped their goal of living sustainably and in the quantitative phase, neighborhood continued to have a strong influence on sustainable transportation practice, regardless of the role of norms and resources. As we mentioned earlier, the neighborhood effect is likely partly one of infrastructure and partly one of a selection factor, or how residents chose where to live. By attracting households with a commitment to reducing consumption and making it easier to choose alternatives to a vehicle, the structure of a neighborhood shapes and is shaped by resources, norms and practices. The qualitative findings reflect that trend: bicycling to soccer games impressed young children and, as discussed elsewhere (Kennedy, 2011), a strong presence of public transit users affects fare structures for families. Yet within the same logic, the norm of parents driving young children to a nearby school in expensive sport-utility vehicles may influence transportation practices as well (recall the lone parent who bicycled with her children to school in suburbia and subsequently chose to move from a suburban to an urban neighborhood). In short, the well-intentioned efforts of dedicated individuals are not enough to present a meaningful challenge to the myriad flaws in suburban design that preclude sustainable transportation practice.

CONCLUSION

The chapter by Gert Spaargaren in this volume notes that social practice theories help to elucidate the limitations of individual responses to global environmental issues such as climate change. In this chapter, we have provided evidence that urban design must be reconsidered if broad changes in sustainable transportation are to take place. In some respects, the central neighborhood represents the limitations of individual action: sustainable transportation in Millcreek is practiced by young households with children and less so by older (possibly long-standing) residents. These younger households have moved to the neighborhood in large part due to the relative accessibility of sustainable transportation alternatives. To encourage other Millcreek residents and the vast majority of Terwillegar Towne residents to shift their transportation practice requires alterations to the urban landscape (or what Spaargaren calls 'demand-side management') and societal reconceptualizations of what constitutes a good place to live. This is not the work of the individual; higher levels of economic and political discourse should be given more stature in the discussion of how neighborhoods serve residents for sustainable systems of provision. Given the importance of the question of how practices recruit new carriers of the practice (Shove and Pantzar, 2005), incorporating neighborhood of residence into future analyses of household-level sustainable practices should prove useful to study interactions between agency, structure and social practices. Broadly, we argue for much more quantitative and mixed-methods empirical work to explore the assumptions of social practice theories, beginning with exploratory research on how quantitative analysis might best be applied.

NOTES

1. With respect to transportation practices, we acknowledge a cautionary note raised by one of the referees of an earlier draft of this chapter that focusing solely on sustainable transportation risks missing related and relevant practices that may shape transportation behavior and neighborhood of residence.
2. Pseudonyms are used throughout the chapter to protect the identity of the participants.
3. Slopes (*b*s) rather than β need to be compared because the latter are standardized within each subsample on the basis of different distributions of, for example, age, income and university education. T-tests were calculated for each pair of slopes, using the following formula: $t = (b_1 - b_2)$ / square root (error variance_1 + error variance_2).

REFERENCES

Birrell, C. (2009). 'Personal use vehicles in Canada: fuel consumption profile and comparative analysis of the 2007 Canadian vehicle survey results', Statistics Canada, Catalogue No. 16–001–M, 9, available at http://www.statcan.gc.ca/pub/16-001-m/2009009/part-partie1-eng.htm (accessed 2 September 2011).

Bourdieu, P. (1977). *Outline of a Theory of Practice*, New York: Cambridge University Press.

Boyd, D. (2003). *Unnatural Law: Rethinking Canadian Environmental Law and Policy*, Vancouver: UBC Press.

Burgess, J., T. Bedford, K. Hobson, G. Davies and C. Harrison (2003). '(Un)sustainable consumption', in F. Berkhout, M. Leach and I. Scoones (eds), *Negotiating Environmental Change*, Cheltenham, UK and Northampton, MA, USA: Edward Elgar, pp. 261–91.

Carmines, E. and R. Zeller (1979). *Reliability and Validity Assessment*, Newbury Park, CA: Sage.

Dietz, T., G. Gardner, J. Gilligan, P. Stern and M. Vandenbergh (2009).

'Household actions can provide a behavioral wedge to rapidly reduce US carbon emissions', *Proceedings of the National Academy of Sciences USA*, **106**(44), 18452–6.

Giddens, A. (1984). *The Constitution of Society: Outline of the Theory of Structuration*, Palo Alto, CA: Stanford University Press.

Hargreaves, T. (2011). 'Practice-ing behaviour change: applying social practice theory to pro-environmental behaviour change', *Journal of Consumer Culture*, **11**(1), 79–99.

Johnson, R., A. Onwuegbuzie and L. Turner (2007). 'Toward a definition of mixed method research', *Journal of Mixed Methods Research*, **1**(2), 112–33.

Kasper, D. (2009). 'Ecological habitus: towards a better understanding of socioecological relations', *Organization and Environment*, **22**(3), 311–26.

Kennedy, E. (2011). 'Ecological citizenship and the social network: observing a virtuous circle in action', *Environmental Politics*, **20**(6), 843–60.

Kennedy, E., N. Krogman and H. Krahn (2012). 'Sustainable consumption and the importance of neighbourhood: a central-urban/suburban comparison', *The Canadian Journal of Sociology*, in review.

Middlemiss, L. (2009). 'The role of community-based organisations in stimulating sustainability practices among participants', Unpublished PhD dissertation, University of Leeds.

Pickett-Baker, J. and R. Ozaki (2008). 'Pro-environmental products: marketing influence on consumer purchase decision', *Journal of Consumer Marketing*, **25**(5), 281–93.

Randles, S. and A. Warde (2006). 'Consumption: the view from theories of practice', in K. Green and S. Randles (eds), *Industrial Ecology and Spaces of Innovation*, Cheltenham, UK and Northampton, MA, USA: Edward Elgar, pp. 220–37.

Reckwitz, A. (2002). 'Toward a theory of social practices: a development in culturalist theorizing', *European Journal of Social Theory*, **5**(2), 243–63.

Røpke, I. (2009). 'Theories of practice: new inspiration for ecological economic studies', *Ecological Economics*, **68**(10), 2490–7.

Schatzki, T. (2002). *The Site of the Social: A Philosophical Account of the Constitution of Social Life and Change*, University Park, PA: Pennsylvania State University Press.

Seyfang, G. (2009). *The New Economics of Sustainable Consumption: The Seeds of Change*, New York: Palgrave Macmillan.

Shove, E. (2003). 'Users, technologies, and expectations of comfort, cleanliness and convenience', *Innovation*, **16**(2), 193–206.

Shove, E. (2010). 'Social theory and climate change: questions often, sometimes, and not yet asked', *Theory, Culture and Society*, **27**(2–3), 277–88.

Shove, E. and M. Pantzar (2005). 'Consumers, producers, and practices: understanding the invention and reinvention of Nordic walking', *Journal of Consumer Culture*, **5**(1), 43–64.

Shove, E., M. Watson, M. Hand and J. Ingram (2007). *The Design of Everyday Life*, New York: Berg.

Sorrell, S. (2009). 'Jevons' paradox revisited: the evidence for backfire from improved energy efficiency', *Energy Policy*, **37**(4), 1456–69.

Southerton, D., H. Chappelis and B. van Vliet (2004). *Sustainable Consumption: The Implications of Changing Infrastructures of Provision*, Cheltenham, UK and Northampton, MA, USA: Edward Elgar.

Spaargaren, G. (2003). 'Sustainable consumption: a theoretical and environmental policy perspective', *Society and Natural Resources*, **16**(8), 687–701.

Statistics Canada (2006). 'Survey of household spending', *The Daily*, 12 December, available at http://www.statcan.ca/Daily/English/061212/d061212b.htm.

Steg, L. and C. Vlek (2009). 'Encouraging pro-environmental behaviour: an integrative review and research agenda', *Journal of Environmental Psychology*, **29**(3), 309–17.

Stern, P. (2000). 'New environmental theories: toward a coherent theory of environmentally significant behavior', *Journal of Social Issues*, **56**(3), 407–24.

Stoddart, M. and D. Tindall (2011). 'Eco-feminism, hegemonic masculinity and environmental movement participation in British Columbia, Canada, 1998–2007: "women always clean up the mess"', *Sociological Spectrum*, **31**(3), 342–68.

Turcotte, M. (2008). 'Life in metropolitan areas: dependence on cars in urban neighbourhoods', *Canadian Social Trends*, No. 11–008, Statistics Canada, Ottawa, available at http://www.statcan.ca/english/freepub/11-008-XIE/2008001/article/10503-en.pdf (accessed 2 September 2011).

Warde, A. (2005). 'Consumption and theories of practice', *Journal of Consumer Culture*, **5**(2), 131–53.

Index